T0311212

AFRICANS
ON STAGE

AFRICANS ON·STAGE

STUDIES IN ETHNOLOGICAL SHOW BUSINESS

Edited by **BERNTH LINDFORS**

INDIANA UNIVERSITY PRESS • BLOOMINGTON & INDIANAPOLIS

DAVID PHILIP • CAPE TOWN

Published in 1999 by

Indiana University Press, 601 North Morton Street, Bloomington, Indiana 47404-3797
USA

and in Southern Africa by David Philip Publishers (Pty) Ltd, 208 Werdmuller Centre,
Newry Street, Claremont 7708, South Africa

www.indiana.edu/~iupress

Telephone orders   800-842-6796
Fax orders   812-855-7931
Orders by e-mail   iuporder@indiana.edu

© 1999 by the authors

All rights reserved

No part of this book may be reproduced or utilized in any form or by any means,
electronic or mechanical, including photocopying and recording, or by any information
storage and retrieval system, without permission in writing from the publisher. The
Association of American University Presses' Resolution on Permissions constitutes the
only exception to this prohibition.

The paper used in this publication meets the minimum requirements of American National Standard for Information Sciences—Permanence of Paper for Printed Library
Materials, ANSI Z39.48-1984.

Manufactured in the United States of America

Library of Congress Cataloging-in-Publication Data

Africans on stage : studies in ethnological show business / edited by Bernth Lindfors.
   p.   cm.
   Includes index.
   ISBN 0-253-33468-3 (alk. paper). — ISBN 0-253-21245-6 (pbk. : alk. paper)
   1. Ethnology—Africa, Sub-Saharan—Exhibitions. 2. Blacks—Africa—Exhibitions.
3. Blacks—Europe—Public opinion. 4. Blacks—United States—Public opinion.
5. Curiosities and wonders—Africa—Exhibitions. 6. Performing arts—Europe—
Exhibitions. 7. Performing arts—United States—Exhibitions. 8. Public opinion—
Europe. 9. Public opinion—United States.   I. Lindfors, Bernth.
GN645.A376   1999
305.8'00967—dc21   98-50551

1 2 3 4 5 04 03 02 01 00 99

ISBN 0-86486-397-7 (pbk. - David Philip Publishers)

CONTENTS

INTRODUCTION

Ethnological show business—that is, the displaying of foreign peoples for commercial and/or educational purposes—has a very long history in Europe, and it became an increasingly common form of enterprise after advances in navigational technology half a millennium ago put Europeans in touch with human communities all over the globe. As the world shrank, traffic in all kinds of exotic goods grew. One reads of live Eskimos being exhibited in Bristol as early as 1501, of Brazilian Indians building their own village in Rouen in the 1550s, of "Virginians" canoeing on the Thames in 1603, and of numerous other native specimens from the New World, Africa, Asia, Australia, and the Pacific Islands being conveyed to European cities and towns as biological curiosities in the centuries that followed (Kirschenblatt-Gimblett 402). In a sense, this trade in odd human bodies was little different from an earlier practice that has continued right up to modern times: the commercial exhibition of *lusus naturae*—human and animal freaks, dead or alive. There appears to be a healthy natural interest in unusual and unnatural beings. Indeed, the stranger the creature, the stronger the draw.

In the nineteenth and twentieth centuries some of the most interesting individuals and groups exhibited in Europe and America came from Africa, or were said to come from Africa. What did the average spectator think of such representatives from the "Dark Continent"? If the display was a dramatic one— that is, if the Africans sang, danced, or acted out events—what opinions did observers form of them as performers and as human beings? How was the spectacle staged, and who organized and managed the show? How authentic were these performances? Where did the performers actually come from? What notions of Africa and Africans were these exhibitions meant to convey?

It should be remembered that the nineteenth century, sometimes called the Age of Darwin, was also the Age of African Exploration. It was the century of Mungo Park, Lander, Speke, Burton, Livingstone, Stanley—an exciting era when the interior of this seemingly mysterious continent was being traversed by Europeans for the first time. The climax of all these strenuous walking tours came with the formal partitioning of Africa by Europe at a conference table in Berlin in 1884–85. So the century that opened with crude geographical exploration ended with adroit territorial expropriation and refined colonial exploitation. And curiously enough, while this process of annexation was going on, slavery was being abolished. In the New World as well as the Old, Africans and their descendants were being released from bondage. Emancipation seemed to suggest that blacks were finally winning the struggle to be recognized as fully human. But if this was true, why were they being deprived of land and liberty in Africa? It is no wonder that the racial tensions generated during this period by changing social and political policies regularly erupted into bloody colonial and civil wars. The Age of Darwin was a century of aggressive imperialism compounded by great biological confusion.

One notion underlying the confusion was the belief that Africans were at least as close to the animal world as they were to the human world, that they probably constituted the "missing link" in the evolutionary chain between apes and men. Many of the earliest scientific observations on Africans offer analogies between them and simian creatures to explain their presumed inferiority to Europeans and Asians. Here is a typical comment from the writings of Baron Georges Cuvier, the most eminent zoologist of his day:

> The negro race is confined to the south of Mount Atlas. Its characteristics are, black complexion, woolly hair, compressed cranium, and flattish nose. In the prominence of the lower part of the face, and the thickness of the lips, it manifestly approaches the monkey tribe. The hordes of which this variety is composed have always remained in a state of complete barbarism. (qtd. in Curtin 231)

On another occasion Cuvier declared that

> It is not for nothing that the Caucasian race has gained domination over the world and made the most rapid progress in the sciences, while the Negroes are still sunken in slavery and the pleasures of the senses. . . . The shape of their head relates them somewhat more than us to the animals. (qtd. in Coleman 116)

This "animality" of Africans was the feature thought to set them apart from the more rational varieties of the human species.

So when the unusual African specimens began to be displayed publicly in Europe and the United States, emphasis often was placed on their kinship with animals. They were identified as missing links or ape men—creatures whose very humanity was in question. Sometimes their bodies were exhibited posthumously in scientific institutions. In the late eighteenth century four Africans were skinned, stuffed, and enclosed in glass cupboards alongside stuffed exotic animals at a Museum of Natural History in Vienna (Debrunner 145). In 1816

Cuvier had plaster casts made of the body of a steatopygous woman known as the Hottentot Venus, and these remained on display at the Musée de l'Homme in Paris until 1982. A 170-year-old stuffed African "chief" is still being exhibited today in the anthropological section of the Darder Museum in Manyoles, Spain. Living Africans were occasionally presented to the public in much the same fashion, the most famous case being that of Ota Benga, a Batwa pygmy who in 1906 was placed in the monkey cage of the Bronx Zoo in the company of an orangutan and a parrot.

Africans of unusual appearance have been showcased in the West not only in anthropological displays but also at places of entertainment, particularly theaters, fairs, amusement parks, and circuses. One finds a group of Bosjesmans (i.e., San) on display at Croydon Fair and later at a hall in London in the 1840s; two diminutive troglodytic "Earthmen" (apparently also San) playing the piano, singing English songs, and dancing at an inn outside London in the 1850s; and a family of albinos from Madagascar being shown at Barnum's American Museum in New York in the 1860s. Pygmies, Amazons, Zulu warriors, and dish-lipped Ubangi women later became popular attractions in circus sideshows, world's fairs, dime museums, and music halls. Several troupes were even invited to Buckingham Palace to perform before Queen Victoria and her children.

Not all these ethnological shows were authentic. When demand exceeded supply, show business entrepeneurs did not hesitate to recruit non-African blacks to masquerade as African savages or wild men. After the Anglo-Zulu wars, pseudo-Zulus appeared regularly in British and American circuses. For more than sixty years, P. T. Barnum and his successors employed a small, microcephalic African American to play the role of "Zip, the What-is-it?"—purportedly a man-monkey captured while swinging from trees in an African jungle. Zip was said to be "without a language" and incapable of learning one, but unlike other ape men, he was not so wild or brutish that he had to be chained, handcuffed, or confined behind bars. Rather, he was docile and "playful as a kitten," the sort of happy, wholesome, domesticated savage who was totally harmless, even among children. William Henry Johnson, one of those who performed as Zip, earned a good living by pretending to be a meek missing link (Cook; Lindfors 12–13).

Such African showpeople, real as well as counterfeit, are featured as the main attractions in this book, but standing just behind them is a supporting cast of managers and impresarios whose efforts to capitalize on spectacular displays of physical and cultural difference share some of the spotlight. The audiences that turned out to see such shows, expecting them to corroborate what they had heard or read about African abnormalities and idiosyncrasies, are also glimpsed in illuminating sidelights. *Africans on Stage* is a book about how these three groups—players, promoters, and spectators—individually and in concert helped to shape European and American perceptions of Africans in the nineteenth and twentieth centuries. The shows that brought them together tended to replicate and reinforce the dynamics of the unequal relationship that had existed between colonizer and colonized, master and slave. Africans were again denigrated, humiliated, dehumanized, and exploited. Transported across the seas, employed in demeaning jobs, blacks labored largely for the benefit of whites and were rewarded mostly with contempt.

The majority of the essays collected here were originally read at an interdisciplinary panel on "African Show Business" convened in recent years at the annual conference of the African Studies Association. They were then expanded and prepared for publication. Since the contributors include historians, anthropologists, folklorists, musicologists, literary scholars, art critics, and freelance writers, no attempt was made to enforce a uniformity of approach to the subject matter. The essays are arranged in chronological order, according to the dates of the performances they described.

First, art historian Z. S. Strother discusses the exhibition in 1810–15 of Sara Baartman, the "Hottentot Venus," against a background of historical misrepresentations of Khoisan peoples in travel books and early ethnological literature. Strother considers especially the iconography of the Hottentot body, continued when Baartman was displayed in England and France. She was increasingly marketed as a biological "type" rather than as a unique freak of nature.

Then Bernth Lindfors examines the public reaction to a troupe of Zulus who performed in London in 1853. In a review ironically entitled "The Noble Savage," Charles Dickens lampooned the show, attacking what he characterized as the bizarre barbarity of native customs, traditions, and manners. His views were influenced not only by what he saw but also by what he heard from a young showman whose lecture introducing the Zulus was based to a large extent on unreliable travellers' tales.

Zulu and San exhibitions are described again in Shane Peacock's investigation of the South African shows brought to England and America later in the nineteenth century by William Leonard Hunt, an enterprising Canadian impresario who billed himself as the Great Farini. Peacock, who has published a full-length biography of Hunt, goes on to discuss his controversial book of exploration, *Through the Kalahari Desert*, in which he claimed to have discovered ancient ruins of a lost city. Hunt set out to educate as well as to entertain, but his shows, by reinforcing racist stereotypes, may have left behind less benign legacies.

Veit Erlmann, an anthropologist and ethnomusicologist, examines the tours to England and North America undertaken between 1891 and 1893 by a group of fifteen South African singers called the African Choir. By singing African and non-African tunes on both sides of the Atlantic, the African Choir became a commodity of empire that contributed to a fiction of global culture. Focusing on dress and dramaturgy, Erlmann demonstrates that late Victorian forms of "African show business" were crucial sites for staging the spectacle of imperial space and time and for simultaneously elaborating and contesting the typology of race and progress as quintessential tropes for ordering knowledge in a time of waning certainties.

Robert W. Rydell, an historian of world's fairs, examines representations of Africa and Africans at American world's fairs, arguing that these exhibits served the purpose of ideological repair, thereby hastening the process of national reconciliation at the expense of people of color, especially African Americans. He contends that the emphasis on the savagery and backwardness of Africans not only helped to rationalize slavery in the American South but also lent legitimacy to American economic penetration of the African continent. However, through their performances Africans often turned showcases of empire into theaters of resistance.

Jeffrey P. Green turns attention to a smaller subject: six pygmies who were displayed in Britain in 1905–07 by Colonel James Jonathan Harrison, a sportsman who had hunted and travelled in the Congo. In off-seasons the troupe lived on Harrison's estate at Brandesburton in Yorkshire, where they interacted socially with local townspeople. It is estimated that before they returned to the Congo, they had been seen by more than a million people, including scientists who measured and photographed them. For many they were a curious entertainment, but those who got to know them perceived them as normal people.

Harvey Blume focuses on a single pygmy, Ota Benga, finding his exhibition at the Bronx Zoo emblematic of the effort of Western science to domesticate a popular notion of the wild man. This project involved presenting a forest African in a setting deemed appropriate to his lifestyle. Anthropologists as well as showmen sought to satisfy an ever-increasing public craving for authenticity. Blume calls this mixture of fact and fabrication Barnumism.

Neil Parsons's subject is another singular individual, Franz Taaibosch, popularly known in the circus trade as "Clicko, the Dancing Bushman." For historians his life reflects the relationship between imperialism and entertainment, for anthropologists it is a saga of racial paternalism and ethnic stereotyping, and for students of theater it is a story that goes to the shamanistic roots of dance-drama. Parsons argues that Taaibosch survived and thrived by drawing upon inner resources that enabled him to reconstruct his psyche, even while alienated from his roots.

David Killingray and Willie Henderson also deal with an unusual performer, but one who was an imposter. Joseph Howard Lee, an African American who renamed himself Bata Kindai Amgoza Ibn LoBagola in order to present himself to the Western public as an African, claimed in his autobiography to have had remarkable adventures in Africa, Britain, America, and Palestine. Though his book was dismissed as a fraud and fantasy, Killingray and Henderson prove that some of what he reported was grounded in fact but embroidered to add interest. His career demonstrates that he was able to play upon his race in a way that opened doors that otherwise would have been closed to him as a black American.

Finally, Robert J. Gordon offers a case study of institutional arrangements that facilitated the public display of "Bain's Bushmen" at the 1936 Empire Exhibition in Johannesburg. Like earlier exhibitions in Britain and elsewhere, it was a commodity spectacle for mass consumption, a show that managed to educate and socialize while the spectators thought they were being entertained. Gordon explains how a sociologically marginal group can occupy an ideological center-stage, visualizing progress yet at the same time anesthetizing concerns of interest to the black majority in South Africa who had been dispossessed of land.

These case studies concern only a few of the hundreds of blacks who over two centuries have been exhibited in the West as ethnologically correct specimens of African humanity. Yet the sample offered here is representative of the rest, illustrating what happens when science and show business converge in anthropological spectacles that are meant to entertain as well as enlighten. In many of these shows fiction overrode fact because the exhibitors wanted to cash in on public curiosity about human diversity. Physical and cultural differences were emphasized and exaggerated, leading spectators to believe that a singular individual or a group was representative of a whole continent of exotic beings with whom they had little in common. As a consequence, Africans came to be perceived as intellectual and moral inferiors—often no better than brutish savages who had not yet climbed beyond the bottom rungs of the evolutionary ladder. Ethnological show business thus promoted and perpetuated racism, pushing whites and blacks further apart by placing them in closer proximity. Africans were put on stage in order to distance them from the rest of humanity.

BERNTH LINDFORS

WORKS CITED

Coleman, William. *Georges Cuvier, Zoologist: A Study in the History of Evolution Theory.* Cambridge: Harvard UP, 1964.

Cook, James W., Jr. "Of Men, Missing Links, and Nondescripts: The Strange Career of P. T. Barnum's 'What is It' Exhibition." *Freakery: Cultural Spectacles of the Extraordinary Body.* Ed. Rosemarie Garland Thomson. New York and London: New York UP, 1996. 138–57.

Curtin, Philip D. *The Image of Africa: British Ideas and Action, 1780–1850.* Madison: U of Wisconsin P, 1964.

Debrunner, Hans Werner. *Presence and Prestige: Africans in Europe.* Basel: Basler Afrika Bibliographien, 1979.

Kirschenblatt-Gimblett, Barbara. "Objects of Ethnography." *Exhibiting Cultures: The Poetics and Politics of Museum Display.* Ed. Ivan Karp and Steven D. Lavine. Washington, D.C.: Smithsonian Institution Press, 1991. 386–443.

Lindfors, Bernth. "Circus Africans." *Journal of American Culture* 6.2 (1983): 9–14.

AFRICANS
ON STAGE

1

Display of the Body Hottentot[1]

Z. S. STROTHER

"What makes the Hottentot so hot?" muses the Cowardly Lion in the film *The Wizard of Oz*. And well might he ask, because for nearly five centuries the Hottentots were the most renowned, the most notorious, of all African societies. The Lion's answer, "Courage," is unusually generous. Hundreds of travellers, who never visited another African society, brought back stories of a people who gobbled like turkeys, who dressed in entrails, who anointed themselves with animal fat, who exposed both infants and the elderly, who worshipped a June bug (or nothing at all), whose women bore an "apron" of skin covering the pubis, and who transformed their men into half-eunuchs. The tale of the Hottentot is a story of willful misunderstanding so persistent and so bizarre that one is tempted to qualify it as a collective hallucination.

Finally, the chimera seemed to take flesh in 1810 with the arrival in London and Paris of Sara Baartman.[2] Under the sobriquet "the Hottentot Venus," Baartman (who suffered from steatopygia, enlargement of the behind) went on to cause a sensation in London, to tour the English provinces, and to travel on to Paris in 1814, where she engaged the interest of the famous Georges Cuvier at the Muséum d'Histoire Naturelle and of the Vaudeville theater. She died in Paris in 1815.[3]

Baartman never entirely disappeared from public consciousness, surviving in a plaster cast on display at the Musée de l'Homme in Paris until 1982 and in occasional snickers in the press.[4] In the late 1970s and 1980s, she began to appear in the burgeoning literature on nineteenth-century exhibitions of people,[5] but it was the discussions of the constructions of sexuality in science and medicine by Stephen Jay Gould (1982) and Sander Gilman (1985) that re-catapulted her to fame. Since then, Baartman has fast become both an academic and a popular icon for black sexuality and its exploitation.

In the 1996 play by Suzan-Lori Parks, "Venus," which received lavish national publicity, Baartman becomes the obsessive love object for the French scientist who "studies" her. During the New York debut, the protagonist wore a revealing costume, formfitted at the top and well padded below, modelled on a contemporary print—not the print that depicts what Baartman actually wore in London in 1810 (fig. 1.10), but the print that depicts how the audience was to imagine her (fig. 1.11). The dilemma of the playwright, playing off the sexuality of her imagined protagonist, while seeking to excoriate her exploitation, highlights the dilemma of many scholars, who have not yet found an easy means of discussing Baartman's experience without replaying the prurience of her initial exhibition. As a compromise, this article will illustrate as few as possible of the demeaning representations of Baartman.

Ironically, Baartman's contemporaries in London and Paris classed the "Hottentot" neither as "black," nor as "sexy." In fact, Baartman's success lay in her status as a figure of the anti-erotic, which allowed her to cross from the "freak show" to the pseudo-educational ethnographic show. It was as the figure of the *anti*-erotic that Baartman was reassuring to a European audience. The "Hottentot" represented a fantasy creature without language or culture, without memory or consciousness,[6] who could never actually threaten the viewer with the sexual power of a "Venus."

From Khoikhoi to Hottentot and Back Again: The Pivotal Role of Language

How did the Hottentots (now known as Khoikhoi) obtain their special place in the European imagination? Anthropologist Michèle Duchet ascribes their notoriety to their position at the Cape of Good Hope, on the important trade route to the east (*Anthropologie* 33). For centuries, Khoikhoi experienced more frequent, and more frequently superficial, contact with Europeans than any other single African population. As Kenneth Parker observes: "In that regard, Philip Curtin's classic location of modern European knowledge of Africa as located in West Africa between the 1780s and the 1840s should be reassigned and relocated at the Cape between the [late] fifteenth and seventeenth centuries" (129). Concerning those early encounters, many scholars have underemphasized the pivotal role of European astonishment at Khoikhoi click languages in the formulation of the Hottentot mythos.

Before European encroachment, the Khoikhoi ("people of people") were successful nomadic pastoralists, ranging over a vast area between Northern Botswana and the Cape of Good Hope. Herds of sheep and cattle numbering in the tens of thousands were visible and tempting to passing ships at the Cape. Nonetheless, irreversible impoverishment of the Khoikhoi rapidly followed the establishment of a rest station by the Netherlands East India Company at the Cape in 1652.[7] Terrible smallpox epidemics and the swift advance of the

Trekboer frontier in the eighteenth century led to the almost total transformation of independent Khoikhoi polities into a landless laboring class dependent on the colony.[8]

Travellers' reports claimed for the Hottentot the role of the most debased group on earth. For example, ship's surgeon Nicolaus de Graaf, who sailed around the Cape in 1640, dismissed them as "wild heathen . . . [whose] customs were more like beasts than men."[9] The position of intermediary between the human and animal realms became entirely institutionalized by the eighteenth century. Diderot's encyclopedia called them "the most barbarous [of the] savages."[10] Bory de St-Vincent listed them as the fifteenth race in a list of fifteen—just above the orangutan (qtd. in Cohen 239). The Larousse Great Universal Dictionary of the Nineteenth Century asserted that "this race appears to be the most ill-favored of all those that populate Africa. The Hottentots lack [both] intelligence and activity."[11] While many writers today collapse the Hottentot into the general history of representations of sub-Saharan Africans, Duchet correctly insists on two *distinct* discourses on "hottentots" and "black Africans" ("Racisme").

It was the European inability to recognize Khoe, with its many clicks, as true language that lay behind the initial creation of a separate discourse on the Hottentots. Although the origins of the word "Hottentot" may never be resolved, it is likely that the word itself testifies to linguistic confusion. Most dictionaries favor derivation from a compound of the Dutch *hateren* (to stammer) and *tateren* (to stutter), formed in response to Khoisan clicks.[12] *Hüttentüt* in Dutch signifies someone who stammers or stutters (Schapera 44). English and French medical literature still defines "hottentotism" ("*hottentotisme*") as a form of extreme stammering.

Because of the pejorative connotations of the word, most scholars today prefer to use the people's indigenous name for themselves, *Khoikhoi*.[13] The change in vocabulary provides convenient markers for this essay in distinguishing between references to the people themselves ("Khoikhoi") and references to their distorted reflection in European discourse ("Hottentot").

Language was central in sixteenth- and seventeenth-century thought because it marked the common frontier separating humanity from the beasts, and the Khoikhoi's acquisition of true language was in doubt.[14] In the influential words of Sir Thomas Herbert, who passed by the Cape in 1627, Khoikhoi speech was

> rather apishly then articulately sounded, with whom 'tis thought they have unnatural mixture, for as what the commentator on Ptolemy observed long since, *humana voce fere carent, ut stridere potius quam loqui videantur*, having a voice 'twixt human and beast makes that supposition to be of more credit, that they have a beastly copulation or conjuncture. (1677 ed., qtd. in Parker 140)

Voltaire went so far as to claim: "The vocal organs are different from ours; they make a stuttering and a gobbling that is impossible for other men to imitate."[15] Popular romancier and playwright Saintine set a short story among the Hottentots in 1825, cannibalizing the travel accounts: "this bizarre and very difficult language resembles no human speech, and, by its hissing, its croaking, its shrill cries, its inarticulate sounds, it appears to serve as the natural link between the language of men and that of the animals."[16] It is first and foremost because they were presumed to lack true human language that the Hottentot was assigned the role of a creature bridging human and animal realms.

As members of sedentary agricultural societies, Europeans were also deeply unsettled by Khoikhoi nomadism, dress, and cuisine. The Khoikhoi custom of rubbing the skin with animal grease led to the oft-repeated depiction of the "stinking and dirty Hottentot."[17] Not being able (or interested) in communicating effectively with the Khoikhoi, Europeans did not understand that the oil (mixed with dried leaves) served as sunblock, body oil, and insect repellent.[18]

The portrayal of the Hottentot proved a considerable problem for illustrators of the travelogues. The history of their visual representation provides rare evidence of the process of familiarizing the unfamiliar, in this case, of transforming the Khoikhoi into the Hottentot. From the sixteenth to eighteenth centuries, the manners of representing Hottentots varied widely as artists struggled to find a vocabulary adequate to their task. By the mid-eighteenth century, a stable configuration had emerged that Sara Baartman would be obliged to act out in dress and in performance on her arrival in Europe in 1810.

Visualizing the Hottentot

In a classic text, art historian E. H. Gombrich has stressed that "[t]o draw an unfamiliar sight presents greater difficulties than is usually realized" (81). This is because an artist "begins not with his visual impression but with his idea or concept . . ." (73). The difficulty lies in producing an image for an unfamiliar subject that evokes a *familiar* body of *conceptual* knowledge. In this case, the serious representational challenge lay in creating an image that would evoke the purported baseness and bestiality of the Hottentot. But how does one fold vocal and olfactory allusions into a visual image? How does one represent a nullity—a "lack" of religion, language, culture?

The first artist known to grapple with the problem was Hans Burgkmair the Elder of Augsburg (1473–c. 1531).[19] In 1508 he published six woodcuts illustrating the travels of a German merchant, Balthasar Springer, who had passed the Cape of Good Hope on a Portuguese ship in 1506. The same year Burgkmair also issued a broadsheet of a couple identified as "Hottentots" (Singer and Jopp) (fig. 1.1).

Fig. 1.1. Hans Burgkmair the Elder of Augsburg. "In Allago,"
woodcut dated 1508, illustrating the travels of German merchant
Balthasar Springer in 1506. London, British Museum.
Photo courtesy of The Warburg Institute, University of London.

Bartholomeu Dias had docked at Mossel Bay only twenty years earlier in 1488, and the inhabitants of the Cape had not yet acquired their reputation (or their name). Burgkmair depicts a Hottentot couple dressed in mantles of fur or skin held together at the neck by leather thongs. Both carry walking sticks and wear leather sandals. The woman wears a sheepskin hat (a sheep's leg hangs down over her shoulder).

Burgkmair's image established the *kaross* (sheepskin mantle) as the "efficient sign" of Hottentot identity. In fact, often one may recognize Hottentots solely by depiction of the mantle. We can understand the resonance of the *kaross* by observing that Burgkmair's broadsheet strongly recalls a reversed image of Dürer's *Adam and Eve* of 1504 both in its composition and in its use of classical quotations for the pose of the figures. Instead of Eve handing the apple to Adam, Burgkmair has revised the action so that the man hands unidentified leaves to the woman. A small son gambols between them in the pose of many a Renaissance cherub. Of late, numerous authors have begun to identify the compositional quotations used in constructing images of Hottentots.[20] Jean Michel Massing notes that such quotations "seem at odds with the cultural context" (44), but Gombrich's emphasis on the *conceptual* nature of visual images needs to be emphasized. Burgkmair is not randomly plagiarizing compositions. By quoting a well-known image, he is assimilating the Khoikhoi to Adam and Eve, newly expelled from the Garden, dressed in garments of skin by the Lord God to hide their nakedness (Gen. 3:21). Burgkmair thereby familiarizes the nomadic foreign society.

Christopher L. Miller has identified the "conjunction of realism and allegory . . . [as] a peculiarly Africanist form of discourse" (14). In this case, close attention to details like the leather thongs or the attempt (unrivalled for centuries) to depict Khoisan coiffure lends credibility to the artist's allegorical interpretation of the Hottentots as a new Adam and Eve. While the artist's image is not unsympathetic, it does imply that the Hottentots have not made any progress since that early period of expulsion, when the first couple were forced to wander before establishing themselves as cultivators. The artist's selection of walking sticks (*kierie*) and sandals also highlights the nomadic pastoralism that so disturbed European visitors.[21] Both attributes point to steady movement over uneven terrain. The *kaross*, stick, sandals, and woman's cap will become stable signs of nomadism and difference in representations of the Hottentots. On her arrival in London, Baartman was anachronistically obliged to adopt them.

THE SAVAGE HOTTENTOT

W. G. L. Randles has pointed to the significance of early hostile encounters between the Portuguese and the Khoikhoi in setting the tone for rancorous descriptions of the latter (150–51). At contact, Khoikhoi stoned Bartolomeu Dias and his men for taking spring water without permission; the Portuguese responded by shooting a Khoikhoi with a crossbow. In 1497, Vasco da Gama was wounded along with several others in an encounter at St. Helena Bay. Antonio de Saldanha was ambushed and wounded in 1503. After his crew kidnapped some children to force barter in cattle, Francisco d'Almeida, the Viceroy to India, was killed in a battle along with fifty others on his homeward voyage in 1510. By this time, the Khoikhoi had established a reputation for military prowess and the Portuguese soon preferred to dock in Mozambique.

Fig. 1.2. "Ein Wilder Man, Bei C. Bona Spei, in Africa." Illustration of the 1595
voyage of Cornelis de Houtman. From Levinus Hulsius, ed., *Erste Schiffart*
(Nürnberg: Levini Hulsij, 1602), facing p. 10. Courtesy of the Beinecke Rare
Book and Manuscript Library, Yale University.

Although English and Dutch merchants established trade in the 1590s, an edgy
wariness lingered from the early years.

The main theme of seventeenth-century images and written accounts is
wildness and savagery. The *Oxford English Dictionary* reports that a savage is
a "person living in the lowest state of development or cultivation; an uncivilized, wild person." The term may also refer to a person who is "[f]ierce, ferocious, cruel."[22] The *OED* describes the standard representation of a savage as
naked, or covered by leaves. The lack of clothes referred by association to a
lack of culture. However, because nudity could *also* signify innocence, through

association with Adam and Eve before the Fall, the naked savage was always a deeply ambivalent visual image and one that was hard to control. In the case of the Hottentot, artists were left struggling without a suitable vocabulary to express the purported cruel and bestial nature of their subject.

One series of images will highlight the problem. Illustrators for the influential voyage of Cornelis de Houtman in 1595 drew on fifteenth- and six-teenth-century images of John the Baptist for the depiction of Hottentots (fig. 1.2). The fiery prophet who lived in the wilderness on a diet of locusts and honey, and who dressed in a coat of camel's hair, was a logical model for assimilating accounts of Hottentot lifestyles, including hunting and gathering (Matt. 3:1–4; Mark 1:6). The artists adapted John the Baptist's iconography of staff (sometimes turned into an assegai for the Hottentots), wiry build, and disheveled hair. The quotation informs the viewer that the Hottentots live *like* John the Baptist.

The problem for illustrators lay in restricting the reading of the image. The fine proportions and reference to Christ's predecessor might mislead viewers. In order to limit the simile, the publisher relies on the caption, which identifies the illustration as "Ein Wilder Man." The editor of a Dutch edition goes further in asserting: "These may well be cannibals, since they eat raw flesh and even the guts and intestines just as they come from the beasts, without cleansing them" (trans. Raven-Hart, *Before Van Riebeeck,* illustration facing 85). The caption also makes reference to language and to smell, but it is the image of eating entrails that will serve as a visual attribute of lawlessness and unrestrained brutality.[23]

In a lavish folio edition from 1599, the illustrator shows the Dutch at work butchering an ox (fig. 1.3). One European offers a Hottentot the present of the entrails. The latter is so eager to consume them that he cannot wait to cook the meat lightly as his colleagues in the background do. He immediately devours the entrails fresh and warm from the animal.

Food taboos are among the strongest cultural markers. In the image of the Hottentot devouring warm entrails, the illustrator has found a resonant metaphor to convey the bestiality of a people who do not know cooking, hence civilization. It is animals who eat raw meat. The inability of the Hottentot to control his animal appetite further underscores the weakness of reason over instinct in his people.

Despite the Hottentot's savage action, the illustration nonetheless is marked by an unsettling tension between the Hottentot's savage *culture* and the beauty of his *body.* European theorists of the time very much desired and expected outer appearance to reflect inner truth. One contemporary traveller wrestled outright with this contradiction: "In a word, these folk are in all ways like the ignorant beasts, except for the noble human form . . ." (qtd. in Raven-Hart, *Before Van Riebeeck* 128).

Fig. 1.3. "Contrafayt der Völcker so an dem Vorgebir oder Capo bonae spei wohnen. (No. VIII)." Illustration of the 1595 voyage of Cornelis de Houtman. From Johann Theodor de Bry and Johann Israel de Bry, eds., *India Orientalis*, pt. 3 (Franckfurt am Mayn: Gedruckt durch M. Becker, 1599), pl. 7. Reproduced from the Collections of the Library of Congress, Washington, D.C.

The illustrator of Sir Thomas Herbert's report on his 1627 voyage is much more successful at resolving the tension of savage culture and human form. The illustrator depicts a European nuclear family unit with man, woman, and child (fig. 1.4). The man is stout and well-muscled. He stands silent, squarely facing the viewer with long assegai held diagonally across the page in an action that blocks the viewer's access to the landscape. The artist thereby conveys the uneasy caution expressed by Herbert and his contemporaries in light of the Portuguese experience of Khoikhoi defense.

While the man is made ridiculous (in European eyes) by the addition of the fanciful hairstyle and cicatrization, it is the woman whose representation reconciles savage culture with savage form. Whereas the man's proportions are naturalistic, the woman's arms are lengthened, her legs shortened and her countenance given a freakish simian cast as she skips up with a handful of bleeding entrails, her mouth open in enthusiastic ululation. She does not look out to address the viewer, but is drawn in profile. She does not even nurse like a European woman, but rather with her "[u]berous dugg stretched over her naked

Fig. 1.4. "A man and woman at the Cape of Good Hope." From Sir Thomas Herbert, *A relation of some yeares travaile, bevnne anno 1626. Into Afrique and the greater Asia* . . . (London: W. Stansby and J. Bloome, 1634), p. 17. Courtesy of the Beinecke Rare Book and Manuscript Library, Yale University.

shoulder" (Herbert 17), a detail oft-repeated in subsequent travelogues (see also figs. 1.6–1.7).

In the chain of being that proposes the Hottentot as the "missing link" between human and animal realms, it is the Hottentot woman who serves as the truly transitional figure between man and ape. A recurrent theme that Herbert repeats is that the women deliver their children (as the beasts do) without pain or need of assistance (qtd. in Raven-Hart, *Before Van Riebeeck* 120). Whatever flaws the men may have (such as the purported excision of a testicle) are attributed to culture, but the woman somehow is different in essence.

10

Namaqua Peuples Nouvellem'decouverts vers le Tropiq. du Capricorne.

Fig. 1.5. "Namaqua Peuples Nouvellemt decouverts vers le Tropiq. du Capricorne." From G. Tachard, *[A] relation of the Voyage to Siam, performed by Six Jesuits* (London: J. Robinson, 1688), fig. vi. Courtesy of the Beinecke Rare Book and Manuscript Library, Yale University.

The radical dissymmetry of Hottentot men and women is the subject for another illustration in the popular travelogue of Guy Tachard (fig. 1.5). The artist (possibly Heinrich Claudius) has represented the man with the profile and physique of the Apollo Belvedere. Only his mantle identifies him as a debased Hottentot. In contrast, the woman is portrayed knock-kneed, with simian proportions and pendulous breasts. The man's demeanor is one of concentration and reserve, indicating faculties of mind absent in the woman with her unfocused eyes and silly grin.

The era of the savage Hottentot was passing. Duchet has observed that exoticism flourishes only when fear of the savage has been vanquished (*Anthropologie* 59).[24] In this case, the day was past when the European felt seriously threatened by Khoikhoi aggression. Historian Richard Elphick has chronicled that the colonists enjoyed a comfortable sense of security by the 1670s due to a rising European population, strict control over firearms, and a series of military victories, 1673–77.[25] During these years, Khoikhoi who had lost their stock were increasingly absorbed into the colony as cheap laborers. The Khoikhoi would again rebel, but the large number of dispossessed workers within and near the colony worked to transform the Hottentot image from brutal savage to hapless simpleton. Elphick reports that "[b]y 1720 the transformation of the Western Cape Khoikhoi into 'colonial Hottentots' was almost complete" (235).

THE ICONOGRAPHY OF INDOLENCE

The new image of the Hottentot in the eighteenth-century travelogues was shaped by the labor requirements of the Dutch colony. To their surprise, the Dutch found that Khoikhoi men were willing to work for nominal sums as herders, but they refused all ill-paid menial and agricultural labor. Khoikhoi recalcitrance was so obdurate that the Dutch began to import slaves, who could be bullied more successfully into performing these tasks. The difficulty of holding a people in their own country scotched early speculations about enslaving the peninsular Khoikhoi. Therefore, the Khoikhoi always retained free status.

The frustrations of the early colonists found vent in the travel literature, including the most influential account of Khoikhoi customs ever published, Peter Kolb's *The Present State of the Cape of Good Hope*.[26] This work, originally published in 1719, became the standard reference tool of Diderot, Voltaire, the Marquis de Sade, and every travel writer.

Kolb gave voice to the colonists' view that Khoikhoi aversion to heavy and poorly paid menial labor sprang from a culture mired in indolence.[27] Kolb writes ironically that the Hottentots cherish their liberty, but only because they are fundamentally lazy:

> If you shake a Stick at a *Hottentot*, who is not in your service, and threaten to compel him to work, he immediately takes to his Heels, and is immediately Miles out of your Reach. The *Hottentots* are the greatest Lovers of Liberty in the World. (Medley translation, 1:322)

However, Kolb goes further and extends a disinclination to work (on Dutch terms) to a *disinclination to think*. In a passage that becomes the touchstone for future writings on the Hottentots (and for speculations on the chain of being), Kolb writes:

> And the first Thing I shall remark in this View of the *Hottentots* is their Laziness. They are, without doubt, both in Body and Mind, the laziest People under the Sun. A monstrous Indisposition to Thought and Action runs through all the Nations of them: And their whole Earthly Happiness seems to lie in Indolence and Supinity. (Medley translation, 1:46)

Other writers extended the equation further still.

Michael Adas has argued that eighteenth-century thinkers ranked societies on the basis of perceived ideas on religion. Hottentots came to represent base zero because they were alleged to have no ideas whatsoever about God or the afterlife. Traveller Nicolas de La Caille asserted that the Hottentots have no god, no idea of prayer, no worship:

> It seems very probable that their great laziness has made them forget the traditions of their ancestors as regards this [religion], since the supreme good for a Hottentot is to do nothing, and even to think of nothing. (41)

Voltaire wrote that the Hottentots had not pushed reason far enough to know a supreme being (*Essai* 308). By the nineteenth century, the Hottentot image was fixed. The writer Saintine reflects it in the popular press in 1826. He describes the Hottentots as a people "who make laziness their only divinity, and whose common maxim is that 'to work is to suffer, and to think is to work.'"[28]

By the mid-eighteenth century, therefore, the Hottentot had solidified in both England and France into a figure nearly without language, certainly without religion, and dangerously close to being without the capacity for thought itself. Thus in English "Hottentot" became a common slur for someone of congenital stupidity (Compact Edition of the Oxford English Dictionary 1971). The slur was often transferred from one colonial situation to another: Ireland. The term was also sometimes used to disparage a person's religious understanding, as when the Methodist John Wesley wrote dismissively: "I found her as ignorant of the nature of religion as an Hottentot" (ibid.). When applied to the Irish, probably both prongs of the epithet were intended.

Curiously, artists found it far easier to respond to the new image of the Hottentot, subject to a "monstrous Indisposition to Thought and Action," than they had to the earlier representations of the wild savage. In the transformation of "Lovers of Liberty" into a people disinclined to think, there is a slippage from culture to nature as yet unresolved. If "Hottentot" came to serve as a colorful epithet for congenital stupidity in the popular imagination, the issue could not be so clear-cut in the learned or "scientific" literature, where such an attribution demanded explanation. Eighteenth-century illustrators found a way out of their representational difficulties through recourse to the cultural emblem of the pipe.

The pipe represented the newest item in Hottentot iconography since Burgkmair had selected the *kaross* in 1508. The short pipe and the Hottentot became inseparable in the European imagination, although the earliest reference to tobacco trading occurs only in 1646. The use of tobacco expanded greatly with the dispossession of the Khoikhoi as part of the payment for wage labor. The Khoikhoi accepted tobacco (with its short pipe) as a mild substitute for *dagga* (Indian hemp, or *Cannabis sativa*), which they had long smoked.[29]

Fig. 1.6. "The Manner in which Hottentot women carry their Children, nurse them, and accustom them to Tobacco." From Pierre Kolb, *Description du Cap de Bonne-Esperance* (Amsterdam: Jean Cautuffe, 1742), vol. 1, facing p. 213. Photo by Z. S. Strother.

Fierce debates had raged in Europe over the status of tobacco as an intoxicating drug and soporific. What amazed European visitors was that women smoked (both *Cannabis* and tobacco) as often as the men.[30] In the English translation of Kolb, the illustrator juxtaposes a detailed drawing of the *Cannabis* plant with a vignette of a seated woman nursing her baby while billows of smoke rise from her nostrils and pipe (illustration facing 163). Kolb remarks: "She is generally smoaking *Dacha* [*sic*] while she has the Child at her Back. The Wind often carries over a great Deal of Smoak full in the Child's

Fig. 1.7. "Prospect of the Country at the Cape of Good Hope." From A. Sparrmann, *Voyage to the Cape of Good Hope*, trans. from the Swedish, 2nd ed., corr. (London: G.G.J. and J. Robinson, 1786), vol. 1, frontispiece. Photo by Z. S. Strother.

Face, sufficient, one would think, to stifle it. She minds not this. Nor, in a little Time, does the Child" (163–64).

In the French edition (fig. 1.6), the artist places two women in the landscape. He underscores the supine pose of the smoking woman through contrast with the vertical alignment of adjacent tree and picture frame. The woman exhales a cloud of smoke that almost obliterates her nursing baby. Another woman strolling by reaches out for a puff and will no doubt join her on the empty rock bench. The ease of the women, each a mother of two, the playful-

15

ness of the children, and the verdant setting along a stream provide a powerful image of a rich country able to satisfy life's needs without much effort. The relaxed pose of the smoking and supine woman makes clear that she is content with a rock to sit on and a tree's shade for her head. The women are *in* nature; they form a part of nature. Eighteenth-century depictions represent Hottentots as integral parts of their environment, which they do not shape or conquer. The woman's intoxication represents an abdication of action. Her companion's willingness to join her represents a fall from agency and culture (she was setting out to do something) to the state of vegetative being.

The costs of this abdication are made explicit in the title-page illustration for another important travelogue, Anders Sparrman's *Voyage to the Cape of Good Hope*, published in English in 1785 and 1786 (fig. 1.7). This artist presents a bountiful vista of a rich land. In the left foreground stands a Hottentot couple. The man holds his spear for hunting, but lingers regretfully over his pipe, which is smoking strongly. A younger man kneels before him, armed with bow and quiver, waiting for his turn with the pipe. The woman, nursing her baby, also seems to be waiting for her turn. The family kraal, nestled into bushes, is depicted behind them, and two adolescent children ride by leisurely on an ox. In the right foreground, two children play with arrows. In the right middleground, a circle of eight round houses corral two cows. The houses nestle in a valley, surrounded by bushes. The darker and verdant planes inhabited by the Hottentots are contrasted formally to the light-filled and rocky distance where European figures are frenetically busy: two pursue a large herd of antelope; another drives an eight-oxen wagon down the steep hill. The Hottentot man's body is turned toward the landscape, toward the hunt, but he pivots back to smoke.

In both images, the representation of the Hottentot turning from productive activity to the "gentle state of intoxication by smoking tobacco" (Sparrman, [London], 1786 1: 205) carried an ideological message. Allegations of indolence justified European appropriation of Khoikhoi land and establishment of their juridical status as minors. The pipe became the potent referent for the Hottentots, lazy in body and mind, who have forfeited their land due to indolence.[31]

THE FAILURE OF THE NOBLE SAVAGE, THE FAILURE OF EROTICISM

As remarked earlier, violent misogyny dominates the description of Khoikhoi women in the travelogues. "The women may be distinguished from the men by their ugliness," asserts William Ten Ryne (qtd. in Schapera and Farrington 115). His pronouncement is blunt, but his sentiment was widespread. In the influential account penned by the Jesuit priest Guy Tachard in

1685, Nama men emerge as an early prototype of the noble savage, long of limb and short of speech: "They are all tall of stature and strong, have good natural sense. . . . [They] weigh their words well before they answer, and all their answers are short and grave" (74). In contrast, the best that can be said of the women is that they are "nasty" and "not so grave as the men" (74). Khoikhoi women are never routinely eroticized, as are women from other African societies, e.g., the Zulu.[32]

In fact, Michèle Duchet argues that European discourse distinguishes "Hottentots" from "black Africans" through claims of critical difference in women's sexuality ("Racisme" 132–34): "Constantly referred to as a *sexed object*, the hottentot woman does not exist as a *sex object [sexual object]*. . . ."[33] Tales of lewd and lascivious behavior are reserved for black women (134). Instead the Khoikhoi woman, although graphically sexed, is not represented as an object of desire—in the travel literature. (The liaisons at the Cape tell a different story; see below.) Instead, an undercurrent of resentment periodically erupts into diatribes directed at face painting, at the use of body oil, and at the body itself of the Hottentot woman.

The two *Voyages* of François Le Vaillant support Duchet's argument. Le Vaillant travelled in the Dutch colony at the Cape, 1781–84, and his subsequent publications established him as the best-read author of the early nineteenth century on Khoikhoi life and customs.[34] Le Vaillant, who began writing in the 1780s, when a new brand of more sentimental travel literature emerged (Pratt 131), very much wanted to cast the Hottentot in the role of the noble savage.

> I had here an opportunity of admiring a free and brave people, valuing nothing but independence; never obeying any impulse foreign to nature, and calculated only to destroy their magnanimous, free, and truly philanthropic character. (*Travels*, 1790, 2: 14)

He emphasizes the distinction between the colonial Hottentots and the "Savage Hottentots" (*Travels*, 1790, 1: 275), who live beyond the colony's borders, in a state of "innocence" (*Travels*, 1790, 2: 124). Knowing the history of Hottentot representation, he asserts: "In an uncivilized state man is naturally good; why then should the Hottentot be an exception to this general rule" (*Travels*, 1790, 2: 125). He rejects the use of tobacco as the degraded symbol of European corruption of these noble people (*Voyage*, 1798, 2: 119).

Le Vaillant's text is fascinating both for what it reveals about the author and for demonstrating the centrality of physical desire in the construction of the noble savage. In his description of Amiroo, "one of the most beautiful savages I had ever seen" (*Travels*, 1790, 2: 4), Le Vaillant sounds almost like a rebuffed lover in his disappointment at the former's cool and self-confident reception: "I was desirous that he might be convinced, by his own experience,

17

that there is a wide difference between a European and a Hottentot" (*Travels,* 1790, 2: 9). Le Vaillant tricks the young man by lending him a gun, which sometimes fires, sometimes not. When he has humbled Amiroo, he can once again wax lyrical about Amiroo's "happy ignorance" (*Voyage,* 1798, 2: 11). It is the beautiful and naked body of the noble savage that is to *embody* a moralizing allegory for the innocent virtues that a corrupted civilization has forgotten. Although Le Vaillant desires to write such an allegory, he is repeatedly thwarted by an inability to eroticize fully his hosts, or more exactly, his hostesses. Like the majority of travellers, he found the typical Hottentot man more impressive than the typical woman.

Le Vaillant's efforts to reform the Hottentot into noble savage met the greatest success among the Gonaqua, who had been incorporated into the Colony only in 1778. His text makes clear how important physical appearance is in this project. He stresses how attractive he finds the Gonaqua, described as darker, taller, with straighter noses (*Voyage,* 1798, 2: 2). (The Gonaqua are often considered intermarried with the Xhosa.) He forms a crush on a sixteen-year-old girl: "her person was slender and elegant, and her shape, formed to inspire love. . . . She was the youngest of the Graces, under the figure of a Hottentot" (*Travels,* 1790, 1: 378). He insists that the girl cease painting her face, oiling her body. Her successful transformation is marked by Le Vaillant's renaming her as "Narina," or "flower." He rejects her true name as senseless and disagreeable to the ear (*Travels,* 1790, 1: 382).

Narina's image is the only fully eroticized representation of a Hottentot woman that I have seen and fits into the history of representations of other sub-Saharan African women (fig. 1.8). Le Vaillant depicts her with Grecian proportions, lowered eyes, and rosebud mouth. The fall of her necklaces draws attention to her tight breasts, also emphasized by the horizontal of her left arm raised in welcome. The figure pivots slightly, directing the viewer into her landscape, and (by extension) into a relationship with her. The artist calls attention to her groin area though the piling up of waist beads, through the sharp, contrasting white beadwork of the cloth covering the pubic area, and through the placement of right hand and basket.

Le Vaillant has stripped the figure of her true name and all the signs of Hottentot identity: hat, *kaross,* face painting, walking stick, or sandals. Her dress is a composite of the dress of different Southern African agriculturalists. Narina's image demonstrates that Le Vaillant can only transform the "Hottentot" into the noble savage by *evacuating all signs of the Hottentot.*

The text also makes crystal clear the role of voyeurism in Le Vaillant's project. He is obsessed with seeing the bodies around him. Le Vaillant purposely stalks some Khoikhoi women who are bathing and uses their embarrassment to eulogize their innate feminine modesty.

Fig. 1.8. "Narina, a Young Gonaqua Girl." From François Le Vaillant, *Travels
into the Interior Parts of Africa* (London: G.G.J. and J. Robinson, 1790), vol. 1,
pl. IV, facing p. 380. Courtesy of the Beinecke Rare Book and Manuscript
Library, Yale University.

Having glided softly between the tree and bushes, I got close to the bank without being perceived, and found them all swimming. . . . When I had surveyed
these female bathers at my leisure, I soon put an end to their sport by firing my
fusee [gun]; upon which they all plunged in the water, leaving nothing above the
surface but the points of their noses. I then seated myself on their clothes which
were heaped together, where I took a pleasure in jeering them; and shewing
them their small aprons one after the other, invited them to come for them.
(*Travels,* 1790, 1: 388–89)

As in the incident with Amiroo, Le Vaillant expresses his phallic superiority as
a man and as a European in firing his gun. He humbles the women, like Amiroo,
in order to be able to praise their innate virtues, in this case, "natural modesty"

Fig. 1.9. "Hottentote à Tablier." From
François Le Vaillant, *Voyage dans l'interieur
de l'Afrique* (Paris, Chez Leroy, 1790), vol. 2,
p. 349. Courtesy of Bernth Lindfors.

(*Travels,* 1790, 1: 393). Le Vaillant's text demonstrates that the noble savage
may only be eulogized from a site of established dominance.

Ironically, Le Vaillant can only demonstrate innate modesty through its
violation. "I myself ought indeed to have blushed" (*Travels,* 1790, 1: 393), he
wrote, but *did not.* The bathing incident is a necessary prologue to Le Vaillant's
project of titillating the reader while establishing the decorous behavior of most
Hottentot women. Le Vaillant ends his travelogue with his *pièce de résistance:*
the unveiling of a woman's genitals—in the purported interests of science (*Travels,* 1790, 2: 350–51). In a fully eroticized passage he stresses the extraordinary
persuasion required to overcome the woman's refusal. Finally, "Confused,
abashed and trembling, she covered her face with both her hands, suffered her
apron to be untied, and permitted me to contemplate at leisure what my readers will see themselves in the exact representation which I drew of it" (*Travels,*
1790, 2: 351).[35] In this passage, Le Vaillant explicitly identifies the reader as his
accomplice in voyeurism and provides an "exact" replica for the reader's own
contemplation. The emphasis on "leisure" emphasizes once again the viewer's
position of dominant power. Neither Le Vaillant, nor the reader, need snatch a
fleeting glance.

The women's resistance to being viewed is necessary to Le Vaillant's project
of transforming the Hottentot into the noble savage, but it does pose a problem
for the artist. In complete contradiction to the psychological violence described

in the text, the accompanying plate (fig. 1.9) seeks to evade any embarrassment the viewer may feel at violating the subject's privacy by rendering the woman complicit in the convention of the Western nude. The artist adapts the composition of the Knidian Aphrodite, who leans on a rock as she disrobes. The woman looks out directly at the viewer but tilts her head in an established pose of erotic submissiveness. She dangles the beaded clothing that she has removed from her left hand as she covers part of her mouth with her right hand. These gestures draw attention by contrast to what she is *not* covering, her breasts and pubis. In addition, the coy tease of the hand at the mouth evokes the sheltered orifice of the vagina.

The language of both the text and the image casts the encounter with this woman as an erotic experience inviting penetration. And yet, what does the viewer find? Le Vaillant was the first traveller to picture the legendary "Hottentot apron," or hypertrophy of the *labia minora* (Schapera 59, 62).[36] Because some Khoisan women develop this condition, and many do not, voyagers bickered over its existence for over 250 years. In the name of "scientific" inquiry, dozens of visitors at the Cape sought to peer up women's skirts and settle the matter to their own satisfaction.

Nicolaus de Graaf made the earliest reference in 1640: "As an ornament the women have in certain places short thongs hanging down, cut from the body" (qtd. in Raven-Hart, *Before Van Riebeeck* 152). The debate took shape over whether the condition, if it existed, was due to nature or culture. De Graaf argued for culture, but sinister speculations soon arose. In 1694, another writer asserted: ". . . [J]ust as they differ in their bestial life from other men, so also Nature has marked them off in this manner" (qtd. in Raven-Hart, *Cape*, 2: 406). After a visit to the Cape, Voltaire's narrator Amabed concludes:

> The more I reflect on the color of these peoples, on the gobbling that they use to make themselves understood instead of an articulated language, on their countenance, on the "apron" of their ladies, the more I am convinced that this race can not have the same origin as we [do].[37]

Those favoring nature found the condition a heaven-sent boon in finally locating difference in the body itself. What first language, then supposed lack of religion, suggested could finally be *represented* for all to see in the genitals of the Hottentot woman.

As self-appointed champion of the Hottentot, Le Vaillant took great pains to argue for a cultural explanation, which he felt explained why only some women manifested the condition (*Voyage*, 1798, 350, 352–53). In an extraordinary passage, Le Vaillant argues that the "famous apron" results simply from fashion, however absurd and extravagant, with the goal of extinguishing lust itself.[38] He asserts that a single glance would suffice to repel the most "monstrous libertine" by turning his passion into laughter. With byzantine sophistry, Le Vaillant connects the practice with "fashion," hence with the foibles of the human race, here used chastely (in contradiction, one understands, to the functions of fashion in France). The Hottentot excess derives from a surfeit of modesty.

Despite Le Vaillant's mental gymnastics, what emerges is graphic evidence of Duchet's claim that the Hottentot woman, *unlike* the black woman, is rendered sexed but not sexy. In Le Vaillant's image and text, the considerable erotic language deployed serves finally to reveal the *absence* of desire. Depicted as an Aphrodite, she can arouse only laughter or horror by contrast. Le Vaillant himself uses the word "ridiculous" to describe the effect of face painting: "Although accustomed to see Hottentots, I never got used to the practice women have of painting their faces in a thousand different manners; I find it hideous and repellent . . . not only ridiculous but foul-smelling" (*Voyage,* 1798, 2:44).[39] More importantly, Diderot's encyclopedia voiced the common assessment of Hottentot women as bearers of a "monstrueuse difformité" (17: 786). It is this image that will linger in the European imagination, not Narina with her rosebud mouth. Le Vaillant's project in rendering the Hottentot as noble savage fails precisely when he is unable to eroticize the nameless and simpering "Hottentot Woman with Apron" ("Hottentote à Tablier").

THE MANUFACTURE OF A HOTTENTOT

> *From the highest to the lowest this people seem fond of sights and monsters.*
> —Oliver Goldsmith, "The Citizen of the World" (248)

The problem of representation of the Hottentot did not end with Sara Baartman's arrival in London. In fact, it only grew worse with the necessity of evoking Gombrich's "familiar body of conceptual knowledge"—all that people thought that they knew about Hottentots—in the display of her body. To make matters more complicated, her display intersected with a venerable system of representation established for the public exhibition of people in the "freak show."

Khoikhoi had gained renewed notoriety in Great Britain due to the definitive British occupation of the Cape colony in 1806. By 1809, British missionaries had won a highly publicized debate within the colony by assigning the Khoikhoi to the special protection of the British government. The British governor was held to stand "in nature of a guardian over the *Hottentot* nation . . . by reason of their general imbecile state . . ." (East, 1816, 195). This dubious protection required the Khoikhoi and other "free coloureds" to enter into service, live at some fixed abode, and carry work passes. It also precluded land ownership. The dispossessed Khoikhoi assumed the juridical status of legal wards in need of discipline and protection.

The following year, around August 1810, Sara Baartman arrived in England in the company of English army surgeon Alexander Dunlop and probably Henrick Caesar, who became her exhibitor (see Bullock's and Solly's affidavits in the appendix).[40] No doubt, Dunlop hoped to capitalize on the British curiosity about its new colony and on the fame of the Hottentots, rendered topical due to the publicity surrounding the recent legislation.

Baartman suffered to an unusual degree from steatopygia, a condition common but by no means restricted to Khoisan peoples. Despite the topicality of Hottentots at that moment in Britain, Dunlop and Caesar clearly chose Baartman rather than some other Khoisan person due to her steatopygia. The initial audience thus fit her easily into the unending production of "freaks" in the capital. The writer of a penny ballad had no doubt on this score:

> But you may ask, and well, I ween,
>   For why she tarries there;
> And what, in her is to be seen,
>   Than other folks more rare.
> A rump she has (though strange it be),
>   Large as a cauldron pot,
> And this is why men go to see
>   This lovely Hottentot.
> ("'The Hottentot Venus': a Ballad" 334)

In Anne Mathews's memoir of actor Charles Mathews, described as a great "sight-seer," the "Hottentot Venus" is included in a list of shows with the "Spotted Boy," M. Lambert (a giant), Count Boruwlaski (a midget), and Miss Crackham (a dwarf) (1). Anne Mathews attributed Baartman's success to the revealing lines of neo-classical women's fashion of the period: "In those days, when *bustles* were *not*, she was a curiosity, for English ladies then wore no shape but what Nature gave and insisted upon. . . . Well, then, a Hottentot Venus [was] in *that* day a novelty . . ." (136–37, *sic*).

The enthusiasm for freaks in the seventeenth, eighteenth, and early nineteenth centuries is something not easily comprehended today. Samuel Pepys once described himself in 1660 as "with child to see any strange thing" (138) and Jonathan Swift immortalized the mania for the extra-small and the extra-large in *Gulliver's Travels*. Eighteenth-century London witnessed an endless succession of dwarves, giants, midgets, Siamese twins, trained monkeys, and curiosities of all kinds (including many inventive fakes). The most successful of these exhibitors established stage personalities, and many acted out special parts or performed tasks thought impossible due to their disability. In these shows, a foreign flavor was especially attractive to spectators: an Irish giant was ever so much better than an English one (Altick 268).

Why were people so attracted to the mutant, the deformed, the ugly? Oliver Goldsmith, writing in the voice of a Chinese philosopher in London, laments:

> By their fondness of sights one would be apt to imagine that, instead of desiring to see things as they should be, they are rather solicitous of seeing them as they ought not to be. A cat with four legs is disregarded, though never so useful; but if it has but two, and is consequently incapable of catching mice, it is reckoned inestimable. . . . (250)

Certainly, the spectators took a positive enjoyment from viewing difference that was so comfortable because a supreme confidence in the ideal underlay it all. Paradoxically, the great age of freaks is also the great age of the art academy and the belief in ideal form.

In an important discussion, literary critic Susan Stewart observes: "Often referred to as a 'freak of nature,' the freak, it must be emphasized, is a freak of culture. His or her anomalous status is articulated by the process of the spectacle as it distances the viewer, and thereby it 'normalizes' the viewer as much as it marks the freak as an aberration" (109). Stewart identifies several tools developed in these spectacles to establish a comfortable distance between viewer and subject. The most important of these is the suspension of dialogue or communication between the two (109–10). The silence of the performer stands in dramatic contrast to the babble of the barker, who acts as translator or interpreter. Secondly, "[w]e find the freak inextricably tied to the cultural other" (109). Thirdly, the freak is "linked not to lived sexuality but to certain forms of the pornography of distance" (110). Baartman's exhibition was pivotal in transferring the tools developed in the freak show to the ethnographic exhibition, which began to flourish in the nineteenth century.

FREAK OR TYPE?

> *For I have always lookt upon it as a high Point of Indiscretion in* Monster-mongers *and other* Retailers of strange Sights; *to hang out a fair large Picture over the Door, drawn after the Life, with a most eloquent Description underneath: This hath saved me many a Threepence, for my Curiosity was fully satisfied. . . .*
> —Jonathan Swift, "A Tale of a Tub" (321–22)

Advertising played an essential role in the promotion of people exhibitions and provides rare evidence for the conditions of their display and reception. Signboards, posters, leaflets, and newspaper advertisements stressed the astounding novelty of the show. What is perhaps surprising to us today in the posters and souvenir prints is the dignity of those depicted. Even in the hands of the caricaturist Rowlandson, the spectators rather than the spectacle come across as truly ridiculous. There is an emphasis on naturalistic detail and perspectival rendering of space. The majority of freaks are depicted frontally or in the traditional three-quarter view used for portraits. Many meet the eye of the viewer and strike self-confident poses. Each conveys a sense of individual personality. The frank gaze and three-dimensional modelling were employed to convince the prospective visitor, through representational analogy, of the subject's authenticity, of his or her existence in real space and time.[41] Baartman's presentation contrasts strongly with this tradition.

Initially, Baartman's exhibitors were conflicted about their publicity strategy. Although the British audience discerned clearly why she had been chosen for exhibition, from the moment of her arrival, Caesar placed a barrage of advertisements in the newspapers that marketed Baartman as a *type*, rather than as a "freak." These ads solicit the attendance of the well-educated, those familiar with the travelogues, by offering a native from the "banks of the Gamtoos" (i.e., on the fringes of the colony):

> a most correct and perfect Specimen of that race of people. From this extraordinary phenomena of nature, the Public will have an opportunity of judging how far she exceeds any description given by historians of that tribe of the human species. She is habited in the dress of her country, with all the rude ornaments usually worn by those people.[42]

The ad asserts that the "literati" have been gratified by "the sight of so wonderful a specimen of the human race." Another ad describes her as "a truly interesting object of natural history" (*MP* 30 April 1811). These advertisements invite the educated viewer to play the role of scientist (or latent anthropologist), and promise to provide for study an accurate type in form, clothing, and behavior.

This is the crucial point at which Baartman's history diverges from that of other "freaks." These latter were usually advertised as being unique and individual; however, Baartman and the spate of ethnological exhibitions that followed her alleged to represent the typical and everyday. In London, Baartman holds a transitional and contested position. Advertised one moment as representing "a most correct and perfect Specimen," she is marketed the next as exceeding any norm: "Her *colour* [*sic*] and formation certainly surpass any thing of the kind ever seen in Europe, or perhaps ever produced on the face of the earth" (*MP* 30 April 1811). In Caesar's most brilliant marketing strategy, he christened Baartman as the "Hottentot Venus," manifesting the "kind of shape which is most admired among her countrymen" (qtd. in Altick 269). The sobriquet joked at Baartman's supposed belief in her own beauty when, as a French play tittered, "With such a form / One can not be a Venus."[43] The sobriquet neutralizes (temporarily) the tension between freak and type by proposing that Baartman represents not a freak, but a rare and desired form of the type.

The prints used as signboards for the "Hottentot Venus" testify to the difficulties of controlling representation of Baartman as the typical Hottentot. *They are unique because Caesar regularly displayed her with two posters, rather*

Fig. 1.10. "Sartjee, The Hottentot Venus. Exhibiting at no. 225, Piccadilly.
[Frederick Christian] Lewis Delin. et. Sculpt. London. Published as the Act
directs March 14th, 1811, by S. Baartman, 225 Piccadilly." From Daniel Lysons,
Collectanea, vol. 1, facing p. 102. By permission of the British Library.
(C.103.k.11, vol. 1, p. 102.) *This print gives the closest approximation of the
outfit in which Baartman was actually exhibited.*

than one.[44] The first (fig. 1.10) displays her in the more typical three-quarter view sanctioned by the long history of "freak" shows. Her exhibition suit is designed to meet (barely) English standards of decency while revealing as much of her figure as possible. The original dress was formfitting and supposed to match her skin tone.[45] The public, wary of fakes, was eager to ascertain that her steatopygia was genuine: "One spectator pinched her, another walked round her; one gentleman *poked* her with his cane; and one *lady* employed her parasol to ascertain that all was, as she called it, 'nattral'" (Mathews 137).

Baartman's costume (as represented) was a pastiche of exotica designed by her exhibitors, fancifully mixing Xhosa or other beadwork with fringed garters, skull cap, and bowed shoes.[46] In the print, she displays the face painting that repelled European visitors to South Africa, exaggerated almost to the point of becoming a mask.[47] The instrument to the right approximates the one-stringed bow used by Khoisan musicians and refers to her "rude" performances of Hottentot music and dance.[48] The elongated and elaborated fringes of her dress may allude to the notorious "Hottentot apron" for those in the know. Baartman's original exhibitors, relying on display of the body of the "freak," did not come equipped with the pseudo-educational paraphernalia of material culture and scenic backdrops that soon developed for people shows in London.[49]

Displaying the body with sufficient respect for English propriety constituted the main obstacle facing Baartman's exhibitors. In the poster, an overly large *kaross* is maintained as a hovering sign of Hottentot identity; however, it has lost its functionality as a piece of clothing. It is not cut as a mantle and is fastened at the neck, which covers the shoulders and obscures the form of the body. No eyewitness account makes reference to it.

Nevertheless, Baartman retains some sense of dignity and humanity in the poster through the pose and three-quarter view adopted by many of her colleagues on the exhibition circuit. The naturalistic portraiture of her face individualizes the image (compare to fig. 1.11). Perhaps her formal pose was perceived as ludicrous in combination with her absurd finery, but it does grant a certain solemnity. The waiting chair, as receptacle for the seat, remains the only discreet reference to steatopygia.

The first poster informs prospective viewers, more or less, of what they will actually see; the second is unique for advising them on *how to interpret what they see* (fig. 1.11). The artist has expunged the opportunity for interaction between viewer and viewed through use of a caricatural silhouette that isolates difference. Baartman is gone.

Instead, the prospective viewer is encouraged to imagine Baartman as the Hottentot, nude, smoking a pipe. The *kaross*, walking stick, shoes, and woman's hat belong to the iconography of the Hottentot as nomad, launched by Hans Burgkmair the Elder in 1508. The artist emphasizes the act of smoking by

Fig. 1.11. "Sartjee, the Hottentot Venus."
London. Published as the Act directs
Septr. 18, 1810, by S. Baartman. Aquatint
(tinted) Vignette Plate-mark 365 x 227
[AM 54/824]. Courtesy of Museum
Africa, Johannesburg. *This print shows
Baartman not as she was exhibited, but as
she was to be* imagined *as the
"Hottentot Venus."*

depicting puffs of smoke emanating from both the bowl of the pipe and her mouth. Its resonance was not lost on local audiences. In 1814, a satirist, profiting from Baartman's exhibition in Paris, imagines her writing a letter home to her cousin:

> My cousin, they say a lot of bad things about the French. The more that one lives with them, the more that one learns to esteem them; but I would not like this nation to be next door to our *kraal*: they would certainly not leave us to smoke in peace. This sweet inaction so dear to the Hottentots . . . is insupportable to [the French man]. . . . ("Variétés" 19 Nov. 1814: 2)

She goes on to contrast the excited volubility of the French with the quiet dispositions of Hottentots: "meditative spirits, we can smoke for entire months without saying a word" (3). Nevertheless, she concludes that she would prefer the French (rather than the British) to govern (3). The connection of smoking with somnolence and the abdication of the right to self-governance continues to drive representations of Khoikhoi.

In the second poster, the Hottentot's skin is darkened and her figure highly sexed with prominent breasts and buttocks, which the artist has ballooned, smoothed, and highlighted against the white sheepskin of the *kaross*. The form of the buttocks is echoed in the curve of the chair behind her that acts as a euphemism for the cupping hand. The prominent fringe again alludes to what the organizers cannot exhibit publicly—the famous "apron" that destroys desire. The face painting acts in a similar fashion to provide a mask that safely distances the viewer from the subject.[50]

As a domestic worker at the Cape, Baartman would not have dressed in this fashion in the early nineteenth century. Indeed, Khoikhoi women had traditionally worn short *karosses* as wrappers. The poster image instead conforms to the language of the travelogues, particularly in reference to the pipe, accented by the billowing smoke. No eyewitness account of Baartman's exhibition refers to the pipe (which would have been remarkable enough in the hands of a woman to attract attention).[51] Instead, the pipe functions as in the travelogues to justify Khoikhoi dispossession through its associations with laziness, somnolence, and economic subjugation. Through the resonance of the pipe, the poster presents the Hottentots as safely subjugated and in need of benevolent supervision on the part of the British government due to their native indolence and idiocy. As a "freak," Baartman would have normalized the spectator as an individual. However, transformed into an ethnographic "type" on display, the Hottentot normalizes and legitimates the British colonial project.

Baartman's second poster cogently demonstrates the tools that Stewart outlined in the development of the freak show. It distances the viewer by silencing, indeed erasing, Baartman. There is none of the portraiture notable in the first version. As "cultural other," Baartman legitimates European society and its hegemony by seeming to present incontrovertible proof in the body that the Hottentot reality conforms to its representation.

Finally, as Stewart observes, the sexuality of the freak belongs to the realm of speculation rather than to "lived sexuality": "It is the possibility of his or her existence that titillates; it is the imaginary relation, not the lived one, that we seek in the spectacle" (111). For this reason, she notes, it hardly matters "whether the freak is alive or dead" (111). Baartman's long tenure as a plaster cast on public exhibit at the Musée de l'Homme provides sad evidence for this assertion. The groping chair and the fringed apron in the poster hint at a sexuality that the puffing pipe, two-dimensionality, and face painting render either monstrous or laughable.

It is not surprising that it was the two-dimensional silhouette of the second poster that caught the fancy of the caricaturists and printmakers.[52] "The Three Graces" (fig. 1.12) illustrates the contrasts outlined above. It depicts three "freaks": Miss Ridsdale ("Only 30″ [inches] high and 35 years old"); Miss Harvey, "the Beautiful Albiness with the silk hair perfectly white and pink eyes"; and "Sartjee," billowing smoke from pipe and mouth. She exclaims, looking at Miss Harvey, "Vat Uggerly tings no like a fine Voman; no Grease about dem like I." Miss Ridsdale and Miss Harvey retain a particularity and

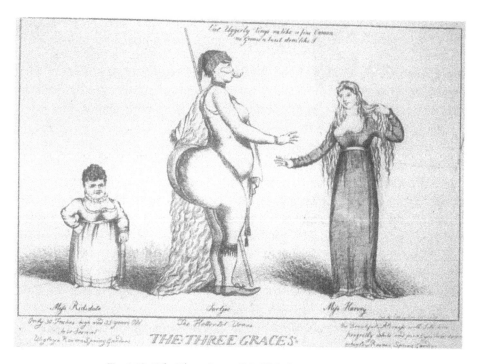

Fig. 1.12. "The Three Graces." Published on 13 Nov. 1810.
© The British Museum.

individuality expunged in the Hottentot, whose pipe and broken English evoke, not Sara Baartman, but the "colonial Hottentot."[53] By parodying the words put into Baartman's mouth, the printmaker suggests that even "freaks" in Europe are more attractive than Hottentot women.

In a spate of English and French caricatural prints, the silhouette of the "Hottentot Venus" is used as a figure for the absence of desire. In a valentine caricature, a cupid rides on her behind, calling out "Take care of your hearts!" In a number of political lampoons, her image is invoked to imply that the butt of the joke knows no limits to his appetite for power, money, or depraved sexual practices.[54] In two French prints, erotic attraction to her body serves to lampoon the depraved taste of the spectators (Rosset 85). The full import of the oxymoron in the sobriquet, "the Hottentot Venus," may now be understood: however highly sexed, the Hottentot woman can never become an erotic threat.

This was also the message of the 1814 Parisian vaudeville play "The Hottentot Venus," by Théaulon de Lambert. Adolphe, a young naïf wounded by the fickleness of French women, and inspired by stories of the noble savage, vows to marry "une femme sauvage." In response, his cousin Amelie passes herself off as the "Hottentot Venus" by dressing up in some brightly colored clothing and by pretending not to know French. Adolphe is charmed—until a chevalier appears bearing a print of the true "Hottentot Venus" (who never appears): "He unrolls the paper and shows the portrait of the Hottentot Venus; everyone gives a cry of terror" ("Il déroule le papier et montre le portrait de la Vénus hottentote; tout le monde pousse un cri d'effroi") (29). A contemporary dictionary connects *effroi* with "an object that inspires horror," such as a "monster" (Morin 368). One glance at the print (most probably the familiar silhouette puffing on her pipe) cures Adolphe of his fantasy. As Le Vaillant warned, a single glance transforms the passion of the most "monstrous libertine" into laughter.

The play offers a comforting view of the dangers of miscegenation. Reviewer after reviewer wrote at length on how far the charms of the actress (Mlle Rivière) surpassed those of the true "Hottentot Venus." One even credits the authors of the play with good business sense in assuring the public that they would *not* see the play's title character: "Gentlemen, we have prudently / Hidden the Hottentot Venus / Behind the features of a cute little face."[55] Another sighs with relief: "The contrast presented by the pretty face of this actress with that of the little monster, whom one should indeed stop exhibiting in public, was a delightful surprise. . . ."[56] Once again, the representation of the Hottentot exorcises the figure of the noble savage by neutralizing desire.

Like the English press, the French press played much on the humor of combining the oxymorons "Hottentot" and "Venus." One newspaper reports that in private salon appearances in 1815, Baartman was lavished with insincere compliments and asked to judge the most affectionate gentleman in the company (Racinet). In ugly, racist, and misogynist comedy, individuals acted out the joke of the printmakers that the Hottentot was too benighted to realize that she *could not be* an object of desire.

ENACTED ETHNOGRAPHY

We earned a living at this time by my exhibiting poor Tonga [a native of the Andaman Islands] at fairs and other such places as the black cannibal. He would eat raw meat and dance his war-dance: so we always had a hatful of pennies after a day's work.
        —Arthur Conan Doyle, *The Sign of Four* (250)

The fact that Baartman's exhibitors felt the need to develop a how-to-read-the-exhibition poster points to a real anxiety on their part that perhaps the body did *not* speak for itself. That concern proved justified as her exhibition became the focus of a lawsuit brought by Zachary Macaulay and other members of the African Institution, an abolitionists' group primarily concerned with repatriating captive Africans to Sierra Leone.

In his sworn deposition, Macaulay recounted how he had paid two shillings to enter the exhibition:

> ... he found a stage of about two or three feet in height erected at one end of the room upon which the said female was exhibited with a small recess at one end of the said stage into which the said female occasionally retired. (PFF 747 [KB1/36], Public Record Office, 1) (see appendix)

At Macaulay's request, Thomas Gisborne Babington and the Dutch-speaking Peter Van Wageninge spent an hour observing the exhibition on 15 October 1810 "with many other spectators." They testified that

> the Exhibitor frequently desired her either to come out of the little recess into which she occasionally walks from off the said stage and to come to him or if she was upon the stage to turn herself round for public exhibition and when he gave these commands it was in the Dutch Language and he gave them in the same manner as he would to any of the brute creation. (2)[57]

All three affirmed that the audience was "invited to feel her posterior parts to satisfy themselves that no art is practiced" (2–3).

Baartman would march out, turn around, and play her instrument, but she refused to give complete consent to her display. Macaulay referred to her "unhappy and dejected countenance," "frequent sighs," her "expressive look of disapprobation which she gives when ordered to exhibit herself" (2). Babington and Van Wageninge described an incident when Baartman was "very morose and sullen and retired into the little recess off the stage and appeared unwilling to come out again when called." Babington testified that the exhibitor lowered the curtain, reached behind it, and "shook his hand" at Baartman, following which he raised the curtain and again called her out to view (2).[58] Baartman's demeanor, interpreted as "sullen," "depressed," and "sad," made viewers uneasy (e.g., Mathews 138–39; "The Hottentot Venus," *Sporting Magazine* Nov. 1810: 82). We cannot know what she thought, but it is clear that she complied reluctantly with instructions for her performance. When this was remarked upon, the politics of abolitionism made the display volatile.

In his defense, Baartman's promoter fell back on the precedent of "freak shows": "And pray, Mr. Editor, has she not as good a right to exhibit herself as an Irish Giant, or a Dwarf, &c. &c." (Cezar letter, 23 Oct. 1810). The court, after providing for Dutch translators, determined that she had (East, 1816; see appendix).

Contemporary audiences were indeed familiar with similar exhibitions from so-called freak shows. However, Baartman's trial reveals the importance of the performer's complicity in consenting to be ogled. As in the conventions of the Western nude, indications of self-awareness or discomfort on the part of the subject must be avoided for fear of exposing the viewer as a predatory voyeur, rather than a connoisseur of art, or a student of natural history.

Macaulay reports that Baartman showed particular reluctance to play her instrument, in other words, to enact the ethnography of the Hottentot (PFF 747 [KB1/36], Public Record Office, 2). While complicity in viewing was important for "freaks," the putative authenticity (the believability) of the developing ethnographic shows also demanded a feigned unawareness of the very act of performance.

We may suspect that covert coercion played a role in Baartman's responses to queries of the court.[59] Nonetheless, the nature of the public display did change: the exhibitor's deportment showed more respect and the exhibition became more "modest" (advertised as suitable for ladies) (MP 12 Dec. 1811). With time, the promoters developed the "educational" element of the show. This direction became particularly clear when Baartman moved on to Paris in 1814.

Her promoters continued to exhibit her with the same two prints,[60] but had developed a smoother covering of scientific language to market her as both type and "Venus." From the earliest advertisement in France, dated 18 September 1814, her promoter evokes knowledge of the works of Le Vaillant by marketing her as a "Hauzanana":

> This extraordinary phenomenon is the only one that has ever appeared in Europe from the Hauzanana tribe. In this woman, as extraordinary as [she is] astonishing, the public has a perfect model of this tribe, which inhabits the southernmost regions of Africa. . . . She wears all the ornaments that serve the tribe to which she belongs as jewelry on holidays.[61]

Le Vaillant alone writes of the Houswaana (a San group) and, no doubt, the sudden attribution of Houswaana ethnicity relates to the fact that Le Vaillant commented on and illustrated steatopygia only in relation to this population.[62] An early newspaper review conveys some of the pseudo-educational patter of the exhibition:

> The woman called by the name of the Hottentot Venus . . . is named Sartjée; she is from the Houzouana tribe, which inhabits a country situated at two hundred leagues northeast of the Cape of Good Hope. . . . She speaks Dutch, English, and her maternal language, in which she sings some songs. . . . Her color is closer to that of the Peruvians than to Africans, whose hair and traits she has. She has preserved the custom of painting her face, and is completely covered by glass beads. She plays a Jew's harp, an instrument which, according to [Le] Vaillant, is well-loved among her people.[63]

In the Parisian exhibition, the reference to "freak" shows is notably absent. Instead, there is a much more assured presentation of Baartman as educational in appearance, dress, and musical performance. One senses that Baartman was exhibited as a living illustration to the two popular Voyages of Le Vaillant.[64]

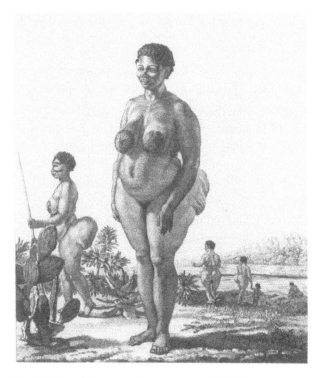

Fig. 1.13. "La Vénus Hottentote. Sara, a woman of the Hottentot race, 25 years old, observed, drawn and painted in the Natural History Museum in March, 1815. . . . [Print] On sale in Paris at Réaux's, Cour des Fontaines, and at Martinet's, Rue du Coq." 42 x 29.7 cm. Engraved by Louis-Jean Allais from the painting by J.-B. Berré, now at the Musée de l'Homme. Cliché Bibliothèque nationale de France, Paris.

This more assured marketing explains somewhat why Georges Cuvier and the scientists at the Muséum d'Histoire Naturelle also chose to examine and present Baartman as a "typical specimen." In March 1815, Cuvier writes "she was obliging enough to strip off her clothes and to allow herself to be painted in the nude" ("elle eut la complaisance de se dépouiller, et de se laisser peindre d'après le nu") (1817, 264). Londa Schiebinger has pointed out the dissonance between Cuvier's account of Baartman's nonchalant acceptance and that of his colleague, Henri de Blainville (170). In the more relaxed format of a talk, which he did not originally envision publishing, the latter revealed Baartman's unease at the crowd of ogling men, her resistance to undressing, and her categorical refusal to allow her observers to closely "examine [her reproductive organs] in a proper manner" ("Sur une femme," 1816, 183, 189). Cuvier's omissions show that for science, like pornography, the appearance of the subject's acquiescence is indispensable if the viewer is not to be exposed as a simple voyeur. In the end, Cuvier's wording betrays something of what is repressed: "dépouiller" can mean "to skin an animal" as well as "to remove someone's clothes by force."

The final product of Cuvier's artists' examination depicts a landscape in which the photographic realism of the woman's three-quarter portrait fuses seamlessly with a beautiful landscape full of such "typical" Venus figures. In the original painting, the artist J.-B. Berré depicts the Venus from five different angles for both information and possession. In the engraving, Louis-Jean Allais kindly numbers the exotic South African flora and identifies them below by their scientific names (fig. 1.13).[65] The women casually stroll by, seemingly engaged in daily life (one is washing her clothes), as though southern Africa were really filled with a race of severely steatopygic women. This European fantasy bears the stamp of one of the world's premier natural history museums.

Ironically, Berré's precise attention to bodily detail captures Baartman in the act of mocking the great scientist by denying him access to what she knew very well he wanted most to see. In his report Cuvier recounts how his team had observed her with such meticulous care as to describe even her pubic hair. Nevertheless, she managed to hide the hypertrophy of the labia minora:

> But at this first inspection, one observed nothing of the most remarkable detail of her organization; she held her apron carefully hidden either between her thighs or more deeply, and it was only after her death that one ascertained that she possessed it.[66]

What the picture captures is Baartman standing at attention, in the very act of hiding through careful and uncomfortable compression of the thighs. In Baartman's gesture of scorn, she refuses to enact fully the body Hottentot, the bearer of ultimate difference, as Cuvier was to represent it. At her death, the scientist triumphed, but Baartman's experience demonstrates, despite significant differences in power, some of the difficulties of controlling the representation of living persons on the exhibition circuit.

Baartman's was the first major ethnological exhibition of the nineteenth century. In her case, despite the inclusion of an occasional dance or song, the gesture towards education lay entirely in the presentation of the body. As with other "freak shows," the difference marked in the body qualified her as an unusual object of "natural history." The entrepreneurs who followed Caesar, however, greatly expanded on the overt educational mission of the exhibitions by adding elaborate props, scenery, demonstrations, and learned lectures that all hammered home the typical nature of the presentation. In the newspaper account of the 1847 exhibition of Bushmen (San), the writer prefers the scenery to the people:

> The curious creatures at the Egyptian Hall are grouped upon a raised stage . . . with a "flat" scene, set vegetation, hanging wood, &c. from the country of the Bushmen, cleverly painted and arranged by Mr. Johnstone. This is a vigorous piece of scenic effect, and greatly relieves the repulsive aspect of the aboriginal group. ("Bosjesmans at Egyptian Hall" 381)

Both advertisements and newspaper reviews stressed the educational value of such shows. They invited the visitors to play the role of scientist, of lay anthropologist.

> Altogether, this is an exhibition of unusual interest and value. The first effect, on entering the room, may be repulsive; but, the attentive visitor soon overcomes this feeling, and sees in the benighted beings before him a fine subject for scientific investigation, as well as a scene for popular gratification, and rational curiosity. (ibid.)

Many of these shows became enormous financial successes (Hagenbeck 20, 25). Elaborate scenic backdrops usually accompanied the performers, which they used in their scenes from "daily life" that included war, hunting, marriage, witch-finding, etc. Performing at set hours, they otherwise sat on the stage, sleeping or smoking.

And what did the lay scientists sitting in the spectator stalls learn? As for Adolphe, the naïve Frenchman who thought to marry a Hottentot, the two-dimensional representation in a print was sufficient to overthrow the noble savage. Charles Dickens gives strong expression to a similar physical revulsion in 1853:

> Think of the Bushmen [exhibited]. . . . Are the majority of persons—who remember the horrid little leader of that party in his festering bundle of hides, with his filth and his antipathy to water, and his straddled legs, and his odious eyes shaded by his brutal hand, and his cry of "Qu-u-u-u-aaa!" [as he acted out a hunting scene] . . . conscious of an affectionate yearning towards that noble savage, or is it idiosyncratic in me to abhor, detest, abominate, and abjure him? ("The Noble Savage," 337)

Dickens's comments are embedded in an argument against aiding Africans while English children starved, but his reaction was widespread. Like Adolphe, Dickens finds that the desire ("affectionate yearning") for the noble savage is overthrown by physical revulsion in the face of the anti-erotic, a revulsion in fact carefully orchestrated by the exhibition itself.

In an uncanny parallelism, the novelist Gustave Flaubert visited the same exhibition when it travelled to France and reports similar responses to the leader of the group, whom he describes as a "type of wild beast . . . making inarticulate cries" (162). He experiences the thrill of seeming "to see the first men on the earth [who] have just been born and creep and crawl still with the toads and crocodiles" (162).[67] And yet, the exhibition leaves him wondering *why* he is drawn to the "savage": "What do I have in me, therefore, that makes me cherish at first sight all that is cretinous, crazy, idiotic, savage? Do these poor characters there understand that I am part of their world? . . . Do they feel some kind of bond with me?" (163).[68] Far from providing an experience of common humanity, the exhibition leaves Flaubert with a sense of profound distance between him and those on display. Despite the active involvement of some performers in elaborating skits for the shows, their general tone served to give Europeans a *physical* experience of their own superiority. It is striking that Dickens, Flaubert, and commentators on Baartman often invoke the evidence drawn from the physical senses of hearing, smell, and touch, as well as vision. Only taste is absent.

In this sense, the people exhibitions diverged from their model in the "freak" exhibitions. As noted above, Susan Stewart has argued that the sexuality of the freak belongs to the realm of the imaginary rather than to "lived sexuality." However, the people exhibitions of the nineteenth century capitalized precisely on the tension between the "imaginary" (the scenery props, the choreographed activities, the exotic costumes) and the lived presence of a person, whom the audience could smell (see Dickens, above) or poke with an umbrella. The body became the signifier of the real, the authentic. Its choreographed presence validated the colonial imagination.

Sometimes the connections with empire were made manifest in the shows. The catalog to a popular and lavish exhibition of Zulus in 1853 ended with an exhortation to emigrate:

> Go to Natal, the field is open for your industry and the reward is certain; there, too, you will become better acquainted with the Zulus, and perchance will have it in your power to assist in the enlightenment of the poor savage, and lend your aid to the civilization of Africa. (*Exhibition* 31)

The ethnographic shows that developed in the course of the nineteenth century perhaps proved the most effective tools of scientific racism. Their enacted ethnography invited spectators "to see for themselves." What they saw was the overthrow of the figure of the noble savage and the open fields of empire.

CONCLUSION

Sara Baartman came to a renewed fame in the English-speaking world when Stephen Jay Gould reinserted her life story into the history of science. Since then, she has become a symbol of imperialist exploitation for many South Africans, and her reclamation a powerful ritual honoring the first inhabitants of the Cape (Koch). Sander Gilman's influential article "Black Bodies, White Bodies," first published in 1985, has also been instrumental in transforming Baartman into a late-twentieth-century icon for the violence done to women of African descent, and in particular, to the representation of their sexuality. Gilman's assertion that "Sarah Baartmann's sexual parts, her genitalia and her buttocks, serve as the central image for the black female throughout the nineteenth century" (216) may be the most frequently cited statement from his article.

In response to the resurgence of interest, an increasing number of women of color have been concerned to reappropriate Baartman's life and voice (see Alexander; Parks; O'Grady; Matus). Photographer Lorraine O'Grady identifies her as one "of our ancestresses most in need of re-vision" (15). One of the most powerful expressions to date of this interest is found in the work of conceptual artist Renée Green. In an interview, Green stated that she has been drawn to the subject by a need to address "[t]he ways in which black women are viewed—there's still this residue of accumulated ideas about animality and sexuality being linked" (Brown 26).[69]

In the installation *Sa Main Charmante* from 1989, the viewer first encounters Baartman, respectfully, as absence (fig. 1.14). Her own thoughts and experiences are unrecoverable. It is her theatrical persona that is invoked by an empty soapbox platform (inscribed "La Belle Hottentote") and by a powerful stage light on the viewer's right, which shines across the "stage." The composition is framed by the klieg light and a mysterious pole on the left. Since both are anthropomorphic in shape and roughly of Baartman's diminutive size, they act like photographic positives highlighting through their presence the absence contained at the heart of the composition.

In the background, a shuttered triptych slows down the viewer's assimilation of the installation by alternating lines from a short biography with quotations taken from Cuvier's dissection report, with its allusions to monkeys and natural history (1817). The viewer eventually becomes curious about the object on the left, which, on exploration, turns out to be a peep-box. The temptation is irresistible. When the viewer peeps, he or she finds that the powerful blast of light from the klieg light illumines one of the most shocking of the caricatural prints made of Baartman's display, "Les curieux en extase" (see note 65). The force of the (unexpected) beam of light shining straight into the eyes requires the viewer to recoil from the image and acknowledge (as Cuvier did not) one's position as voyeur.

In Gilman's article, a certain historical slippage has obscured the circumstances of Baartman's exhibition and its contemporary reception. Gilman is careful to argue that "*[i]n the course of the nineteenth century* [my emphasis], the female Hottentot comes to represent the black female *in nuce*" (206). He argues that the work of J. J. Virey in 1819 and 1824 in France is pivotal in establishing a racist medical discourse in which black women were represented as lascivious, with oversized sexual organs (212–13). Building on Cuvier's dissection report, "Virey cites the Hottentot woman as the epitome of sexual lasciviousness" (212–13). Gilman argues that Hottentot women's genitalia were firmly inscribed in European medical discourse by the mid-nineteenth century (218).

Fig. 1.14. Renée Green. *Sa Main Charmante*. 1989. Mixed media installation.
Roush Fund for Contemporary Art, 1991. Allen Memorial Art Museum,
Oberlin College, Oberlin, Ohio. Approx. 70 x 88 x 63.5 in.

Gilman is not interested in Baartman's exhibition, but in the mid- to late-nineteenth-century appropriation of Baartman's body for medical discourse. Consequently, he occasionally argues backwards from the later century to make blanket assertions that cannot be supported for the time of her exhibition in 1810–15, such as: "while many groups of African blacks were known to Europeans in the nineteenth century, the Hottentot remained representative of the essence of the black, especially the black female" (206). In fact, for four hundred years, those fantasy creatures the Hottentots were usually considered a separate species from "the black race," primarily because of language, but also because they were considered *undersexed*, since their men were reputed to have only one testicle and their women a barrier of flesh guarding their modesty. Reports of Hottentot lasciviousness are rare indeed. More typical is Le Vaillant, contrasting the Hottentots with their "air of reserve" to the "blacks . . . who give themselves up to pleasure" (*Travels*, 1790, 2: 120). The historical imperatives that required substantial reworking of a long-lived myth following the publication of Cuvier's dissection report merit further study.

This essay has been concerned with understanding the circumstances of Baartman's historical exhibition. A long history of travelogue literature on the Hottentot shaped both her literal display and her reception. The travel literature presages the problems of the ethnographic show circuits in controlling representation of the body. For over two centuries, artists trained to render the ideal body struggled to convey savagery in the nude. Finally, after 1652, the smoking pipe emerged as an iconographic sign par excellence of indolence and mental sloth to justify the theft of Khoikhoi land.

Although Baartman was originally recruited for the so-called freak show circuit, her exhibitors in Britain soon experimented with advertising her as a "perfect type" of Hottentot. When Baartman appeared in Britain, a celebrated victory for missionaries in South Africa had claimed special ward status for Khoikhoi, based on their putative "imbecilic nature." People thronged to see the famed creature, the Hottentot, who spoke a bestial tongue, and who stood midway between human and animal realms (Altick 268–69). The pseudo-educational patter became much more assured in France and set the tone for the spate of nineteenth-century ethnographic exhibitions to follow.

Far from representing Baartman as a lascivious creature, her display acted as an apotropaic device mocking the threat of interracial marriage and relationships. This is the dehumanizing message of most of the English caricatural prints—that only the most depraved and ludicrous could take Baartman seriously as a woman and as a sex partner. Le Vaillant, the self-proclaimed champion of the Hottentot and the model for Baartman's display in France, argues that a "single glimpse" of the apron is enough to transform the "wildest passion" of "the most monstrous libertine" into "the most uncontrollable laughter" (*le rire le plus inextinguible*) (*Voyage*, 1798, 2: 351). Exhibitors of ethnographic shows choreographed an experience of the body designed to disclaim *other* experiences of the body. Although Baartman's position is highly charged sexually (regard the groping hand disguised as a chair in fig. 1.11), public discourse "protests too much" in denying the very possibility of all such attraction.

It is fitting that Baartman does not appear in person or as a character in *La Vénus hottentote*, the 1814 vaudeville play that bears her sobriquet. She appears only in image. At the close of the piece, the young man who has sworn to marry a Hottentot is shown a portrait of the "true Hottentot Venus." One presumes that the poster unrolled at the *dénouement* is based on the second and most popular of Baartman's exhibition posters: the one that shows the audience how they are to imagine the Hottentot (fig. 1.11). In that image, the Hottentot is nearly naked, well endowed with female secondary sexual characteristics, but comfortingly anti-erotic. The puffing pipe, the face painted with gunpowder, the nomad's walking stick, the oversized cap, and most of all, the dangling fringed "apron" all safely distance the threat of sexual power by rendering it ludicrous. As a reviewer summarized the ending: "They explain laughing; Adolphe abjures his crazy ideas, and marries his [French] cousin."[70]

APPENDIX

THE FOLLOWING IS THE RESULT OF THE EXAMINATION OF THE
HOTTENTOT VENUS—27TH NOV. 1810

She does not know when she left her native place she being very young when she came to the Cape: the Brother of her late Master, Peter Cæsar, brought her to the Cape: she came with her own consent with Peter Cæsar and was taken into the service of Henrick Casar [*sic*] as his nursery maid; she came by her own consent to England and was promised half of the money for exhibiting her person—She agreed to come to England for a period of six years; She went personally to the Government in Company with Henrick Cæsar to ask permission to go to England: Mr. Dunlop promised to send her back after that period at his own expence [*sic*] and to send the money belonging to her with her—She is kindly treated and has every thing she wants; Has no complaints to make against her master or those that exhibit her: is perfectly happy in her present situation: has no desire whatever of returning to her own country not even for the purpose of seeing her two Brothers and four sisters: wishes to stay here because she likes the Country and has money given her by her Master of a Sunday when she rides about in a Coach for a couple of hours—Her father was in the habit of going with Cattle from the interior to the Cape and was killed in one of those Journeys by the "Bosmen." her [*sic*] mother died twenty years ago—she has a Child by a Drummer at the Cape with whom she lived for about two years yet being always in the employ of Henrick Cæsar; the child is since dead—She is to receive one half of the money received for exhibiting herself and Mr. Dunlop the other half—She is not desirous of changing her present situation—no personal violence or threats have been used by any individual against her; she has two Black Boys to wait upon her: One of the men assists her in the morning when she is nearly compleatly attired for the purpose of fastening the Ribbon round her waist—her dress is too cold and she has complained of this to Henrick Cæsar who promised her warmer Cloathes; Her Age she says to be twenty two and that her stay at the Cape was three years—To the various questions we put to her whether if she chose at any time to discontinue her person being exhibited, she might do so, we could not draw a satisfactory answer from her—She understands very little of the Agreement made with her by Mr. Dunlop on the twenty ninth October 1810—and which Agreement she produced to us—The time of Examination lasted for about three hours—and the questions put to her were put in such a language as to be understood by her.—and these Deponents say they were informed by the said female that she could neither read or write.—

[signed] S SOLLY
JN. GEO. MOOJEN

King's Bench

[Copy of the sworn deposition of Samuel Solly, representative for Zachary Macaulay, and John George Moojen, representative for Alexander Dunlop and Henrick Caesar, dated 28 Nov. 1808 [*sic*], recounting their three hour interview with Baartman in Dutch on 27 Nov. 1810 at her residence in Duke Street, Saint James's Square. The interview took place in the presence of James Temple, Esq., Coroner of the Court, and the solicitors for each party, and in the absence of Dunlop and Caesar. PFF 723 (J18/462), Public Record Office.]

TRANSCRIPTS OF THE SWORN AFFIDAVITS FILED
DURING THE TRIAL OF 1810.

Zachary Macaulay of Birchin Lane London Merchant Thomas Gisborne Babington of the same place Merchant and Peter Van Wageninge of Water Lane Thames Street London Gentleman Severally make oath and say and first this Deponent Zachary Macaulay for himself saith that he is Secretary to an Institution called the African Institution the object of which is the civilization of Africa and the said Zachary Macaulay having understood from different public advirtisements [sic] and otherwise that a native of south Africa denominated the Hottentot Venus of a most extraordinary or unnatural shape was publicly exhibited for Money in Piccadilly he was desirous if possible of learning under what circumstances she came to England and whether she was made a public spectacle with her own free will and consent or whether she was compelled to exhibit herself and was desirous of returning to her own country as the said Institution would be anxious in that case to restore her to her Country and friends and therefore this Deponent Zachary Macaulay as Secretary to the said Institution went on Thursday the eleventh day of this present Month of October to Piccadilly in order to see the female in question and having paid two shillings was admitted into the room where she is usually exhibited And this Deponent saith that he found a stage of about two or three feet in height erected at one end of the room upon which the said female was exhibited with a small recess at one end of the said stage into which the said female occasionally retired And this Deponent saith that the said female was cloathed in a dress resembling her complexion which is very dark and her dress was so tight that her shapes above and the enormous size of her posterior parts are as visible as if the said female were naked and the dress is evidently intended to give the appearance of her being undressed And this Deponent further Saith that he entered into conversation with the person who exhibited the said female and made many enquiries respecting her and the Exhibitor informed this Deponent that she was a female of the Hottentot Tribe and that he had brought her from the Cape of Good Hope having obtained her from the Dutch Boors who came from the interior down to the Cape and that he had made an agreement with the Government at the Cape and they had given him permission to take her to this Country And this Deponent saith that upon the Exhibitor informing him that he brought her to England with the consent of the Government at the Cape he was much surprized and said what did Lord Calledon [sic] who is Governor at the Cape give permission for her being brought to England and the exhibitor answered that he did and upon being interrogated if Lord Calledons permission was in writing the exhibitor said it was and upon being further asked if Lord Calledon knew that she was brought to this Country to be exhibited he answered Oh! Yes, Yes, upon which this Deponent Being [several words are crossed out and initialed "ES"] in the habit of corresponding with him and doubting the truth of these assertions stated to the Exhibitor that he wished to see the permission which Lord Calledon had signed for her being brought to England as he knew his hand writing upon which the Exhibitor said what wont you believe my word, I have already told you that he has signed it and I shall give you no further satisfaction or conversation to this effect passed between the Exhibitor and this Deponent at the time aforesaid And this Deponent saith that he proceeded to ask further questions of the said Exhibitor relative to the said female but the Exhibitor excused himself from giving any more information respecting her by saying I do not choose to have so many questions put to me or words to that effect And this Deponent Saith that during the time he remained in the room he paid particular attention to the conduct and behaviour of the said Exhibitor and also of the said female and he says that the said Exhibitor sometimes would call the said female to him, and when she came would desire her to turn round and would invite the spectators to feel her posterior parts and at other times if she was at a distance from him would desire her to turn round in order that every body might see her extraordinary shape if in the Recess he would call her out for exhibition and in fact she is exhibited to the public in the same manner that any animal of the brute creation would be exhibited And this Deponent saith from the unhappy and dejected countenance of the same female and from the expressive look of disapprobation which she gives when ordered to exhibit herself and from her frequent sighs he considers the said female is unhappy in her situation and that she is under the restraint and controul of her exhibitor and is deprived of her liberty And this Deponent further saith that during the time he was in the room, the Exhibitor gave to the said female a musical Instrument somewhat like a guitar and desired her to play upon it and upon that occasion he particularly observed that the said female by her looks gave evident signs of mortification and misery at her degraded situation in being made a spectacle for the derision of the bystanders without the power of resistance And this Deponent further saith that the said African Institution are willing to take the said female under their care and protection and to bear all expences of restoring her to her Country and friends if they are permitted to do so And these Deponents Peter Van Wageninge and Thomas Gisborne Babington severally say that at the request of the said Zachary Macaulay they went on the fifteenth day of October now instant [?] to see the said female in Piccadilly aforesaid and having paid two shillings each they were admitted into the said room and found her exhibited upon a stage as described by the last Deponent And this deponent Peter Van Wageninge saith that he is a native of Holland and being informed by the exhibitor that the said female could speak the Dutch language although not perfectly well, he this Deponent put many questions to the said female and amongst others he enquired of her whence she came whether she had any relations whether she was happy and comfortable here and whether she was desirous of returning home all which questions were asked in the language in which the exhibitor spoke to the said female but the said female would not answer any of such questions And both these Deponents Peter Van Wageninge and Thomas Gisborne Babington say they remained in the room with the said female with many other spectators, for nearly an hour and during that time she never spoke but the Exhibitor frequently desired her either to come out of the little recess into which she occasionally walks from off the said stage and to come to him or if she was upon the stage to turn herself round for public exhibition and when he gave these commands it was in the Dutch Language and he gave them in the same manner as he would to any of the brute creation—If she was in the little recess his order was "come out," if upon the stage "come here" or "turn round" just as he might wish and the said female obeyed the orders in the same manner that animals of the brute creation obey similar commands—that whilst these Deponents were present they heard the said female utter several deep sighs evidently as from a being whose mind is distressed and which her countenance strongly shews her to be And these Deponents Peter Van Wageninge and Thomas Gisborne Babington say that the said female is called by the Exhibitor towards the persons standing round the stage and they are invited to feel her posterior parts to satisfy themselves that no art is practiced—And these Deponents Peter Van Wageninge and Thomas Gisborne Babington do verily believe from the dejected appearance of the said female and from the obedience which she pays to the commands of her exhibitor that she is compleatly under restraint and controul and is deprived of her liberty And these Deponents further severally say that during the time they were present the said female at one time appeared very morose and sullen and retired into the little recess off the stage and appered unwilling to come out again when called by the Exhibitor and the Exhibitor felt it necessary on that occasion to let down a curtain which when drawn separates the stage and little recess from the other part of the room And this Deponent Thomas Gisborne Babington saith that the Exhibitor after the curtain was let down looked behind it and held up and shook his hand at her but without speaking and he soon afterward drew up the Curtain and again called her out to public view and she came forward again upon the stage And these Deponents severally say they are informed and believe that the said females' [sic] name is Saartgee and that the name of the person who has the possession of her is Henrich Cesar—

[signed] Zachary Macaulay
Thos. Gisborne Babington
P. van Wageninge

Sworn by the above named Deponents Zachary Macaulay
Thomas Gisborne Babington and Peter Van Wageninge at
my chambers in Serjeants Inn Chancery Lane London this
seventeenth day of October one thousand eight hundred and ten Before me

[illegible signature]

[PFF 747 (KB1/36), Public Record Office.]

IN THE KINGS BENCH

William Bullock of Piccadilly in the County of Middlesex Proprietor of the Liverpool Museum maketh Oath and Saith that some time in or about the month of August—he this Deponent was applied to by Mr. Alexander Dunlop who this Deponent believes either is or was an Army Surgeon and who stated that he had then lately arrived from the Cape of Good Hope, to purchase of him a Camelopard [sic] [giraffe] skin of great beauty and considerable value but the price being greater than this Deponent chose to give no bargain was then made although he afterwards had a subsequent interview with the said Alexander Dunlop and purchased the skin And this Deponent further Saith that the said Alexander Dunlop in the course of conversation with this Deponent informed him that he was in possession of a Hottentot Woman whom he had brought from the Cape of Good Hope informing this Deponent at the same time that he was under an engagement to return her to the Cape of Good Hope in two years and he the said Alexander Dunlop expressed to this deponent previous to the time he this Deponent purchased the said Camel-opard Skin that he would rather dispose of the whole concern together meaning thereby as this Deponent understood and verily believes the said Skin and the Hottentot Woman but when he purchased the said Skin the said Mr. Dunlop he remarked that as he had disposed of the other part of the concern (meaning thereby as this Deponent understood and believes the said Hottentot Woman) to advantage, if he would make him a handsome offer for the said skin he should have it a bargain, the said Mr. Dunlop at the time this Deponent was in treaty for the said Skin stating the extraordinary shape and make of the Woman and that she was an object of great curiosity and would make the fortune of any person by exhibiting her (for the said two years) to the public, but this Deponent feeling that such an exhibition would not meet the countenance of the public declined acceding [?] to Mr. Dunlops proposal and only purchased the skin And this Deponent further Saith that the said Alexander Dunlop and the said Hottentot Female and also Henrick Cæsar who now exhibits the said Female came to England from the Cape of Good Hope in the same Ship as this Deponent verily believes And this Deponent further saith that the said Alexander Dunlop Henrich [sic] Cæsar and the Female lately (and (as he believes) now live together in the same House in York Street Piccadilly and he has since been informed by the said Alexander Dunlop that he has been so unfortunate as to sell and dispose of his Interest in the exhibiting of the said Hottentot Woman and that he has now next to nothing to do with her (meaning the said Hottentot Woman—

[signed] W BULLOCK

Sworn in Court this
twenty first day of November
one thousand eight hundred
and ten ———   By the Court
[PFF 723 (J18/462), Public Record Office.]

47

IN THE KINGS BENCH

Arend Jacob Guitard of Sweeting's Alley
Royal Exchange Notary Public maketh oath and saith that at the request
of Mr. Alexander Dunlop of Duke Street St. James, he this deponent made a
translation from The English into the Dutch language of an agreement made
between the said Alexander Dunlop and Sarah or Saartje Baartman otherwise
called The Hottentot Venus, That he This Deponent read the said agreement
twice plainly and distinctly to the said Saartje Baartman, and that it appeared
to him this deponent, that she understood the contents thereof and was there-
with satisfied.—And this deponent further saith that he put several questions
to the said Saartje Baartman as to her being contented with her situation and
whether she was duly supplied with good eat and drink to which she replied in
the affirmative And this deponent also asked the said Saartje Baartman whether
she preferred either to return to the Cape of Good Hope or stay in England and
that she replied—Stay here.

[signed] AJGUITARD

Sworn before me
at my Chambers Serjants Inn
Chancery Lane the
27th day of November 1810
[illegible signature]
[PFF 723 (J18/462), Public Record Office]

NOTES

1. I am grateful to Anne Higonnet for bringing the story of Sara Baartman to my attention years ago, to Christopher L. Miller and Eugenia W. Herbert for comments on an earlier draft, and to Bernth Lindfors for great generosity in sharing both numerous references and his enthusiasm for prints. Jonathan Reynolds offered critical encouragement. Andrea Henderson gave me the means to hurdle a paralyzing impasse. Archival research in London and Paris was funded by summer grants from the Dept. of the History of Art, Yale University, in 1983 and 1984.

Part of this material was presented as the paper "Display of the Body Hottentot" at the 37th Annual Meeting of the African Studies Association, Toronto, 3 Nov. 1994, as part of the panel *African Show Business*, chaired by Bernth Lindfors.

2. Contemporary documents frequently cite Baartman's name as "Saartje," or "little Sara" in Dutch ("Saartjie" in Afrikaans). Dr. Sandra Klopper has kindly informed me of the fact that diminutives were often "used in the nineteenth century to differentiate slaves and people of colour . . . effectively relegating adults to the status of children" (personal communication with the author, 25 Nov. 1997). For this reason, I have preferred to use the adult form of the name, "Sara," in the essay.

3. Baartman's death is variously reported as between 29 Dec. 1815 and 1 Jan. 1816. Probably Georges Cuvier, who performed her dissection, is the best informed. He reports 29 Dec. 1815 (1817, 265).

4. For example, Théophile Gautier dismissed Gustave Courbet's *Baigneuse* in the Salon of 1853 as "une sorte de Vénus hottentote" (2).

5. For example, see Altick, Drimmer, and Lindfors.

6. In this sense, the Hottentot embodies the most extreme form of European discourse on Africa, as described by literary critic Christopher Miller in *Blank Darkness*. See, in particular, chap. 1 for the role of "nullity" in this discourse (17–18, 27).

7. For this history, see Elphick, *Khoikhoi*; and Elphick and Giliomee, *The Shaping of South African Society*.

8. Today, most of the descendants of the Khoikhoi make up part of the so-called Griqua, Basters, and Cape Coloured populations in South Africa. Their culture has been creolized with Dutch, Indonesian, Xhosa, and many other elements (Barnard 193–98). The Nama of Namibia constitute the one surviving cultural unit that has preserved the language (Khoe). Their population numbers about 90,000 (Barnard 176).

9. Translated from the 1701 edition of Nicolaus de Graaf's *Reisen* by Raven-Hart (1967, 154).

10. "les sauvages les plus barbares" (Diderot, ed., article "Athée," *Encyclopédie*).

11. ". . . cette race paraît être la plus disgraciée de toutes celles qui peuplent l'Afrique. Les Hottentots manquent d'intelligence et d'activité" (Larousse 19.1, article "Hottentots" 406).

12. E.g., *Webster's New International Dictionary of the English Language*, 2nd ed. Another suggestion traces derivation from a Khoikhoi dancing refrain (Nienaber 89). Some recent scholars have favored the latter explanation, perhaps because it appears in travel accounts (Elphick 180; Barnard 9). Both proposals follow the model traced by Miller for Africanist etymologies in arguing for a phonological link to "the language that the writer sees as most authentic" (in this case, Dutch or Khoikhoi) and in granting the naming function to an outside, dominant subjectivity (12).

13. Barnard gives a concise overview of the labyrinthine debate over terminology of Khoisan peoples (7–11). Since the orthography of the Nama, the only surviving Khoikhoi group, has modernized, Barnard prefers the spelling "Khoekhoe" (7), but as a non-specialist I have retained the established "Khoikhoi."

14. It is perhaps worth noting that no person of European descent became truly fluent in a click language before the twentieth century.

15. "Les organes de la voix sont différents des nôtres; ils forment un bégaiement et un gloussement qu'il est impossible aux autres hommes d'imiter" (Voltaire, *Essai* 2: 308).

16. ". . . cette langue bizarre et si difficile dont n'approche aucun parler humain, et qui, par son sifflement, son croassement, ses cris aigus, ses sons inarticulés, semble être la liaison naturelle entre le language des hommes et celui des animaux" (Saintine 213–14).

17. Andrew B. Smith points out the irony of this appellation, given the bathing habits of seventeenth- and eighteenth-century Europeans (10).

18. Because Khoisan skin has little adipose tissue, it dries and cracks easily in the arid South African climate (Schapera 60). The skin lotion kept it soft and supple. In addition, the Khoikhoi also wore the oil as Europeans wore gold in conspicuous consumption (Elphick 60–61).

19. Singer and Jopp, and Massing.

20. See, for example, Bassani and Tedeschi; Massing 44; and Poeschel 60.

21. Andrew B. Smith notes that the *kierie* served originally as a fighting stick, but that it came to signify "walking stick" in the nineteenth century (79). In rare drawings of contemporary Khoikhoi life made in the late seventeenth to early eighteenth century, the *kierie* seems multifunctional. Men use it for herding sheep and cattle; both men and women may carry one as a walking stick or as a pole for carrying bundles. In the travelogues, illustrators interpret *kierie* as walking or drovers' sticks. What Burgkmair depicts as sandals are more accurately translated as leather moccasins (A. Smith 60).

22. "Savage," *Compact Edition of the Oxford English Dictionary*, 1971 ed.

23. A. Smith is apparently working independently on a parallel project (12).

24. One notes the same process at work in representations of the Xhosa. As long as they were fighting the British, men like Lt. Col. John Graham described them as "horrid savages" (qtd. in Elphick and Giliomee 315). See also the illustration for "The Kaffir War," *Illustrated London News* 25 July 1846: 52.

25. Richard Elphick, "The Khoisan to c. 1770," in Elphick and Giliomee 12–14.

26. Peter Kolb (1675–1726), a German astronomer, was sent by Baron Krusick, chancellor to the King of Prussia, to the Cape of Good Hope in order to make astronomical observations and records of the natural history. He lived there from 1705–12 and recorded his findings in *Caput Bonae Spei Hodiernum* (1719). Important English and French translations appeared in 1731 and 1741, respectively.

Kolb provides the most complete picture of Khoikhoi customs extant, although his account is marred by numerous errors. His work gained additional influence by inspiring the account of Hottentot religion given in the Abbés Antoine Banier and Le Mascrier's *Cérémonies et coutumes religieuses des peuples idolâtres* (1728). The elaborate illustrations for this set of books, provided by Bernard Picart, made it a European best-seller for a century.

27. Professor of General Literature John M. Coetzee anticipates my argument by noting that there are few references to Hottentot idleness before the foundation of the East India Company station in 1652 (89). He then asserts that one might infer that this rhetoric stems from "the refusal of the natives to be drawn into the economy as wage laborers" (91). Coetzee, however, rejects this interpretation because "the denunciation of Hottentot idleness belongs not so much to the discourse of the *rulers* of the Cape . . . as it does to the rudimentary anthropological discourse of travel literature" (91–92). In a complex argument, he holds instead that the bourgeois emphasis on work has distorted the representation of "Hottentot" culture, first by condemnation, now by claiming "work" that did not exist. "If the Hottentot did not absorb the ideology of work in a generation, we cannot expect the Western bourgeois to shed his allegiance to it in a day. It would be particularly rash to expect the modern researcher and writer to respond more generously than his ancestors to a way of life so indolent that, in its extreme form, it presented him with *nothing to say*. The temptation to claim that there is something *at work* when there is nothing, is always strong. . . . The challenge of idleness to work, its power to scandalize, is as radical today as it ever was" (94).

I strongly disagree with Coetzee. First of all, the travel literature of this period is not "rudimentary anthropological discourse" in any meaningful sense. Travellers like Kolb seldom communicated directly with the Khoikhoi. Their "informants" were the farmers, small businessmen, and administrators who were frustrated at Khoikhoi resistance to menial labor. It is *their* voice we hear in Kolb's claim below that not even physical threats prevail on Khoikhoi, who can take to their heels. Work and travel passes will eventually be enforced on the Khoikhoi in their own country to curtail this free choice. The attacks on Khoikhoi indolence begin after the foundation of the colony because this is when Khoikhoi labor becomes critical. Notably, the San, located farther away, become less associated with idleness, despite their hunting and gathering lifestyle, until the frontier moves to meet them.

28. ". . . qui font de la paresse leur seule divinité, et dont la maxime commune est que travailler c'est souffrir, et que penser c'est travailler" (Saintine 205).

29. The Khoikhoi probably imported *dagga* originally from the Swahili trade on the East African coast. They probably also knew tobacco from early Portuguese trade, but originally reserved it for use as snuff (Shaw 277).

30. See seventeenth-century sketches in A. Smith (35, 42–43).

31. Interestingly, in texts, the drunken Hottentot was almost as popular a figure as the smoking Hottentot, but rarely appears to my knowledge in illustrations. Elphick reports that Dutch farmers often paid Khoikhoi workers a dram of alcohol per day in addition to bread and tobacco (165). The smoking pipe conveyed much more economically the desired image of *passive* and unthreatening indolence than did the bottle with its associations of raucous and potentially violent activity.

32. This practice continued into the age of photography. In a selection of photographs of Zulu women published by Virginia-Lee Webb, the compositions are composed specifically to draw attention to the women's breasts, as are the beaded ornaments (possibly photographers' props) that direct the viewer's eye to both the breasts and hidden pubis. The women assume the pose of "bedroom eyes." Likewise, in a photo of a woman passing as "Assambola, die Zuluprinzessin," the photographer Carl Guenthers depicts his subject very much in erotic undress in the studio (Goldmann 91).

33. "Constamment désignée comme *objet sexué,* la femme hottentote n'existe pas comme *objet sexuel . . .*" (Duchet, "Racisme" 132).

34. (*François Le Vaillant* 114). The first *Voyage* was originally published in 1790; the *Second Voyage* was published in An 4 [1796]. Immediate English translations accompanied both editions.

Mattys Bokhorst has proposed Johann Lebrecht Reinold as the artist who worked over Le Vaillant's sketches of Khoikhoi into their final form (*François Le Vaillant* 2: 111). Le Vaillant was also the poet Baudelaire's uncle.

35. Translation from Le Vaillant, *Travels,* 1790, 2: 351. "Alors, confuse, embarrassée, tremblante, et se couvrant le visage de ses deux mains, elle laissa détacher son petit tablier, et me permit de contempler tranquillement ce que le lecteur verra lui-même dans la copie fidèle que j'en ai tirée, et qui forme l'objet de la planche que je joins ici" (*Voyage,* 1798, 2: 349).

36. Le Vaillant made four watercolors. One was published in his first French edition, but the others have remained censored. The South African government reproduced all of his paintings with the exception of these four (*François Le Vaillant* 131–32).

37. "Plus je réfléchis sur la couleur de ces peuples, sur le gloussement dont ils se servent pour se faire entendre au lieu d'un langage articulé, sur leur figure, sur le tablier de leurs dames, plus je suis convaincu que cette race ne peut avoir la même origine que nous" ("Lettres" 448).

38. "Oui, lecteur, ce fameux tablier n'est qu'une mode, une affaire de goût, je ne dirai pas dépravé; les signes de la pudeur n'en sauroient constituer l'essence; mais original, mais extravagant, mais, si l'on veut, absurde, et tel que *sa seule vue suffiroit au plus monstrueux libertin pour chasser de son esprit toute idée d'une atteinte profane*; et, trompant d'une façon nouvelle et trop claire le raffinement de ses besoins, feroit succéder le rire le plus inextinguible aux transports de la passion la plus effrénée" (*Voyage,* 1798, 2: 351, emphasis mine). Le Vaillant's reasoning has precedence in the work of Sir Thomas Herbert, who claimed in 1634 that "[m]ost [men] have but one stone, the other is forced away in their infancie, that Venus allure them not from Pallas" (15).

39. "L'habitude de voir des Hottentotes ne m'a jamais familiarisé avec l'usage où elles sont de peindre la figure de mille façons différentes; je le trouve hideux et repoussant . . . non-seulement ridicule, mais fétide" (*Voyage*, 1798, 2: 44). Considering the degree to which French women of the period painted their faces, I admit to bafflement at the degree of disgust expressed by Le Vaillant and his contemporaries to Khoikhoi practice.

40. See Kirby (1949, 59) for speculation on the elusive Caesar.

41. For examples of the posters discussed, see Isherwood, Monestier, Frankcom, and Musgrave.

42. *Morning Post*, 20 Sept. 1810: 2, emphasis mine. A similar version appears in the *Morning Herald*, 20 Sept. 1810: 1.

43. "Avec une telle figure / On ne peut être une Vénus" (*VH* 29). "Figure" can be translated as either "form" or "face."

44. Verneau reports the survival of the posters in 1916 (178). Avalon reproduces both in the French journal *Aesculape* in 1926 (284–85). *Aesculape* reproduces the profile view again in 1950 ("Un portrait": 216), and the three-quarter view in 1952 (Kirby, "La Vénus Hottentote": 15). It is possible that the later reproductions were made from the same photographic prints used in 1926.

The present whereabouts of the posters are unknown. Kirby places them in the Musée de l'Homme in 1953 ("More about" 129). I did not see them during a visit to the Musée de l'Homme and Muséum d'Histoire Naturelle in 1983. Nor have I been able to confirm their existence through correspondence.

The posters (preserved under glass) are described as showing aquatints of Baartman cut out and pasted onto pastel backgrounds that depict Baartman standing against an interior wall, near a chair (Avalon 284–85; Kirby, 1952, 15; Kirby, 1953, 129). The prints illustrated for this article in figs. 1.10 and 1.11 are close approximations to the illustrated posters.

45. According to Zachary Macaulay (a motivated witness), Baartman "was cloathed in a dress resembling her complexion . . . and her dress was so tight that her shapes above and the enormous size of her posterior parts are as visible as if the said female were naked and the dress is evidently intended to give the appearance of her being undressed" (PFF 747 [KB 1/36], Public Record Office, 1) (see appendix). Baartman's one voiced complaint in her interview of 27 Nov. 1810 was that her dress was "too cold" (PFF 723 [J18/462], Public Record Office, 2) (see appendix). In a preemptive strike, the defending counsel advised the court that Baartman was "clothed in a dress of cloth as well as silk" ("Law Report," *TL* 29 Nov. 1810: 3 and "Law Intelligence," *MC* 29 Nov. 1810: 3). When Lord Ellenborough dismissed the lawsuit brought against her exhibitor, claiming unlawful restraint, he advised the plaintiffs that "offense to decency," if it existed, could be grounds for prosecution ("Law Report," *TL* 29 Nov. 1810: 3). Such charges were never made (East, 1816, 195). Readers should keep in mind that contemporary women's fashion also clung to the figure, a fact many caricatures lampooned. See, for example, the print from 1810, "The [Three] Graces in a high wind."

46. The garters may be intended to invoke anachronistically the dried rawhide leggings once worn by Khoikhoi women (A. Smith 33 ff.). The shoes probably allude to moccasins (Smith 60).

47. While Le Vaillant commented on face painting in the hinterland in the 1780s, it is highly unlikely that Baartman ever availed herself of the fashion in her work as domestic worker and nanny.

48. In his deposition, Macaulay describes it as "somewhat like a guitar" (appendix).

49. Already by 1822, William Bullock had launched a fully formed ethnographic exhibition of Laplanders at his commercial museum, including displays of artifacts, dioramas, and

even reindeer. It was a huge success, which earned one hundred pounds per day for six weeks (Timbs 320). For unusually comprehensive prints of the exhibition, see "A Collection of Handbills, Newspaper Cuttings and Other Items Relating to . . . the Egyptian Hall . . . 1820–1896," Guildhall Library, London [Granger 2.5.7].

50. The European response to Khoikhoi face painting remains consistent from the seventeenth to nineteenth centuries. Herbert wrote that it rendered the women "Monsters to all civill eyes" ("Some yeares" 17). The review to Baartman's exhibition in Paris in 1815 highlights a similar response to face painting (misread as cicatrices): "Ce nom de Vénus avait reveillé en moi des souvenirs mythologiques assez tendre. . . . Ah! Messieurs quelle terrible Vénus! . . . [elle a] d'horribles cicatrices sur la joue, faites avec de la poudre à canon, en forme d'enjolivements" (Musard 1815: 2–3).

51. De Blainville observes that Baartman did not smoke (1816, 189).

52. Many writers (and the costume designer for Parks's play *Venus*) have mistakenly read fig. 1.11 and its descendants as the literal and naturalistic representation of Baartman's exhibition in London. As observed above, conforming to English laws of public decency, Baartman was exhibited in a flesh-tinted dress. Eyewitness Ourry confirms this fact also for the Parisian exhibition (3–4).

Subsequent reproductions grow progressively more brutal. The print "Sartjee The Hottentot Venus, from Gamtoos River, South Africa" is very close to a reversed version of the exhibition poster, but the modifications are telling. The smoke has been accentuated and Baartman's lips protrude in caricatural fashion. The artist has dropped her arm to reveal more of her breast, now marked by an erect nipple. The pursed lips and slack hold on the walking stick contribute further to the representation of an imbecilic and lazy nature.

53. English printmakers call attention to the pipe, often billowing smoke from the bowl, in "Astronomical Phœnomenon. An Exact Representation of THE PLANET VENUS . . ." (1810) ("Plays and the Theatre" 176); "Love and Beauty" (British Museum no. 1444a); "Neptune's Last Resource"; "A Pair of Broad Bottoms"; "Love at First Sight" (British Museum no. 11578); etc. I thank Dror Wahrman for bringing the unusual first print to my notice.

54. For example: "A Pair of Broad Bottoms" (1810) (Altick, fig. 85); "Love at First Sight" (1810) (George 8, No. 11577: 947–78); "Prospects of Prosperity" (1810) (Altick, fig. 86); "Neptune's Last Resource" (1811?) (George 9, No. 11748: 38–39).

For sly newspaper innuendos, see the *MH* 23 Nov. 1810, *MP* 7 Nov. 1810. For political satire on Lord Grenville, see *MP* 5 Nov. 1810, *MP* 9 Nov. 1810. For more on the political caricatures, see Altick 271–72; Lindfors, "Hottentot Venus," "Afterlife," and especially "Bottom."

55. "Messieurs, nous avons prudemment / Caché la Venus hottentote / Sous les traits d'un minois charmant" (couplet d'annonce, qtd. in Martainville 1814, 4).

56. "Le contraste qui présentait la jolie figure de cette actrice, avec celle du petit monstre qu'on devrait bien cesser d'expose [*sic*] en public, a procuré une si agréable surprise . . ." (*GF* 21 Nov. 1814). Another reviewer writes confidently that he would not do the actress the insult ". . . de la comparer un instant avec celle que chacun peut voir pour 15 sous. Il y a plus d'une différence entre Mlle Rivière et son modèle étranger. Une jeune et jolie actrice comme elle ne peut avoir aucun rapport avec une *Vénus sauvage*" (*JGF* 21 Nov. 1814). Or economically: "On pourrait reprocher [*sic*] à Mlle. Rivière de mal représenter une *Hottentote*, car elle est fort jolie" (*QP* 20 Nov. 1814).

57. The newspaper embellished the language of this account and invented a cage: "The Hottentot was produced like a wild beast, and ordered to move backwards and forwards, and come out and go into her cage, more like a bear in a chain [*sic*] than a human being"

("Law Report," *TL* 26 Nov. 1810). The *Times* account has misled many writers, e.g., Gould (1982, 21) and Wiss (17).

58. An anonymous letter writer claimed that the exhibitor "holds up a *stick to her, like the wild beast keepers* [*sic*], to intimidate her into obedience" ("An Englishman," 12 Oct. 1810).

59. It is also possible that Baartman used the trial to advantage to bargain for better terms and was satisfied with her (new?) arrangements (see appendix). Kirby has suggested that, faced with a trial, Dunlop cleverly drew up a contract with Baartman, which was dated 29 Oct. 1810, but antedated to 20 Mar. 1810 ("More about" 125–26). The existence of the contract weighed heavily in favor of the defendants.

60. "Feuilleton," *GF* 7 octobre 1814; "Feuilleton," *GF* 24 octobre 1814. An advertisement notes that (as was common for "freak" shows), her promoter sold souvenir copies (*AAA* 18 septembre 1814).

61. "Ce phénomène extraordinaire est le seul qui ait jamais paru en Europe, de la tribu d'Hauzanana. Dans cette femme, aussi extraordinaire que surprenante, le public a un modèle parfait de cette tribu qui habite les régions les plus méridionales de l'Afrique. . . . Elle porte sur elle tous les ornemens [*sic*] qui servent de parure, dans les jours de fête, à la tribu à laquelle elle appartient" (*AAA* 18 septembre 1814). See also: *AAA* 28–31 octobre 1814.

Curiously, either in reference to the "sullen" demeanor that provoked the English trial, or out of deference to perceived French tastes, much emphasis is placed on promoting Baartman's engaging personality: "La Vénus Hottentote diffère beaucoup de caractère de sa nation, ordinairement très morose, par sa douceur, son affabilité et ses manières engageantes" (*AAA* 18 septembre 1814). See also: *JGF* 22 septembre 1814.

62. Le Vaillant, *New Travels,* 1796, 3: 180–82, pl. 18. Georges Cuvier and subsequent writers have asserted that Baartman was San ("Bushman") based on Cuvier's questionable reading of ethnicity in the body (Cuvier, "Extrait," 1817). Some have grown even more specific: Wiss states that she was !Kung (11), and Kirby speculates that she was of "mixed stock" (1949, 55). Unless new documents surface, I do not know how any claim to ethnicity may be supported. For the arguments of this article, all that matters is that Baartman served as a representation of the "Hottentot."

63. "La femme désignée sous le nom de *Vénus Hottentote* . . . se nomme Sartjée; elle est de la tribu *d'Houzouana,* qui habite un pays situé à deux cent lieues dans le nord-est du cap de Bonne-Espérance. . . . Elle parle le hollandais, l'anglais, et sa langue maternelle, dans laquelle elle chante quelques chansons. . . . Sa couleur est plutôt celle des Péruviens que des Africains, dont elle a les cheveux et les traits. Elle a conservé l'habitude de se peindre la figure, et est toute couverte de grains de verre. Elle joue de la guimbarde, instrument que, selon *Vaillant,* et très affectionné de ces peuples" (*JGF* 22 septembre 1814; and *QP* 23 septembre 1814).

64. For example, a satirist placed a letter in the "Variétés" column of the *Journal de Paris* (7 Nov. 1814), in the voice of "Sartjée" writing to her cousin. Clearly drawing on the illustration of "Hottentot Woman with Apron" from Le Vaillant, and on his argument about a surfeit of modesty, the satirist has Baartman recount how she had counseled her French women friends to adopt Hottentot fashion. They answered that Hottentot customs were "too natural and hid nearly nothing." "What modesty," responds Baartman. "And also what prejudice! Do we not have an apron that descends nearly to our knees . . . ? Besides, they could always elongate it a little, if they found it too short. . . ."

65. We know that Réaux, the showman (reputedly an animal trainer) who was handling Baartman's exhibition, demanded a report on the observations by the zoologists and other scientists (Kirby, "'The Hottentot Venus'" 320). Since his name figures as vendor on the print, he may also have required a product of the artists' efforts in remuneration.

This engraving (or even one of the profile drawings made at the Jardin des Plantes) appears to have served as a model for one of the few caricatural prints that does not draw on the second poster as its inspiration: "Les curieux en extase" (illustrated in Gould, *Flamingo* 305), published 28 Oct. 1815 (Rosset 85). Gould misreads the print and gives an incorrect date (305). For a more accurate description, see Rosset or Ourry.

66. "Mais à cette première inspection l'on ne s'aperçut point de la particularité la plus remarquable de son organisation; elle tint son tablier soigneusement caché; soit entre ses cuisses soit plus profondément, et ce n'est qu'après sa mort qu'on a su qu'elle le possédoit" (Cuvier, 1817, 265).

De Blainville believed that he had caught a glimpse of the condition when Baartman was walking or bent over but notes "dans la station verticale" they could observe absolutely nothing (1816, 187). One senses the immense care that Baartman exerted to thwart the men around her.

67. "Il me semblait voir les premiers hommes de la terre; cela venait de naître et rampait encore avec les crapauds et les crocodiles" (Flaubert 162). Thanks to Bernth Lindfors for bringing this remarkable text to my attention.

68. "Qu'ai-je donc en moi pour me faire chérir à première vue par tout ce qui est crétin, fou, idiot, sauvage? Ces pauvres natures-là comprennent-elles que je suis de leur monde? . . . Sentent-elles, d'elles à moi, un lien quelconque?" (Flaubert 163).

69. I thank curator Amy Kurland of the Allen Memorial Art Museum for sharing this interview with me and for showing me the installation on very short notice.

70. "On s'explique en riant; Adolphe abjure ses folles idées, et se marie avec sa cousine" (Martainville, 20 Nov. 1814: 4).

BIBLIOGRAPHY

AAA	*Affiches, Annonces et Avis Divers ou Journal Général de France*
GF	*Gazette de France*
JDM	*Journal des Dames et des Modes*
JGF	*Journal Général de France*
JP	*Journal de Paris*
JR	*Journal Royal* (Paris)
MC	*Morning Chronicle* (London)
MH	*Morning Herald* (London)
MP	*Morning Post* (London)
QP	*La Quotidienne* (Paris)
TL	*Times* (London)
VH	*La Vénus Hottentote, ou Haine aux Françaises.* By Marie Emmanuel Guillaume Marguerite Théaulon de Lambert. Paris: Chez Martinet, 1814.

ARCHIVES AND MUSEUM COLLECTIONS

British Library. Daniel Lysons, "Collectanea; or a Collection of Advertisements and Paragraphs from the Newspapers, Relating to Various Subjects," Vol. 1. Unpublished scrapbook (c.103.k.11).

Manchester Cathedral (formerly Collegiate Church) Baptismal Register. Dec. 1, 1811 (Entry no. 2689).

Musée de l'Homme, Paris. Painting by Berré (1815). Silhouette profile in pencil by Huet (1815). Cast, skeleton, etc.

Muséum d'Histoire Naturelle (Jardin des Plantes), Paris. Watercolors by de Wailly and Huet (1815).

Public Record Office, Chancery Lane, London. J18/462 PFF 723; KB 1/36 PFF 747. Affidavits deposed at the Court of the King's Bench during the 1810 trial.

PART I: PRIMARY SOURCES ON THE EXHIBITION OF S. BAARTMAN (IN CHRONOLOGICAL ORDER)

1810

"The Hottentot Venus." Advertisement. *MP* 20 Sept.: 2.
"The Hottentot Venus." Advertisement. *MH* 20 Sept.: 1.
"An Englishman." Letter. *MC* 12 Oct.: 3.
Cezar, Hendric [*sic*]. "The Hottentot Venus." Letter. *MC* 13 Oct.: 3.
"Humanitas." "Female Hottentot." Letter. *MC* 17 Oct.: 3.
"A Man and a Christian." Letter. *MP* 18 Oct.: 3.
Cezar, Hendric [*sic*]. Letter. *MC* 23 Oct.: 4.
"Humanitas." "Female Hottentot." Letter. *MC* 24 Oct.: 3.
"White Man." Letter. *MP* 29 Oct.: 3.
"The Hottentot Venus." *Sporting Magazine* (London) 37.218 (Nov.): 81–82.
"The Hottentot Venus and the Grenvilles." *The Satirist, or, Monthly Meteor* 1 Nov.: 424–27.
"The Hottentot Venus and the Grenvilles." *MP* 5 Nov.: 1.
"When a Certain Money-getting Manager. . . ." *MP* 7 Nov.: 3.
"De Hottentot Fenus [*sic*]." *MP* 9 Nov.: 3.
"There is great reason to believe. . . ." *MP* 10 Nov.: 3.
"A few evenings since. . . ." *MH* 23 Nov.: 3.
"Law Intelligence; Court of King's Bench, Sat., Nov. 24; The Hottentot Venus." *MC* 26 Nov.: 3.
"Law Intelligence; Court of King's Bench, Sat., Nov. 24; The Hottentot Venus." *MP* 26 Nov.: 3.
"Law Report; Court of King's Bench, Sat., Nov. 24; The Hottentot Venus." *MH* 26 Nov.: 3.
"Law Report; Court of King's Bench." *TL* 26 Nov.: 3.
"Law Intelligence; Court of King's Bench, Nov. 28; The Hottentot Venus." *MC* 29 Nov.: 3.
"Law Intelligence; Court of King's Bench, Nov. 28; The Hottentot Venus." *MP* 29 Nov.: 3.
"Law Report; Court of King's Bench, Nov. 28." *MH* 29 Nov.: 3
"Law Report; Court of King's Bench, Nov. 28," *TL* 29 Nov.: 3.
"The Hottentot Venus and the Grenvilles." *The Satirist, or, Monthly Meteor* 1 Dec.: 550–54.
"The Venus." Satiric Poem. *MP* 1 Dec.: 4.
"The Hottentot Venus." Satiric Poem. *MH* 12 Dec.: 3.

1811

"Sartjee to the Satirist." *The Satirist, or, Monthly Meteor* 1 Feb.: 164–66.
"The Hottentot Venus." Advertisement. *MP* 30 Apr.: 1.
"The Hottentot Female." *Wheeler's Manchester Chronicle.* 7 Dec.: 4.
"The Hottentot Female." *Aston's Exchange Herald.* 10 Dec.: 4.
"The Hottentot Female." *MP* 12 Dec.: 3.
"That beautiful, amiable object. . . ." *Cowdroy's Manchester Gazette* 14 Dec.: 4

1814

Théaulon de Lambert, Marie Emmanuel Guillaume Marguerite. *La Vénus Hottentote, ou Haine aux Françaises, Vaudeville en un acte.* Paris: Chez Martinet, 1814.
"Paris: La Vénus hottentote." Advertisement. *AAA* 18 Sept.: 15.
"Feuilleton: La Vénus hottentote." Advertisement. *JP* 18 Sept.: 1.
"Paris: On montre pour trois francs . . . la Vénus Hottentote." *JP* 22 Sept.: 2.
"Paris: La femme désignée sous le nom de Vénus Hottentote." Description of the exhibition. *JGF* 22 Sept.: 3.
"Paris." Description of the exhibition. *QP* 23 Sept.: 2.
"Nouvelles des Théâtres." Play preview. *JP* 26 Sept.: 3.

"Variétés." *JGF* 26 Sept.: 1.

"Variétés: La Vénus hottentote." Note on exhibition and preview of play. *GF* 30 Sept.: 1087.

"Variétés." Rev. of exhibition posters. *GF* 7 Oct.: 1114.

"Feuilleton: *La Vénus Hottentote*." Advertisement. *GF* 24 Oct.: 1.

"Paris: *La Vénus Hottentote*." Advertisement. *AAA* 28 Oct.: 15; 29 Oct.: 15; 30 Oct.: 14–15; 31 Oct.: 15–16.

"Variétés: Sartjée ou la Vénus hottentote, à son cousin." Satire. *JP* 7 Nov.: 2–4; 19 Nov.: 2–4.

"Le Vaudeville." Play preview. *GF* 8 Nov.: 1241.

"Feuilleton: La Vénus Hottentote." Advertisement. *GF* 16 Nov.: 1273.

D.C.y. [*sic*]. Rev. of *VH*. *QP* 20 Nov: 4.

"Paris." Rev. of *VH*. *JGF* 20 Nov.: 3.

Martainville, A. Rev. of *VH*. *JP* 20 Nov.: 2–4.

Rev. of *VH*. *GF* 21 Nov.: 1291.

Rev. of *VH*. *JGF* 21 Nov.: 3–4.

Rev. of *VH*. *Journal des Débats, Politiques et Littéraires* 21 Nov.: 3–4.

Rev. of *VH*. *JR* 22 Nov.: 2–3.

Rev. of *VH*. *JGF* 21 Nov.: 3.

"Paris." Rev. of *VH*. *JDM* 25 Nov.: 511.

1815

M. Musard l'emigré. "Feuilleton." Satire. *QP* 15 Jan.: 1–3.

"La Vénus Hottentote." Advertisement. *JP* 22 Jan.: 1.

"Paris: La Vénus hottentote civilisée." Advertisement. *AAA* 22 Jan.: 15; 24 Jan.: 7; 26 Jan.: 15.

"Mélanges: *La Vénus hottentote*." Note on exhibition. *JGF* 23 Jan.: 3.

"La Vénus hottentote." Announcement of a new caricature. *JP* 25 Jan.: 4.

"La Vénus Hottentote." Description of a private exhibition and fictional conversation. *JDM* 25 Jan.: 37–40.

"Spectacles: La Vénus Hottentote." Advertisements. *AAA* 27–31 Jan.: 16; 1–8 Feb.: 16.

"Nouvelles: On dit que la Vénus Hottentote va faire un journal." Satire. *QP* 5 Mar.: 4.

"Feuilleton: La Vénus hottentote." Advertisements. *JP* 6 Mar.: 1; 25 Mar.: 1; 21 July: 1; 22 July: 1; 2 Aug.: 1; 31 Aug.: 1.

"Paris: La Vénus hottentote." *QP* 11 Sept.: 3–4.

"Paris: La Vénus hottentote." Obituary. *JGF* 31 Dec.: 2.

1816

de Blainville, Henri. "Sur une femme de la race hottentote." *Bulletin des sciences, par la Société philomatique de Paris.* 183–90.

East, Edward Hyde. *Reports of Cases Argued and Determined in the Court of King's Bench,* AMENDED BY Thomas Day. Vol. 13. Hartford: Hudson & Goodwin. 195–96. "The case of the Hottentot Venus."

"Chronique de Paris." *Mercure de France* Jan.: 334.

"Paris." Obituary. *JP* 1 Jan.: 2.

"Nouvelles de Paris: La Vénus hottentote est mort." Obituary. *QP* 1 Jan.: 4.

Obituary. *Annales Politiques, Morales et Littéraires* 3 Jan.: 2.

"Paris" and "Petite Chronique." Satire and gossip. *JP* 8 Jan.: 2–3; 8 Apr.: 4.

"Semaine Dernière: On assure que les savans qui dissèquent au Jardin du Roi la Vénus hottentote." Obituary. *JGF* 8 Jan.: 4.

"Paris has now to deplore . . ." *MP* 10 Jan.: 3.

"Variétés." Satire. *L'Ambigu* 10 Jan.: 38–40.

"In the place where. . . ." *MP* 15 Jan.: 3.

1817

Cuvier, Georges. "Extrait d'observations faites sur le cadavre d'une femme connue à Paris et à

Londres sous le nom de Vénus Hottentote." *Mémoires du Muséum d'histoire naturelle* 3: 259–74.

1838

"Ourry" [E. T. Maurice?]. "La dernière planche. . . ." *Musée de la caricature,* ed. E. Jaime. Paris: Delloye. 3–4.

1839

Mathews, Anne. *Memoirs of Charles Mathews, Comedian.* Vol. 4. London: Richard Bentley. 136–39.

PART II: SECONDARY SOURCES ON THE EXHIBITION OF S. BAARTMAN

Alexander, Elizabeth. *The Venus Hottentot.* Charlottesville: University Press of Virginia, 1990.

Altick, Richard D. *The Shows of London.* Cambridge: Harvard University Press, 1978.

Avalon, Jean. "Sarah, la 'Vénus Hottentote.'" *Aesculape* 16 (1926): 281–88.

Brown, Elizabeth A. "Social Studies." *Allen Memorial Art Museum Bulletin* 44.1 (1990): 6–57.

Chambers, Robert, ed. "The Hottentot Venus." *The Book of Days.* 1862–64. Detroit: Gale Research Company, 1967. 621–22.

Drimmer, Frederick. "The Hottentot Venus." *Body Snatchers, Stiffs and Other Ghoulish Delights.* New York: Fawcett Gold Medal, 1981. 137–56.

Fontenay, Elisabeth de. "Flee, Unhappy Hottentots." *Diderot: Reason and Resonance.* 1981. Trans. Jeffrey Mehlman. New York: George Braziller, 1982. 91–100.

Fusco, Coco. "The Other History of Intercultural Performance." *English Is Broken Here.* New York: New Press, 1995. 37–63.

Gautier, Théophile. "Feuilleton: Salon de 1853." *La Presse* 21 juillet 1853: 2.

George, Mary Dorothy. *Catalogue of Political and Personal Satires Preserved in the Department of Prints and Drawings in the British Museum.* Vols. 8–10. London: British Museum Publications, Ltd., 1978.

Gilman, Sander L. "Black Bodies, White Bodies: Toward an Iconography of Female Sexuality in Late Nineteenth-Century Art, Medicine and Literature." *Critical Inquiry* 12.1 (1985): 204–42.

Gould, Stephen Jay. *The Mismeasure of Man.* New York: W. W. Norton, 1981.

———. "The Hottentot Venus." *Natural History* 91.9 (1982): 20–27.

———. "The Hottentot Venus." *The Flamingo's Smile.* New York: W. W. Norton, 1985. 291–305.

Gratiolet, Pierre. *Mémoire sur les plis cérébraux de l'homme et des primates.* 1854.

"'The Hottentot Venus': A Ballad." Appendix D. *Circus and Allied Arts.* Ed. R. Toole-Stott. Derby, England: Harper and Sons, 1962. 333–36.

"Une Image de la Vénus Hottentote." *Aesculape* 19 (1929): 113.

Kirby, Percival R. "The Hottentot Venus." *Africana Notes and News* 6.3 (1949): 55–62.

———. "La Vénus Hottentote en Angleterre." *Aesculape* 33.1 (Jan. 1952): 14–21.

———. "More about the Hottentot Venus." *Africana Notes and News* 10.4 (1953): 124–34.

———. "The 'Hottentot Venus' of the Musée de l'Homme, Paris." *South African Journal of Science* 50.12 (July 1954): 319–22.

———. "A Further Note on the Hottentot Venus." *Africana Notes and News* 11.5 (Dec. 1954): 165–66.

Koch, Eddie. "Bring Back the Hottentot Venus." *Weekly Mail and Guardian* 15–22 June 1995: 13.

Lindfors, Bernth. "'The Hottentot Venus' and Other African Attractions in Nineteenth-Century England." *Australasian Drama Studies* 1.2 (1982): 82–104.

———. "Circus Africans." *Journal of American Culture* 6.2 (1983): 9–14.

———. "The Bottom Line: African Caricature in Georgian England." *World Literature Written in English* 24.1 (1984): 43–51.

———. "Courting the Hottentot Venus." *Africa* (Rome) 40 (1985): 133–48.

———. "The Afterlife of the Hottentot Venus." *Neohelicon* 16.2 (1989): 293–301.

———. "Hottentot, Bushman, Kaffir: Taxonomic Tendencies in Nineteenth-Century Racial Iconography." *Nordic Journal of African Studies* 5.2 (1996): 1–30.

Matus, Jill. "Blonde, Black and Hottentot Venus." *Studies in Short Fiction* 28.4 (Fall 1991): 467–76.

O'Grady, Lorraine. "Olympia's Maid." *AfterImage* 20.1 (Summer 1992): 14–15, 23.

Parks, Suzan-Lori. "Venus." Play presented at the Yale Repertory Theatre (New Haven, Conn.) and Joseph Papp Public Theatre (New York), 1996.

"Plays and the Theatre." Catalogue. London: Jarndyce Booksellers, Summer 1995.

"Un Portrait de la Vénus Hottentote." *Aesculape* 31.11 (Nov. 1950): 216.

Racinet, Auguste. *Le Costume historique.* Vol. 2. Paris: Librairie de Firmin-Didot et Cie, 1888. N. pag.

Regnault, Félix. "La Spondylolisthésis de la Vénus Hottentote." *Bulletins et Mémoires de la Société d'Anthropologie de Paris* 5 (6th series) (1914): 233–35.

Rosset, Anne-Marie. *Un siècle d'histoire de France par l'estampe (1770–1871): Collection de Vinck. Inventaire Analytique.* Vol. 5: 85–86. Paris: Bibliothèque Nationale, 1938.

Schiebinger, Londa. *Nature's Body.* Boston: Beacon Press, 1993.

Verneau, R. "Le centième anniversaire de la mort de Sarah Bartmann." *L'Anthropologie* 27 (1916): 177–79.

Wiss, Rosemary. "Lipreading: Remembering Saartjie Baartman." *Australian Journal of Anthropology* 1994.5 (1 and 2): 11–40.

PART III: RELATED MATERIAL

Adas, Michael. *Machines as the Measure of Men.* Ithaca: Cornell University Press, 1989.

[Banier, Antoine l'Abbé, and M. l'Abbé Le Mascrier, eds.] *Cérémonies et Coutumes religieuses des peuples idolâtres, représentées par . . . Bernard Picart.* Tome 2, pt. 1. Amsterdam: J. F. Bernard, 1728.

Barnard, Alan. *Hunters and Herders of Southern Africa: A Comparative Ethnography of the Khoisan Peoples.* Cambridge: Cambridge University Press, 1992.

Bassani, Ezio, and Letizia Tedeschi. "The Image of the Hottentot in the Seventeenth and Eighteenth Centuries." *Journal of the History of Collections* 2.2 (1990): 157–86.

"The 'Bosjesmans,' or Bush People." *TL* 19 May 1847: 7.

"The Bosjesmans, or Bush People. Now Exhibiting at the Egyptian Hall." [1847] Promotional pamphlet. British Library.

"The Bosjesmans, at the Egyptian Hall, Piccadilly." *Illustrated London News.* Vol. 10 (12 June 1847): 381.

"Bushmen Children or Pigmy Race!" Handbill, Egyptian Hall. D137.13 (1845). Archives Dept. Westminster City Libraries.

"Bushmen Children." *Illustrated London News* 7.175 (6 Sept. 1845): 160.

Coetzee, John M. "Anthropology and the Hottentots." *Semiotica* 54.1/2 (1985): 87–95.

Cohen, William B. *The French Encounter with Africans.* Bloomington: Indiana University Press, 1980.

Conolly, John. *The Ethnological Exhibitions of London.* London: John Churchill, 1885.

De Bry, Johann Theodor, and Johann Israel de Bry, eds. *India Orientalis,* pt. 3. Franckfurt am Mayn: Gedruckt durch M. Becker, 1599.

Delon, Michel. "Corps Sauvages, Corps Étranges." *Dix-huitième Siècle* 9 (1977): 27–38.

Dickens, Charles. "Amusements of the People." *Household Words* 1 (1850): 57–60.

———. "The Noble Savage." *Household Words* 7.168 (11 June 1853): 337–39.

Diderot, M., ed., and M. D'Alembert. *Encyclopédie, ou dictionnaire raisonné des sciences, des arts et des métiers.* Neufchastel: Samuel Faulche, 1765.

Doyle, Arthur Conan. *Study in Scarlet and the Sign of Four.* New York: Berkeley Publishing Corp., 1975.

Duchet, Michèle. *Anthropologie et histoire au siècle des lumières*. Paris: François Maspero, 1971.

———. "Racisme et Sexualité au XVIIIe Siècle." *Ni juif ni grec*. Ed. Léon Poliakov. Paris: Mouton, 1978. 127–38.

Elphick, Richard. *Khoikhoi and the Founding of White South Africa*. Johannesburg: Ravan Press, 1985.

Elphick, Richard, and Hermann Giliomee, eds. *The Shaping of South African Society, 1652–1820*. London: Longman Group, 1979.

Exhibition of Native Zulu Kafirs: Descriptive History. London: John Mitchell, Royal Library, 1853.

Flaubert, Gustave. "A Louis Bouilhet." *Oeuvres Complètes. Correspondance*, vol. 2, ed. René Descharmes. Paris: Librairie de France, 1923. 162–64.

François Le Vaillant: Traveller in South Africa and His Collection of 165 Water-Colour Paintings (1781–1784). Cape Town: Library of Parliament, 1973.

Frankcom, G., and J. H. Musgrave. *The Irish Giant*. London: Duckworth, 1976.

Goldmann, Stefan. "Zur Rezeption der Voelkerausstellungen um 1900." *Exotische Welten. Europaeische Phantasien*. Wuerttemberg: Institut fuer Auslandsbeziehungen Wuerttembergischer Kunstverein, 1987. 88–93.

Goldsmith, Oliver. "The Citizen of the World; or, Letters from a Chinese Philosopher Residing in London to his friends in the East." 1760. *The Works of Oliver Goldsmith*. Vol. 3. New York: Jefferson Press, 1900.

Gombrich, E. H. *Art and Illusion*. New York: Pantheon Books, 1961.

Gordon, Robert J. *The Bushman Myth: The Making of a Namibian Underclass*. Boulder, Colo.: Westview Press, 1992.

———. "The Venal Hottentot Venus and the Great Chain of Being." *African Studies* (University of Witwatersrand) 51.2 (1992): 185–201.

Hagenbeck, Carl. *Beasts and Men*. Abr. ed. Trans. Hugh Elliot and A. G. Thacker. New York: Longmans, Green, 1909.

Herbert, Sir Thomas. *A relation of some yeares travaile, begvnne anno 1626. Into Afrique and the greater Asia....* London: W. Stansby and J. Bloome, 1634.

———. *Some yeares travels into divers parts of Asia and Afrique*. Rev. and enlarged. London: Printed by R. Bip for I. Blome and R. Bishop, 1638.

Hirschberg, Walter. *SchwarzAfrika*. Graz, Austria: Akademische Druck-u. Verlagsanstalt, 1962.

Hulsius, Levinus, ed. *Erste Schiffart*. Nürnberg: Levini Hulsij, 1602.

Isherwood, Robert M. *Farce and Fantasy: Popular Entertainment in Eighteenth Century Paris*. New York: Oxford University Press, 1986.

"The Kaffir War." *Illustrated London News* 25 July 1846: 52.

Kennedy, R. F., ed. *Catalogue of Prints in the Africana Museum*. Johannesburg: Africana Museum, 1975. H161–70.

Kolb, Peter. *Caput Bonae Spei Hodiernum*. Nuernberg: Peter Conrad Monath, 1719. Other editions consulted: *The Present State of the Cape of Good-Hope*. Trans. Guido Medley. 2 vols. London: W. Innys, 1731; *Description du Cap de Bonne-Esperance*. Amsterdam: Jean Catuffe, 1742; *Beschreibung des Horgeburges der Guten Hoffnung*. Frankfurt and Leipzig: Peter Conrad Monath, 1745; *Unter Hottentotten (1705–13): Die Aufzeichnungen von Peter Kolb*. Basel: Horst Erdmann Verlag, 1979.

La Caille, Nicolas Louis de. *Travels at the Cape, 1751–53*. Trans. R. Raven-Hart. Cape Town: A. A. Balkema, 1976.

Larousse, Pierre, ed. *Grand Dictionnaire universel du XIXe Siècle*. 1873. Genève-Paris: Slatkine, 1982.

Le Vaillant, François. *Voyage de M. Le Vaillant dans l'intérieur de l'Afrique*. Paris: Chez Leroy, 1790. Other editions consulted: *Travels into the Interior Parts of Africa*. London: G. G. J. and J. Robinson, 1790; *Voyage de F. Le Vaillant*. Paris: Desray, An VI [1798].

———. *Second Voyage dans l'intérieur de l'Afrique*. Paris: H. J. Jansen, An 4 [1796]. Other edition consulted: *New Travels into the Interior Parts of Africa*. London: G. G. J. and J. Robinson, 1796.

Massing, Jean Michel. "Hans Burgkmair's Depiction of Native Africans." *Res* 27 (Spring 1995): 39–51.

Miller, Christopher. *Blank Darkness: Africanist Discourse in French*. Chicago: University of Chicago Press, 1985.

Morin, Benoît. *Dictionnaire Universel des Synonymes de la Langue Française*. Vol. 1. Paris: Dabo-Butschert, 1833.

"The Most Extraordinary Exhibition of Aborigines." Advertisement. *The Athenaeum* 7.1020 (15 May 1847): 521.

Nienaber, G. S. "The Origin of the Name 'Hottentot.'" *African Studies* 22.2 (1963): 65–90.

"Our Weekly Gossip." *The Athenaeum* 28 May 1853: 650.

Parker, Kenneth. "Telling Tales: Early Modern English Voyagers and the Cape of Good Hope." *The Seventeenth Century* 10.1 (Spring 1995): 121–49.

Pepys, Samuel. *Diary*. 1660. Ed. Robert Latham and William Matthews. Vol. 1. London: G. Bell and Sons, 1970.

Ploss, Hermann, Max Bartels, and Paul Bartels. *Woman: An Historical, Gynaecological and Anthropological Compendium*. 1885. London: William Heinemann Ltd., 1935.

Poeschel, Sabine. *Studien zur Ikonographie der Erdteile*. Scanea: Richard A. Klein, 1985.

Pratt, Mary Louise. "Scratches on the Face of the Country; or, What Mr. Barrow Saw in the Land of the Bushmen." *Critical Inquiry* 12.1 (1985): 119–43.

Randles, W. G. L. *L'Image du Sud-Est Africain dans la Littérature Européenne au XVIe Siècle*. Lisboa: Centro de Estudos Históricos Ultramarinos, 1959.

Raven-Hart, Major R. *Before Van Riebeeck: Callers at South Africa from 1488 to 1652*. Cape Town: C. Struik, 1967.

———. *Cape of Good Hope, 1652–1702*. 2 vols. Cape Town: Balkema, 1971.

Saintine, X. -B. "La Vengeance: Le Hottentot-Boshi." *Contes Philosophiques*. 1825. Paris: Ambroise Dupont et Roret, 1826. 203–44.

Schapera, Isaac. *The Khoisan Peoples of South Africa: Bushmen and Hottentots*. London: George Routledge and Sons, 1930.

Schapera, Isaac, and B. Farrington, eds. and trans. *The Early Cape Hottentots*. Cape Town: Van Riebeeck Society, 1933.

Shaw, M. "Native Pipes and Smoking in South Africa." *Annals of the South African Museum* 24.5 (Aug. 1938): 277–302, plates 85–99.

Singer, Ronald, and Werner Jopp. "The Earliest Illustration of Hottentots: 1508." *South African Archaeological Bulletin* 22 (June 1967): 15–19.

Skotnes, Pippa, ed. *Miscast: Negotiating the Presence of the Bushmen*. Cape Town: University of Cape Town Press, 1996.

Smith, Andrew B. *The Khoikhoi at the Cape of Good Hope: Seventeenth-Century Drawings in the South African Library*. Cape Town: South African Library, 1993.

Sparrman, Anders. *A Voyage to the Cape of Good Hope*. Translated from the Swedish. 2nd ed. corr. London: G. G. J. and J. Robinson, 1786. Other editions consulted: *Voyage to the Cape of Good Hope*. Dublin: R. Marchbank, 1786; *Reize naar de kaap de Goede Hoop*. Leyden, Amsterdam: Luchtmans and Bruijn, 1787; *Voyage au Cap de Bonne-Espérance*. Trans. M. Le Tourneur. Paris: Buisson, 1787.

Stewart, Susan. *On Longing*. Durham: Duke University Press, 1993.

Swift, Jonathan. "Gulliver's Travels" and "A Tale of a Tub." *Swift*. New York: Random House, 1934.

[Tachard, Guy]. *[A] Relation of the Voyage to Siam, performed by Six Jesuits*. London: J. Robinson, 1688.

Timbs, John. *Curiosities of London*. London: Longmans, Green, Reader and Dyer, 1868.

Voltaire, François Marie Arouet. *Essai sur les moeurs et l'esprit des nations*. Ed. René Pomeau. 2 vols. Paris: Garnier, 1963.

———. "Les Lettres d'Amabed." *Romans et Contes*. Paris: Garnier, 1967.

Webb, Virginia-Lee. "Fact and Fiction: Nineteenth-Century Photographs of the Zulu." *African Arts* 25.1 (1992): 50–59, 98–99.

Zulu Kafirs. Last Few Days in London. [1853] Promotional pamphlet. British Library.

2 Charles Dickens and the Zulus

BERNTH LINDFORS

On 15 December 1852 a steamer, the *Sir Robert Peel*, left Durban carrying passengers and cargo bound for Cape Town. Among those on board were A. T. Caldecott, a prominent merchant from Pietermaritzburg; his son C. H. Caldecott; and, in the steerage compartment, thirteen Zulus whom the Caldecotts were taking to London for the purpose of exhibiting them to the English public. The Caldecotts claimed that these were the first "Kafirs from the Zulu country [to be] exhibited in England" and that it had long been A. T. Caldecott's wish

> that the English public should be gratified with a sight of the interesting savages, by whom he was surrounded in the fertile and flourishing colony of Natal. On various occasions he has endeavoured to form a party to accompany him across the ocean to Great Britain, but their own reluctance, their fear of the voyage, the difficulties to be overcome before the colonial government would permit them to embark, and other causes, rendered for a while all his efforts nugatory. By dint of continual perseverance; by telling the poor fellows the grand sights which awaited them; by engaging one this month and another the next; and by promising to each a good and just reward for their services, he was at length fortunate enough to secure eleven men, a young woman and a child. But the consent of the people themselves was not all that had to be obtained. It was necessary that the British government should sanction their removal. Mr. Caldecott memorialized the authorities accordingly. Fortunately the circumstances of having been thirty-three years in Africa, and of his being known as a merchant of respectability, and a highly honourable man, influenced the government in his favour. (Caldecott 4–5)

However, since trafficking in slaves had been outlawed by the British government barely nineteen years before, the Colonial Office in Natal granted Caldecott's request only "on condition that he [enter] into a recognizance, binding himself in a sum of £500 and two sureties of £250 each" to guarantee that the natives accompanying him would do so voluntarily, would be well treated on the voyage and in England, would be reported and, if necessary, produced to the Secretary of State for the Colonies, would be paid for the services they performed, and would be brought back to Durban no later than eighteen months after their arrival in England (4–5). To all these conditions Caldecott readily agreed, and early in January 1853, after exhibiting his troupe in Cape Town for a few days, he sailed with them out of Table Bay on a ship headed for London, arriving there in March after more than two months at sea.

There was good reason to suppose the English public would be curious about the Zulus. Reports of the military prowess of this tribe had been filtering back to England since the days of Shaka thirty years before. Dingane's (Dingaan's) massacre of the Boer leader Piet Retief and some of his followers in 1838 and the devastating retaliation of the Boers at the battle of Blood River later that same year probably were still remembered by British adults who had been following the fortunes of Europeans in South Africa. In 1840 Dingane was overthrown by Boers working in alliance with his brother Mpande (Panda) who, as the new king of Zululand, granted them most of the territory south of the Tugela river, territory which the British annexed in 1843 as the Colony of Natal. From 1848 to 1851, the year just preceding the visit of Caldecott's Zulus to London, more than 2,700 British immigrants had arrived in Natal. The first substantial books about Natal and its peoples had started to appear in London in the 1830s, and during the period of the Great Trek (1835–44) there were frequent reports in the press about frontier skirmishes and full-scale "Caffre" wars. So there must have been considerable curiosity in Britain about the aggressive natives who inhabited this remote corner of the empire and occasionally created problems for white settlers.

But even without such a reputation, the Zulus would have been an interesting novelty in Victorian England. Blacks had been seen in London for centuries and were becoming quite numerous in the city by the middle of the nineteenth century, but most of these early residents and visitors were ex-slaves from North America or the West Indies—blacks, in other words, who had become Westernized to some extent. Africans and other so-called "primitive peoples" were still a relatively rare sight in even the most cosmopolitan European capitals, and it was not uncommon for exhibitions to be held to display such peoples to audiences that had only heard or read of their remarkable appearance and strange habits. They were the human equivalents of unique specimens in a botanical garden or metropolitan zoo and were treated rather like visitors from outer space. The science of ethnology was just getting established in Britain in the 1840s, and learned professors as well as uneducated laymen would flock to these exhibits to study the latest arrivals from exotic lands overseas. During the months that the Zulus were on stage in London, there were competing exhibitions of such peoples as the "Earthmen" (a pair of diminutive individuals described in the *Illustrated London News* as "pigmies from Southern Africa" [6 Nov. 1852: 371–72] who lived in holes in the ground, but subsequently identified by a medical doctor and member of the English Ethnological Society as "Bushman-Troglodytes, or Troglodyte-Bushmen" who lived in natural caves rather than in ordinary Bushman habitations) (Latham 149), and the "Aztec Lilliputians" (whose reported "capture" in an "alleged mysterious city lately discovered in Central America" was dismissed by at least one newspaper as a "cock and bull story" [*The Examiner* 9 July 1853: 439], and was later thoroughly discredited by the Secretary of the English Ethnological Society, who regarded these dwarfish creatures as nothing more than profoundly retarded and deformed children hauled up for public display by mercenary hucksters) (Latham 120–37, 297). Yet each of these three unusual groups—Earthmen, Aztec Lilliputians, and Zulus—was honored by being summoned to give a command performance at Buckingham Palace for Queen Victoria and her children. They were sought out by Crown and commoner alike.

The Zulus became one of the most popular shows in London during the summer of 1853. Caldecott, a canny businessman, had spared no expense in mounting the exhibition. He had rented St. George's Gallery (formerly known as the Chinese Museum) at Hyde Park Corner for the performances, and had hired Charles Marshall, one of the most highly regarded painters and set designers of his day, to paint authentic scenery which could be changed mechanically to suit the time, place, and action depicted—a rather recent innovation in stage technology. Two months were spent preparing the troupe for the first performance, on the evening of 16 May, and daily advertisements were placed in leading papers and journals throughout the exhibition's three-month run in London.

These efforts paid off handsomely. When the show opened, performances were given every evening at 8, and Wednesday and Friday afternoons at 3. By 1 June, a third matinee had been added, and three weeks later there were afternoon and evening performances daily. To provide background information on the Zulus and Natal, Caldecott's son wrote a thirty-two-page pamphlet entitled *Descriptive History of the Zulu Kafirs, Their Customs and Their Country, With Illustrations,* which was sold for sixpence during performances at the Gallery. But even this was not enough to satisfy London's appetite for so unusual an attraction. On 25 July, the *Times* carried an announcement by Caldecott that

> In consequence of the increasing interest excited by this extraordinary and pleasing EXHIBITION, arrangements have been made to meet the public wishes, by which visitors will be allowed to see and converse with this interesting tribe daily from 11 to 1 o'clock, during the remaining period of their performance in London.

Before the troupe left in mid-August to tour France, Germany, and some of the English provinces, a second pamphlet on them had been published which reprinted several enthusiastic reviews of their performances and provided more information on the sanguinary history of the Zulus under "warlike and ambitious" Essenzingercona (Senzangakhona), "terrible" and "despotic" Chaka (Shaka), "cruel and treacherous" Dingarn (Dingane), and "their present king, Panda [Mpande], [who] is to a considerable extent imbued with civilization, [having] got the good sense to prefer trading to fighting" (*Final Close* 3–6).

What helped to make the Zulu exhibition more popular than other ethnographic displays was the fact that it was an extremely dramatic performance, not a static sideshow. The performers acted out incidents said to be typical of Zulu life and did so with great fervor. The advertisement placed in the *Times* on the day the show opened stated that the exhibition would illustrate "in an extensive and unexampled manner this wild and interesting tribe of savages in their domestic habits, their nuptial ceremonies, the charm song, finding the witch, hunting tramp, preparation for war and territorial conflicts" (16 May 1853: 4). To explain some of the scenes, Caldecott's son served as interpreter and master of ceremonies, lecturing briefly on Zulu customs and traditions before they were enacted on the stage.

The earliest review of the "Caffres at Hyde-Park-Corner" (as they came to be called), appeared in the *Times* two days after the maiden performance. It is worth quoting in full because it is typical of the response of British theater critics to this novel entertainment:

> Although there have been several attempts to render Caffre life familiar to the English public through the medium of exhibitions, nothing in this way has been done so completely or on so large a scale as the new exhibition opened on

THE MEAL SONG.

Monday evening in the rooms formerly occupied by the Chinese museum. Eleven Zulu men, with a woman and a child, are assembled into a company, and instead of performing one or two commonplace feats, may be said to go through the whole drama of Caffre life, while a series of scenes, painted by Mr. Charles Marshall, gives an air of reality to the living pictures. Now the Caffres are at their meal, feeding themselves with enormous spoons, and expressing their satisfaction by a wild chant, under the inspiration of which they bump themselves along without rising in a sort of circular dance. Now the witchfinder commences his operations to discover the culprit whose magic has brought sickness into the tribe, and becomes perfectly rabid through the effect of his own incantations. Now there is a wedding ceremony, now a hunt, now a military expedition, all with characteristic dances; and the whole ends with a general conflict between rival tribes. The songs and dances are, as may be expected, monotonous in the extreme, and without the bill it would be difficult to distinguish the expression of love from the gesture of martial defiance. Nevertheless, as a picture of manners, nothing can be more complete; and not the least remarkable part of the exhibition is the perfect training of the wild artists. They seem utterly to lose all sense of their present position, and, inspired by the situations in which they are placed, appear to take Mr. Marshall's scenes for their actual abode in the vicinity of Port Natal. If 11 English actors could be found so completely to lose themselves in the characters they assumed, histrionic art would be in a state truly magnificent. (18 May 1853: 8)

Other reviewers singled out many of the same features of the exhibition for comment—the excellent scenery, the impressive physical appearance of the Zulus, the spirited and uninhibited acting. A columnist in *The Athenaeum*, after noting how the physiognomy of the Zulus differed from that of West African Negroes, went on to say, "Most of the men have a fine muscular developement [*sic*], and they exhibit considerable strength in some of their exhibitions on the stage. One thing is very striking in these performances—that is, the almost perfect dramatic effect with which these wild men play their parts" (28 May 1853: 650). The reviewer for *The Spectator* was equally impressed with the "considerable dramatic propriety" of the performances, but found several of the scenes highly amusing:

> The Zulus—fine well-formed men, of fleshy frames but attenuated legs—get up the quarrel, and discuss the chances of war, with a great appearance of being in earnest about it all. In this point, and in its lifelike character, to which the accessories contribute, the exhibition transcends all others we have witnessed of the kind. The charm-song and the proceedings of the witch-finder or "smeller out" were especially expressive and forcible in their pantomime. As for the noises— the howls, yells, hoots, and whoops, the snuffling, wheezing, bubbling, grovelling, and stamping—they form a concert to whose savagery we cannot attempt to do justice. (21 May 1853: 485)

The Illustrated London News initially mentioned the exhibition as a "picturesque drama [consisting of] a series of scenes which charm by their spirit and *vraisemblance*" and often excited laughter by depicting incidents "more amusing than anything in a farce" (21 May 1853: 399), but in its next issue displayed on its front page a sketch of one of the scenes in the show, gave brief biographical details on several of the performers, and elaborated on what it had found particularly entertaining:

> After a supper of meal, of which the Kaffirs partake with their large wooden spoons, an extraordinary song and dance are performed, in which each performer moves about on his haunches, grunting and snorting the while like a pair of asthmatic bellows . . . but no description can give an idea of the cries and shouts—now comic, now terrible—by which the Kaffirs express their emotions. The scene illustrative of the preliminaries of marriage and the bridal festivities might leave one in doubt which was the bridegroom, did not that interesting savage announce his enviable situation by screams of ecstasy which convulse the audience.
>
> The Zulus must be naturally good actors; for a performance more natural and less like acting is seldom if ever seen upon any stage. (28 May 1853: 409)

The "Zulu Kafir Exhibition" was obviously good theater and deserved to become a smash hit.

On 26 May, after the show had been on for a week and a half and the first

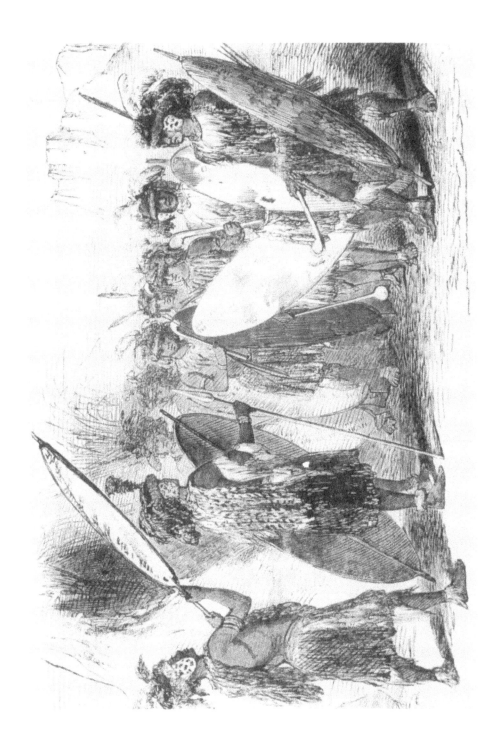

rave reviews had appeared, Charles Dickens went to see it, inviting his friend John Leech to accompany him (qtd. in Dexter 462–63). Dickens may have been in need of relaxation, for he was terribly overworked at the time. Not only was he writing the final chapters of *Bleak House* in monthly installments and the middle chapters of *A Child's History of England*, but he was also quite busy editing *Household Words*, a popular weekly journal he had launched in 1850. As might be expected in such circumstances, the Zulus turned out to be more than mere transitory entertainment for him; they became grist for his prolific mill. Shortly after witnessing their performance, he wrote a humorous essay entitled "The Noble Savage" which appeared in the 11 June issue of *Household Words*. Though he made reference to such peoples as the "Ojibbeway" Indians and the Bushmen who had been on display in London earlier, he focused his attention primarily on Caldecott's Zulus, using them as hilarious examples of the ignobility of uncivilized man. The essay has been called "one of the most effective philippics of our language" (Crotch 85), and there can be no doubt that Dickens, with his incomparable flair for comic exaggeration, achieved his aim of debunking the Romantic myth of the "noble savage," but today this piece of writing is seldom commented on by scholars or teachers of Victorian literature, possibly because the views expressed in it are embarrassing and offensive to a contemporary sensibility.

Here is how the onslaught begins:

> To come to the point at once, I beg to say that I have not the least belief in the Noble Savage. I consider him a prodigious nuisance, and an enormous superstition. His calling rum fire-water, and me a pale face, wholly fail to reconcile me to him. I don't care what he calls me. I call him a savage, and I call a savage a something highly desirable to be civilised off the face of the earth. I think a mere gent (which I take to be the lowest form of civilisation) better than a howling, whistling, clucking, stamping, jumping, tearing savage. It is all one to me, whether he sticks a fishbone through his visage, or bits of trees through the lobes of his ears, or birds' feathers in his head; whether he flattens his hair between two boards, or spreads his nose over the breadth of his face, or drags his lower lip down by great weights, or blackens his teeth, or knocks them out, or paints one cheek red and another blue, or tattoos himself, or oils himself, or rubs his body with fat, or crimps it with knives. Yielding to whichsoever of these agreeable eccentricities, he is a savage—cruel, false, thievish, murderous; addicted more or less to grease, entrails, and beastly customs; a wild animal with the questionable gift of boasting; a conceited, tiresome, bloodthirsty, monotonous humbug. (337)

From here Dickens goes on to grumble about the way some people whimper over the savage "with maudlin admiration" and pretend that "the tenor of his swinish life" is preferable to "the blemishes of civilisation." He cites the "miserable jigs" of the Ojibways and the "horrid" pantomimes of the Bushmen as evidence of the degenerate nature of such peoples, and then reinforces his argument by taking a long look at the Zulus.

> There is at present a party of Zulu Kaffirs exhibiting at the St. George's Gallery, Hyde Park Corner, London. These noble savages are represented in a most agreeable manner; they are seen in an elegant theatre, fitted with appropriate scenery of great beauty, and they are described in a very sensible and unpretending lecture, delivered with a modesty which is quite a pattern to all similar exponents. Though extremely ugly, they are much better shaped than such of their predecessors as I have referred to; and they are rather picturesque to the eye, though far from odoriferous to the nose. What a visitor left to his own interpretings and imaginings might suppose these noblemen to be about, when they give vent to that pantomimic expression which is quite settled to be the natural gift of the noble savage, I cannot possibly conceive; for it is so much too luminous for my personal civilisation that it conveys no idea to my mind beyond a general stamping, ramping, and raving, remarkable (as everything in savage life is) for its dire uniformity. But let us—with the interpreter's assistance, of which I for one stand so much in need—see what the noble savage does in Zulu Kaffirland. (339)

It is apparent that Dickens relied heavily on the ethnographic information supplied in young Caldecott's lecture, but he supplemented what he heard with his own observations on the Zulus in action. It is interesting to compare the descriptions of Zulu life and customs in Caldecott's later pamphlet (which presumably grew out of his lecture) with Dickens's version of how these wild creatures conducted their affairs. The accounts were often quite similar, though Dickens had a tendency to stress graphic details and toss in amusing asides to his readers.

For instance, young Caldecott, after describing the land, racial background, and material culture of the Zulus, devoted one entire chapter of his booklet to Zulu "Laws and Government" and another to "Zulu Characteristics." Since he based his remarks on Nathaniel Isaacs's *Travels and Adventures in Eastern Africa, Descriptive of the Zoolus, Their Manners, Customs, with a Sketch of Natal* (1836), it is perhaps best to begin with Isaacs's account and to observe how this was transmuted via Caldecott into vintage Dickens. Isaacs regarded the Zulus as "the most extraordinary people in existence" and "zoolacratical government" as

> the most incomprehensible government with which any known nation on the face of the earth is conversant. . . . Its outline, however, may be said to be perfectly simple—namely, despotic. . . . It is monarchical, it is true; but apparently neither hereditary nor elective, the succession depending on the murder of the existing monarch, which usually takes place when he begins to exhibit either of those two signs of age—wrinkles or grey hairs. In this case, the criminal who performs the bloody deed, or directs its execution, is perhaps a son or

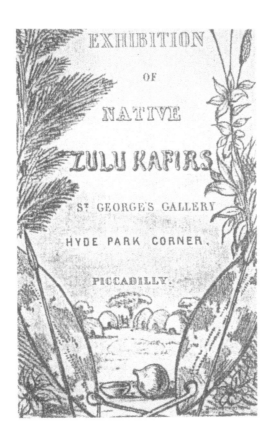

some other member of the royal family. When the throne has become vacant by the sacrifice of the monarch, it usually happens that civil disputes settle the succession. . . . When the monarch is firmly seated on his throne—which is seldom or never accomplished without, as it were, wading through blood to it—he becomes an absolute king, or "Inquose." His name then becomes sacred, and adoration is paid to it. . . . The power of the monarch is indeed not only despotic, but even atrocious; for he can command indiscriminate massacres by his nod. . . . [His warriors] are a morose, sullen, savage set of monsters, fit only for deeds of darkness and for the devastations of war; and these are their sole occupations. (294–96)

As for religion, Isaacs says simply, "[The Zulus] have none" and "are unquestionably the most superstitious creatures on the face of the earth" (297–98).

That young Caldecott followed Isaacs very closely, at times even slavishly, can be seen quite plainly in his description of Zulu government as most nearly resembling "a perfect despotism":

The king is absolute; there is no liberty of the subject; a nod from the monarch consigns any one to death, no matter whether guilty or innocent. At the command of his ruler a father must murder his own unoffending child, brother must slay brother, or a husband destroy his wife. Appeal is death to the appealer. It is a monarchical government, but apparently neither hereditary nor elective. The succession depends on the murder of the existing sovereign, which

THE COMBAT.

usually takes place when he begins to exhibit the signs of age. The criminal who performs the deed, or directs it, is usually the son, or some other member of the royal family. When the throne has become vacant by the sacrifice of the monarch, a dispute and some additional murders settle the succession. . . . When the king becomes firmly seated on the throne, he is called an "Inkosa." His name then becomes sacred, and adoration is paid to it. (19)

In his chapter on "Zulu Characteristics," young Caldecott also asserted that "In his present savage state [the Zulu] has very little idea of morality and none whatever of religion. Behind his agreeable outward bearing, he conceals the most vindictive feelings, and a capacity for perpetrating the most atrocious cruelty. Impulsive, emotional, and excitable even to frenzy, he makes no effort to control his impulses, nor at any time reasons upon the abstract justice of his deeds" (21–25).

Dickens compressed all this information into a brief paragraph which conveyed the essence of what he had learned from Caldecott about Zulu law, government, and character:

The noble savage sets a king to reign over him, to whom he submits his life and limbs without a murmur or question, and whose whole life is passed chin deep in a lake of blood; but who, after killing incessantly, is in his turn killed by his relations and friends, the moment a gray hair appears on his head. All the noble savage's wars with his fellow savages (and he takes no pleasure in anything else) are wars of extermination—which is the best thing I know of him, and the most comfortable to my mind when I look at him. He has no moral feelings of any kind, sort, or description; and his "mission" may be summed up as simply diabolical. (336)

Dickens then went on to poke fun at the way Zulu marriages were contracted. Here his description seems to be based as much on the performance he saw as on the lecture he heard. Young Caldecott's written account also appears to owe a great deal to personal observation, though portions of it were taken directly from his two primary sources, Isaacs's *Travels* and Capt. Allen F. Gardiner's *Narrative of a Journey to the Zoolu Country in South Africa* (1836). Here is how Caldecott introduces the subject of marriage:

A Zulu marriage festival is a very noisy and animated affair. Preliminary matters having been gone through, the bridegroom, in company with his friends, seats himself, and waits the arrival of the bride, who comes escorted by the people of her tribe. She is tastefully attired; her hair being decorated with feathers, in imitation of a coronet, and her skin well oiled and polished for the occasion. Rows of beads in varied colours are suspended round her neck, and she brings many strings of beads with her. The overture is as often made by the women as the men. The bride's father usually sends a cow with her as a present. When she arrives in the presence of her future husband, she and her attendants perform a dance, accompanied with as large an amount of noise as they can conveniently get up for the occasion. It is the aim of the lady, on this occasion, to appear as agile as possible in the presence of the bridegroom's friends, and that which she may lack in grace she compensates for in expertness. The ballet being finished, and all present being satisfied with the lady's performance, her friends proceed to settle the important business of how much she is worth. They value her at six cows. Her lover offers three: the offer is rejected. Very much clattering and haranguing takes place, but at length the bargain is struck at the price originally demanded; and the bridegroom is made a happy man by the gain of a wife and the loss of his six cows. (25)

Dickens turns this "very noisy and animated affair" into a raucous unmusical comedy in which the bridal barter and "ballet" are pictured as uninhibited haggling punctuated by earsplitting ejaculations and frenzied foot stomping.

If he wants a wife he appears before the kennel of the gentleman whom he has selected as his father-in-law, attended by a party of male friends of a very strong flavor, who screech and whistle and stamp an offer of so many cows for the young lady's hand. The chosen father-in-law—also supported by a high-flavored party of male friends—screeches, whistles, and yells (being seated on the ground, he can't stamp) that there never was such a daughter in the market as his daughter, and that he must have six more cows. The son-in-law and his select circle of backers, screech, whistle, stamp, and yell in reply, that they will give three more cows. The father-in-law (an old deluder, overpaid at the beginning) accepts four, and rises to bind the bargain. The whole party, the young lady included, then falling into epileptic convulsions, and screeching, whistling, stamping, and yelling together—and nobody taking any notice of the young lady (whose charms are not to be thought of without a shudder)—the noble savage is considered married, and his friends make demoniacal leaps at him by way of congratulation. (336)

Dickens gets even more dramatic when describing Zulu witchcraft, a subject calculated to amuse a Victorian public skeptical of the efficacy of any form of non-European divination. Young Caldecott, who shared this prejudice with his London audience, may have helped to shape Dickens's negative attitude toward Zulu sorcery, but it is apparent that the spirited enactment of a witch hunt by Caldecott's troupe made a very powerful impression on him, one which he tried to replicate for others in onomatopoeic prose. Before looking at Dickens's account, however, let us see how young Caldecott presented this custom, which he frankly regarded as "singularly absurd":

The Zulus believe illness to be always the result of witchcraft. When any of their tribe are taken ill, the services of the *Inyanger* or witch-finder are called into requisition, to *nooker* or smell out the *Umtugartie* or witch, who has caused the illness of the invalid. They abhor the tiger-cat, or *Imparker*, as they call it, and believe it to be as necessary a companion to the witch of Zulu, as a black cat is thought by some people, to be indispensable to the witches of more civilized nations. The witch-finder, or *Inyanger*, makes his appearance, attired very demoniacally in shaggy strips of fur; all the people seat themselves before him. He dances in their presence, flinging himself about in the wildest manner imaginable; then smells the ground, and eventually pouncing upon one of the party present, declares him to be the person who has bewitched the sick man. The *Inyanger*'s assertion is unhesitatingly believed, and the denounced individual is at once hustled away by his neighbours, and beaten to death with their knobkerrees. It is almost needless to add that these Inyangers are the vilest impostors. (27–28)

Dickens substitutes a grizzly bear for the leopard (or "tiger-cat" as it was called in South Africa then) and spells phonetically all the Zulu words introduced by young Caldecott, but otherwise his account is fairly faithful to the substance and tone of his source. It differs mainly in its dramatic immediacy and hilarious sound effects.

When the noble savage finds himself a little unwell, and mentions the circumstance to his friends, it is immediately perceived that he is under the influence of witchcraft. A learned personage, called an Imyanger or Witch Doctor, is immediately sent for to Nooker the Umtargartie, or smell out the witch. The male inhabitants of the kraal being seated on the ground, the learned doctor, got up like a grizzly bear, appears, and administers a dance of a most terrific nature, during the exhibition of which remedy he incessantly gnashes his teeth, and howls:—"I am the original physician to Nooker the Umtargartie. Yow yow yow! No connexion with any other establishment. Till till till! All other Umtargarties are feigned Umtargarties, Boroo Boroo! but I perceive here a genuine and real Umtargartie, Hoosh Hoosh Hoosh! in whose blood I, the original Imyanger and Nookerer, Blizzerum Boo! will wash these bear's claws of mine. O yow yow yow!" All this time the learned physician is looking out among the attentive faces for some unfortunate man who owes him a cow, or who has given him any small offence, or against whom, without offence, he has conceived a spite. Him he never fails to Nooker as the Umtargartie, and he is instantly killed. In the absence of such an individual, the usual practice is to Nooker the quietest and most gentlemanly person in company. But the nookering is invariably followed by the butchering. (336)

Dickens's next subject was the Zulu "Praiser" whom young Caldecott described as a "Poet-laureate" and a

> most uncouth-looking individual, dressed in the skin of a leopard, or a tiger-cat, the head of the animal forming his own head for the nonce, and his occupation being to utter, through the leopard's mouth, and in very deep-toned words, the attributes and excellencies of his super-excellent monarch. The more he disregards the laws of punctuation in performing his duty, the better he acquits himself. We subjoin a portion of his eulogy, printing the epithets as they are spoken, without any intervening pauses—"Thou who art as high as the mountains thou noble elephant thou black one thou who art as high as the heavens thou who art the bird who eats other birds thou who art the great cow and the peace maker! &c. &c. &c. (27)

Dickens anglicizes the praise-song and throws in a few more animals unknown in the African subcontinent, but again captures the vigor and spectacle of the Zulu performance at Hyde Park Corner.

> There suddenly rushes in a poet, retained for the purpose, called a Praiser. This literary gentleman wears a leopard's head over his own, and a dress of tigers' tails; he has the appearance of having come express on his hind legs from the Zoological Gardens; and he incontinently strikes up the chief's praises, plunging and tearing all the while. There is a frantic wickedness in this brute's manner of worrying the air, and gnashing out "Oh what a delightful chief he is! O what a delicious quantity of blood he sheds! O how majestically he laps it up! O how charmingly cruel he is! O how he tears the flesh of his enemies and crunches the bones! O how like the tiger and the leopard and the wolf and the bear he is! O, row row row row, how fond I am of him!"—which might tempt the Society of Friends to charge at a hand-gallop into the Swartz-Kop location and exterminate the whole kraal. (337)

The last example Dickens gives of the culture of this uncultured people is their colorful preparation for battle. A war song had been performed as part of the show at St. George's Gallery, and Dickens, as usual, based his description of the custom both on what he had seen and on what he had heard from young Caldecott, whose booklet put it this way:

> War is the principal business of a Zulu Kafir. Before going to battle the king calls a council of his chief men. He appears among them arrayed in a mantle of tigers' tails, and with an attendant behind him holding a shield above his head. The particulars of the projected campaign are detailed, and one warrior after another steps forward to give his advice. Though in the presence of his monarch, he does not speak coolly, nor conduct himself with modesty, but utters his opinions with a howl, emphasizes them with a jump, and bangs his shield with his assagai to enforce their justness, and the strength of his own convictions. When, at length, the place of action is determined upon, the warriors rush off at once to where the conflict is to take place, singing with savage glee their war song on the way. (28–29)

Now here is Dickens expanding upon the subject:

> When war is afoot among the noble savages—which is always—the chief holds a council to ascertain whether it is the opinion of his brothers and friends in general that the enemy shall be exterminated. On this occasion, after the performance of an Umsebeuza, or war song—which is exactly like all the other songs—the chief makes a speech to his brothers and friends, arranged in single file. No particular order is observed during the delivery of this address, but every gentleman who finds himself excited by the subject, instead of crying "Hear, Hear!" as is the custom with us, darts from the rank and tramples out the life, or crushes the skull, or mashes the face, or scoops out the eyes, or breaks the limbs, or performs a whirlwind of atrocities on the body, of an imaginary enemy. Several gentlemen becoming thus excited at once, and pounding away without the least regard to the orator, that illustrious person is rather in the position of an orator in an Irish House of Commons. But, several of these scenes of savage life bear a strong generic resemblance to an Irish election, and I think would be extremely well received and understood at Cork. (337)

Dickens followed this up with a paragraph playfully suggesting other parallels between the ceremonies of the noble savage and the practices of civilized man in Europe, but he returned to his main theme in his concluding statement:

> My position is, that if we have anything to learn from the Noble Savage, it is what to avoid. His virtues are a fable; his happiness is a delusion; his nobility, nonsense . . . and the world will be all the better when his place knows him no more. (339)

Although it sometimes appears so in this essay, Dickens was not really recommending genocide. He was very much the Victorian pragmatist striving to puncture an inflated Romantic conception of the dignity of "primitive" peoples. The Zulus were simply a convenient case in point, a group so far removed from Europe in custom and culture that they could easily be held up as examples of an underdeveloped race obviously in need of moral improvement and mental refinement. Dickens did not suggest that such peoples be exterminated; rather, he wanted them "civilised off the face of the earth." He believed in cultural, not literal, genocide.

Yet is it interesting to note with what contempt Zulu customs, traditions, and institutions were viewed by the London audiences who saw this troupe perform. The performers obviously overstepped the boundaries of Victorian decorum when they sang and danced, but their antics presumably would not have provoked so much hilarity among spectators with cultural traditions more closely akin to those of the performers themselves. Underlying the reactions of Dickens and other English viewers was a broad streak of undisguised racism, a belief that the Zulus were morally and mentally inferior to Europeans. The numerous comments on their smell, their bizarre modes of dress (and undress), their noises, their monotonous songs, rabid incantations, and wild, demoniacal dances betray an arrogant assumption that the Zulus were overgrown children of nature who had not yet developed the inhibitions, self-discipline, and manners that distinguish more civilized folk. They were savages pure and simple, primitives in the raw.

Of course, one cannot blame the Victorians for being so ethnocentric. Nineteenth-century Europe, with its numerous civil and international wars, was not exactly a showcase of ethnic tolerance, and inadequate opportunities for meaningful face-to-face cultural contact with representatives of the non-Western world hindered Europeans from learning much about the human beings who inhabited the rest of the globe. There were no documentary films or television specials to bring more accurate images of foreign peoples to the drawing rooms of London. The Zulus were therefore merely a spectacle, a carnival act consciously designed to play up their abnormalities—i.e., their radical deviation from European norms of dress and behavior. It would be ethnocentric of us to expect audiences who saw them almost a century and a half ago to react with a more modern sensibility and to come away from such a performance with a richer understanding and appreciation of Zulu culture.

Indeed, one wonders if this would be possible in Europe or America even today. There is strong evidence to suggest that it would not. If we examine public reactions to more recent black South African performances in London and New York, we find remarkable echoes of those antiquated Victorian attitudes.

The second black South African musical that managed to reach the London stage was *King Kong*, a jazz opera set in Johannesburg's shantytowns, which ran for more than eight months at Princes Theatre in 1961. Though the script was written and produced by white South Africans, though the setting was urban rather than rural, though the hero was an Othello-like boxer who strangled the woman he loved and then committed suicide, drama critics yielded to the temptation to fasten on what seemed to be the crudest aspects of an animated performance. The London *Times* called it "a piece of naive but vital indigenous art" and went on to say:

> The naivety, the rhythm and the vitality have a characteristic colour and manner of their own. They seem to be conditioned by the particular locality to which the characters belong; and it is perfectly easy to take what appear to us as stage clumsinesses in our stride and to yield ourselves up to the rhythm and the vitality.
>
> Mostly the dances are frankly erotic, with the dancers using their hips and legs, or they are war dances with the gangsters seeking to strike terror with their foot movements. The songs are always strongly, if seldom melodiously, sung. . . . There is also a wildly uninhibited gangster dance culminating in a murder and an enchanting wedding hymn warmly lit and beautifully dressed which also culminates in a murder. (24 Feb. 1961: 17)

Except for the gangsters, this almost sounds like a revival of the "Caffres at Hyde-Park-Corner."

King Kong was a harbinger of things to come. In the 1970s, no fewer than four Zulu musicals were brought to London, and all received similar reviews. In 1972, *Umabatha*, an attempt to tell the story of Shaka as a super-sanguinary Macbeth, met with this startled response:

> Before the murder, Mabatha (Macbeth) takes snuff and sneezes; an approved method of achieving second sight, which brings him the vision of an assegai. His letter to his wife is communicated as a drum message. And the three witches are transformed into *sangomas* (witch-doctors) who upset all Western notions of the sinister by conducting jolly dances round the cauldron shaking with seemingly innocent laughter. The most surprising thing about the whole show is its apparent good humour. . . .
>
> The dances are built on a uniform beat to a short melodic fragment, and when one of these ostinatos starts building up the stage really catches fire. The shields go down to the ground while a leader whirls demoniacally in the foreground, executing high-kicks up to his chin, and bringing in the group with a pounding one-footed beat.
>
> The effect is as stunning visually as it is to listen to: a mass of moving skins and weapons transforming separate members into a single indomitable animal, bent on celebration, joy, or killing, but unstoppable no matter what its objective. (*Times* 4 April 1972: 6)

Singing, dancing, and drumming were also singled out as the most impressive features of *Kwa Zulu*, a musical that opened in London in July 1975 (see *Times* 25 Aug. 1975: 7; *Sunday Times* 3 Aug. 1975: 24). But an even more enthusiastic response greeted the musical gyrations in *Ipi-Tombi*, which premiered a few months later in London and had a long run before going on tour. The *Times* called it "all ululating leaps, steatopygous flourishes, and tableaux of warriors framed in russet skybroth silhouette" which added up to "an evening of exotic escape" (20 Nov. 1975: 10). The *Sunday Times* went further, hailing it as a

> thrilling production, presented with a verve, an *éclat*, a technical brilliance, a richness of voice in the singing, an excitement and a precision in the dancing which I do not believe that even the best American musical could rival. It is a riot of colour and movement, yet it is as controlled as the changing of the Guard. Every member of the huge cast is superb. (23 Nov. 1975: 35)

Ipi-Tombi did not win such unrestrained applause when it traveled to New York in January 1977. The fact that the show was picketed by anti-apartheid groups may have made some critics think twice about the political significance of the atmosphere of joy, happiness, and innocence being conveyed by the black performers, but it did not stop a few reviewers from indulging in the usual clichés about African atavism. The dances, *Time* magazine exclaimed,

> illustrate how close to nature some Africans apparently still are. The gestures, the rhythms and the sounds indicate an unbroken totemic relationship with animals. The members of the troupe slither like snakes, stalk like the great cat family of the jungle, stamp and trumpet like elephants. This is all done with an agility, grace and energy that is breathtaking. The lead drummer (Junior Tshabalala) plays with galvanic fervor and propels the best number in the show, a warrior dance, into a Dionysian frenzy. (24 Jan. 1975: 35)

Dickens would have loved it. Such a performance would have proved to him that savages are no nobler now than they were a century and a half ago, thereby reinforcing his belief that "between the civilized European and the barbarous African there is a great gulf set" (Dickens, *Niger Expedition* 133).

This Victorian notion lingers even today, fed by an entertainment industry that capitalizes on anachronistic racial stereotypes. Hollywood films, television travelogues, best-selling novels, and popular magazines continue to carry images of Africa and Africans that deliberately emphasize the exotic at the expense of the ordinary. In such media one is far more likely to see resurrections of Tarzan than revelations of Tanzania. So powerful an ethnocentric compulsion to discover savages at every bend of the river, to define the "Dark Continent" as the benighted antithesis of the enlightened West, reveals that Dickens is not dead yet.

WORKS CITED

Caldecott, C. H. *Descriptive History of the Zulu Kafirs, Their Customs and Their Country, with Illustrations*. London: John Mitchell, 1853.

Crotch, W. Walter. *The Touchstone of Dickens*. London: Chapman and Hall, 1920.

Dexter, Walter, ed. *The Letters of Charles Dickens*. Vol. 2. Bloomsbury: Nonesuch Press, 1938.

Dickens, Charles. "The Niger Expedition." *Miscellaneous Papers*. Vol. 1. New York: Scribner's, 1908.

———. "The Noble Savage." *Household Words* 11 June 1853: 337–39.

Final Close of the St. George's Gallery, Hyde Park Corner, Piccadilly. Zulu Kafirs. Last Few Days in London. [London: n.p., 1853].

Isaacs, Nathaniel. *Travels and Adventures in Eastern Africa, Descriptive of the Zoolus, Their Manners, Customs, with a Sketch of Natal*. 1836. Cape Town: Struik, 1970.

Latham, R. G. "Ethnological Remarks upon Some of the More Remarkable Varieties of the Human Species, Represented by Individuals Now in London." *Journal of Ethnological Science* 4 (1856): 149.

3

Africa Meets the Great Farini

SHANE PEACOCK

The so-called "Dark Continent" drew its share of eccentric Europeans to its "undiscovered" regions in the eighteenth and nineteenth centuries, but few, if any, matched Guillermo Antonio Farini. His life was a whirlwind of adventures, his attention shifting from one exploit to another, as he explored each subject and then moved on. Africa and African people came into his rotating gaze in the late 1870s, and though he would exhaust this interest within a decade, his impact on the burgeoning business of African exhibitions was substantial.

He was afflicted to some degree by the racism of his time, but unlike some of his contemporaries, he did not emphasize the supposed inferiority of the people he exhibited. A consummate showman with a touch of genius and a preference for frightening his audiences, he had created many show-business sensations, and when Africans graced his performances, he made them stars too; thus his shows were a disservice to people whom he had not set out to slander.

William Leonard Hunt, who would come to call himself Farini, likely saw very few people of African descent during his formative years. He was born on 10 June 1838 in Lockport, New York, but was actually the son of Canadian parents and grew up in the little towns and countryside of southern Ontario. Here, slavery had long been outlawed[1] and the population was relentlessly Anglo-Saxon Protestant. Many, like Willie Hunt's mother, were United Empire Loyalists, Americans who had stayed loyal to the crown at the time of the U.S. revolution and had fled north to find huge lots of land virtually handed to them by the king. They thus became pseudo-aristocrats by virtue of their holdings and immediately considered themselves the upper class and the moral arbiters of the infant society they began to create; anyone non-English, non-Protestant, and especially nonwhite fell distinctly below them on their social pecking order. Since the Scottish, the Irish, and Roman Catholics were so poorly regarded, it was no surprise that North American Indians, who had occupied this land before them, were accorded a place only slightly higher than the animals; people of African descent, though free in this new world, were so rarely seen and so obviously nonwhite that they were similarly disrespected.

Bill Hunt was a rebel in this society almost from the instant he was born into it. Blessed, or cursed (as his parents felt), with extraordinary energy, he was constantly in trouble: at school, at home, and on the muddy roads of the villages. Brainy, muscular, and imaginative, he found life in southern Ontario monotonous and restrictive. For him, only the travelling American circuses, which visited the area once or twice during the summers, full of exotic feats and people, could momentarily explode the drudgery. But the unadulterated thrills it gave him were frowned upon by his parents and their friends, who considered circus people low and their shows immoral.

Bill secretly visited the circuses and then set out to learn the feats he witnessed. This he did extremely well, and by the time he was twenty-one years old, despite having been diverted into medical studies by his father, he was an accomplished amateur wire walker, acrobat, and strongman. When he debuted as Signor Farini (he took the name of an Italian war hero and political leader, because using his own would have shamed his family) on a "high rope" in the little town of Port Hope in 1859, he was an immediate sensation. But his father, who was conveniently out of town during the performance, essentially disowned him for his actions.

Farini then took to the road, on a swashbuckling, careering life of adventure, exchanging the morality of his childhood for passionate adulthood. Convinced that his parents had lived false lives, he wanted to live truthfully. He loved excitement and thought that, deep down, so did everyone else; he vowed to give people what they really wanted, on stages throughout the world.

Though he had only been a professional wire walker for ten months, in 1860 he challenged the legendary Blondin, who claimed that no other man could cross the gorge at Niagara Falls. As huge crowds came to watch and newspapers around the world wrote of the treacherous duel, Farini matched Blondin feat for feat. When the Frenchman stood on his head on his 900-foot rope above the whirlpool, Farini did the same on a cable more than twice that length upriver closer to the falls; when the veteran walked with a man on his back, the upstart carried a taller and heavier man; and when the great man brought out a stove and cooked an omelette at mid-wire, the rebel lugged a washing machine across and did his laundry 180 feet above the eddying river.

His versatility in the pursuit of excitement was astonishing. After several years of high-wire adventures, he expanded his repertoire to feature acrobatics, strongman displays, and trapeze exhibitions, as well as lectures to his audiences about physical fitness. Once he even stilt-walked along the edge of the

Fig. 3.1. Signor Farini ca. 1864, about the time of the Niagara stilt
walk and the Chaudière Falls high-wire feat.

American Falls at Niagara, just to see if it could be done. He also sought adventure with the Union Army in the American Civil War; travelled to Europe, Asia, Africa, and Australasia; became the lead artiste in the famous Flying Farinis trapeze show; and created circus headliners in "Mademoiselle Lulu" (who could jump thirty feet into the air from solid stage boards and was actually a man, Farini's adopted son, in drag), and "Zazel the Human Cannonball," who performed Farini's classic invention. He also presented many famous freaks. So extraordinary were the dangerous feats his protégés performed and so mesmeric was his presence that a rumor circulated that he was the model for George Du Maurier's evil character Svengali.[2] But Farini was much more than a showman; he was an inventor with at least one hundred patents to his credit (among them folding theater seats), an explorer, an author, a respected horticulturist, and a linguist who could speak seven languages; and in old age he was a painter, a financier, and a businessman.[3]

It was in mid-career, just after he turned forty, that he became interested in Africa. He had been retired from performing for nearly a decade and was in full Svengali mode, sporting a long, black beard, and scaring audiences who came to the dark, glass-roofed interior of the huge Royal Westminster Aquarium in downtown London where he presented his sensational shows. The Aquarium was not always a successful venture, but whenever Farini had it in his grip, it thrived.

Situated across Broad Sanctuary from Westminster Abbey, "the Aq" had been created in 1876 as a kind of cultural institution, complete with libraries and educational exhibitions; it hosted elegant concerts as well as lectures by esteemed scientists. Exotic fish were also meant to inhabit its numerous tanks, their mere presence an enlightenment to the gentlemen and ladies who would gaze at them. But such a mandate had little general appeal and within six months the Aquarium's financial losses were mounting. Its well-heeled board of directors sought out the one man in all of the empire who could create the sort of show-business sensations that could vastly improve their fortunes in an instant. Much to the disdain of "respectable" people (many of whom surreptitiously enjoyed his shows), Farini then gave them what they wanted.

The acts he was creating for his many protégés in those days were mostly gymnastic, though many were of a decidedly sensational sort. Like his own performances of an earlier time, his athletes seemed to be testing the limits of human accomplishment; indeed, it sometimes appeared as though "The Great Farini" was actually trying to make them fly. Restricted in his activities as a child and taught that life had limitations (both moral and physical), he was determined to push the envelope.

At the Aquarium he began things, literally, with a bang. The human cannonball act, never seen before by stunned London audiences, drew tens of thousands. Farini stood at the cannon, looking evil in his black beard, commanding the sweet, beautiful young Zazel to enter the mortar, and lighting the fuse to a great flourish, sending her across the Aq's great hall into a net of his own invention. Despite protests from moralists, Londoners (and the Prince of Wales, who was enthralled) wanted more. Farini, almost erotically charged both by the thrill of such acts and by the challenge of digging further into his mind to invent even more spectacular ones, was happy to oblige.

Soon there was Pongo the Gorilla, a frightening animal from the "dark continent," presented as the only gorilla in captivity; then there were white whales (belugas), never before seen indoors in England; and even a "mermaid," one of those sirens of the sea who called sailors into watery graves (though Farini's was, as he admitted from the outset, actually a manatee). And he had more than animals: his human beings still flew through the air, causing his spectators the greatest of unease. Besides shooting performers out of cannons, he projected them horrifying distances from "human catapults," taught them to dive ghastly heights from ceiling to floor, and even presented a woman (of African descent) named LaLa "the Black Venus," who hung upside down from a trapeze bar with a cannon in her mouth as it was ignited and fired. The exhibition of unusual human beings, presented not for what they did, but for who they were, wasn't far behind.

The freak show had existed, in one form or another, for a long time before Farini presented his first "human curiosity." In fact, the activities of its practitioners are recorded as far back as medieval English fairs. It was experiencing a major growth spurt in the late 1870s: dime museums, some even luxuriously appointed, with classy clientele and wealthy owners, were sprouting up in the burgeoning urban centers, especially in the Bowery in New York City. So when Farini began his brief involvement with this sort of entertainment, he was riding a wave of public interest, not creating one. However, with his showman's verve, he certainly contributed to its popularity; and his reputation, his intelligence, and his ability to deceive his audiences also helped to give it a sort of legitimacy. He immediately attracted some of the world's most sensational freaks to his fold: Millie-Christine, the Two-Headed Nightingale, who were a pair of African American conjoined twins born to southern slaves; Herr Haag the Elastic-Skin Man, who could pull the skin from his chest up over his head; Captain Costentenus, who boasted that an oriental khan had ordered him stripped naked, tied to the ground, and tortured by a beautiful woman with "7,000,000 punctures of the quivering flesh," rendering him "the world's most tattooed man"; dwarfs with extraordinary names like Baron Littlefinger, Count Rosebud, and the Countess of Lilliput; and the "Leopard Boy," a piebald young man who, it was claimed, came from a white African tribe. And in the early 1880s Farini invented his own freak, "Krao the Missing Link," a simianlike little girl destined to become one of the greats of her profession.

Africa, exotic and freakish to much of the Western world, happened into the news just as Farini was hitting his stride as a freak merchant. It had been of intense interest to people outside its borders for several centuries, and intrigue grew in the mid-Victorian period as the manly feats of men like Livingstone, Stanley, and Burton were celebrated far and wide in the "civilized" world. But early in 1879 Africa was news for less celebratory reasons: when the impis of the Zulu King Cetshwayo fell upon a regiment of the British army at Isandhlwana in the south and killed eight hundred of Her Majesty's soldiers, Africans shot to the Empire's front pages with the speed and impact of a Zulu-thrown assegai. The Anglo-Zulu War would be won by the British within a few months, but Isandhlwana was not the only shocking blow inflicted on the victors. On the first day of June the son of the exiled Emperor of France, who had been trained in military schools in England so he might one day return triumphantly to his homeland as Napoleon IV, was in a small group of British soldiers who were attacked by Zulus. "Loulou" fought bravely but fell under a hail of eighteen assegais. On the home front the citizens of the empire on which the sun never set reeled from the news. African people, whom the English had for the most part considered mentally and physically inferior, were outsmarting and butchering their brightest young men. Though Zulus were still not accorded much true respect, they began to rise in the British public's mind as larger-than-life warriors of nearly superhuman capabilities.

The wizard of the Westminster Aquarium, the Great Farini, saw an opportunity. There was almost a sense of glee in the speed and style with which he immediately brought Britain's deadly enemies into their midst and onto their respectable stages (to perform war dances), while English soldiers were still dying at the hands of such frightening foreigners.

Farini's shows, going all the way back to his Niagara crossings, were designed to give audiences jolts and to put them in touch with the most intense of their emotions. He was convinced that most people, especially his parents and the "respectable" citizens who had criticized him as a child and often condemned his thrilling acts as an adult, were fakes, afraid to look certain truths in the face. He once proclaimed, "I courted peril because I loved it, because the very thought of it fired my soul with ardour, because it was what others were afraid to face."[4] In early 1879 Farini showed the British public what they claimed they were afraid to face: those monstrous Zulus.

The buildup began in March when he presented the "Zulu Kaffir Boy," the first in a series of increasingly spectacular living African exhibitions. Later in the month the Aq featured "Umgame, the Baby Zulu," and in April Farini tempted citizens with the "Maravian Wild Women," Pawchee and Flycheia Letiaway, who were advertised as the "dusky daughters" of a Maravi chief, kidnapped from their central African home in their youth by the warlike Zulus. Though not the enemies themselves, these two women, aged twenty and twenty-three, generated some interest, mostly because Farini presented them in a way that connected them to the war. The Aq's publicity machine told the public that:

> The manner in which they illustrate the method of killing their war victims is in itself enough to strike terror into the stoutest heart. The fiendish reality of their war dances and songs is marvellous in its true and horrible intensity. (*Times* 14 April 1879: 1)

But customers were not yet truly offended by what they saw, and it was Farini's experience that it was often only when the public claimed that they were genuinely outraged that they were really interested and a show could be a sensation. The London *Times* spoke of the "two savage African women" rather benignly (15 April 1879: 6), and the *Daily Telegraph* wrote that the exhibition had "at least the recommendation of being well-timed and throwing some light on the manners and customs of barbarous nations" (15 April 1879: 6).

Farini was an intelligent man with an endlessly inquiring mind, and he often tried to educate his audiences as he thrilled them. There is no doubt that he was trying to enlighten them a little with these "ethnological" exhibitions, and it is equally undeniable that he was occasionally racist and condescending in his characterizations of the Africans he employed. But as the above quotations from England's two most respected newspapers indicate, the press had nothing on him. It is instructive to look at these comments since they are not meant to make any sort of point or to sensationalize: Africans are factually "savages" from a "barbarous" continent, no questions asked. This is the atmosphere in which Farini worked. The press certainly never took him to task for racism, mostly because they were incapable of detecting any in his style of presentation. When he offended them, it was usually because he scared them, thrilling them just a little more than they wanted.

Later that year he was ready to really offend. In May, while the war still raged, he sent his associate and veteran circus man Nat Behrens to southern Africa to do the unthinkable: sign some genuine Zulu men, warriors even, to come to London to be shown to the British public. (A few years later a booklet entitled *The Zulu Spy,* written by Hercules Robinson and published in New York, claimed that it was Farini himself who had gone to the war front that summer and had ridden dangerously back and forth between the opposing armies seeking adventure, even challenging and defeating legendary white Zulu leader and traitor John Dunn with his fists. It was also claimed that the Zulus whom Farini signed were the actual men who had killed the Prince Imperial. Though there is a very slight chance this is true, there does not appear to be any hard evidence that Farini was in Africa at that time, and the fact that this booklet was used as promotional material for "Farini's Zulus" on P. T. Barnum's Greatest Show on Earth renders the story even less credible.)

Behrens found six men willing to come to London with him and, on instructions from Farini, took the utmost care to prove to everyone that these Zulus were the real thing, and most importantly, that they had come willingly. A letter was even published in the London papers confirming as much, signed at the police station in Durban by George James Forrester, Sergeant of the Licensed Native Labourers. Forrester also admonished Behrens in print to "Take good care of the boys and bring them back safe" (*Daily Telegraph* 8 July 1879: 1). Not satisfied with that, Farini made sure that Behrens had every crew member and passenger on the *Balmoral Castle* sign a statement confirming that the six men on board with them were genuine Zulus and had come from Africa. Some of these passengers were citizens of considerable reputation. Sir Theophilus Shepstone, the Secretary of Native Affairs in Natal, also put in writing for public consumption that one of these Zulus was the eldest son of Chief Somkali.

Royal Aquarium.

FARINI'S FRIENDLY

ZULUS

Who were originally brought over by Mr. N. BEHRENS,
FROM SOUTH AFRICA for MR. G. A. FARINI.

PRINCESS AMAZULU, AND THE YOUNG CHIEF INCOMO!

Zulu Table d'Hote at 6.30.

Such brilliant showman's tactics ensured that London was waiting to see the Zulus and that a good-sized crowd came to the Southampton docks in late June to watch them disembark (a crowd American showman W. C. Coup outrageously estimated at 100,000 in his autobiography). Farini, perhaps growing wary that government officials would not be as thrilled as the general public, let it be known that they were "friendly Zulus," loyal to the British crown.

But the government, still shamed by the death of the young Napoleon, and not yet able to defeat the Zulus, viewed this prospective Farini show with contempt. Though they did not legally bar his exhibits from entering the country, the Secretary of State for the Home Department (R. A. Cross, who had also tried to censor the human cannonball act) made it known that Zulus, friendly or not, were not welcome. Officials also made this abundantly clear to the board of directors at the Royal Westminster Aquarium. And so, with the Zulus veritably en route to their debut, the show was cancelled.

Farini was enraged. A rebel from birth and an outsider wherever he lived, he was not accustomed to give in to authority. He considered his Zulu exhibition to be something that the British public needed to see: a palpable truth, Zulus in flesh and blood who should be witnessed and understood in person, not declared anathema. And of course, it was a hell of a good show.

By the first week of July he had negotiated a deal with a rival venue, St. James's Hall at Piccadilly and Regent Street, to unveil "Farini's Friendly Zulus" to London. Fittingly, this popular theater was famous for its blackface minstrel shows.

They opened on 8 July and the crowds came in droves, thrilled by the mere presence of these exotic men but particularly excited by the spectacle of the terrific throws of their assegais, which they buried deep into targets. Whether any members of the big crowds or packs of reporters ever imagined the five-inch blades of these deadly spears tearing into the youthful bodies of their own soldiers or the hallowed flesh of the Prince Imperial is a question that is worth considering, though it probably will never be answered.

From time to time the Zulus played tourists in London that summer of 1879. They were always accompanied by their hosts, and often, it seemed, journalists were invited to be part of the party. One outing involved a trip to the zoo. Farini knew that Victorians, some of whom still believed that Africans were only a few links superior to apes in the chain of being, would be fascinated to read what ensued; indeed, the trip may have been arranged as a sort of promotion. Frank Buckland, a friend of Farini and an eminent writer on zoological subjects (as well as freaks and ethnological exhibitions) reported that the Zulus were intrigued by the sight of wild animals in cages and that the "chief," entranced by a particularly beautiful young lady who served him at the refreshment department, made enquiries concerning how many cows her father would accept in exchange for her (Bompas 378).

When the war ended the following month, the Aquarium immediately set aside its high moral standards and brought "the Only Genuine Zulus" to the Aq. Here they stayed to the end of the year and into 1880, a show-business sensation. Soon Farini added five more Zulu men to his show. They had apparently come to him via a Parisian showman who had treated them badly, and were wary of white men. When another London impresario, anxious to capitalize on Farini's success, offered them more money, they tried to leave the Aquarium and were only thwarted when Farini confiscated their clothing (he also claimed that he did so in order to prevent them from wandering the streets of London alone, where mischief could befall them). The Zulus, apparently not without legal advice, proceeded to take their dynamic boss to court.

The case was given great play in the newspapers, and something of the relationship between the Zulu men and Farini was revealed. Their complaints apparently had nothing to do with harsh treatment, nor did they seem in the least concerned about being displayed like animals before the public; they were merely dissatisfied with their salaries. Farini replied that he would not force the men to remain with him and would pay their way back to Africa if they wanted to leave, but that they had had full understanding of the details of their contracts when they signed them, and therefore, while he would let them work in non-show-business professions in England, he would under no circumstances allow another English showman to exhibit his legally contracted performers. The Zulus, on the other hand, still concerned by their treatment at the hands of their French employer, were tentative about the rebuff Farini had given them when they inquired about bettering their situation. Understandably, they did not see why they were not free to take the best financial offer presented to them. A few sympathetic Englishmen, like Theophilus Shepstone and the son of the famously liberal Bishop of Natal (Colenso), appeared in court speaking to the Zulus in their native language and helping them understand the proceedings, but a more typical response to their dilemma came from the *Daily Tele-*

graph, which offered the racist opinion that the men were obviously just lazy, unprepared to work at anything. One can't help but wonder how this white English journalist would have fared had he been suddenly deposited into southern Africa and subjected to the subtleties of Zulu law and culture. But in those days all sides knew little of each other and it showed in both their actions and words. Calling the men "wretched creatures" and "savages," the reporter said they should be:

> turned adrift into the streets for a day, and then taken up for the first misdemeanour they committed and punished like ordinary criminals. So far they have been enjoying life vastly, living on the police-court poor-boxes, and successfully defying their employers' efforts to make them fulfil their contract. Whether . . . [they] will eventually . . . [be persuaded] to be honest remains to be seen, but meanwhile London is threatened by an impi of outrageous Zulus, determined to live here, but equally determined not to work. (*Daily Telegraph* 7 Jan. 1880: 5)

By contrast, Farini, who soon settled amicably with his employees, seemed a relatively benign force. He even found some humor, and some publicity, in the court case, immediately advertising that his new show consisted of "discontented Zulus, who are now becoming contented" (*Daily Telegraph* 7 Jan. 1880: 1).

But that wasn't the end of Farini's association with Zulu exhibitions, though the next phase was hastened by unwanted influences. By 1880 he was under extreme pressure from various government powers attempting to pass legislation that would ban his "dangerous performances" (it should be noted that the exhibition of human beings was never considered unfit for the public and was therefore never part of this legislation). P. T. Barnum was simultaneously urging him to come to the United States. So in the spring of 1880 he left England and brought several of his famous acts to The Greatest Show on Earth; among them were four of the Zulus.

Americans, without any personal involvement in the war in southern Africa, had only a few preconceived notions about Zulu people and certainly didn't regard them with horror. A satirical article in the 23 August 1879 *New York Clipper* (complete with a caricature depicting them as pitch-black, bug-eyed, thick-lipped, and childlike) had even presented Farini's Zulus as harmless, as much in danger from the excesses of Western life as from their own savageness (180). Nevertheless, when Dingando, Possomon, Maguibi, and Ousan ran into the circus ring in front of a big crowd in New York City that April, dressed in full battle costume, they stirred and even frightened a great many spectators. Farini had their targets set up at one end of the ring, just in front of a portion of the audience, and when they hurled their assegais, they struck terror into the hearts of many nearby spectators. The fascinated news-

paper reporters called them "copper-coloured men" and liked to write about their colorful ostrich feathers and the scantiness of their attire, referring to them as nearly naked. They also seemed incapable of not mentioning their well-developed and apparently not unattractive physiques.

Throughout that year, and during the following two seasons in America with W. C. Coup's New United Monster Shows (of which Farini was part owner) and in the 1882 Barnum show, Farini's Genuine Zulus played on the biggest stages in the world. The circus was approaching its golden age and crowds of 10,000 for a single performance were not uncommon. Farini's intention was to give Americans a show unlike any they had ever seen before, to thrill them just as he had with the human cannonball act. But he (and each of his performers) was also creating a misconception: that all Zulus were savage warriors.

Those three years in America produced several intriguing incidents. In late May 1880 in Detroit, one of the Zulus, a "chief," dressed himself in American street clothes and left the show unannounced. That evening he was said to have been seen enjoying a drink at a local saloon, but it wasn't until a few days later that he was found by Barnum's men, across the Canadian border at "a negro settlement" in Windsor (*Detroit Evening News* 29 May 1880: 4). Farini was an accomplished linguist and had apparently acquired a smattering of Zulu. One of his employees was dispatched to Windsor to speak to the chief and shortly thereafter, apparently without coercion of any sort, he agreed to return to the show when it played Chicago on 1 June. The reason for his hiatus in Detroit was never publicized, and he never again felt inclined to leave.

For Coup's shows Farini supplied the "Only Female Zulus ever brought to America," a footrace between a Zulu and a North American Indian was sometimes run on the hippodrome track, and the circus's banners and advertisements often featured huge drawings of the Zulus in full war costume, making for curious sights on the front pages of frontier town newspapers. In Barnum's 1882 show, the invidious concept of comparing African natives with animals was brought to a new low when Zulus were occasionally featured running in competition with horses. Later that season, on 21 August in Rome, New York, a stir was created when a Zulu child was born; the show's route book described the occasion:

> Arrival into the world of the first American Zulu born in captivity, to use a Jumbonian expression. Signor Farini was delighted, as there is a chance now of one of his many apprentices becoming President of this great republic.

Though Farini ended his direct association with the giant American circuses after 1882, he continued to manage several Zulu exhibits into the mid-1880s and booked some of them with U.S. circuses, including Barnum's. In an 1884 interview he remarked that he once had had thirty-three Zulus working for him, divided into three troupes, and on the very day of the interview still had a dozen in his employ. Though he was not the first showman to exhibit Zulu people (they had been to England as early as 1853), he certainly did it in the most spectacular way. Who else but Farini would have graphically shown the English how to brutally murder an Englishman with a spear, at the very moment when fathers, sons, and brothers were being similarly butchered? His Zulu shows were the best of their kind, if such a phrase can be used, and his performers (and they certainly were such) appear to have worked willingly and under at least tolerable conditions. It also seems apparent that his Zulus were actually who he claimed they were, a fact of note since it was not uncommon for Victorian promoters to exhibit "exotic Africans" who were really from places like Hoboken or the Bronx. There are many stories of such hoaxes. W. C. Coup told a particularly interesting one, in which Farini himself was either knowingly or unknowingly complicit:

> About 1882 a very tall specimen of the African race walked into an Eastern museum looking for work. He was actually over seven feet in height, and had never been on exhibition. Knowing that his value as a negro giant would be but little, the proprietors resolved to introduce him as a monster wild African. After

consulting Rev. J. G. Woods' *Illustrated History of the Uncivilized Races,* it was determined to make a Dahomey of the tall North Carolinian. A theatrical costumer was set to work to make him a picturesque garb. A spurious telegram was issued, purporting to be from Farini of London, stating that the Dahomey giant had sailed with his interpreter from London and would arrive in Boston on or about a certain date.

The man, with his interpreter, was then taken by train to Boston, from which city they, in due time, wired the museum proprietor of their arrival. That telegram was answered by another telling them to take the first Fall River boat for New York City. The press was then notified, and the representatives of five New York papers were actually sent to the pier the following morning to interview the distinguished stranger from Dahomey. The man had been well schooled, and pretending not to know a word of English, could not, of course, converse with the reporters. But his interpreter managed to fill them up very comfortably. At all events, long and interesting accounts of the "snuff-coloured giant from Dahomey" appeared in most of the dailies, and for several weeks this Dahomey was the stellar attraction at that particular dime museum. The advent of summer and its consequent circus season closing the city museums, the Dahomey "joined out" with a side show in which, for successive seasons, he posed as a Dahomey giant, a Maori from New Zealand, an Australian aborigine and a Kaffir. This man's success was the initiative for a score of other negroes, who posed as representatives of any foreign races the side-show proprietor wished to exhibit. (47–49)

Farini was back at the Royal Aquarium in London by 1883 and his interest in Africa, stimulated by his contact with Zulus, was still growing. The following year he sent W. A. Healey, his right-hand man at the Aq, to the southern part of the continent to persuade a different sort of African native to come to London. These people, six of whom returned with Healey from the area of the southern Kalahari Desert, were presented at the Aq as "Earthmen," "pygmies," or "yellow dwarfs," but they were better described as Bushmen and most accurately as San, the short-statured indigenous people of the Kalahari who had lived in southern Africa for 15,000 years and had been pushed into residing in the desert by the intrusion of Europeans. The six individuals who made their debut at the Westminster Aquarium that year were described in the following way:

> N'Co N'Qui, a kind of captain or chief, and a giant in his own country, aged thirty-five years, height 4 feet 6 inches.
> N'Arbecy, the chief's wife, still taller, height 4 feet 6 1/4 inches, aged forty years.
> N'Fim N'Fom, the chief's favourite dancer, aged twenty-four years, height 4 feet 1 inch.
> N'Co, a fine shot and good hunter, not afraid of tackling a lion single handed, aged 19 years, height 4 feet 1 1/2 inches.
> N'Icy, the daughter of two fine specimens that ran away, aged twelve years.
> N'Arki, the son of the chief, aged six years, and still nurses. (Qtd. in Clement 178–82)

STALKING THE OSTRICH. / REJOICING OVER A SLAIN ANIMAL / METHOD OF HUNTING

They were presented in "Farini's Desert in the Aquarium," a show that featured them stalking a lion and an ostrich, shooting poisoned arrows, building their homes in anthills and, of course, performing war dances. Their shows were accompanied by a great deal of literature and many lectures, detailing their appearance, customs, and history. This was all part of Farini's "aggrandized" style of ethnological exhibitions and freak shows, in which he attempted to give some scientific integrity to his presentations. For example, his "Krao, the Missing Link," then a sensation, was never exhibited as a leering, ugly freak, but instead as a gentle young girl discovered in southeast Asia, whom scientists were asked to examine, and whom Farini educated and adopted. At this point in his life, he was actually beginning to shed his former fascination with terrifying his audiences, and his impending marriage to a German lady of high breeding and social caste helped to push him toward a less sensational style of showmanship.

He did teach his Victorian spectators something about the San people, though he occasionally made errors, both intentional and unintentional, and was certainly motivated by show-business principles as well as by scientific ones. For example, he made the bizarre statement that the African "dwarf's" yellowish skin color was due to extended habitation underground and, as Robert Bogdan has pointed out, he showed his exhibits in leopard-skin shorts, so they would look primitive and perhaps animal-like next to the Aquarium's elegantly attired white lecturers (189). However, while the San people were obviously not presented as equal to English citizens, the Farini show did not make their supposed inferiority its main focus. He gave audiences a sort of grade-school, Anglocentric education about Africans while displaying them as human exhibits, a murky elucidation that one might argue was worse than no education at all.

The "Earthmen" exhibition was not a typical Farini show. Unlike the Zulu presentation, it lacked danger and sensation; and though Farini was moving away from that to some degree, it was still unusual for him to give the public something without much adventure in it. San people were first brought to England more than thirty years earlier, and though his show was an involved, exotic one that tried to give the British the sense of actually being in the Kalahari, it really made little "progress" either scientifically or theatrically over the exhibits of the 1850s. In fact, in some ways it repeated the earliest shows. It did do well at the box office, like almost all of his shows, and that is its major legacy. Farini himself did not seem nearly as interested in this show as he had been in the Zulus, which perhaps accounts for some of its imitation of the tired and racist presentation methods of an earlier time.

Though it has been said that "Farini's Dwarf Earthmen" were first exhibited at Coney Island, New York, and even that he actually discovered them there being presented by another showman, no evidence for that has been found, and it is almost certain that they debuted in September at the Aq and then crossed the Atlantic for New York City appearances at Steinway Hall in December. There the *New York Clipper* reviewed them with typical nineteenth-century white man's chauvinism, displaying superficial knowledge of Darwin's theories and very little else:

> Their conversation is similar to the chatter of monkeys, yet it is said they are intelligent in their own way . . . their heads (are) narrow and unintellectual. (13 Dec. 1884: 613)

The "Earthmen" toured the eastern United States that year and throughout 1885, appearing in the most prestigious dime museums, like the luxurious Austin and Stone's in Boston, and Kohl and Middleton's in Chicago. At the latter city the "Queen" of the group gave birth, but the baby died. A great deal was written about the San's reaction: it was said they painted themselves, chanted, and shrieked in grief. It was also reported that they were terribly distraught by the fact that their child was buried in the ground.

But Farini had no influence, either good or bad, on his employees' troubles in Chicago. By that time he was far away, in Africa, deep in the Kalahari Desert.

Though this would be the pinnacle of his fascination with Africa, it was, curiously, also the beginning of the end. As with many of his interests, his African period had started slowly, then built to a climax, and would soon evaporate, as if he had experienced everything he wanted and needed a new challenge.

Unlike most show-business impresarios or freak show promoters, Farini was capable of doing almost every feat he masterminded. For example, though some thought him cruel for asking a young woman to allow herself to be shot from a cannon, there is no question that he would have done it himself (and likely had in rehearsal) and had many times in his youth performed feats that were much more dangerous. Similarly, he wasn't just a merchant of exotic human exhibitions; he travelled to most of the places where his exhibits originated and sometimes even arrived in person, in jungles or deserts, to persuade people to come home with him.

The wonderful stories he had heard about the Kalahari from natives and friends, of seas of sand, undiscovered diamonds, ranch lands, and unusual people, were irresistible. By January 1885 he was on board an ocean steamer with Lulu (his adopted son and protégé) and a Baster guide, and within another two months he was on a covered wagon in the midst of a perilous journey through parts of the Kalahari few people had ever visited. But he was undaunted: it was unparalleled adventure and that was what he lived for.

During the course of the seven-month trip, he met a great variety of people: English, Boers, Germans, Malays, Basters, Khoikhoi, San, Zulus, and others. Part way through he encountered several "pygmies" who he claimed were of unique appearance; he was fascinated by their peculiarities and convinced them to return with him to London. (He said he found them in the Lake N'Gami region and called them "M'Kabba" dwarfs, though they may have been Koba.) He described them as averaging just slightly more than four feet in height, and he recalled their strange customs of tattooing themselves with a blue dye and amputating the first joint of each little finger. He also commented, with typical Farini irreverence, that their projecting stomachs made them look like "so many dwarf aldermen of the desert" (253). It is difficult to ascertain who these people really were, and whether Farini fabricated some of their unusual characteristics. But coming face to face with Africans in their homeland was just a very small part of his trip. So many other things caught his interest: he searched for diamonds, scouted ranch lands, explored rocky falls, hunted wild animals, ate everything the natives offered him, examined and carefully pressed flora and fauna, and nearly killed himself and his companions at least once or twice. And all the while he recorded what he saw in a diary and on his return wrote a book entitled *Through the Kalahari Desert,* which would be published in five countries in three languages.

Though this journey would give him his fill of Africa, and he would start to wind down his African exhibitions upon returning to London, incidents during its course give insights into Farini and his approach to the "Dark Continent."

The first concerns one of the most intriguing stories in Farini's storied life. He claimed that when he was far into the unmapped depths of the desert, he stumbled upon the ruins of an ancient civilization, in a place where history records no such African culture. It was as if he had found Atlantis, peeking up through the sands.

Though his book was a success and was reviewed in many major publications, leading him to be invited to speak at both the Royal Geographical Society and the Berlin Geographical Society (he did, in German), little notice was taken of the book's brief account of his strange discovery. But in the twentieth century "the Lost City of the Kalahari" has become one of the enduring legends of southern African lore. Two books have been entirely devoted to it (Clement, Goldie), while many others mention it, and dozens of expeditions have been organized to find it, some government sponsored, others including eminent professors, anthropologists, adventurers, and even a famous author (Alan Paton). Searches have been conducted by jeep, car, truck, and airplane; aerial photographs have been examined and reexamined. The bizarre stories of many individuals, both native and white, have been recorded, many asserting that they have seen the mystical ruins and others even claiming that they house hidden treasures; Farini's biography has even been included in the *Encyclopaedia of Southern Africa*. But no one has ever found his city.

In a strange way the legend of the Lost City of the Kalahari is part of Farini's African entertainment legacy. Many believe he fictionalized parts of his book and that the lost city ruin was a particularly ingenious invention. Others, some of whom have searched for it and are well informed, take the ruin very seriously and think it will be found some day. But whether it really exists or not sometimes appears to be beside the point: it is a marvellous story, a spectacular story, and Farini set it in Africa. He knew that Western civilization was deeply fascinated by the "Dark Continent," and whether he was exhibiting its peoples or creating a legend situated in one of its most mysterious regions, he exploited the spectacle Africa provided. The Lost City of the Kalahari, among other things, is a show-business sensation.

But there is another, perhaps more important insight into Farini's attitude toward Africa and its peoples that can be gleaned from his account of his Kalahari exploration. This concerns the question of his racism. His book contains many observations and comments that we in the twentieth century (and even some in the nineteenth century) would consider racist, and yet even a casual reading turns up contradictions. In fact, some are so striking that one might even build a case for Farini as an antiracist.

Early in the book he makes numerous comments about the laziness and uselessness of certain natives and is caustic in his criticism, but it soon becomes evident that the color of one's skin does not excuse anyone from his wrath. The Boers, for example, are given a constant flogging, and he undoubtedly despises them with a passion that supersedes anything he feels for natives. He is especially hard on them for the way they treat Africans and becomes so disturbed about it that he occasionally can barely find the adjectives: for example, one dishonest Boer who tried to con him was characterized as one of many ". . . honourable, blackmailing, religious, sanctimonious, upright, thieving scoundrels" (82).

Another intriguing moment occurs when Farini and his party arrive in the dusty diamond town of Kimberley after an arduous trek and are told by the owner of their hotel that Gert Louw, their Baster guide, must sleep in the stables. Basters are actually the mixed descendants of Boers and Hottentots, but the owner is adamant that a "black man" will never sleep inside the doors of his establishment. Farini then vociferously intercedes on Gert's behalf, a noble action that very few Victorian white men would have dared. Indeed, by the time Farini has finished putting his case to the owner, Gert is sleeping in his boss's hotel room, and in fact is bunked down in the coolest part of these decidedly hot accommodations. Within a few weeks Farini is bristling at Gert's laziness but does so on the basis of his actions, not his skin color. Farini thought just about everyone lazy, and relative to his own approach to life, he was likely correct.

When white officials at the Kimberley mines told him that thievery was rife and its practitioners were natives, he wrote in his diary that he felt they were being wrongly accused. And when he saw natives abused and disrespected in urban centers, he wrote:

> The black man is not improved by a veneer of civilization. The real "savage," who has never been in contact with the whites, has a certain amount of honour and chivalry about him, and one cannot help admiring him; but the half-Christianized black is a lying, lazy scoundrel, without a spark of self-respect. . . . (75)

Upon his return to England he wrote this surprisingly tender passage in his book:

> . . . the poor Bushman is hardly dealt with. The big game is driven from the country by the Boers and their flocks; the small game he cannot hunt, as his poisoned arrow and bows are always taken from him; so he is obliged to steal

some of the flocks to exist, for which he is punished by depriving him of his liberty which he loves so well. Is it a wonder he resists capture so desperately? But the march of civilization has no ears for the cries of those poor wretches whom it crushes if they stand in its way. (442)

These words come from the same man who exhibited Zulus and San people on freak-show stages and in 1864 had supported George McClellan's presidential bid against Abraham Lincoln in part because he was against the emancipation of the slaves (though it must be noted that his opposition likely had more to do with the speed and nature of the decision, rather than with any support for the institution of slavery); the same man who said of a grass-covered stretch of the Kalahari, "In the hands of an energetic white race this country could surely be made one of the most productive grazing lands in the world" (159). So a somewhat contradictory picture arises.

The answer to the problem seems to be that Farini possessed some of the prejudices of his time, but nothing that was truly deep-seated. In fact, if he had been questioned concerning the equality of races, he might have even turned out to be somewhat liberal, relative to his contemporaries. But he was obsessed by adventure, by anything or anyone who struck him as unusual, and by the excitement that a really powerful show-business sensation could generate. Those passions tended to override any other concerns.

He had also grown up in a secluded world where black people truly were exotic. It had been a society that believed fervently in human hierarchies, and while he detested such beliefs, preferring to think that human beings should be judged by their actions and not their heritage, he still inherited these notions somewhat; he was never free from the assumption that the Anglo-Saxon way was usually the superior way. Nor was he above the Victorian habit of judging groups of people by characteristics found in a few of their number (an approach to others which our own era has not completely shaken). This, combined with his inexorable pursuit of excitement, allowed him to present his Zulu and San shows without questioning whether or not they might be detrimental to the individuals thus exhibited.

He was certainly not the worst of African exhibitors, and his African shows occupied only a brief period in his extraordinary life. But his showman's skills brought African people to the forefront in an explosive way, not necessarily to be looked down upon, but unfortunately, not to be considered equals either.

After a respite of nearly a decade, Farini had a brief and final fling with another style of entertainment that, while not originating in Africa, had taken a long and circuitous route from there, and certainly affected the public image of people of African descent. This was blackface or burnt-cork minstrelsy. In

September 1894 the board of directors of the famous Moore and Burgess Minstrels asked Farini to take charge of their company. Believe it or not, this was considered a prestigious position. In fact, this style of entertainment was thought to be family-oriented, and the legendary Moore and Burgess troupe were renowned for the great numbers of ladies who attended their shows at a time when most musical hall fare was considered beneath such delicate observation.

Many of the most talented popular singers in the Victorian era performed in blackface, undaunted by such tunes as "Happy Little Niggers," "The Popping Coon," and "The Darkey's Jubilee," and the Moore and Burgess Minstrels were one of the biggest sensations in London for nearly three decades. They performed downstairs at St. James's Hall (where Farini's Friendly Zulus had made their debut), packing people into their nine-hundred-seat theater every night, bringing their audiences to such fevered enjoyment that the stomping of feet sometimes nearly drowned out the more elegant entertainments upstairs (such as, in the early years, lectures by Charles Dickens).

When Farini received the offer from the Moore and Burgess directors, he was in the midst of many other adventures. Just a few years earlier he had drawn 65,000 people to an outdoor London venue to see a parachute jump (he co-invented what was then the most effective version of the modern parachute) and would soon move on to other strange and diverse pursuits, like writing a book about growing begonias, becoming the vice president of a gold mining company, and experimenting with a tubular steel boat that spun like a huge rolling pin as it sailed. He would spend only six months as a blackface minstrel manager. He once said while exploring the Kalahari, "I would put up with anything for the novelty of the thing" (179). It seems that big-time minstrel music, like African exploration and daredevilry over the Niagara gorge, provided what he needed.

Farini spent the first three decades of the twentieth century, as he aged from sixty-two to ninety, far from Africa and African entertainments, but still in pursuit of novelty. He continued inventing, became an accomplished painter and sculptor, and played the stock market with abandon. During the First World War he lived with his wife in Germany, behind enemy lines. Perhaps because such an existence wasn't enough intrigue for his eighty-year-old mind, he filled his days translating articles from German and other European newspapers and writing down his feelings about the war from Germany's perspective. When he was finished, he had written an astonishing thirty-seven volumes.

Back in Port Hope by 1921, he approached his ninth decade at full speed, driving himself relentlessly, rising in the mornings to rotate his scalp, do his exercises, eat his yogurt, and take seven-mile bicycle rides on unpaved roads to help harvest the crops on his farms. Many of his hours were spent at his easel, where he often recorded in vivid colors some of the bizarre scenes he had witnessed during the whirlwind tour that had been his life. Whatever he was searching for, he never found, but when he finally died on 17 January 1929, a few weeks into his ninety-first year, he left behind one of the most extraordinary life stories the world has ever known.

It is important to view Farini's involvement with African exhibitions within the context of his many diverse adventures, of other ethnological shows, and of the time in which he lived. The day after Farini's fifteenth birthday, gained in the backwoods of a southern Ontario rural community, Charles Dickens, the great conscience of the most "civilized" nation on earth, published his thoughts concerning an African exhibition he had just seen at Hyde Park, London. He said of the Zulu:

I call him a savage, a something highly desirable to be civilised off the face of the earth . . . he is . . . cruel, false, thievish, murderous; addicted more or less to grease, entrails, and beastly customs; a wild animal with the questionable gift of boasting; a conceited, tiresome, bloodthirsty, monotonous humbug. . . . My position is, that if we have anything to learn from the Noble Savage, it is what to avoid. (337–39)

Every era has individuals as wonderful and terrible as Dickens and Farini. Life for such people is a race: the Englishman flying through marathon walks in the streets of London, staring at the poor he found everywhere in rags, his mind so overflowing with ideas and sympathies and emotions that it seemed his fifty-eight years on earth were all he could stand; and the inimitable Farini, forever searching and exploring, hungry for any excitement, intrigue, or danger he could find, and so inexhaustible at the end he seemed like that ancient character in one of Beckett's plays, the one who cries out "MORE!" when she thinks she may die.

Farini wasn't an evil person, nor was he a saint. He was curious and passionate to a fault. He may have never even noticed, as he raced through life, that he sometimes knocked people down.

NOTES

1. Though slavery did exist for a short while in Canada, its practice was certainly never nearly as widespread as in the United States, and it was abolished in 1833.

2. Mrs. Lucy Buck in *The Radio Times* (London, 1933). See notes in Clement 192.

3. For details about Farini's life, see Peacock. A thorough bibliography for this book is at the Ganaraska Region Archives in Port Hope, Ontario. For extensive primary sources, see the Farini Papers in the Archives of Ontario, Toronto.

4. Autobiography, ms., Farini Papers, Archives of Ontario, Toronto, n. pag.

WORKS CITED

Bogdan, Robert. *Freak Show: Presenting Human Oddities for Amusement and Profit*. Chicago: U of Chicago P, 1988.

Bompas, George C. *Life of Frank Buckland*. London: Smith, Elder and Co., 1885.

Clement, A. J. *The Kalahari and Its Lost City*. Cape Town: Longmans, 1967.

Coup, William Cameron. *Sawdust and Spangles*. Chicago: Herbert S. Stone and Co., 1901.

Dickens, Charles. "The Noble Savage." *Household Words* 11 June 1853: 337–39.

1882 Route Book. P. T. Barnum's Greatest Show on Earth.

Farini, G. A. *Through the Kalahari Desert: A Narrative of a Journey with Gun, Camera and Note-book to Lake N'Gami and Back*. London: Sampson, Low, Marston, Searle, and Rivington, 1886. Cape Town: Struik, 1973.

Goldie, Fay. *Lost City of the Kalahari: The Farini Story and Reports on Other Expeditions.* Cape Town: Balkema, 1963.

Peacock, Shane. *The Great Farini: The High-Wire Life of William Hunt.* Toronto: Viking, 1995.

Robinson, Hercules. *The Zulu Spy: Giving an Authentic History. Farini's Genuine Zulus, One of the Many Leading Features of the Barnum and London Circus.* New York: New York Popular Publishing Co., 1881.

4

"Spectatorial Lust"
The African Choir in England, 1891–1893

Veit Erlmann

In September 1891, a young black South African woman named Charlotte Manye made the following statement in a London monthly magazine:

> Let us be in Africa even as we are in England. Here we are treated as men and women. Yonder we are but as cattle. But in Africa, as in England, we are human. Can you not make your people at the Cape as kind and just as your people here? That is the first thing and the greatest. But there are still three other things that I would ask. Help us to found the schools for which we pray, where our people could learn to labour, to build, to acquire your skill with their hands. Then could we be sufficient unto ourselves. Our young men would build us houses and lay out our farms, and our tribes would develop independently of the civilisation and industries which you have given us. Thirdly, give our children free education. Fourthly, shut up the canteens, and take away the drink. These four things we ask from the English. Do not say us nay. (256)

Charlotte Manye's statement appeared in *The Review of Reviews*, a liberal monthly edited by William T. Stead, erstwhile editor of the *Pall Mall Gazette* and a leading figure of Britain's "New Journalism." It came in the course of a remarkable venture, during what in retrospect must count as one of the most fascinating moments in the history of black South Africa and as a major turning point in its musical history in particular: the tours to England and North America undertaken between 1891 and 1893 by a group of fifteen African singers called the African Choir. But these tours not only marked a dramatic juncture in the culture and consciousness of a handful of South Africans. They also initiated a drama of truly global dimensions, one whose acts were set in places as far apart as Kimberley in South Africa, London, and Cleveland, Ohio, and whose dramatis personae included individuals as varied as Queen Victoria, South African black leader John Tengo Jabavu, a Glasgow ship builder, the principal of one of the leading South African black colleges, and bishops of the African Methodist Episcopal Church. Likewise, the scripts through which this drama was acted out consisted of texts as diverse as American minstrel tunes and Negro spirituals, Sesotho press reviews, the earliest known forms of Christian hymns sung in Xhosa, English concert reviews, and travel accounts written in Sesotho.

As Manye's statement suggests, the venture was first and foremost designed to secure metropolitan support for an industrial school in Kimberley in the Cape Colony, an idea which the celebrated Fisk Jubilee Singers from Tennessee had made a *cause célèbre* during their 1870s world tours, and that another African American group, touring South Africa in 1890 as the Virginia Jubilee Singers, had instilled in the minds and hearts of black audiences. As for the school itself, it was to somehow follow the example of Lovedale College—one of the country's premier mission schools and alma mater to several members of the African Choir—in providing modernizing Africans with the skills needed in a rapidly advancing world economy. But the tours also had implications of a broader political nature, as Charlotte Manye's remarks also show. They were to enlist imperial succor against the rising tide of antiliberal sentiment in South Africa and the combined efforts by mining capital and the Cape colonial administration to divest themselves of some of the mid-Victorian premises of the colonial order ("civilized rule for civilized men") and to undermine Africans' position as autonomous producers and citizens.

The venture failed dismally. After a two-year tour of the British Isles, losses of more than £1,000 had been incurred, and with most musicians ill and eventually abandoned by their white agents in London, the whole enterprise ended in a fiasco. In addition to the financial disaster, other problems that contributed to the failure of the enterprise were the fact that Paul Xiniwe, a senior choir member, had impregnated fellow singer Sannie Koopman, and, above all, the animosity between the Kimberley-based members of the choir and the Lovedale group. The explanations proffered for this rift varied. Pianist Lilian Clark somewhat predictably ascribed it to ethnic frictions between Xhosa and Basotho, whereas Paul Xiniwe explained the whole disaster in the terms under which the enterprise had originally been conceived: as a political campaign against white settler paternalism. The idea of using a choir to raise funds for a technical school, he maintained, had been "simply a fine rolling phrase" to catch the unwary, and he accused the managers of having "bolstered and pampered" the Kimberley girls.[1]

Be this as it may, it is not my aim here to unravel the knot of "untoward happenings," as officious Lovedale historiography later was to call the tangle of perspectives, interests, and narratives making up all these various disputes (Shepherd 57). For whatever the cause of the failure may ultimately have been, it was not due to ethnic rivalry, unsound management, and white callousness alone. The conflicting notions of modernity, Africa, and the West highlighted by the tour of the African Choir were every bit as much inscribed into the chimera of the "civilizing mission," and as such into the very late-Victorian order of knowledge and global imagination.

SPECTACLE AND THE GLOBAL IMAGINATION

In what follows I trace these remarkable transatlantic episodes and discuss a broad range of issues arising from the intertwined histories, experiences, and narratives of people on both sides of the Atlantic. I shall contend that the narratives, ideas, and practices of the global age—a period which in my view begins in the 1890s—are imaginations of a special kind, different from earlier fantasies by virtue of a number of wide-ranging developments in domains such as technology, mass media, and aesthetics. More specifically, my argument proceeds from the hypothesis that this culture, like all socially constituted realms of practice and meaning taken for worlds, is an imagined totality. Global culture is a fiction that is united not so much by things such as international trade, multilateral agreements, or the institutions of modern society, as by a regime of signs and texts. In other words, it is through new forms of narrative, physical sensations, and bodily practices that new and infinitely more complex power relations manifest themselves.

Of course, these new global narratives are not fictitious in the sense that, as some have suggested, *il n'y a pas de hors-texte.* My interest is not to demonstrate that outside the text there is only a further text, and that the world and social life are nothing but a web of signs and simulations, hermetically self-referential and devoid of any meaningful connection with human action. Nor do I think that these imaginings are, as Niklas Luhmann somewhere has defined culture, mere "islands of understanding" amidst a sea of restlessly self-generating systems and subsystems. If the shock of modernity, as Jean-François Lyotard has shrewdly remarked, is the recognition that so little about reality is real, we nevertheless do not all live in illusory worlds (24). Rather, what has changed is the measure of the real and, hence, the aim of an ethnography of the global imagination must be to examine why and in what way people's measures of the real change. For clearly, it is no coincidence that modern technologies of simulation and an aesthetics of the surface begin to make progress at precisely the moment when nineteenth-century imperialist expansion opens up a global horizon for Western inspection. Empire is at heart a society of the spectacle. But the total narratives arising from these new technologies are more than "dramatic falsification," as one of the earliest critics of imperial expansion, John A.

Hobson, called the discourse and ideology of imperialism (215). The "spectatorial lust" of the imperial mind, as he puts it, does not so much veil and misrepresent imperial conquest and the triumphant capitalist world market. Rather, empire and unreality constitute each other in ways rooted in the deepest layers of modern consciousness. The opening of the world as a site for the modeling of Western and African identities and its simultaneous self-enclosure in panoramic superficies go hand in hand. From the beginning of the nineteenth century, the emerging modern world system and the systematic conquest of the universe by the bourgeois gaze have been continually rehearsed and glorified in forms of what Walter Benjamin called "hundred percent image-space" (*Gesammelte Schriften* 309): first the panorama, then film, and finally cyberspace. Like these, the fictions and performances examined here are actual *symbolon*, binding elements that enable growing numbers of modern actors living in increasingly complex and spatially disconnected worlds to imagine themselves as being part of a variety of local, regional, national, or even global ecumenes.

More particularly, the episode that I examine was part and parcel of late-Victorian epistemology and consciousness—and, to be sure, of a corresponding imperial practice—which Thomas Richards has subsumed under the image of an "imperial archive." In the age of empire, Richards argues, we see the rise of the first information society in history, in which the engineers of colonial domination, in a very real sense, built a paper empire, a fiction of a nation in overreach that is kept together not by force or civil control but by knowledge and the ordering of data. This new synthesis of knowledge and power persistently sought to incorporate the colonized on terms which, albeit frequently contested, ultimately met with their approval. The cultural and historical premise for such approval, I argue, rested not on the imposition of a Western social model and epistemology but on the coauthoring of global identities at home and on the periphery. In other words, the African belief in Western fictions of modernity and progress was worked out through Western assumptions about Africans as they were in turn enabled by African stagings of something taken for an African past.

Having thus prepared the ground for a more detailed discussion of the shows of the African Choir themselves, let me propose a brief look at the members of the tour. There were two sets of singers: a first set that gathered in Kimberley when the African Choir was formed, and a second, much larger group that eventually left for England. The story begins in September 1890 with a concert in the Beaconsfield Townhall by Charlotte Manye, Titus Mbongwe, and one Miss Gwashu. The concert, together with the even more spectacular appearance in the town of Orpheus McAdoo's Virginia Jubilee Singers, prompted a number of white residents to try their hands at a similar venture that they called the African Jubilee Singers (Erlmann, *African Stars* 21–53). Several weeks later and after a series of auditions, singing lessons, and meetings with local politicians, a choir was formed that included former Lovedale student Wellington Majiza, as well as Hoffa and Paul Sinamela, Charles Mzozoiyana, Mbikazi Nobengula, Thomson Sepurn, George Polisa, Charlotte and Kate Manye, Miss Bibyle, M. Keyi, and Annie Sanders. Although little is known about most of these early recruits except for the Manye sisters and the Sinamela brothers, it is probably correct to assume that the original cast represented a fair cross section of the younger, 1860s generation of Kimberley's Fingo location, by then South Africa's most self-consciously modernizing African community. The whole group was directed by two white professional performers, Walter Letty and John Balmer, who had come to South Africa from England but whose precise background is unclear.

Most of these members, for equally unknown reasons, soon withdrew from the enterprise, leaving Letty and Balmer with only the Manye sisters, Mbikazi Nobengula, and Wellington Majiza to embark on a tour of the Cape Colony in January of the following year. There, after a hasty cruise of the Eastern Cape, the group was enlarged by Johanna Jonker, Sannie Koopman, and, after a flying visit to Lovedale College, a number of erstwhile students, including Paul Xiniwe, his wife Eleanor, his son John, his nephew Albert Jonas, Frances Gqoba, John Mbongwe, George McLellan, Samuel Konongo, and Neli Mabandla. Back in Kimberley to finalize the deal and to enlist high government patronage, the promoters persuaded Josiah Semouse and the white pianist Lilian Clark to join the group, and with their fifteen-piece ensemble eventually left Kimberley on 15 April 1891 for one of the most extraordinary episodes in the early history of black South Africa's encounter with the West in the West.

In England, things at first went surprisingly well. Queen Victoria received the Choir at Osborne, and concerts in London and other major centers were well patronized and generously reviewed in the press. In fact, glancing over the press coverage of the tour, one is struck by the sense of genuine admiration for the vocal talents displayed by the South Africans. But this positive response was less surprising than it may seem. For what the concerts confirmed, after all, was precisely the outcome of Dickens's notorious prognosis several decades earlier that the Zulus would better be "civilised off the face of the earth (337)." And thus it was in this vein that one London critic believed that concerts such as those given by the African Choir "ought to put a final end to the stale calumny that an African Christianised is an African spoiled" (*Bradford Daily Telegraph* 10 Sept. 1891).

Not all sections of the British public, however, appear to have shared this view. The music, to some critics, was simply too European. "[T]he value and interest of the pieces performed," the weekly magazine *South Africa* complained, "are considerably reduced by the inevitable European harmonies . . . suggestive rather of an English tonic sol-fa class than of savage strains" (4 July 1891: 17). *The Musical Standard* seconded: "[I]t is pretty obvious that the South African singers have in the process of civilization adopted more or less the European scale, to say nothing of European harmonies" (11 July 1891). Of course, the disaffection was not about musical grammar alone. Voiced though it mostly was from within more openly antimissionary and antiliberal factions of the metropolitan press, the disappointment indicated a more deep-seated ambiguity at the heart of late-Victorian imperial doctrine.

Until the mid-nineteenth century, attempts at justifying the "civilizing mission" rested on the notion that Africans' inferiority and barbarism were rather to be attributed to environmental predicaments than to racial deficits. In fact, the work of the early evangelical missions in the Eastern Cape—just like much, although by no means all, of the colonial public discourse about "natives," colonization, and Christianization—consisted precisely in vindicating Africans' innate capacity for civilization. If whites and blacks did not occupy the same positions on the ladder of racial evolution, the latter could at least hope that, with time and "proper" (i.e., white) guidance, they too would eventually climb to the upper steps of this ladder. The broader changes within British society and consciousness at the end of the nineteenth century changed all that. What then came to dominate popular discourses at home and in settler society was a more blatantly racist variant of the imperial rhetoric, one that declared Africans' "benighted" condition as permanent, intrinsic. For instance, Rider Haggard, one of the most popular writers of popular fiction about South Africa, author of such phenomenally successful novels as *King Solomon's Mines* and *She,* mused in 1877 that civilization, "when applied to black races, produces effects diametrically opposite to those we are accustomed to observe in white nations; it debases before it can elevate." And, "as regards the Kafirs it is doubtful, and remains to be proved, whether it has much power to elevate them at all" (96).

As a result of this shift toward social Darwinism, jingoism, and "scientific racism"—a shift that had prompted the tour of the African Choir in the first place—the tour touched upon one of the epistemological nerve centers of the Victorian global imagination itself. If, in the early days of empire, difference—the fact, namely, that some people were found to be uncivilized and therefore standing in need of colonial guidance—had been the *raison d'être* for the civilizing mission, scientific racism destroyed the moral justification on which imperial expansion rested. In other words, if the civilizing mission took difference as its point of departure, it was in the uppermost interest of the whole operation to efface the very difference on which it was built. The disappointment about the lack of "exotic" elements in displays of African identity such as the concerts of the African Choir would thus seem to veil the fact that the colonial powers had long backtracked from the civilizing mission.

Spectacle and the Crisis of Imperial Knowledge

All of this becomes perhaps nowhere clearer than in an article on "The Music of Africa," a review of a concert given by the African Choir in England. Written by one E. Gowing Scopes, the text appeared in December 1891 in *The Ludgate Monthly*, a rather obscure London magazine located on the liberal end of Britain's political spectrum. Before I examine some of the implications the shifts in metropolitan constructions of Africa have had in the field of African "show business" and how these shifts hinged upon the spectacle of the commodity, let me quote a number of extended passages from "The Music of Africa." In the middle of the article, the reviewer offers a detailed list of the pieces performed by the African Choir:

> "Ulo Tixo Mkulu," is the first music known to have been sung by Christian Kaffirs, and the original composition of Mtsikana, the first convert amongst the Amaxosa tribe.
>
> "Singame wele" (we are twins), is a song and dance. The natives are exceedingly fond of singing and dancing, and this item is typical of how they spontaneously, and at any time, commence their amusements. The lead is generally taken by a bass voice, but is never begun in exactly the same way.
>
> The choir sing a short story in the Kaffir language, giving a striking illustration of the clicks used in the native tongue. It is adapted to the music of Schumann's "Merry Peasant."
>
> The typical Kaffir wedding song is purely native, and the harmonies have not been, in any way Europeanized; it is sung at the wedding feast by the friends of the bridegroom. The bride, whose sobs can be heard amid the general rejoicing, is finally led away by two of the guests to her husband's "mgwelo" which awaits her. At some of the marriages the festivities are kept up days and nights without cessation.
>
> "Mgwelo engena tentyi" is a wayside Kaffir song and dance. When traveling by bullock waggon in Africa, the oxen are unyoked at intervals and allowed to graze and rest, or are outspanned—as the local term has it. This scene is supposed to take place when the Kaffirs are seated round their fires, awaiting the time for inspanning, whilst the oxen are grazing and the skoff is boiling in the "pot."
>
> "Lutukela" is a duet, composed by a Kaffir. The style of this piece is very popular amongst the natives, they are fond of accompanying solos with their voices, and, as a rule, take the parts very clearly, without any training whatever.
>
> Kaffirs are very fond of mimicry, and are always ready to pick up anything to imitate. An item entitled the "Kaffir Travesty," is a purely Kaffir song, and is their idea of the English street cry of "Hot Cross Buns!" Its origin is doubtful.

"Molokoda" means good-bye. The natives of South Africa, when travelling in parties, have a singular habit of singing—keeping time to the melody with their feet. Standing upon a hill, you can hear their peculiar chant when the band is miles away. "Molokoda" is a representation of the effect produced by the gradual approach and disappearance of one of these parties, who have just left their kraals to go into the towns in search of employment. Perfect stillness, on the part of the audience, is necessary during the singing of this piece.

"On the Mountain" is a quintette. It was requested that the choir should give a little more English in the programme; this quintette has, therefore, been introduced in response to this request, and to please those who are so fond of their mother tongue.

"Lovedale" is a Kaffir solo with vocal accompaniment. It is another composition of a Kaffir, and describes the beauties of the country surrounding Lovedale College, Cape Colony, where seven of the choir were educated. It is also another illustration of the native fondness for vocally accompanied solos.

"Does anybody here know the Big Baboon?" is a solo and chorus. It was specially composed for the African Native Choir by James Hyde, Esq., King Williamstown (one of the, if not the first musician in South Africa), after he had attended one of their concerts given in his town.

"Africa" is a Kaffir quartette. The London *Times*, in criticising the African Choir Concert, said: "A quartette, or rather a solo accompanied by three voices, bore so close a resemblance to Rossini's 'Cujus animam' that it is difficult to accept it as a specimen of native music at all." But this quartette is the composition of a Kaffir who had never heard of Rossini or his "Stabat Mater," and did not dream that such a selection as 'Cujus animam' was in existence. It is descriptive of how the natives hum some portions of their songs.

"Good News" is another English piece, but one given in true Kaffir style.

"Send the Light" is a solo and chorus, the words and music having been composed expressly for the European tour of the African Choir, by gentlemen in South Africa who were wishful the enterprise should be a success.

It is easy for us today to dismiss a text such as this as the product of a rather insignificant literary mind in an obscure magazine. But a whole range of themes run through this inventory of songs, the relevance of which to my subject matter becomes immediately apparent. Among other things, the reviewer reproduces typical Victorian stereotypes such as those about Africans' mimetic capabilities and their innate inability for higher forms of cognition. And, like the European public generally, he too confuses the songs of America's black slaves, represented here by "Good News," and African music. More important than these slurs and glitches, however, is the list of song titles itself, its cataloglike character and the tone of supposed objectivity suggesting a familiarity with a series of curious items and, beyond this, a mastery of a supreme organon of global knowledge.

But the passage quoted also sets the scene for another fundamental aspect of the global imagination that I want to explore here. What I mean by this will become apparent when we consider the context in which this document of late-

Victorian global gnosis and curiosity appears. It is framed by reflections of a kind not uncommon in late-Victorian society, reflections about the moral foundations of the imperial order and, beneath these, about the ever more precarious relationship between order, power, and knowledge. "Let an African explorer or novelist," the *Ludgate Monthly* article begins, "Stanley or Haggard will do, write up the details, in gory language, of some sickening barbaric custom, and it will produce upon the civilized mind a sense of shuddering thankfulness that we have risen above the ignorance of these native tribes. Perhaps we have."

> In our present highly cultivated state we cover ourselves with clothes, excepting only our handsome faces; walk upon level pavements that the lower classes have laid down for us, and partake of our meals from clean plates, on the strict understanding we do not put our knives to our mouths. Most families keep servants to cook and bring in the meals—it is not decent to do this sort of thing for one's self. The servants, of course, have to feed without assistance, but that cannot be helped, as it is impossible for all to be highly civilized at once. . . .
>
> There are some weak-minded individuals who have raised the very absurd question as to whether a system of warfare that places a thousand men in an iron boat in order that they may be immediately afterwards blown into fragments by the kindly aid of a torpedo, is quite the best way of feeding the fishes or justifying civilization; in fact, whether it is a very great improvement upon some of the pastimes of barbarism from which we shrink with horror. But such reasoning as this is childish and opposed in principle to the best interests of the country. Civilization towers high above these effeminate thoughts.

The ironic tone in this passage of course indicates that the writer is merely introducing a rhetorical device to create a contrast with what then follows. For he goes on to relate a report he had read in a Cape newspaper about a "smelling out" ceremony "among some native tribe up the country" in the course of which a young girl, having been smelled out by the medicine man of the tribe as the evildoer, was "put to death by perforating her body with seventeen assegais." And so our author promptly asks himself whether Rider Haggardism, after all, was not more than mere fiction, and missionary work more than a need of the past. But it is not long before the initial doubts about his society return:

> Is there nothing at home that compares with this strange custom? Are there not men among us given to "smelling out" their fellows, and, under the pretext of some social offence, so embittering their victims' best friends that they stab and stab again with a virulence more deadly than poisoned steel? But it is a civilized medicine man, it is the assegai of the tongue and public press.

All these grave concerns, the writer then discloses, were brought home on a "peaceful, Lancashire country town Sunday" during a dinner table conversation with choir director Letty that pressed on him the notion that the answer to all his doubts was knowledge. And thus, after more causerie and all manner of disparaging anecdotes about the Boers and the annexation of the Transvaal, the article launches into the descriptive part quoted above. It finally ends on a note of optimism which, in the context of the feverishly racist and jingoist climate of the 1890s, must be read as a well-intentioned attempt to rescue the mid-Victorian civilizing mission. The natives, Scopes concludes, "constitute a living band of witnesses as to the power of Christian civilization on the raw material of African humanity."

> The better one knows these men and women the narrower seems to be the gulf between our high civilization and the low barbaric life which they are supposed to represent.

The call for the maximization of knowledge and the integrity of the channels of communication came at a time when late-Victorian society had lost precisely its absolute confidence in the possibility of positive knowledge. Scientists were among the first to articulate such doubts. It was new disciplines such as thermodynamics that dismantled comprehensive mechanical worldviews and that raised serious doubts about the knowability of the world. Entropy, the gradual disintegration of closed systems into increasing disorder, became a metaphor for the random and arbitrary character of all knowledge and even of social life itself (Myers).

For many late-Victorians, as Thomas Richards has shown, what the entropy of the universe really meant was the end of the British Empire. As early as 1884, in a lecture aptly entitled "The Storm-Cloud of the Nineteenth Century," no less a person than Ruskin had perceived a storm gathering over the head of Britons, a menace that would not so much bring about the sudden death of empire than its slow entropy in an amorphous flow of events governed by the laws of chance and statistics, a process which Richards calls "order by fluctuation." "The empire of England," Ruskin closed his lecture, "on which formerly the sun never set, has become one on which he never rises" (qtd. in Richards, *Imperial Archive* 87).

As much as thermodynamics may have shattered the belief in the possibility of a comprehensive system of knowledge, control over knowledge continued to be the single, most widely believed foundation of modern society and, in fact, of the state itself. Knowledge was inconceivable without the state just as the question of the state was a question of knowledge. In short, as Richards puts it, "the integrity of the channels of external communication was essential to the welfare of the Empire" (*Imperial Archive* 74). Beyond this, the transformation of the public sphere of the eighteenth century into a site of and for the spectacle was the primary process that redefined the relationship between power and knowledge. Through a network of public spaces like museums and world fairs and such events as the concerts of the African Choir, the disjointed data—the evidence of difference—could be reunited and through them the waning confidence in some notion of an overarching order of things rekindled. The center of all these rituals of empire, however, was the commodity and through it, a new way of looking at the world. It is this strange osmosis of the commodity and the gaze that we must now examine.

THE ORGANIZATION OF THE VIEW

Much research has been undertaken in recent years to unravel the logic and historical genesis of consumer society. Expanding on Marx's notion of commodity fetishism, Benjamin's concept of the wish-image, and other critical approaches to capitalist commodity production, scholars have demonstrated that modern consumer society is essentially a social order in which the commodity becomes, as Jean Baudrillard puts it, "a total *medium*, as a *system of communication* administering all social exchange" (*Critique* 146). But more than the fact that things govern social interaction, what characterizes consumer society is how objects come to occupy social life in such a way that the whole society is turned into a stage for the fictions it has created for its commodities. In short, to use Guy Debord's famous formulation, modern capitalist society is a "society of the spectacle," an order that concentrates all attention, all consciousness, on the act of seeing the commodity (12).

The historical roots of this society lie deep in the nineteenth century. Almost one hundred years before the countries of advanced capitalism became regarded as consumer societies, the "Great Exhibition of the Industry of All Nations" at London's Crystal Palace in 1851 had inaugurated the cultural forms of consumerism. Long before the economies of the West had begun to produce a vast surplus of goods, this first world's fair had illustrated the fact that spectacle and capitalism, aesthetics and production, had become indivisible. As Thomas Richards writes in *The Commodity Culture of Victorian England: Advertising and Spectacle, 1851–1914*, by the second half of the nineteenth century the representation of the commodity had become an integral component of production. The spectacle of the commodity was no longer the distorted mirror of production: it was the capitalist *mode* of production. In other words, what the Crystal Palace exhibit prefigured was an economic regime that produces "signs, signs taken for wonders, signs signifying consumption" (16). And in doing so, Richards goes on to state, the exhibition further formulated the foundations of a semiotics of the commodity spectacle. It laid down the liturgical rules. Richards himself lists six such principles: an autonomous iconography for the object, the figuration of a consuming subject, the invention of the myth of the abundant society, and so on—by which the commodity was to be worshipped. Although the implications for the colonial world of this new semiotics of the commodity spectacle have not been fully explored, I have to limit myself here to two things. First, I am interested in the imperial dimension of these "giant new rituals of self-congratulation," as Eric Hobsbawm calls them (*Capital* 32). Second, I want to show how the production of signs as a global mode of production was paralleled by a production of differences and mirror images in a broad range of related spectacles and performance genres.

Four decades after the "Great Exhibition," world's fairs had expanded on an unprecedented scale, and by the time the Chicago fair of 1893 opened its gates, these spectacles had established themselves as something more than just celebrations of bourgeois power and "sites of pilgrimages to the commodity fetish" (Benjamin, *Gesammelte Schriften* 151). World's fairs in the age of empire had turned into major platforms of the global imagination on which the idea of empire, progress, and the commodity all appeared rolled into one. Total events of this sort were predicated upon carefully orchestrated stagings of spaces, global actors, and goods that spoke not so much of the world as it is as of how the West wished to perceive it.[2] Thus, the architectural design and site planning portrayed a humanity divided by "race"—a concept as deeply entrenched in popular Western consciousness as that of "progress"—and a world in which nations occupied fixed places determined by the host country. The layout of the Turkish quarter at the Universal Exposition of 1867 in Paris, to take but one representative example, was deliberately irregular to create an "authentic" and "picturesque appearance" that was in line with Western fantasies about the Orient (Çelik 61).

The goods on display, for their part, were the tangible expression of empire as an organized system of manufactured objects rather than as a set of social relations based upon domination and submission. Just as Mungo Park and his sponsors had envisaged it, commodities were to be bearers of the "civilizing mission," magically dissolving boundaries and local identities all by themselves. Along with cloth, mirrors, and clocks, soap especially was thought of as a kind of sesame yielding untold treasures and opening up vast empires: both spiritual ones in which outer cleanliness would signal a person's inner purity, and more worldly ones in which a healthy social body—like "national hygiene," a key euphemism for class hierarchy—was taken to be a consequence of personal hygiene. Furthermore, soap was also the key to a whole new form of racist ideology that Anne McClintock calls commodity racism (131–54; cf. Richards, *Commodity Culture*, chap. 3). Soap staged a global drama in which the Victorian home became the site for the production of racial difference and fantasies of imperial progress, while the colonial space in turn became domesticated.

Goods of non-Western origin were similarly pressed into service as part of a unitary landscape of discourse and practice, creating what Carol Breckenridge has called a Victorian ecumene; a new object-centered mythology of British global power. More particularly, as Breckenridge's analysis of Indian artifacts at world's fairs and other types of colonial collections nicely demonstrates, this new ecumene entailed more than a transformation of visual culture and a disciplining of the popular gaze. It also staged a whole typology and history of goods, technologies, and human bodies in which the colonies were said to represent an aesthetically imposing and yet outdated phase of universal evolution. Contrasting, for instance, the Indian and the American courts at the Crystal Palace exhibit, Breckenridge shows how India featured sumptuous technologies associated with feudal power—artisanal products such as weapons, jewels, and royal paraphernalia. The display of these objects foregrounded the human body in suggesting that the royal body that used them *was* the body politic rather than a private reality. The American display, by contrast—with its Morse telegraph, surgical instruments, and other implements—highlighted production and associated aesthetic technologies of practicality that required, but did not directly relate to, the human body. By elevating objects to ends in themselves, the American exhibit thus implicitly argued for a more rational, and hence superior, Western relationship to the world.

Lastly, the domesticated subjects themselves who were regularly displayed as an integral part of the proceedings in "colonial pavilions" or "native villages" were the most prized commodity of them all. Reduced to little more than living specimens, physical embodiments of the grand scheme of things, and beings produced by European imperial superiority, these flesh-and-bone images became mere stations on the revolving canvas of the imperial panorama.

Finally, along with all the contentment and imperial aplomb, these shows also provided the ideological cement needed to diminish domestic discontent and to contain radical mass action. Even if by that time very few visitors were able to afford the things on display, the sight of the amassed commodities served to rally the crowd of spectators behind the banner of progress and imperial expansion. While many commentators have been inclined to consider these and other manifestations of "social imperialism" as propaganda and a deliberate strategy on the part of the ruling classes "to address the masses" (Hobsbawm, *Empire* 105–106), more recent research indicates that this form of social engineering was inherent in the logic of the commodity spectacle itself. For the masses did not only gaze at the spectacle, they also looked at themselves. For the first time, the spectacle of mass production made the crowd feel as a unity, as an audience reveling in the glory of its own centrality. And thus there resulted from the combined effects of commodity fetishism and the new strategy of manufacturing popular consent what Eric Hobsbawm has called a "common frame of social psychology," a specifically imperial form of popular global imagination that bound together the Royal Tournament and the illuminations on the seafront of Blackpool, Queen Victoria, and the Kodak girl (*Empire* 106; cf. MacKenzie).

Another major form of public culture concerned with the entangled visions of Europe and its colonial subjects was the series of exotic shows introduced to the British public early in the nineteenth century. Of the Africans displayed in these spectacles, one Sara Baartman, touring England and France as the "Hottentot Venus," gained a particularly pitiable reputation. Afflicted with steatopygia and excessively developed genitalia, the South African woman became the object of much speculation about Africans' place in the "great chain of being" (Lindfors, Altick). A similar response awaited a troupe of "Zulu Kafirs" that visited London in 1853, and several others following them. But no matter how many Africans came to England, what the British public was able to see in such shows was anything but Africans. By the mid-nineteenth century, Africa, as a concept and object of Western knowledge, had been elaborated as part of the making of Europe's self-consciousness, and was shaped by a cascade of narratives and other discourses of difference in which the continent had served as the symbolic antithesis to the main tenets of liberal, enlightened Europe. Thus, rendering such spectacles of African bodies up to metropolitan public scrutiny not only defined, once and for all, African identities in terms of what knowledge the West produced about them. These shows also organized the procedures and modes by which vast sectors of metropolitan society were to consume the "African" as thing, as something that could be experienced—touched, seen, smelled—by the unleashed senses of bourgeois panoramic apperception.

Another form of nineteenth-century popular culture expressed these fantasies about the Dark Continent and black people generally perhaps even more glaringly: the blackface minstrel theater. Probably no mode of representation took the white imagination of Africa and the black "race" to greater popularity and more grotesquely distorted forms than the songs and sketches of the "burnt-cork" show. Closely connected with slavery, the minstrel theater had emerged in the United States at the beginning of the nineteenth century, and by the mid-1800s had come to occupy a central position in the popular cultural practices of North America and throughout the British Empire (Toll, Lorimer). Although minstrel shows contributed significantly to racist and imperialist discourse and provided the single most important source of "knowledge" about black people, their main impact on nineteenth-century ideology lay in the way in which their racial stereotypes reinforced core fantasies of Victorian society about itself and, as Eric Lott has argued, conveyed a sense of "how precariously nineteenth-century white people lived their own whiteness" (23–50). Within the British context, for instance, the pastoralism of plantation songs and scenes aimed not so much at depicting happy darkies relishing their bondage than at celebrating the sweet joys of a rural life long lost in a country in which the majority of the population lived in cities (Pickering). Similarly, the two classic roles of the ragged Jim Crow and the slick Zip Coon spoke of the division between town and country in industrial England, just as much as the portrayal in minstrel shows of sensuous, aggressive, and boisterous blacks set up a radical contrast to the dour piety and reserve of Victorian respectability (Pickering 214).

Needless to say, Africans in South Africa, too, had acquired detailed knowledge about Europeans, given the latter's long-standing presence and dominance in South Africa itself. And ironically, it was again minstrelsy that served as the principal medium of cross-cultural imagination and self-definition. English and American minstrel troupes had been touring South Africa from as early as the 1850s, and throughout the latter half of the century most South African towns —including Kimberley of course—had a thriving amateur minstrel scene (Erlmann, *African Stars* 30–32; Malan 366–68). Blacks soon absorbed the format and aesthetic of the minstrel stage so that by the 1890s most mission schools (but possibly not Lovedale) sponsored their own minstrel performances. Thus, the aesthetics of the minstrel stage not only enabled whites to fantasize about blacks, but in turn also helped blacks to define themselves in opposition to whites. Because the constrained conditions of imperial rule restricted black parody of white behavior to more hidden means of expression, Africans often had few alternatives other than manipulating the representations whites had created of them. Although much of this cross-cultural trafficking of images and fictions of race remains obscure at this stage, one figure of the minstrel stage seems to have been particularly crucial in providing a template for such re-inscriptions. In one of the many ironic twists of the global, interracial imagination, black South Africans transformed the "coon," the fashion-conscious, urban, emancipated black male, into a hero. Beginning in the 1920s urbanizing Zulu-speaking migrant workers reworked the songs and dances associated with the minstrel stage into their own distinct blend of modern "town" music called *isikhunzi* (Erlmann, *Nightsong*). As crucial and counterhegemonic as such African attempts at the definition of a positive self-identity may have been, it is this promiscuous mix of mirror images that made up the consolidated symbolic world of the empire. And it was this peculiar racial unconscious of the world's fair, the exotic show, and the minstrel stage that not only formulated their own grammar, but also produced new modes of perception, new regimes of visuality.

Two types of colonial spectacle—the colonial exhibition as such and the missionary exhibition—illustrate this well. The epitome of the first of these spectacles, one that had barely closed its doors before the arrival of the African

Choir, was the Stanley and African Exhibition of 1890. In that year Henry M. Stanley had returned from central Africa, where he had led a "private" expedition ostensibly to "rescue" Emin Pasha, the British empire's Governor of Equatoria. It was primarily because of such ventures and the publication of Stanley's best-selling books *Through the Dark Continent* (1878) and *In Darkest Africa* (1890) that the *Times*, no doubt echoing the popular mood of the time, was able to proclaim that "Africa in one or other of its phases is on everybody's mind and in everybody's mouth" (qtd. in Coombes 3). As for the content of the show, the organizers—representatives of the British aristocracy and middle class with vested interests in Africa—had put particular emphasis on the philanthropic and humanitarian aspect of Stanley's mission and of imperial expansion as such. As the catalog of the exhibition put it:

> Frightful wrongs to be wiped out, deeds of high surprise to be achieved, virgin countries to be commercially exploited, valuable scientific discoveries to be made, myriads of people steeped in the grossest idolatry . . . these are some of the varied elements which have thrown a glamour and fascination over Africa and taken men's minds captive. (Qtd. in Coombes 81)

We wince, to be sure. Yet when such exhibitions are compared with the second type of colonial spectacle—shows depicting the "mission field"—the differences concern rhetoric rather than subject matter and ideology. If we follow Annie E. Coombes's careful analysis, the roots of these events can be traced to ethnographic collections belonging to missionary societies—the London Missionary Society, a mission enormously active in southern Africa, was among the first to establish a museum for its own ethnographic collection—but it was only after 1882 that missionary exhibitions became regular events promoting the activities of various missions (Coombes 161–86). Often these events were designed to demonstrate the African's skill as a manufacturer, and thereby had to be seen as part of a broader strategy of gaining government support for the growing number of technical and "industrial" schools the missionary societies were setting up throughout Africa. At the same time, missionary exhibits disseminated a more benign image of Africa and the African that carefully cultivated a distinctive, though by no means uninterested, position on the colonial enterprise. Of course, the strategy was a contradictory one in that it declared that imperial conquest and the redemption of the African for the "civilizing mission" were not irreconcilable projects. But because they made no effort at concealing these contradictions, Coombes concludes, such events were "distinct, both in kind and in degree, to their colonial counterpart." Because of the benevolent character of the missionary shows, they were spectacles "of a very different nature" in which the African, though a spectacle, could still be differentiated from the African displayed at the colonial exhibition.

Perhaps they were, perhaps not. While there is certainly an element of truth in this regarding the *objects* being depicted at these exhibits, the available evidence might equally suggest a more complicated and simultaneously more uniform picture in relation to the viewing *subjects*. For both types of exhibitions rested on the same aesthetic of the panorama and simulation. And like the world's fairs, both were important arenas for the figuration of the global consumer. Modeled, for instance, in the image of "virgin countries" passively waiting to be explored, and offering the visitor through simulated forests and an explorer's camp the experience of finding "himself" "in the heart of Africa," the Stanley exhibit actually turned the spectator into an actor in the drama of world politics. Likewise, missionary exhibits constructed a sphere of tacit complicity with the imperial project by putting the visitor in a mediating position between Africans demonstrating their potential for "development" and the imperial powers. The difference between both types of spectacle, then, was probably one of degree rather than substance in that they appealed to different strands of British imperial ideology and staged different roles for the visitors: a distanced position vis-à-vis "myriads of people steeped in idolatry" in the colonial show, and a more engaging and mediating one in the missionary exhibit.

I have dwelt at length on a number of global spectacles because they lead us directly to an aspect of modern consciousness that only becomes clear once it gains *global form*. For, I repeat, there is a good deal more to the drama of the commodity than mere social control or the production of exotic identities. The world's fair and other associated forms of public culture such as the colonial exhibit and the minstrel show, I would argue, reveal what Stephan Oettermann has recognized as one of the chief dialectical configurations of nineteenth-century panoramic consciousness. Like the panorama—which, after all, formed one of the main attractions featured at world's fairs—these forms of public culture not only liberated and directed the ascendancy to global dominance of the bourgeois gaze, they also incarcerated it again (9). Together, world's fairs, colonial shows, and missionary exhibits not only conjured up fantasies of a human cosmos in movement, dreams of what Jean Baudrillard calls an infinitely expandable "perspectivist space." They also attempted to close up again the space of being and evolution by confining the probing gaze that had produced these total vistas of space and time in the first place (Benjamin, *Passagen-Werk* 238). As a result, they ended up creating the spectacle of a society that was not only global, but whose very spherical, centripetal structure also prevented it from seeing itself. By closing up the horizon to a *tableau vivant* and by populating it with objects and subjects to be contemplated from the center, all these different types of world spectacle inaugurated a scopic regime in which the bourgeois vision ultimately ended up seeing only that with which it had encircled itself.

Furthermore, the nature of knowledge and the idea of truth as such in turn also came to be reshaped by the world's fair–type spectacles. While the panoramic gaze may have piled up all around itself enormous quantities of pieces of reality and neatly arranged these into a total prospect, by the late nineteenth century it became clear that there was no longer a center for all these bits of knowledge. Thus, while celebrating an immensely widened universe of people, signs, and goods, these universal rituals of autohypnosis also effectively masked the sharpening crisis of the imperial knowledge that was to unite all this immense diversity under one system of communication. Troubled by the blurred boundaries of order and chaos, fact and fiction, world's fairs inaugurated a type of hypnotic, inward-turning autism that characterizes the societies of late capitalism to this day. While it may be true, as Michel Foucault has consistently argued, that this social order is rather one of surveillance in which "the play of signs defines the anchorages of power" (217), I would add that what the panoptic view lays bare is everything there is; the world that opens up before it is not the real world, but a world made for visual consumption, a world of commodity images. In the early world exhibitions, a world was beginning to take shape in which images mediate all social existence, in which the world is not put on exhibit, but rather grasped as though it were an exhibition.

A similar view is taken in Timothy Mitchell's fascinating account of the colonization and representation of Egypt in nineteenth-century world's fairs and colonial politics. World's fairs, Mitchell argues, did not so much exhibit the world as engineer a particular relationship between the individual and a world conceived and grasped as though it were an exhibition. What resulted from these events was not just a new vista of the Orient, but a world rendered up to the individual according to the way in which it could be set up before him or her as an exhibit. The colonial nature of the nineteenth-century world's fairs thus consisted less in their celebration of the global hegemony of Western economic and political power than in their redefinition of the nature of knowledge. What was to be rendered in them was the idea of the "world-as-exhibition," the fact that truth was to rest on what Heidegger called "the certainty of representation" (Mitchell 13).

Egyptian visitors to Europe and to the French Expositions Universelles of the 1860s to 1880s, for instance, found this obsession with the visual to be the single most important aspect of the West. "One of the characteristics of the French is to stare and get excited at everything new," an Egyptian scholar wrote in the 1820s. Other Egyptian travellers, writing later in the century, frequently commented upon themselves becoming the object of European curiosity, and spent much time and energy describing the panoramas and dioramas and the phenomenon of *le spectacle* generally (for which they knew of no Arabic equivalent). All these technologies of the spectacular revealed a European preoccupation with, as one Middle Eastern author put it toward the end of the nineteenth century, *intizam al-manzar*, the organization of the view. The significance of these glimpses of the West from outside becomes particularly apparent when set in relation to prevailing Western assumptions about an alleged lack of curiosity among Asians, assumptions which suggest that staring and the intellectual curiosity that it is said to express are simply the unfettered relation of a person to the world. Yet Mitchell is right to point out that, read against the background of what the Middle Eastern writers of the nineteenth century found to be an unnatural European behavior, the Western way of addressing the world, far from being based upon rationality, entails "a certain theology of its own" (2–5, 12).

The question of modern Western theologies evokes of course Marx's famous phrase about the "theological whims" of the commodity and provides another interesting point of convergence with the South African ethnographic evidence. As Mitchell notes, the irony in Marx's theory of commodity fetishism was that while it claimed the power of capitalism to rest on the phantasmagoric misrepresentation of the actual social relations that produced alienation in the first place, it left representation itself unquestioned. Marx—and with him numerous theorists of media consumption and popular culture who followed—accepted absolutely the distinction between a realm of representations and something called external reality. Yet at the same time, they failed to examine "the novelty of continuously creating the effect of an 'external reality' as itself a mechanism of power" (Mitchell 18–19). They could not see that, as Debord nicely sums it all up, the spectacle of the commodity "is the very heart of society's real unreality" (13).

By now it should be clear that the whole point about the "theology" of modernity and its celebration in colonial spectacles—be they world's fairs or concerts by "native choirs"—was the question of the "certainty of representation." In a period of growing doubts about the empiricist foundations of the late-Victorian global imagination, colonial spectacles fabricated an order of knowledge, a system of objective truths validating, and in turn being validated by, an idea of subject and object as two distinct realms of reality. In an age of collapsing mechanical world models, colonial spectacles set up a frame of truly global dimensions in which European consumers were able to fancy themselves as what Max Weber called "cultural beings" who "take a deliberate attitude toward the world and lend it significance" (256). The result of this was a perfectly closed world: the order and security of colonialism rested on the certainty of this distinction, while in turn the unassailability of the society of the spectacle depended on colonialism. Projects such as the African Choir, to finally return to our South African story, not only highlighted the considerable contradictions inherent in the missionary cause and the impossibility of reconciling in the 1890s the worldly strand of imperialist realpolitik with the politics of sub-jugation under the Cross. More significantly, through them the Western specta-tors took up their deliberate posture and figuratively associated the object world with other spaces, other times, unfamiliar to the inquiring subject and yet fa-miliar to it at the same time.

In the remainder of this essay I shall focus on dress and dramaturgy as crucial sites for staging the spectacle of imperial space and time and for elabo-rating and, at the same time, contesting the typology of race and progress as quintessential tropes for ordering knowledge in a time of waning certainties.

"AFRICA CIVILIZED AND UNCIVILIZED"

The African Choir, as we have seen from the *Ludgate Monthly* review, performed the first half of the program donned in "native" dress but wore sober Victorian dress in the second half—quite literally illustrating, as the *Irish Times* had it, "Africa Civilized and Uncivilized" (15 March 1892). When word about this sartorial scheme leaked back to South Africa, Lovedale missionaries immediately denounced the wearing of *karosses* as "mischievous" and "bar-barian," blaming the managers for this decision and claiming that none of the choristers had ever worn it at home. "This costume would do occasionally," the *Christian Express* fretted, "but it is a mistake otherwise, and physically and morally dangerous." Morija missionary H. Dieterlen chimed in, charging that the singers had "exposed themselves" to the Europeans. Choir manager Edwin Howell, as manager of London's famous vaudeville Alhambra Theatre well-versed in matters concerning gaudy dress, promptly refuted the charge, arguing that "the decision as to dress was not solely the act of the Managers, but the natives themselves were consulted and approved of the dress worn in every particular." And, he added, "they simply wear their skins over their ordinary clothing. . . . On many occasions when the Managers wished it otherwise, they preferred appearing with bare feet."[3]

Such quibbles over skins and footwear may appear as rather trivial to us. In the nineteenth century, however, such arguments over clothing, costumes, and the moral dangers of wearing animal skins bespoke a whole world view, a complacent metropolitan discourse about morals and markets, spiritual salva-tion and social distinctions. From the first, European missionaries, already promi-nent interlocutors in this discourse at home, made clothing one of the most morally charged mediums of their message. By restyling the outer shell of the "heathen," they reasoned, they would reform and salvage the inner self of the newly converted.

But the missionary project of bodily reform was not as simple as it may seem. Nor was it passively received by those who were to become the object of reform. The nature of capitalist commodity aesthetics makes dress and fashion major and complex arenas for the retooling, not only of individual identities, but also of culture itself as meaningful practice. Formerly, social life and the place within it of things and objects such as clothing constituted a world whose order was not one of appearance or of a systematically coded linkage between things. This was a world in which things and bodies entered into a variety of associations with each other that, while certainly being richly expressive and (*pace* Max Weber) culturally saturated, were not mediated by signs. Thus these associations did not form a code separate from the things themselves, and hence, the idea of knowledge as a code or system of meanings to be applied to the material world did not exist. Nor did, correspondingly, the notion of a thing *per se* occur. In a sense, there was no "nature" (and hence no "natural body")— the great signified through which the enlightened subject and its codes of operational finality came to be in the first place (Baudrillard, *Mirror* 54). What was there, by contrast, were social relations that worked through numerous and complex concatenations of sameness and difference permeating the world (Mitchell 61). Similarly, the relationship between a piece of clothing and the body that it covered was not primarily mediated by some dualism between a signifier and its signified. Rather, by wearing a certain item of clothing a person became part of a field of practice in which the bodies, physical and social, and the garment as "social skin" mutually actualized and inscribed each other without either of them being the primary source of meaning.

The rise of the commodity and, more specifically in our case, of the European textile industry changed all that. It not only restructured the relations of production of India, Egypt, the southern United States, and a host of other cotton-growing regions, but also created new patterns of consumption within Europe itself and, within this redesigned landscape of social relations, production, and consumption, it brought about a new sense of corporeality and bodily sensation and, in fact, of what it meant to have a body. As the work of John and Jean Comaroff on concepts of work and labor among the Tshidi Barolong of South Africa has shown, the colonized subjects increasingly came to experience wage labor as a gradual weakening of the idea of work as the primary measure of personal value (155–80). Instead, industrial labor required the physical operation and interaction of bodies increasingly cut loose from any referentiality in nature. At the same time, the domestic sphere ceased to be a place where the body might reside for itself. The "house," the quintessential atom of the social universe, has become no more than a site of consumption, severed from the direct appropriation of the earth and physically segregated from the sphere of production: the mines and the factories. And it is this contradiction between production and consumption that mutilates the body. The distance of the body from the workplace only generates more need and the necessity to return to work in order to satisfy it. Unable to find a home, the body "roams" in a never-ending pursuit of satiation. Unleashed and abandoned to its devices, it eventually comes to be perceived as an afflicted, homeless thing whose pathology in turn indicates the disturbed social order.

If, then, in the final analysis, capitalist production reduced the body to a status as thing, it was through this process of reification that the body was able to enter the drama of signification. Disconnected from the web of echoes, traces, and similarities that made up the pre-industrial world, the body acquired significance. It became the object of a new regime of signs that were contained, ordered, and codified in the commodities used to clothe it. Commodity relations create a world in which symbols take over the role of things in the sense that order and meaning come to wholly depend on the introduction of a distinction between signifiers and signified, a division in which the body becomes a mere referent for the commodified images of itself. Bodily experience becomes veiled behind an endless array of images to be gazed at. Ultimately, then, what commodity production altered was signification. Or, better still, modern industrial society reorganized the creation of meaningful life, which had formerly arisen out of specific contexts of practice, by subjecting the relationship between things and bodies, mind and matter, to Weber's "deliberate posture." What emerged from the mid-nineteenth century, then, was a consolidated regime of spectacular signs in which clothes, signs taken for wonders, were to conjure up total visions of being itself.

Although it is difficult to ascertain whether and to what extent the members of our two choirs shared their Egyptian predecessors' sense of European "spectatorial lust," the failure of the choirs and the conflicts that contributed to them would seem to suggest that it was particularly in terms of seeing and being seen that Britons and South Africans developed conflicting and yet mutually implicated notions of modernity and world order. One aspect of the performances where this can be clearly seen at work is the use of dress as a metonymic gesture, as a spectacle within the spectacle. For the whole point about the "native" dress was precisely to illustrate how much Victorian models of "universal history" and the chorister's own personal history coincided, thanks to the "civilizing mission." The change from native dress to Victorian clothing in the two parts of the performance was to be a serious demonstration in progress of the progressive history of their wearers.

This allegoric device—very common in nineteenth-century representations of progress—was complemented by and in a sense even depended on another metonymic strategy by which an unknown and chaotic outside world came to

Fig. 4.1. "Africa Civilized." The African Choir, 1891.

Fig. 4.2. "Africa Uncivilized." The African Choir, 1891.

be organized as a "reality" available for objective scrutiny and classification. The photographs of the African Choir in figs. 4.1 and 4.2 show this quite clearly. While the symmetrical positioning of the choir for the camera in fig. 4.2 conforms to the standard Victorian format, and as such is clearly reminiscent of the "trophy" method in museum displays of foreign implements and weapons (typically framed by two Europeans), the garments displayed in this and the other photograph (fig. 4.1) convey a similar message of difference. Foremost among these items were woolen blankets such as the one donned by several women. Blending Western forms of fashion with some modified, indigenous form of apparel, these blankets are themselves the key vehicles and symbols of the entanglement of local communities with the world economy. And, as we shall see in due course, they were the means to protest an order that relegated them to the status of exotic specimens.

By the late nineteenth century, industrially manufactured blankets had largely replaced skin cloaks and similar kinds of precolonial overdress throughout Southern Africa. Two major differences, however, can be observed in the way in which these items were combined with other forms of European attire and, more important perhaps, in the social position of their wearers. Thus, by the second half of the nineteenth century the term "blanket" had already become firmly integrated into the lexicon of Southern Nguni as the designation of rural non-Christians that distinguished them from Christianized "school" people. The other major difference concerns the gender-marked use of blankets. Although men—and here especially the migrant workers—increasingly exchanged blankets for precolonial garb and extravagantly interchanged these with European clothes, it was women whose changing position in colonial society was increasingly becoming associated with woolen blankets. Although, on the face of it, they were transformations of precolonial skin aprons and cloaks and, as such, in time became key emblems in a sort of generic Southern African "folk costume," the blankets were anything but a sign of the "conservativism" South African men like to see in their womenfolk. In reality, as the work of John and Jean Comaroff has demonstrated, blankets and headscarves were the product and visible sign of a very "modern" process: of the feminization of the countryside, in the course of which "native" women were made into guardians of the rural homestead and into premodern counterparts of European women, set apart from modern centers of production in increasingly devalued rural and domestic enclaves (43).

Apart from the blankets, the photographs reveal one further marker of "native" identity: the ostrich feathers and the beadwork sported by some of the men; the bracelets of some of the women; the leopard skins worn by the Manye sisters, Josiah Semouse, and some of the other male performers; and most prominent perhaps and somewhat incongruous, the tiger skin and head on the floor. The point about "native" identity is worth noting, because this was precisely what the choir's entire appearance was meant to represent. Thus, choir manager Howell may not have been too far off the mark when he suggested that the choir was not wearing the dress "as in Africa." Rather, what some of the singers were wearing was a sign of what, in the imperial lexicon of the late nineteenth century, was taken for Africa.

Beyond this, the "native" dress was a form of representation that at once familiarized and distanced. As an allegory, by making the part stand for the whole, it made "Africa" familiar and knowable. Yet the same leopard skin, as a generic type of "African" clothing, distanced its users from a specific locale and tradition, and in doing so, substituted representation for historical practice. Ultimately, of course, this strange oscillation rested on a type of knowledge and on an "organization of the view" that could only have been possible as a result of the Western modern preoccupation with objects and their significance (Stewart 139–45).

Interestingly, the photographs discussed also reveal certain elements in the sartorial scheme of the African Choir that are at odds with these rhetorical devices of familiarity and distance. For in these pictures we see the actors playing with difference in unforeseen ways that seem to hint at the possibility of reversing the received subject-object relationship of the colonial order. Note, for instance, that the beadwork worn by some of the women, but most notably by Charlotte Manye on the far right, strongly resembles English jewelry of the day. Similarly, Eleanor Xiniwe (seated in the center) appears to be wearing some sort of Western gown. Even more important than this outright appropriation of the coded commodities of empire is the bricolage of Victorian and "African" sartorial elements in some of the women's couture. This bricolage could mean several things. First, there is the possibility, strongly hinted at by Howell's statement, that the performers, like many other Africans involved in the emerging international show business, "knowingly exploited a presentation of self and identity which reappropriated and transformed anticipated western assumptions about the African and Africa and which was calculated to have a particular effect in Britain" (Coombes 107–108).

Second, black women in South Africa were never simply the passive consumers of foreign goods made available by the new global market. Although a strangely concocted costume fixed them in a marginal and premodern position as "folk," it is precisely through such a costume that women like Charlotte Manye and Eleanor Xiniwe may have expressed, as the Comaroffs have written of women elsewhere in Southern Africa, an "aura of independence and reserve": a "locally-tooled identity" that, while it might have made them hostage to a newly politicized "tradition," also "spoke of an attempt to limit their dependency on the market" (51–52).

Finally, the rapid decay of African independent power and the ensuing radicalization of the 1880s led some African intellectuals to reexamine the "heathen" past and to tentatively explore other expressive media in which to articulate their growing uneasiness with the imperial variant of modernity. A decade later, as liberals in the Eastern Cape began to turn to chiefs and headmen as agents of social control, spectacles of "tribal" culture—although still shunned by the missionaries—were no longer solely regarded as "heathenish" and, at the same time, came to be accepted as more than mere folklore.

In conclusion, clothes were an immensely ambiguous symbolic terrain that could serve quite varied intellectual and political projects. At the very least, the story of the African Choir and the role of "spectatorial lust" in their performances illustrate how deeply the imperial order and the global imagination of Africans and Europeans were intertwined with the "spectatorial lust" of commodity production and the society of the spectacle.

NOTES

1. For full details, see: *Imvo Zabantsundu*, 14 and 21 Jan. 1892; *Christian Express*, 1 Feb., 1 March, 1 Aug., 1 Nov. 1892; *Cape Mercury*, 22 March 1892; *Review of Reviews*, Sept. 1892; *South Africa*, 18 June 1892.

2. A substantial amount of literature on world's fairs has become available in recent years. Among the best accounts I have found are Çelik, Greenhalg, and Rydell.

3. *Christian Express* 2 Nov. 1891: 170; *Leselinyana* 1 Dec. 1892; *Christian Express* 1 March 1892: 35.

WORKS CITED

Altick, Richard D. *The Shows of London*. Cambridge: Harvard UP, 1978.
Baudrillard, Jean. *For a Critique of the Political Economy of the Sign*. St. Louis: Telos Press, 1981.
———. *The Mirror of Production*. St. Louis: Telos Press, 1975.
Benjamin, Walter. *Gesammelte Schriften*. Band 2, 1. Frankfurt am Main: Suhrkamp, 1989.
———. *Das Passagen-Werk: Français*. Paris: Editions du Cerf, 1989.
Breckenridge, Carol. "The Aesthetics and Politics of Colonial Collecting: India at World Fairs." *Comparative Studies in Society and History* 31.2 (1989): 195–216.
Çelik, Zeynep. *Displaying the Orient: Architecture of Islam at Nineteenth-Century World's Fairs*. Berkeley: U of California P, 1992.
Comaroff, John, and Jean Comaroff. *Ethnography and the Historical Imagination*. Boulder: Westview, 1992.
———. "Fashioning the Colonial Subject: The Empire's Old Clothes." Unpublished ms.
Coombes, Annie E. *Reinventing Africa: Museums, Material Culture and Popular Imagination in Late Victorian and Edwardian England*. New Haven: Yale UP, 1994.
Debord, Guy. *The Society of the Spectacle*. New York: Zone Books, 1994.
Erlmann, Veit. *African Stars: Studies in Black South African Performance*. Chicago: U of Chicago P, 1984.

———. *Nightsong: Performance, Power and Practice in South Africa.* Chicago: U of Chicago P, 1996.

Foucault, Michel. *Discipline and Punish: The Birth of the Prison.* New York: Vintage, 1979.

Greenhalgh, Paul. *Ephemeral Vistas: The Expositions Universelles, Great Exhibitions and World's Fairs, 1851–1939.* Manchester: Manchester UP, 1988.

Haggard, Rider. "A Zulu War Dance." *Gentleman's Magazine* July-Sept. 1877: 96–107.

Hobsbawm, Eric. *The Age of Capital, 1848–1875.* London: Weidenfeld and Nicolson, 1975.

———. *The Age of Empire, 1875–1914.* New York: Pantheon, 1987.

Hobson, John A. *Imperialism: A Study.* Ann Arbor: U of Michigan P, 1965.

Lindfors, Bernth. "The Hottentot Venus and Other African Attractions in Nineteenth-Century England." *Australasian Drama Studies* 1.2 (1982): 83–104.

Lorimer, Douglas A. "Bibles, Banjoes and Bones: Images of the Negro in the Popular Culture of Victorian England." *In Search of the Visible Past: History Lectures at Wilfrid Laurier University 1973–1974.* Ed. Barry M. Gough. Waterloo, Ontario: Wilfrid /Laurier UP, 1975.

Lott, Eric. "Love and Theft: The Racial Unconscious of Blackface Minstrelsy." *Representations* 39 (1992): 23–50.

Lyotard, Jean-François. *Le postmodern expliqué aux enfants.* Paris: Editions Galilee, 1986.

MacKenzie, John M., ed. *Imperialism and Popular Culture.* Manchester: Manchester UP, 1986.

Malan, Jacques P., ed. *South African Music Encyclopedia.* Vol. 4. Cape Town: Oxford UP, 1986.

McClintock, Anne. "Soft-soaping Empire: Commodity Racism and Imperial Advertising." *Travellers' Tales: Narratives of Home and Displacement.* Ed. George Robertson et al. London: Routledge, 1994.

Mitchell, Timothy. *Colonising Egypt.* Cambridge: Cambridge UP, 1988.

Myers, Greg. "Nineteenth-Century Popularizations of Thermodynamics and the Rhetoric of Social Prophecy." *Energy and Entropy: Science and Culture in Victorian Britain.* Ed. Patrick Brantlinger. Bloomington: Indiana UP, 1989.

Oettermann, Stephan. *Das Panorama: Die Geschichte eines Massenmediums.* Frankfurt am Main: Syndikat, 1980.

Pickering, Michael. "Mock Blacks and Racial Mockery: The 'Nigger' Minstrel and British Imperialism." *Acts of Supremacy: The British Empire and the Stage, 1790–1930.* Ed. J. S. Bratton et al. Manchester: Manchester UP, 1991. 179–236.

Richards, Thomas. *The Commodity Culture of Victorian England: Advertising and Spectacle, 1851–1914.* Stanford: Stanford UP, 1990.

———. *The Imperial Archive: Knowledge and the Fantasy of Empire.* London: Verso, 1993.

Rydell, Robert W. *All the World's a Fair: Visions of Empire at American International Expositions, 1876–1916.* Chicago: U of Chicago P, 1985.

Scopes, E. Gowing. "African Music." *Ludgate Monthly* Dec. 1891: 107–12.

Shepherd, R. H. W. *Lovedale South Africa, 1824–1955.* Lovedale: Lovedale Press, 1971.

Stewart, Susan. *On Longing: Narratives of the Miniature, the Gigantic, the Souvenir, the Collection.* Baltimore: Johns Hopkins UP, 1984.

Toll, Robert. *Blacking Up: The Minstrel Show in Nineteenth-Century America.* New York: Oxford UP, 1974.

Weber, Max. "'Objectivity' in Social Science." *Sociological Writings.* Ed. Wolf Heydebrand. New York: Continuum, 1994. 248–59.

"Darkest Africa"
African Shows at America's World's Fairs, 1893–1940

ROBERT W. RYDELL

In the centre of the enclosure is the theatre, if such can be called a large, open shed, unwalled, with thatched roof and floor of rough planking. Here is the strangest sight among all the spectacular wonders of the plaisance. At one end are grouped the musicians, all of the Dahomeans, all lean and lank, and all supremely hideous. . . . It is in truth a barbaric spectacle, and the more so as many of the performers are women, the amazons of western Africa, trained for the service of the king and esteemed as the choicest of his troops.[1] —Hubert Howe Bancroft, *The Book of the Fair*

Beginning with the 1893 Chicago World's Columbian Exposition and continuing through the world's fairs of the 1930s, representations of Africa and Africans were prominent features at American world's fairs. So interwoven were fairs and African shows that by the beginning of the twentieth century it was difficult to imagine a world's fair without some kind of display featuring Africans.[2] By the close of the 1930s, however, a subtle shift had occurred. American fairs continued to represent Africa, but not with Africans. What happened?

In broad outline, my argument can be previewed as follows. At America's Victorian-era fairs, African exhibits served the purpose of ideological repair, serving to hasten the process of American national reconciliation at the expense of people of color, especially African Americans. In the words of the caption to one illustration of an African woman featured on display on the Chicago fair's Midway Plaisance, slavery had "not been an unmixed blessing." With their emphasis on the savagery and backwardness of Africans, African shows reinforced this message. At fairs held during the Great Depression, shows representing Africa continued to foster images that lent legitimacy to segregation, but their primary emphasis shifted to provide support for American economic penetration of the African continent. Earlier images of "savagery" did not disappear. Rather, these images were refashioned to support the central tenets of modernization theory, especially the conviction that "development" along Western lines was in the best interests of Africans and Americans alike. By the close of the 1930s, the easiest way to imagine African "development" was to imagine a continent without Africans or to envision a continent with African laborers working for American corporations. These were precisely the representational strategies adopted by the promoters of the 1939 New York World's Fair. But the story of African shows at world's fairs, as much as it is a story of representation *and* ideological innovation within burgeoning visions of American empire, is not quite as seamless as it might appear. Through their performances, Africans put on display at America's fairs often rewrote scripts and turned showcases of empire into theaters of resistance.[3]

African shows at American fairs did not appear out of thin air. They owed their existence to a world of popular entertainments increasingly shaped by the active intervention of anthropologists. Indeed, ever since George Cuvier had dissected the genitalia of the "Hottentot Venus" in 1815, European anthropologists had developed a positive passion for exhibiting Africans. The reasons for this commitment to the exhibition medium were twofold. First, anthropologists sought to wed their profession to specific national, imperial ambitions and thereby demonstrate their usefulness to the state. Second, they sought to educate the public about the applicability of social Darwinian insights to social struggle at home and imperial expansion abroad. Nowhere in Europe did that passion bear more fruit than in France, especially in the ongoing displays at the Jardin d'Acclimatation that featured so-called native villages from Senegambia, western Sudan, and western Africa. The popularity of these villages inspired French anthropologists to become involved in one of the grandest colonial displays ever arranged—the exhibit of colonial villages at the 1889 Paris Universal Exposition, where the contrast between the dwellings of "savages" and Eiffel's monumental tower underscored the distance between "savagery" and "civilization."[4]

The financial and ideological successes of the colonial displays at the Paris fair fired the imagination of two generations of American exposition builders. Between the 1893 Chicago World's Columbian Exposition and the fairs held on the eve of America's entry into the First World War, American world's fairs had ethnological villages, many of which depicted Africans. The Dahomeyan Village at the 1893 Chicago fair set the standard (fig. 5.1).

This village was the brainchild of Xavier Pené, an amateur French geographer and professional labor contractor. Born in the early 1840s in France, Pené came of age along the west coast of Africa. Virtually nothing is known of his family or early years, except that he pinned his own future to developing

Fig. 5.1. "Xavier Pené [?] with Dahomeyan Villagers." From Trumbull White
and William Igleheart, *The World's Columbian Exposition, Chicago, 1893*
(Philadelphia and St. Louis, 1893), p. 581. Courtesy Department of Special
Collections, Henry Madden Library, California State University, Fresno.

Africa's resources, and established himself as an explorer and ivory trader. By
the early 1880s, he was also trading in human beings, running what one newspaper whimsically termed "an employment agency on a large scale." Specifically,
he supplied individuals of the Krooman tribe to French railroad interests constructing a railroad across the isthmus of Panama where, the newspaper assured its readers, the Africans "were fed and paid well, for unskilled labor, by
the contractors, and Mr. Pené got only fair compensation for his trouble in
engaging them." Perhaps because he believed his compensation was only fair,
perhaps because he determined wider markets could be found for African art
objects, perhaps because of his interest in African geography and ethnology, or,
most likely, because of some combination of all of these reasons together with
his knowledge of the spectacular success of the African villages at the 1889
Paris fair, Pené linked his fortunes to the emerging profession of imperial showmanship.[5]

In 1892, Pené travelled to Chicago and tried to persuade World's Columbian Exposition officials to award him an African village concession. As excited as they were about making living anthropology displays a leading feature of their fair, Chicago's exposition promoters were evidently nonplused by his proposal to construct an African village at the fair along the lines of the colonial shows that had been featured at the Paris exposition. To his surprise, exposition officials told him that since "negroes were no novelty in America" they had little reason to believe that the show would be successful. Despite this initial reaction, Pené persisted. He undoubtedly reminded exposition authorities of contemporary press coverage of the French wars in Dahomey and of Sir Richard Burton's earlier account of Dahomeyan women warriors, the fabled "Dahomeyan Amazons." Then Pené played his ace in the hole: the French government's enthusiasm for and tacit endorsement of his scheme. On 15 July 1892, the exposition directors reversed themselves and awarded Pené a contract for a concession that would have far-reaching consequences for American images of Africa.[6]

That these images would be carefully constructed and laden with ideological direction was clear from the start. The contract exposition that officials hammered out with Pené made clear that the village would be located on the Midway Plaisance, the mile-long appendage to the exposition that simultaneously functioned as a living ethnology museum and commercial strip. To satisfy the anthropological requirements of the midway, Pené agreed to construct an authentic, or "faithful," representation of a Dahomeyan village inhabited by at least sixty Dahomeyans, half of whom would be women, especially Amazon warriors. The contract also stipulated that the village include a "king or chief" and that the people on display agree to perform "military maneuvers," "modes of combat," and religious ceremonies on a daily basis. To satisfy the for-profit demands of the fair, the contract also mandated that the people on display agree to produce and sell gold and silver jewelry and that their wares, along with other "objects of curiosity," including works of art and various natural resources, be displayed and sold in a museum—really a colonial gift shop—that would be part of the village installation.[7]

Once he received the contract, Pené embarked immediately for Africa where he recruited sixty-seven individuals, four from the French Congo, four from French Guinea, and fifty-nine from Benin. For an eight-month commitment, the adults received 100 francs per month, and children—there were only two—half that amount. One adult, listed as a jeweler, received 160 francs each month, while another, listed as a chief and guide, received 150 francs for his help recruiting Pené's performing subjects.[8]

When they arrived at the fair, the Dahomeyans were put on display in a village setting that had been constructed at the end of the mile-long Midway

HE WAS NO CHICKEN.

Fig. 5.2. "He Was No Chicken." *World's Fair Puck*, no. 6 (1893): 73.
Courtesy Chicago Historical Society.

Plaisance by local Chicago laborers prior to the Dahomeyans' arrival. Placement of the village at a point far removed from the "civilized" splendor of the White City was hardly accidental, for the Midway, in addition to serving as an avenue of commercial pleasures, was also organized as an outdoor museum that popularized Darwinian notions of racial progress from "savagery" to "civilization."[9]

Placed at the end of the midway, the Dahomeyan Village was intended to convey a specific message within the overall ideological landscape of the fair. As one guidebook explained: "The habits of these people are repulsive; they eat like animals and have all the characteristics of the very lowest order of the human family. Nearly all the women are battle-scarred; most of them are captives." Cartoonists gave their own slant to this theme, urging their audience to think of Africans as virtually interchangeable with simians (fig. 5.2).[10]

Pené did everything he could to reinforce the impressions that fairgoers received of his wards being beyond the reach of "civilization." According to one newspaper, he made them hold pint bottles of beer while they danced.[11]

Another characteristic of the Dahomeyan Village came into sharper relief several months later when a smaller version of the Dahomeyan Village travelled to the Midwinter Exposition in San Francisco. There the lure of the show became more explicitly sexual, as illustrated by the pyramid of bosoms featured in the official souvenir publication of the fair (fig. 5.3).[12]

Clearly, the Dahomeyan Village concessions represented not so much Africa and Africans as the pornography of power that Raymond Corbey and others have noted was so vital to the efforts of imperialists trying to build public support for their expansionist schemes. That is exactly the point that Pené underscored in his report to French colonial officials. His motivation in organizing the Dahomeyan Village in Chicago, he explained, had less to do with personal profit than with "a more elevated goal: *l'intérêt Colonial,* and also the interest of the indigenous people who had been able to judge, for themselves, the grandeur of France, and the progress of civilization in the United States, Portugal, Spain, etc."[13]

No doubt Pené was motivated by his devotion to French imperial interests, but his show also reinforced the racial politics of the United States by putting the finishing touches on dominant ideological rationalizations of America's post-Reconstruction-era nation builders. Two decades after the close of the Reconstruction period in American history, when whites in the North and South had been reunited at the expense of former slaves, the Dahomeyan Village offered what seemed like visible proof of the need for denying African Americans political, social, and economic equality. In the eyes of the Newberry Library's Frederic Perry Noble, the lessons about Africa taught at the fair could have practical consequences for the future of American race relations. "What

Fig. 5.3. "A Pyramid of Dahomey Women." *Official History of the California Midwinter International Exposition* (San Francisco, 1894). Courtesy National Museum of American Art.

might not the American negro accomplish for Africa if himself baptized with the missionary spirit!" he exclaimed. Perhaps, he fantasized, dipping into the rhetoric of the colonization movement of the antebellum decades, as many as 700,000 carefully selected African Americans could be persuaded to return to Africa to "establish lighthouses of civilization amid inland seas of savagery."[14]

The messages that Pené's Dahomeyan Village sent were reinforced by the exhibits of Africa assembled by another explorer, May French-Sheldon. Her substantial collection of African artifacts was concentrated in the ethnological section of the Woman's Building, and won praise—and awards—from exposition officials. She was lauded by the *Chatauquan* as the fair's "White Queen" and praised for having subdued African "savages." Yet, while there is little doubt that her exhibits had the effect of complementing Pené's concession, French-Sheldon took pains in her own lectures to argue that Africans were not subhuman and could be civilized. The issue for her, as it was for Frederic Perry Noble, was not whether Africans could be civilized, but how.[15]

These issues obviously interested white Americans. And because arguments about Africa and Africans carried implications for African Americans and the future of race relations in the United States, they also interested, and troubled, African Americans. Frederick Douglass, the aging former slave and outspoken advocate of civil rights who was serving as Haiti's official representative at the fair, condemned the Dahomeyan Village. It was, he wrote, "as if to shame the Negro [that] the Dahomians are also here to exhibit the Negro as a repulsive savage." Then, in a speech evidently delivered on the occasion of the opening of the Dahomeyan Village, Douglass applauded the Africans' "dance and ceremonies, which, he remarked, were all on the same principle, if not quite so well developed, as those of people living nearer to civilization." On the occasion of a special "Colored People's Day" set aside for African Americans, he tried to reverse the terms of the show's ideological effect. "We have come out of Dahomey into this," Douglass proclaimed, referring to the World's Columbian Exposition. "Measure the Negro," he insisted. "But not by the standard of the splendid civilization of the Caucasian. Bend down and measure him—from the depths out of which he has risen." Douglass obviously struggled with his terms. He valued African cultural forms that were so badly misrepresented in the Dahomeyan Village. But he could not free himself from the dominant discourse of "civilization" and "savagery."[16]

The full force of the ideological construct on display at the 1893 Chicago and 1894 San Francisco fairs hit at the 1901 Buffalo fair, where a coterie of local lawyers and business interests financed a show called "Darkest Africa," proposed once again by that intrepid labor-contractor-turned-showman, Xavier Pené. Their contract spelled out the details of the show: "the ground plan in a general way to consist of groups of typical huts of at least twenty-five different races or tribes of Africa south of the Senegal River, the Desert of Sahara and Egypt. . . ." Furthermore, the contract made clear that the Africans selected for the show were "to present the racial peculiarities and customs [of their tribes] . . . subject to the approval of the Director General." To lend scientific legitimacy to his enterprise, Pené, before proceeding to Africa, secured commissions from the Smithsonian Institution and the Buffalo Society of Natural History with the understanding that artifacts brought to the fair as part of the show be left with the Buffalo museum. This validation from two prestigious museums cinched the knot between science and showmanship—a conjuncture that became apparent for all to see when the exposition actually opened.[17]

As I have noted elsewhere, no world's fair was ever more explicitly organized around ethnologically grounded social Darwinian ideas about racial hierarchy. For instance, the Buffalo exposition grounds were mapped according to a social Darwinian theory of progress. Visitors entered the fairgrounds through Delaware Park, a state of nature, and proceeded to climb the rungs of civilization until they reached its climax in the exposition's Electric Tower. Just in case anyone missed it, these lessons were driven home architecturally by color-coding buildings according to an overtly racist chromatics. That is, structures closest to the entrance were decorated in "savage" colors. The Electric Tower, by contrast, was painted and illuminated in "more refined" hues of light green and blue. As was the case at the 1893 fair, what bound the whole together were anthropology exhibits. The Buffalo fair featured an Ethnology Building (its interior was color-coded, with brighter colors near the bottom giving way to softer hues at the top) with a large sign near the entrance stating that the anthropology exhibits continued on the midway. There visitors could find Native Americans, Mexicans, Filipinos, Africans, and African Americans represented in ethnological ghettos, along with a caged Chimpanzee named Esau, presented as "the missing link."[18]

From the moment they arrived in Buffalo, Africans were imprisoned in the categories of preexisting racist tropes that invited visitors to compare and contrast Africans and African Americans. The *Buffalo Express,* for instance, spared little hyperbole in its description of the Africans' arrival in Buffalo: "From the mysterious inland of Darkest Africa came 98 persons to the exposition yesterday, who are as black as the ace of spades, black as ebony, black as dulled tar, black as charcoal, black as cinders, black as crows, black as anything that will convey to the mind absolute undiluted sunless, moonless, starless blackness. Night is pale beside them. American mulattos seemed well-nigh white when compared to them." To drive the contrast home, the newspaper told a story about an encounter that supposedly took place between African Americans performing in the Old Plantation concession and Africans in the Darkest Africa show. According to the newspaper, two African Americans, Henrietta and her husband, Tannie, walked over to the African village "to see our ancestries," as Aunt Henrietta explained to the "fat, jolly darky" who accompanied her. "We was like that befo' our ancestries kemmed over," she continued. Then, taking note of her husband's fascination with unclothed African women, she commanded: "Turn yo' back, yo' Tannie an shet yo' eyes." As was the case in Chicago, the invitation to gaze at Africans was simultaneously an invitation to reflect on the alleged racial backwardness of African Americans.[19]

The lessons of the exposition generally and of the show specifically were not lost on many visitors. "[C]ivilization is not national but racial," one of America's leading cultural critics, Hamilton Wright Mabie, asserted in the pages of *The Outlook*. An educator, after seeing the "Darkest Africa" show, recorded this impression in the *New York Times*: "Nothing else I have ever seen conveys such an impression of wild savagery. . . . One understands at last what a really wild man is; the Indians are conventional citizens beside them. One understands also what a foe civilization is to the physical man; how the brain had been cultivated at the expense of the teeth, the muscles, the physique." Then, shifting the tone, but not the substance, of her comments, she concluded: "And yet, when someone in whom they have confidence speaks to them, the way their faces light up is instructive. . . . In fact, while they were wild men, and their war dances betrayed the ferocity of savages, they did not impress one as wicked or vicious any more than an animal is wicked or vicious."[20]

Demeaned in the popular press and openly ridiculed by visitors, the "Darkest Africa" show once again anchored the racist ideology embedded in the exposition's blueprint for the future. Anthropologized as "savages," Africans on display at America's Victorian-era fairs helped cement herrenvolk ideas about race and democracy that, in post–Civil War America, had reunited white Americans by debasing African Americans.[21] These shows, and similar ones at succeeding fairs in St. Louis and San Diego, were not innocent of exploitative intentions commonly associated with economic imperialism, but the overriding function of these world's fair shows was to use Africans to buttress the arguments for segregation that the U.S. Supreme Court had sanctioned in its notorious 1896 decision in *Plessy v. Ferguson*.

Two additional points need to be made about this first generation of African shows at America's world's fairs. First, these shows had modular dimensions that made them easy to recreate in communities across the United States. Second, despite the exploitative intentions of their sponsors, these shows were also sites of resistance to the imperial intentions of Pené and his world's fair sponsors.

The modular dimensions of African shows were clearly revealed by a how-to-create-your-own-midway pamphlet that appeared right after the 1893 fair closed. Written by Annie Meyers Sergel and called *The Midway: A Burlesque Entertainment*, the pamphlet encouraged community and school groups to stage their own African village show. How could a community group recreate the Dahomeyan Village in the absence of real Africans? The author made this suggestion:

> These distinguished foreigners should be impersonated by quick witted young men, dressed in black tights, with blackened faces and fantastic wooly wigs. The wildest decoration in the way of ballet skirts, feathers, flowers and colored paint should be indulged in. . . . Wild war dances, songs, and cake-walks should be arranged as entertainment. . . . If possible the booth should be built to have a raised platform over the entrance and the villagers may howl and dance upon it, as in the original, to the delight of all passers-by.

To add to the authenticity of the performance, the pamphlet advised organizers to give participants names like "Tobroro, Kellowmpargum, Tabmboughorn, Tabatkingman, Parshmpomba, Driggajumey, Postororogm, Sidleeorump, Strekelamgn, Longgmurnys, Leonaymyneys, Anderosnynngg, Raoydggm and other dark lights." As Sergel's pamphlet made clear, show-business entrepreneurs saw in the African shows an opportunity for sustaining the tradition of blackface minstrelsy within American culture.[22]

There is no doubt that African shows were freighted with ideological intention and meaning. But were these shows successful in their efforts to manipulate representations of Africans to serve the ideological ends of exposition sponsors? The answer, I think, is yes, but with this caveat.

Try as they might, the promoters of the Dahomeyan Village concession at the 1893 fair were not entirely successful in controlling the ability of African performers to impart their own meaning to their performances. As Gertrude Scott explains in her examination of the Dahomeyan Village at the 1893 fair, the Dahomeyan women were overheard by another concessionaire who claimed to understand what they were really chanting during their participation in the daily parade of "ethnological types" up and down the Midway Plaisance. The concessionaire's account bears quoting:

> A good many people imagine, I suppose [that the women] are sounding the praises of the Exposition or at least voicing their wonder at the marvels they have seen since coming to this country. But the fact is that if the words of their chants were translated into English they would read something like this: "We have come from a far country to a land where all men are white. If you will come to our country we will take pleasure in cutting your white throats."

No doubt the Dahomeyans were exploited by exposition officials. They were held as virtual slaves by Pené who, in theory, paid their wages to their chiefs. But, if the account just mentioned is true, Africans on display in these shows were not entirely stripped of their ability to preserve their basic human dignity. Some, like the women just mentioned, resisted through language. Others, like one of the Africans in the Darkest Africa concession at the Buffalo fair, decided to convert to Christianity, to the delight of Buffalo's missionaries, but refused to participate in the show's "fetish dance" after his conversion. Pené accused the man of laziness. In reality, he was "making do," using the means available to him to resist the "iron cage" of race into which he was shoved.[23]

The first generation of American world's fairs established African shows as centerpieces of these imperialistic extravaganzas. The second generation of America's fairs, the fairs of the Great Depression, followed suit as African shows continued to be featured midway attractions that lent legitimacy to the social and political construction of apartheid in the United States. But there was an important shift in the ideological function of these shows. In addition to stressing the distance of American "civilization" from African "savagery," African shows at the fairs of the 1930s now raised the possibility of incorporating Africa under the spreading shade of America's neo-imperialist umbrella. There is no doubt that Africans put on display remained objects of ridicule, but there was a shift in the rhetoric of display. At America's Victorian-era fairs, representations of Africans and Africa had been largely relegated to the midway as anthropological attractions. At the fairs organized during the Great Depression, midway representations of Africans and Africa were re-presented under the sponsorship of corporations.[24]

The exposition that took the lead in recasting American images of Africa was another Chicago fair—the 1933–34 Century of Progress Exposition. As was the case with the World's Columbian Exposition forty years earlier, much of the inspiration for this fair came from European (fig. 5.4), particularly French precedent—in this case the 1931 Paris Colonial Exposition. After seeing the colonial complexes at the Paris fair, Chicago's fair planners became more convinced than ever that their fair should include a broad range of colonial villages sponsored by European imperial powers. But as economic chaos and political conflict in Europe forced European governments to scale back their plans for participating in the fair, Chicago planners determined that they would have to develop village concessions on their own. When several Africans along with several African Americans proposed a show for the fair called "All Africa," exposition authorities jumped at the possibilities and encouraged the show's proponents to submit their ideas for review.

Information on the All-African Company is sparse, but it evidently owed its creation to two Africans living in the United States who saw in show business, especially the creation of African shows at fairs, the possibility of "improving the conditions of the natives of Africa in their own land" through increased commercial relations with the United States. Pointing to the success of African shows at the earlier generation of American fairs, Modupe Paris, one of the founders of the All-Africa Company, proposed bringing twenty-five Africans to the Century of Progress Exposition to "exhibit the smelting of iron ore, to have the iron made into weapons, amulets, charms, etc., by the native artificers, and the products sold to the public as souvenirs." At night, the Africans would "give concerts and dances typical of the life of the natives in Africa itself." To pull it off, exposition authorities told the show's backers that they would have to raise at least $125,000 to guarantee its feasibility.

This is no small sum today. It was an enormous amount of money in the Great Depression. Modupe Paris and his partners hoped to raise money from different governments and corporations. When these efforts fell through, Paris's group became the object of a successful—and one is tempted to say, hostile—takeover by several enterprising whites involved in an import/export business.

Fig. 5.4. Postcard, "African Village." Antwerp Exposition Internationale Coloniale, 1930. Author's Collection.

They proceeded to remove Paris from the directorship and incorporated their operation as the "All-Africa Corporation," issued stock worth $500,000, and set in motion plans to make the show an outright concession devoid of all philanthropical ambitions.

Their plans, which expanded to include representations depicting African Americans, open a window on white American interwar fantasies about Africa. After entering the show, which occupied five hundred feet of prime lakefront terrain, "distinguished guests from all over the world" could be entertained in "the charming and romantic Arabian Cafe" and be entertained by "a Bedouin Sheik and his retinue of servants." Then, the project description continued, "you may go to the African Explorers Club where you will see hundreds of trophies of many African wild game hunts. . . ." Ordinary visitors would have much to see as well. An auditorium and theater would feature "the best that can be offered and produced by African and American negro talent." In "Frederick Douglass Hall," visitors would encounter the "achievements of the colored race."

As appealing as these attractions might have been, the show's central drawing card was the twenty-foot-high boardwalk broken periodically by "parasol-protected tables and chairs." "Under the Board Walk on the north end," the concessionaires enthused, would be "cages for a number of wild animals, lions, leopards, etc. To the east of these cages are storage rooms and space for savage native Africans who occupy the native villages, or Kraal, situated in the southeast part of our grounds." Once in the Kraal, which was surrounded by jungle, visitors could see: "A savage native making a dugout canoe; American boys throwing real African spears at a stuffed lion . . . A Protestant Mission . . . A Catholic Mission . . . [and] an African wild game hunters outfit post. . . ." As they proceeded along the boardwalk, fairgoers could encounter "the snake charmers, the JuJu man, the witch Doctor, the Firewalkers, Dancers, Beggars, Vendors, musicians, fortune tellers, shopkeepers," not to mention a minaret. And to cool off, visitors could ride "real dugout canoes" on the Nile-Congo Ride.

As its promoters summed up their fantasy-filled show, this "African Exhibit will be dignified, inspiring, authentic and highly educational. There will be fun and laughs . . . and not a few real thrills. This African Exhibit pertains to about one-seventh of the land of this world—the richest, darkest, most interesting, and most unusual land and people in the whole world."

Their plans were ambitious. In fact, they were too ambitious for the fair's organizers, who refused to agree to demands that profits from the show's concessions go primarily to its backers. Together with protests from African Americans, who were already enraged over the discriminatory employment policies at the fair, disputes over profit sharing led to the show's demise late in the fall of 1932.[25]

With only a few months remaining before the exposition's opening, exposition authorities did not abandon their dreams of representing Africans within their century-of-progress show. They turned to a master carnival showman, freak-show promoter, and Broadway impresario, Lou Dufour, and his partner, Joe Rogers, who promised to deliver an African village concession. They were as good as their word. Through his contacts in the entertainment world, Rogers knew of an African dance troupe that was stranded in Chicago. He also knew of an animal importer, Warren (not Frank) Buck, who could deliver an assortment of wild animals from Africa. By opening day, the concession, complete with a Coconut Grove Restaurant, was ready for business. Sadly for the concessionaires, the show proved "too tame" for fairgoers. Undaunted, Dufour flew to New York City, and persuaded an African American entertainer, Bob Lucas, who had danced with the popular Ubangi troupe a couple of years before, to help in hiring native Africans living in Manhattan to travel to Chicago to jazz up the concession. Jazz it up they did. Lucas had distinguished himself with the Ubangis by putting a hot sword in his mouth and walking on hot coals. He proceeded to train his new employees in these skills and, as Dufour put it, "the revised show was a real ball of fire."[26]

The hit of the Darkest Africa show, however, was not the Africans. Rather, it was a white explorer named Captain Callahan, who, while on a mission for the German government, had supposedly run afoul of a group of Africans who were insulted by his refusal to marry a local woman. They were so incensed, according to Dufour, that the head of the tribe "took out a sharp knife and removed Callahan's private parts, in total." Callahan survived, found gainful employment on the carnival circuit, and provided Dufour and Rogers with the chief attraction for their show. This was the spiel delivered to visitors to lure them inside this attraction within the Darkest Africa concession:

> Ladies and gentlemen . . . on the inside of this enclosure you will see and hear Captain Callahan, that brave and durable man who was so horribly tortured by a ferocious group of savages in the Cameroons, who were about to fling his ravished body into a steaming pot of boiling water, after a sadist beast had decapitated his penis and testicles. Please, please, just stop to think—what a terrible, despicable crime! On the inside you will hear from the very lips of Captain Callahan how he was rescued from those ruthless cannibals. Now, please listen very carefully: everyone is invited to come in, this being the understanding—that the captain will be on an elevated stage. He will remove his robe. And after you see with your own eyes that the captain is absolutely devoid of sexual glands as I am now stating—then, and only then, will you be expected to pay fifty cents to the cashiers as you pass out through the turnstiles. . . .

In retelling this tale, Robert Bogdan notes that the "'Darkest Africa' exhibit was booked as an educational display."[27] It was also seen by a reported 250,000 people and featured special ceremonies for visiting dignitaries like Charles G. Dawes, former U.S. Vice President and ambassador to England.[28]

So what are we to make of these two exhibits—one planned, but never realized, the other barely planned, but opened to the public for the run of the fair? Clearly, they were minted as coins of the emerging neo-imperialistic realm that reinvented Africa as a playground filled with people not to be taken too seriously, except perhaps as anthropological specimens fit for pleasures of touristic voyeurism. There was, of course, a sinister logic at work here. If "savage" Africans existed only to amuse or instruct, there was no need for Americans to consider the fullness of their humanity or the complexity of their cultures, and there certainly was no need to accord Africans control over their destiny, much less over their natural and cultural resources.

The next step followed in due course. Representations of Africa at the 1939 New York World's Fair emphasized how corporations would modernize "the dark continent" by putting Africans to work. For instance, the Victoria Falls exhibit, organized by the British South African Company and placed on the exposition's midway, illustrated "the scenic beauties of the Colony and describes its leading industries—tobacco-growing, gold-mining, and agriculture."[29] Featuring a 186-feet-by-22-feet working replica of Victoria Falls, the exhibit exoticized the British imperial mission. "As you walk up a curved ramp toward the door of the main section of the building," the guidebook informed visitors, "the dull roar drums louder in your ears until it becomes vast thunder. You are in the heart of Africa." Once inside the show, visitors could browse through displays of "native arts and crafts, Bushman paintings, animal heads and war weapons" and walk into a grass hut and there imbibe "the atmosphere of the 'Dark Continent'. . . ."[30] What distinguished this show from its antecedents was that Africans were nonexistent, rendered extinct, as it were, from a continent that tourists could enjoy and corporations could exploit at will.[31]

A parallel line of representational logic unfolded in the Firestone Factory and Exhibition Building and in the Firestone-sponsored rubber exhibit at the same fair. Central to both exhibits were displays depicting "modern Firestone rubber plantations in Liberia." As one piece of promotional literature explained: "Actual work of gathering latex on the vast Firestone plantation . . . is dramatized ingeniously to tell the story of how Firestone initiative transformed thousands of acres of jungle land into cultivated plantations—all in the course of a few short years." Dioramas drove home the message that Africans were best suited for work on rubber plantations that generated the raw materials necessary for modern American consumer comforts (fig. 5.5). In addition to its dioramas, the Firestone building included a working tire factory and displays of rubber products "ranging from women's foundation garments and bathing suits to rubber tie plates for reducing noise and vibration in subways."[32]

Fig. 5.5. "Firestone Exhibit, New York World's Fair." Century of Progress/World's Fair Collection, Manuscripts and Archives, Yale University Library.

To fit Africa even more firmly into corporate-driven neo-imperialist visions, Firestone, with the help of the Smithsonian Institution's National Zoo, upgraded its exhibit for the 1940 version of the New York World's Fair by organizing a fake jungle habitat complete with "the pygmy hippopotamus, the pygmy elephant, fierce forest leopards and colorful harness antelopes together with various species of chimpanzees, monkeys and gay-plumed birds. . . ." As visitors proceeded along the "native trail," they experienced the "rhythmic throb of tom-toms mingled with native mumbo-jumbo" and saw firsthand "native huts of dried clay with thatched roofs and scores of strange articles used by the people of this distant land. . . ." After making their way through "the tangled mass of plant life, which challenged the perseverance of Firestone engineers," visitors arrived at a "modern rubber plantation where trees in orderly rows are tapped for latex." But that was only the introduction to Firestone's modernization fantasy:

> Neat bungalows replace primitive huts; modern roads supersede forest trails; and electricity pierces the blackness of the African night. Here visitors see a reproduction of the processes of gathering and preparing rubber as it is carried on daily by the 15,000 native workers employed by Firestone on its Liberian plantations.

Once they left the plantation scenes behind them, visitors moved directly to the tire factory, where scenes of modernizing America, including the Firestone Singing Color Fountain, left little doubt that Firestone's involvement in Liberia was essential for the continued "progress" of the United States and its culture of consumerism.[33]

In the "world of tomorrow," the motto of the 1939 New York World's Fair, African shows laid bare the modernizing and neo-imperial strategies of America's world's fair promoters. No less than skyrides and stratoships, streamlined modern buildings and toasters, nylon stockings and television, African shows at America's "coloniale moderne" fairs of the 1930s, like the "Darkest Africa" shows at America's Victorian-era expositions, continued to shape the way Americans were taught to think about "progress" and "civilization." No less important, these shows encouraged Americans to think of Africa's "development" apart from its people and cultures. Visitors to the New York World's Fair might easily have asked if there were any Africans left in Africa—a question that, however conducive for building popular support for the modernization of Africa according to blueprints laid down by corporate sponsors of the fairs, hardly prepared Americans for understanding the postcolonial remapping of Africa by Africans themselves.

NOTES

1. Hubert Howe Bancroft, *The Book of the Fair,* vol. 2 (Chicago: Bancroft, 1895), 878.

2. To date there has been very little work done on African representations at American world's fairs. There are, however, several suggestive studies of African representations at French and English fairs. See, for instance, William Schneider, "Colonies at the 1900 World's Fair," *History Today* 31 (1981): 31–34; Jean Angelini, "L'Exposition nationale coloniale de Marseille 1922" (Ph.D. diss., Université d'Aix, 1971); Sylviane LePrun, *Le Théâtre des Colonies: Scénographie, acteurs et discours de l'imaginaire dans les expositions 1855–1937* (Paris: l'Harmattan, 1986); Jonathan Woodham, "Images of Africa and Design at the British Exhibitions between the Wars," *Journal of Design History* 2 (1989): 15–33; Annie E. Coombes, *Reinventing Africa: Museums, Material Culture and Popular Imagination in Late Victorian and Edwardian England* (New Haven: Yale UP, 1994), esp. chaps. 5 and 9; Burton Benedict, "Rituals of Representation: Ethnic Stereotypes and Colonized Peoples at World's Fairs," *Fair Representations,* ed. Robert W. Rydell and Nancy E. Gwinn (Amsterdam: VU UP, 1994): 28–61. Benedict argues that, over time, so many different Africans were displayed at fairs that the undifferentiated image of "the African" gave way to a more complex image.

3. The quotation is from the souvenir publication entitled *Oriental and Occidental: Northern and Southern Portraits. Types of the Midway Plaisance* (St. Louis: N. D. Thompson, 1894), n. pag.

4. On Sara Baartman, the "Hottentot Venus," see Richard D. Altick, *The Shows of London* (Cambridge: Harvard UP, 1978); and Stephen Jay Gould, "The Hottentot Venus," *Natural History* 91 (1982). My own work, especially *All the World's a Fair* (Chicago: U of Chicago P, 1984), details the involvement of anthropologists in American fairs. See also George W. Stocking, Jr., *Victorian Anthropology* (New York: The Free Press, 1987); Fatimah Tobing Rony, "Those Who Squat and Those Who Sit: The Iconography of Race in the 1895 Films of Felix-Louis Regnault," *Camera Obscura* 28 (Jan. 1992): 262–89.

5. "Met in Buffalo," clipping, *Buffalo News* 23 Sept. 1900, Pan-American Exposition Scrapbooks, Buffalo and Erie County Historical Society.

6. "The Story of the Midway Plaisance," *Inter-Ocean,* qtd. in Gertrude M. Scott, "Village Performance: Villages at the Chicago World's Columbian Exposition" (Ph.D. diss., New York University, 1991), 283. My own analysis draws heavily on Scott's insights.

7. Contract between Xavier Pené and World's Columbian Exposition, 15 July 1892, carton 283, dossier 1887, Archives d'outre mer, Généralités.

8. Pené, letter to Louis Henrique, 24 Dec. 1893, ibid.

9. There is a growing literature on the Midway Plaisance. One should compare the interpretations offered by Rydell, *All the World's a Fair,* chap. 2, with James Gilbert's *Perfect Cities: Chicago's Utopias of 1893* (Chicago, 1991); Curtis M. Hinsley's "The World as Marketplace: Commodification of the Exotic at the World's Columbian Exposition, Chicago, 1893," in *Exhibiting Cultures: The Poetics and Politics of Museum Display* (Washington, DC: Smithsonian Institution Press, 1991), 344–65; and Meg Armstrong's "A Jumble of Foreignness," *Cultural Critique* (Winter 1992–93): 199–250. See also Scott 284 on the construction of the village.

10. John J. Flinn, comp., *Official Guide to the Midway Plaisance* (Chicago: The Columbian Guide Company [1893]), 30.

11. Unidentified newspaper clipping, Charles Harpel Scrapbooks, Manuscripts Division, Chicago Historical Society.

12. On the Midwinter Exposition, see Rydell, "Rediscovering the 1893 Chicago World's Columbian Exposition," in *Revisiting the White City*, comp. Carolyn Kinder Carr et al. (Washington, DC: National Museum of American Art and National Portrait Gallery, 1993), 57–58. Raymond Corbey's work in visual anthropology is especially important here. See his "Alterity: The Colonial Nude," *Critique of Anthropology* 8 (1988): 75–92; and "Ethnographic Showcases, 1870–1930," *Cultural Anthropology* 8 (1993): 338–69.

13. Pené, letter to Henrique, 24 Dec. 1893.

14. Frederic Perry Noble, "Africa at the Columbian Exposition," excerpt from *Our Day* (Nov. 1892): 2, 7, New York Public Library. On the colonization movement, see George M. Frederickson, *The Black Image in the White Mind* (New York, 1971), 8–11.

15. For an analysis of French-Sheldon's work, see T. J. Boisseau, "'They Call Me *Bebe Bwana*': A Critical Cultural Study of an Imperialist Feminist," *Signs* 21 (1995): 116–46; and Jeanne Madeline Moore, "Bebe Bwana," *American History Illustrated* 21 (1986): 36–43. See also Fannie C. Williams, "A 'White Queen' at the Fair," *The Chautauquan* 18 (1893): 342–44.

16. Frederick Douglass et al., *The Reason Why* (privately printed, 1893), 9; "The Jubilee Day Folly" and "The World in Minature," *Indianapolis Freeman* 2 Sep. 1893; "Opening of the Dahoman Village," *Chicago Tribune* 30 May 1893: 2.

17. "Briefs of Pan-American Concession Contracts," 52–53, box 5, Frederick W. Taylor Papers, Department of Special Collections, UCLA; "Going After Native Africans," clipping, *Buffalo Courier* 18 Oct. 1900, Pan-American Scrapbooks; "X. Pené Has a Commission," clipping, *Buffalo Courier* 18 July 1900, Pan-American Scrapbooks; "An African Village," *Buffalo Express* 31 March 1901, Pan-American Scrapbooks.

18. Details of the 1901 fair are drawn from Rydell, *All the World's a Fair*, chap. 5.

19. "From Darkest Africa," clipping, *Buffalo Express* 11 June 1901, Pan-American Scrapbooks.

20. Hamilton Wright Mabie, "The Spirit of the New World as Interpreted by the Pan-American Exposition," *The Outlook* 68,10 (10 July 1901): 529; Minnie J. Reynolds, "Exposition as an Educator," *New York Times* 6 Oct. 1901: 24. See also the promotional pamphlet issued by Pené, which provides a detailed description of the village: *Darkest Africa: Real Life in a Real African Village*, n.p., vertical files, Department of Special Collections, Henry Madden Library, California State University, Fresno (cited hereafter as CSUF).

21. On "Midway Day" at the fair, an immense parade of midway performers took place. For this occasion, the managers of the "Old Plantation" concession arranged a float depicting "a slice from a huge watermelon with the heads of singing darkies for seeds." Following the float was "a company of colored young men and maidens, dressed ready for a cakewalk." See "Grand Success of Midway Day," clipping, *Buffalo Commercial* 3 Aug. 1901 n. pag., Pan-American Scrapbooks.

22. On the concept of America as a "modular" culture, see Jay Blair, *Modular America* (New York: Greenwood Press, 1988); Annie Meyers Sergel, *The Midway: A Burlesque Entertainment . . . Full Directions for Producing and Conducting It Upon the Most Extensive Plan or on a Limited Scale* (Chicago: The Dramatic Publishing Company, 1894), n. pag., CSUF.

23. Scott, "Village Performance" 297–98; Michel de Certeau, *The Practice of Everyday Life* (Berkeley: U of California P, 1984); Ronald Takaki, *Iron Cages: Race and Culture in 19th-Century America* (New York: Alfred A. Knopf, 1979).

24. On the fairs of the interwar period, see Rydell, *World of Fairs* (Chicago: U of Chicago P, 1993).

25. Details about this show come from the Records of the Century of Progress Exposition, General Correspondence, file 1, 190–92, Department of Special Collections, University of Illinois, Chicago. See also Rydell, *World of Fairs* 165–171.

26. Lou DuFour, *Fabulous Years: Carnival Life, World's Fairs, and Broadway* (New York: Vantage Press, 1977), 60–70. I am also indebted to Robert Bogdan's *Freak Show* (Chicago: U of Chicago P, 1988) for filling in details of this show. See also the account in Burton Benedict, *The Anthropology of World's Fairs* (Berkeley: Scholar Press, 1983), 51–52.

27. Bogdan, *Freak Show*, 196–97.

28. Charles H. Williams, "'Darkest Africa' at 'A Century of Progress,'" *Southern Workingman* 62 (Nov. 1933): 436.

29. *Official Guide Book. New York World's Fair, 1939* (New York: Exposition Publications, Inc., 1939), 114.

30. Ibid., 54.

31. It is worth noting that "animal expert" Frank Buck organized a concession at the New York fair called "Frank Buck's Jungleland," which included some African animals, but primarily featured animals and humans from Malaysia.

32. "From Firestone Factory and Exhibition Building. World's Fair. New York," n.d., file 56, 33, Manuscripts and Archives, Century of Progress—New York World's Fair Collection, f. 56. Yale University Library.

33. "Wild Animals to Feature Jungle at World's Fair," n.d., ibid.

A Revelation in Strange Humanity
Six Congo Pygmies in Britain, 1905–1907

JEFFREY P. GREEN

In 1865 the *Household Monthly* of London, noting that "Men's minds often appear to have been haunted with the desire of converting Nature's slightest freaks into irrefutable evidence of the truth of their own quaint fancies" (537), stated that diminutive humans had been mentioned in Swift's *Gulliver* and in *Sinbad the Sailor,* as well as in the writings of Homer, Aristotle, Pliny, Milton, and John Mandeville. In 1890, after explorer-traveller Henry Morton Stanley's *In Darkest Africa; or the Quest, Rescue and Retreat of Emin, Governor of Equatoria* was published, Europeans had evidence that people who, in maturity, were very much shorter than themselves, did indeed dwell in the heart of darkest Africa.

Stanley's book soon sold 150,000 copies in English; there were editions in Dutch, French, German, Italian, and Spanish (*Dictionary of National Biography* 392). The book's endpaper maps name the Ituri forest region as "Darkest Africa." On his three journeys through "the trackless depths" of the Ituri, he met with "pythons, puff adders, horned and fanged snakes," and so many insects that enumerating them all "would require a whole book" (Stanley 355, 357). Survivors among his white companions on the three-year journey published their accounts; so did relatives of two who had died. Six titles appeared in 1890, four in 1891, others in 1893 and 1898. Stanley's 1887–89 trans-Africa journey was probably the best-documented account of European travellers in Africa and certainly had an impact on European perceptions of Africa and Africans at the end of the nineteenth century.

As Stanley and Emin walked toward the Indian Ocean, they met German soldiers travelling west (Hall 328; Stoecker 98–99); the imperial age in tropical Africa had started in earnest. Africa was the last inhabited continent to be known to people of other lands, and while its darkness was very much in the imaginations of European peoples, its secrets were being revealed to outsiders as the twentieth century dawned.

The firepower that European explorer-travellers had used to cross Africa also enabled them to kill lion, buffalo, elephant, and crocodile. Big game was Africa's attraction for James Jonathan Harrison, who went to the Congo in 1904 "to try for that rare animal the okapi." The rains drove him out, he wrote in 1905. His photographs of pygmies, Harrison recalled, "caused so many friends at home to ask why I could not bring some of these pygmies to England, and I was thus first led to think of doing so" (Harrison, *Life* 7).

While much of what passes for the history of Africa is really the history of Europeans in Africa, it is necessary to focus on Harrison, for he was responsible for bringing six African pygmies to Britain. Harrison was born 8 July 1857 and educated at Harrow and Oxford. His family lived at Brandesburton Hall, in southeast Yorkshire, which they had rebuilt in 1872. It sat in parkland just off the main street of Brandesburton, a large gravel-digging and farming village on the road from Beverley to the North Sea coast at Bridlington.

His father, Jonathan Stables Harrison, who was to die aged eighty in 1917, had the property, including eleven farms (but not the hall and its grounds), in a trust, perhaps because of his son's expensive hobbies. He had been a deputy lieutenant of Yorkshire, an honorary but prestigious role; his wife, Eliza, was a daughter of George Whitehead of York, another deputy lieutenant. Both were magistrates, a reflection of their social status. Young Harrison, following his expensive education, joined the cavalry in 1884, entering a militia regiment that was very chic. The *Army List* shows he was a lieutenant in the Princess of Wales's Own Yorkshire Hussars. By 1895, he had become a captain and, by January 1902, one of the regiment's four majors. Some of his colleagues served in the South African war (1899–1902), but Harrison never saw action. He retired with the honorary rank of lieutenant colonel in September 1904.

Social life in such an elitist regiment, along with the costs of horses, grooms, and uniforms, would have been a drain on Harrison's finances. So were the big-game hunting trips which he started in 1885, and the collection of trophies which filled Brandesburton Hall. He had been in Bermuda, North and South America, Canada, and southern Africa by the time he wrote the preface, in October 1892, to his privately printed *A Sporting Trip through India: Home by Japan and America.* By 1893 he had crossed the Rockies and passed through San Diego, Yosemite, Salt Lake City, Chicago, Niagara, and Washington, D.C. One album shows that he was in "central Africa" from June to December 1896. Another, from 1899–1900, is labeled "Abyssinia–Lake Rudolph–Uganda." A companion on this trip, which included meeting the Emperor Menelik, was Percy Powell Cotton, whose massive *A Sporting Trip through Abyssinia* was published in 1905 by Rowland Ward. Ward's taxidermy business in central London was kept busy by Harrison, who is named in Ward's *Records of Big Game* (1899).

Harrison had a semi-scientific interest in the animals he slaughtered. Ornithologist W. R. Ogilvie Grant of London's Natural History Museum listed Harrison's bird discoveries from the Lake Rudolph region in *Ibis* in April 1901. The chestnut-headed sparrow lark, *Pyrrhulauda harrisoni*, has since been renamed. The painted or woolly bat, *Kerivoula harrisoni*, and Harrison's pygmy antelope, which was described in Thomas's *Annals and Magazine of Natural History* for 1906, seem to have retained his name.

It was natural that the European discovery of the okapi in 1901 (Johnston 347) in the rain forests of the Congo would interest Harrison. He travelled via Egypt and the Sudan and reached the Congo Free State in March 1904. His diary for 4 March records "Saw my first pygmy man—quite a quaint looking object." By 12 April Harrison was on a river that flowed toward the Atlantic. On 29 April 1904, he was at Boma, the capital of the Congo Free State. He had 257 kilos of ivory with him, which would have defrayed some of his expenses, but, as Britain's acting consul reported to the Foreign Office, neither an okapi nor a white rhino (FO 123/436).

On his return to England, Harrison wrote to the London *Times*. His letter, published on 10 June, the day after parliament had debated consul Roger Casement's February report on the nature of the administration of the Congo, stated that he had read that report while in Africa. He praised the administration of King Leopold (who was king of the Belgians and owner of the Congo in his own right) and said he had been "armed as a rule with a camera, umbrella, and, at times, a collecting gun," while in British-governed regions such expeditions had been attacked. He remarked that English and American travellers, as well as Catholic missionaries, had praised the Free State administration.

Harrison angered Casement (Inglis 98, 101, 142) and continued to annoy members of E. D. Morel's Congo Reform Movement with statements such as his letter of 1 October 1904 in the *Times*. Morel, whose weekly *West African Mail* became crucial in the campaign to remove the Congo from Leopold's personal control, wrote to the London *Morning Post* on 14 July 1905 to advise its readers that Harrison was "an aggressive controversialist" who had said that the British government's confidence in Casement "was a most unfortunate error." Casement wrote to Morel that Harrison was an "addlepated dwarf impresario" (Louis 271), for the colonel's six pygmies were now entertaining Londoners.

Harrison had not found it easy to get the six to England. It took from 27 February to 10 March 1905 before Harrison got seven volunteers. One of the females was later thought to have measles and was sent back on 20 March. The others, carried in hammocks or riding on donkeys, reached Wadelai. A telegram sent via Mombasa was published in the *Times* on 21 March. Travelling by Nile steamer, they reached Khartoum, where the news was cabled to England on 11 April and published in British newspapers.

This attracted Sir John Kennaway, veteran politician and president of the Church Missionary Society. Thus the British foreign secretary, Lord Lansdowne, cabled the de facto ruler of Egypt, Lord Cromer, asking on what conditions were the pygmies being brought to England; did they understand those conditions, and was their health likely to suffer (FO 141/390)? A medical examination in Cairo revealed that only two were fit; all were sent to hospital. Harrison was interviewed by Lord Cromer. The news that the pygmies were in hospital, published in the *Pall Mall Gazette* on 28 April, led Lansdowne to cable Cairo again. By now the *Daily Mail* indicated that the Foreign Office would not permit the six to continue their journey. Lansdowne met Harrison, who had rushed to London via Italy, and expressed his distaste for the exploitation, but the six were not British subjects and he could do nothing.

The *Daily Mail* interviewed Harrison in London on 25 April; its report was copied by the *Beverley Guardian*. "Thousands of people will be glad of a chance of seeing what they have read about so much." Harrison also said that the "little people" had volunteered. In Cairo, after one of them had been interviewed in Swahili, the view had been that "if the pygmies had their choice they would return to their forests" (FO 141/390).

It seems likely that before he went to Africa, Harrison had entered into a contract with the Moss-Stoll Empire theater circuit, whose London flagship was the Hippodrome, where the six appeared from Monday, 5 June 1905. The Africans travelled to England on the cargo boat *Orestes,* which docked in London on 1 June. The Sudanese who accompanied them appears with them in a photograph in the *Illustrated London News* of 10 June 1905. A white man is with the six in a commercial postcard, "Colonel Harrison's African Pigmies [*sic*]" (fig. 6.1), and in one of two other poses published in *The Sphere, The Graphic,* and the *Penny Illustrated Newspaper* of that date.

Newspaper reports of their arrival in London are so similar that it seems likely that a press release had been circulated. Reviews of the Hippodrome show were published in theatrical papers such as *The Era* (10 June: 19), *The Encore* (15 June: 7), *The Referee* (11 June: 4), and in the daily papers.

The Hippodrome manager, Fred Trussell, quoted from them in advertisements, such as that in the *Standard* on 7 June: "A more mannerly, inoffensive, and retiring little party could not well be imagined. It is a most interesting study of the ultra-primitive" (*Morning Post*); "The most remarkable thing about the Pygmies was their childlike shyness. They all stood like schoolchildren who were being applauded for reciting" (*Daily Mail*); "Savages untouched by European customs and just as in their primeval forests. Attracted vast and interested

Fig. 6.1. Colonel Harrison's African Pigmies [*sic*]. One of several publicity photographs used by the British press in May–June 1905, this picture was posed on the ship bringing the Africans from Egypt. A commercial postcard. The identity of the white male is unknown. Collection of Bernth Lindfors.

crowds. These curious people are well worth a visit" (*Daily Telegraph*). A photograph of them on stage was published in the *Penny Illustrated Newspaper* (17 June: 371) with the caption "The little folk were tremendously alarmed when the picture was taken, and it would be very dangerous to make a second attempt."

The pygmies appeared on the stage against a backdrop of a tropical forest. The Africans were in front of four huts, described as "wigwams" by the *Era* and as "kraals" by the *Referee*. Three of the males were armed with spears and bows and arrows. Both females were seated. The fourth male "had charge of a tom-tom." To the beat of that drum, the senior African or "chief" "began a low, dirge-like chant" and the three males danced. The applause from the audience made them stop.

The six must have been instructed to continue dancing when the thousand or so in the audience banged their hands together, for that difficulty was not mentioned after the first reviews. However, the Africans did not spring into a performance as soon as the curtain rose. The *Referee* of 11 June noted they were "very uncertain and wayward, and that sometimes it seems doubtful whether they will dance or do anything to oblige" (4). The *Globe* of 7 June

Fig. 6.2. The pygmies as performers on the London stage, 1905. The sender of one card wrote, "Tried to snapshot some of them, but they were too sharp for me. I nearly got shot myself," having seen them at Barmouth, on the coast of Wales, in the late summer of 1906. Collection of Bernth Lindfors.

reported that they wore "only girdles of long grass fastened around their waists, and necklaces of beads" and noted that their showman had to explain that no one could be certain of the length of their performance (9). The *Encore* of 15 June commented that "they do not seem to recognise that they are being made a show of" (7). The *Magnet* of Leeds, a theatrical weekly, referred to them on 10 June 1905 as "that weird band of little people from a strange land" (5).

A different view of the African entertainers emerges from the memoirs of William Hoffman, a working-class Londoner born in Germany, who had been Stanley's servant on the *In Darkest Africa* journey. In a letter to Stanley's old friend Henry Wellcome, dated 30 May 1905, Hoffman wrote, "Some time ago I answered an advert, regards to look after the Stanley Pygmies it was one who could speak Kiswahli, and know their ways. I should think as I have lived with them in the Aruwimi forest and know their ways and habits I would have a chance. I shall feel extremely obliged if you know Col Harrison to please help me [sic]" (Royal Geographic Society). He told Wellcome on 10 July, "I am charge of the pygmies what Sir H M Stanley discovered in 1887. I saw Lady Stanley when she came to see them [sic]" (Royal Geographic Society). Stanley's widow had recommended Hoffman to Harrison.

Thirty-three years later a heavily ghost-written book, William Hoffmann's [sic] *With Stanley in Africa*, had as its final twelve-page chapter "The Pygmies Come to England." "Usually they were very good-tempered in public and did everything I told them, only indulging now and then in a hoarse chuckle of amusement, or uttering some guttural aside in their own language. But on a few occasions, and for some reason I could not fathom, they refused to perform, sitting instead on their little chairs and grimacing broadly, and nothing I could do made them alter their minds. Such behaviour affected me more than anybody else, for it meant that I had to lengthen my lecture to fill up the allotted time" (Hoffman 273–74).

The study of theatrical entertainers must avoid uncritical acceptance of contemporary comments, which can often be the result of publicity handouts. Reviews are equally doubtful sources unless the reviewer's experiences and bias are known. When entertainers are of a different culture, as with Africans in Britain, we must ask what knowledge and expectations existed among the audiences. Hoffman appears to be a source that is both informed and independent. But, as with the ghost-writer's work in his *With Stanley in Africa*, we must take anything Hoffman wrote with caution. Stanley's odd relationship with Hoffman has fascinated biographers, who noted that Stanley did not mention him by name in his *In Darkest Africa*. He had been accused of theft and other crimes, was dismissed after a court-martial, yet accompanied Stanley to South Africa at the end of the century. Hoffman, usually misspelled Hoffmann, cannot be trusted.

Neither can we trust Lady Stanley or Henry Wellcome, who, in 1904–07, were busy protecting the legend of Henry Stanley by purchasing photographs, an early autobiographical manuscript, and other documents (Hall 338–39). Wellcome, a London-based American pharmaceutical millionaire and collector, purchased documents from Hoffman in 1907 and in 1932. One of them is entitled "How the Pygmies were discovered who are now in this country," with a pencil amendment from "are now" to "were." The eight pages, not in Hoffman's scrawl but written by a scribe, describe Hoffman's role from page four. "When I took charge of them at the London Hippodrome they were mere skeletons, especially the old lady who underwent a serious operation on an old spear wound which had formed. Since then she has gained two stone [28 pounds] in weight. When people came to see them in their rooms they would shrink up in a corner, but there is no shyness about them now. It is really wonderful how they took to the stage work; indeed Mr Arthur Walcott had a very difficult task when he first put them on the stage. Just fancy these little people landing off a steamer in the Thames and taken straight to face a huge audience. At first they would hardly do anything but they were great favourites with all the artists and staff especially Mr F. Trussel [sic]. After we left the Hippodrome to go on tour they often wished they would be back. They called the Hippodrome the 'ushibey' that is house of music. They have been a great success in the provinces and have made great friends of some of our music-hall stars" (Wellcome).

The British, despite the initial publicity, reviews, and the Hippodrome's advertising, which called the pygmies "ape-like," "absolute specimens of primitive creation," "the most curious race in the world," asserting that "they prefer, it seems, to inhabit trees" and that their dances "seem intended to imitate the play of monkeys," began to see the six entertainers as "a revelation in strange humanity," as the Era was to comment on 5 August 1905 (19).

The first glimpse of the Africans being perceived as people was in the Referee of 17 June, when its reporter commented, "I took tea with them on Wednesday afternoon." A week before, the Variety Theatre had indicated that they were to be seen by the king in the near future. The bone-scrunching, unwashed, cannibal Africans had been taken to the Foreign Office on Thursday, 8 June, to meet Francis Villiers and other officials.

The pygmies visited parliament, where they were photographed by Sir Benjamin Stone. One group picture, with both Harrison and Hoffman, is dated 29 June 1905 (National Portrait Gallery) (fig. 6.3). Others have later dates. That it was indeed within the first weeks of the six alleged savages being in London is strongly suggested by the Southern Weekly News of Saturday, 24 June 1905 (16), which reported on the pygmies who had travelled by motor car to the Sussex town of Crawley, twenty-five miles south of London, the previous Sunday. One of the females is absent from Stone's 29 June photograph, and as

Fig. 6.3. Visiting the houses of Parliament, Westminster, 29 June 1905. Posed with eight members of Parliament. Photographer Sir Benjamin Stone wrote, "They were armed to the teeth with their weapons of war, tiny bows and arrows and spears. These children of primitive nature were certainly sleek and healthy. They seemed bright and intelligent." James Harrison stands behind Mongonga, the shortest African. Wearing a derby, not the top hats of the elite, is William Hoffman, who had crossed the Congo with explorer Stanley in the 1880s. He was the interpreter until the late summer of 1906. Courtesy National Portrait Gallery, London (reference 22270).

the Sussex paper reported, one had undergone an operation and was unable to accompany the five; that only one African woman was in Stone's 29 June photograph suggests it was indeed taken at the end of the Africans' first month in England. The photograph and a report of the excursion to Crawley show that the "primitives" were mixing with members of parliament and riding in motor cars to a semi-rural location *armed to the teeth with bows and arrows, and spears.*

There may have been strong men ready to pounce if the five attacked the members of parliament, but Crawley, a town of some five thousand, had its two police officers occupied keeping the large crowd away from the George Hotel. Yet those arrows were poisoned. The local reporter repeated the usual nonsense about their ages, insisted that pygmies married at eight, were in the prime of life at twelve, and wrote that those in the Harrison group were from different tribes. "They appear to be more intelligent than most coloured people we are acquainted with. There is nothing unpleasant about their appearance; in fact, apart from his colour, one of the number would be considered quite good-looking."

The Africans wore British-style clothes, necessary as the cars were not enclosed. They held a reception at the hotel before taking an after-lunch nap; their meal, expected to be raw meat, was "a very matter of fact one" of boiled mutton and rice. "Knives and forks were used as if to the custom born."

Mongonga "perched himself at the window, and whether he or the crowd outside was the more amused is an open question. At any rate each had a good view of the other, and all seemed perfectly satisfied with the result." The 23 June *Variety Theatre*'s report noted that "a small but obstreperous boy was successfully hurled across the road" by one of the police officers, and that the sixteen cars carried reporters, the pygmies, and Harrison (6).

On 6 July, thirty-seven days after they had disembarked from the *Orestes*, the six Africans were driven to Buckingham Palace to entertain royalty. It was a birthday party for Princess Victoria. This was reported in Harrison's local weekly, the *Beverley Guardian* (22 July 1905: 7), and elsewhere. "The pygmies undoubtedly achieved the triumph of the afternoon. Although the little people have been in London for some weeks, they have scarcely advanced in civilisation at all, beyond picking up a few phrases like 'Good-night, sir,' and 'Good morning,' which they repeat automatically without any appreciation of their meaning." There were 150 guests, and other entertainments, including a baby elephant from the Royal Italian Circus. Queen Alexandra was present but her husband was absent. Mongonga, "the 'jolly boy' of the four," attempted "to kill an old cock sparrow with his spear."

The reporter, in criticizing the Africans for their small knowledge of English, failed to note that the fully armed alleged savages had been close to the family of the king-emperor. The pygmy entertainers were not a threat despite their origins, weapons, race, and other differences.

The stage show, twice nightly, with the bogus forest backdrop and alleged war dance, was one presentation. The African entertainers were still seen by many as uncivilized savages, but they had been trusted enough to be armed in the presence of royalty, legislators, the curious citizens of Crawley, members of the press on that Sussex safari, and people who visited them at their lodgings.

Helping Hoffman was his wife, Elizabeth "Jani" Jane Hoffman. They stayed with the six Africans at 5 North Crescent, a brief cab ride from the Hippodrome. Lady Stanley visited on 19 July, and within a few weeks so did some people related to Edmund Barttelot, who had been Stanley's second-in-command in the Congo in 1887–88. It had been his death in Africa that had led to some challenges to Stanley's account of events. Walter Barttelot's *Life of Edmund Musgrave Barttelot* (1890) had been "written in a spirit of virulent animosity against Stanley," according to the *Dictionary of National Biography*'s entry on Stanley.

Hoffman wrote to Stanley's widow, advising that "they are still after the details of the fate of their relative" and asking him to visit them. This shocked Lady Stanley, who wrote to Wellcome on 15 August that Hoffman was "a weak, untruthful man" who should never have consented to go near the Barttelots.

On 28 July the pygmies reached Beverley by train and rode off in a private bus hired by Harrison. That weekend they were at the center of affairs, for Harrison had three thousand visitors to the Hall, including over one thousand who had bicycled, to see the Africans: 1,267 paid extra to look at the trophies.

The following week they were a little to the west, at Market Weighton, where they entertained at Londesborough Park. Lord Londesborough, married to a daughter of the Duke of Beaufort, owned over 52,000 acres and five homes— Londesborough Park was one of them. The Africans again arrived by train and travelled in Harrison's car where one "enjoyed himself tootling the horn." Lady Londesborough's garden fete was an expensive affair, with military bands, a play, and the pygmies. "Hundreds of people paid them a visit, and many stayed to see them dance. They seemed to thoroughly enjoy themselves, mixing with the crowd when not seated on the platform. One smoked a cigarette, others ate chocolate or grapes with evident delight, and from children's toys all of them seemed to gain a great delight," reported the *Scarborough Post* on 1 August (3).

Their "curious dances" were one of their attractions. Rabbits were released from sacks for the pygmies to hunt. This, described briefly in the *Era* (2 Sept. 1905: 20), was recalled in 1977 by Annie Mowthorpe who, at the age of thirteen, had witnessed the swiftness and skill of the Africans (Neave). She recalled that the Africans were accommodated in a metal bungalow, originally

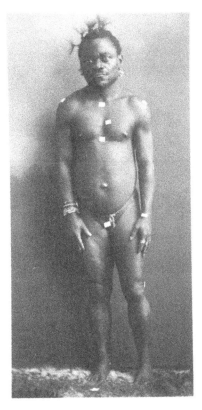

erected for the police who accompanied King Edward, when Prince of Wales, to the house. A rabbit, with a pygmy's arrow still in it, was stuffed and kept as a souvenir. One of the Africans killed two running rabbits with his arrow, noted the *Era*.

The country folk of mid-Sussex and now of Yorkshire would have respected such skills even if they were possessed by "Niggers on a small scale," as a Crawleyite had been heard to remark.

Their host, Lord Londesborough, welcomed them back on 27 August, the day after they finished at the Hippodrome. To have an enormously wealthy earl meet their private train, and to mix with Yorkshire people, was quite different from their time at the Hippodrome and their meetings with old Africa hands such as Harry Johnston, who had chaired the Anthropological Institute's investigation of the pygmies, which had been completed by mid-September, duly reported in the *Beverley Guardian* (6) and the *African World* (247) on 16 September 1905. While no published report has been traced, there are anthropometric photographic poses of the pygmies, taken by the elite London photographic studio W. and D. Downey (Edwards 130; Wright) (see figs 6.4–6.5).

We can believe William Hoffman's comment that they "objected to a crowd of men prodding and poking them, and peering into their mouths for no other reason than to see how they differed from white men" (Hoffman 278). The *Entr'Acte*, a London theatrical weekly, reported on 17 June

Figs. 6.4–6.5. Royal Anthropological Institute, London.

Fig. 6.6. The Africans on stage. Taken in 1905. The sender, a semi-literate, scrawled, "I have sent you one of these photo to pick a nice fancy man how do they suite you I thought their face would be fetching what lovely faces they got." Collection of Bernth Lindfors.

1905 (6), "The South African Pigmies held a reception to anthropologists the other day at their quarters near the London Hippodrome. The guests were received quite graciously, until the curiosity of the scientists became rather irksome. The two lady pigmies modestly and flatly refused to be measured, and the attempt had to be abandoned. Mongonga, the tom-tom instrumentalist, was respectfully requested to open his mouth for throat examination. With some show of reluctance he consented, being unable to resist a proffered banana. His gape was an alarming revelation. Fully expanded, his capacious mouth seemed large enough to crunch an average-sized apple at one bite."

Downey's studio took other poses, one of which was published as a commercial postcard by Beagles & Co. It named the six—Mongonga, the chief Bokane, Kuarke and Amuriape (the two women), Mafutiminga, and Matuka. Harrison's yellow-covered book was published in London in 1905, selling for one shilling.

Other souvenirs of the African entertainers, although not available until the spring of 1906, were five phonograph records made for the Gramophone Company, London. These single-sided, ten-inch, 78-rpm shellac discs were extremely fragile, and just four have been traced, although the masters were stored and have been copied for London's National Sound Archive. Two begin with an English male voice declaring it to be 25 August 1905. The masters were sent to Hanover, Germany, where the shellac discs were pressed. GC 11269 and GC 11270 are described as "ORIENTAL TALKING," and GC 14196 and 14197 as "ORIENTAL VOCAL," for the company did not know how else to classify them.

The discs were announced in the January-February 1906 catalog as "records of the language and Folk Songs [sic] of this remarkable tribe of dwarfs who inhabit the forests of Central Africa." In addition to forgetting to consider why the phonograph-owning public would purchase recordings of short people who could not be seen, another marketing error was the fourth and final sentence: "Their language is quite unknown, and they have created the greatest interest in anthropological and scientific circles."

The catalog states that discs 14196 and 14197 were the folk songs, duets by Bakani "the chief" and Matuka (fig. 6.7). Disk 14197 has drumming, too. Disc 11270 was "Conversation between two 'Pygmy Ladies,' punctuated by laughter"; 11269 was a conversation between Bakani "and Mongongo, the Interpreter"; while 1310 was "The Pygmy Language: Conversation between Matuka and the Interpreter." The disc labels differ from the catalog listings: the senior African is spelled "Bokani," and 11269 has the conversation between Bokani, "and Mongongo with Interpreter." This dialogue is in Swahili, despite the claim that all the discs were in an unknown language. Hoffman spoke Swahili, as did Mongonga and Bokani.

Fig. 6.7. Recorded in London in August 1905, five fragile shellac discs went
on sale in early 1906. Courtesy Wood End Museum, Scarborough.

Mongonga was reported in the *Beverley Guardian* of 2 September 1905
(6) to have "fallen violently in love with a pretty fair-haired girl who is employed as a typist by the Gramophone Company," and to have pointed out the
lady with "a deadly-looking spear." It was stated that the masters of the recordings would be offered to the British Museum.

The six went to the Natural History Museum in London, where they
were photographed in the grounds. The museum's photo is labeled "Central
Africa Belgian Congo. Pigmies [*sic*]" but, as Leopold retained possession of his
Free State until 1908, perhaps these identifications were added later. Certainly
the man named as "Dr. R. Murray-Leslie (Doctor in charge of pygmies)" is
Colonel Harrison. The doctor, a specialist in tuberculosis, was named by
Hoffman as chest specialist to attend the Africans (Hoffman 278) and was
listed in early June 1905 as part of the Anthropological Institute's committee
under Harry Johnston.

A second picture, of Bokani and one of the women, has a bow and arrows, but not the nose-stick decorations that he and both women had in the
group photograph (which has two males with spears, and two with bows and
arrows). The Africans wear the same costume as at Westminster. A full-page
photograph of them in this British style appeared in the *Tatler*, 26 July 1905:
"the much-discussed pigmies from the Congo. The little folk in their Sunday-
suits" (121). It was a Downey studio photograph.

The museum had and still has the skeletons of three Mbuti pygmies. One had been presented by Harry Johnston, whose memoirs recall that when he was governor of Uganda, his staff found a German attempting to take more than twenty pygmies to be exhibited in Paris. Seven pygmies were taken to Johnston at Entebbe; one died in May 1900. That individual's skeleton was at the museum (Johnston 344–45), where it was registered in 1901. Colonel Harrison had known about the German, for the *Beverley Guardian* of 6 May 1905 had reported the colonel's account that this group, abducted from the Ituri forest, remained with the German and "will not return to their own people." Johnston's autobiography admitted that because "the imprisonment of Europeans was not, at that time, a convenient thing," the German had merely been heavily fined.

The myths and legends that Europeans created about Africa are reflected in the fact that the other two skeletons had been donated by Emin Pasha in 1887 (Kruszynski)—and it was in 1886 that Stanley had started to organize the "rescue" of Emin, the official motive for his expedition, which took Hoffman and Stanley from England in early 1887.

Another aspect of the six pygmy entertainers as people emerged from this area of search. Rosemary Powers, who has worked at the museum since 1955, recalls that a woman who had been a nurse told her that she had nursed the younger woman pygmy and that they had later become friends. "The younger woman made a second visit to London and sold programmes at one of the great exhibitions" (Kruszynski). That recollection fits the facts uncovered for 1907, as will be seen.

The Hippodrome weeks were over; it was now September 1905, and the six pygmies probably settled down at Brandesburton Hall. Their entertainment work is known to have recommenced by mid-October, for the *Beverley Guardian* of 9 September advised the six would be in that town on Saturday, 14 October, and on that date carried an advertisement of the "Special Visit." The town's assembly rooms were to have two "receptions," at 7:15 and 8:15, with tickets on sale at a shop in the main square. Reserved seats were one shilling and sixpence (three times the price of Harrison's book, thirty-six times the cost of a stamp to mail a postcard anywhere in Britain). The *Guardian*'s review appeared on 21 October (5). The Hoffmans were with them, and Bill Hoffman told the audience about "the life and habits of these strange nomadic tribes." One of the Africans was ill, it was noted.

The advertisement stated that the Africans had appeared "before their Majesties at Buckingham Palace." This bold claim that both the king and the queen had seen them was to be repeated. That advertising was in the Yorkshire area, where the Africans were entertaining in halls and theaters. They were at Driffield on 16 October, then York and Lincoln. The *Lincolnshire Chronicle* of 13 October said they had "been honoured by a command to appear before the

King and Queen," and told the inhabitants of that cathedral city that the Africans were to be at the Central Hall, at 2:45, 3:45, 7:15, and 8:16 [sic]. Tickets were available at a music shop in the main street.

From 23 October the six African entertainers were back on the Empire group's circuit. They opened in Manchester's Hippodrome, performing twice daily and three times on Tuesday, Wednesday, and Saturday. The publicity claimed they had appeared before the king and queen.

We are now able to see ignorance similar to that noted in the London press in May and June. Because the pygmies moved on every week there was less time for reflection by the reviewers. The pygmies "from the morasses of Central Africa" were still top of the bill, among ten or more other acts.

There were five Africans on stage in the city of Manchester in the last week of October 1905. The *Manchester City News* review of 28 October said they were "interesting as curiosities, but disappointing as entertainers" (7). The drum and the singing were still there, but the five "did their best to hide their faces from the audiences." The gallery, where the cheap seats were, expressed its derision. The *Manchester Evening News* (24 Oct.: 6) had reviewed the first show: "a source of great and wondering interest. Until they began talking—or rather twittering—among themselves, and to shuffle about in a native dance these mysterious visitors seemed scarcely human at all." At the end of their act, three or four of them kissed their hands and said "good-bye." "Except for these things the Pygmies seemed scarcely human." The reviewer thought they were not more intelligent than the trained baboon on a bicycle which was a later turn. Even the Manchester critic for London's *Era* reported that the ape was "particularly clever" (28 Oct. 1905: 10).

The previous day had seen *Smith's Liverpool Weekly* carry an advertisement for the pygmies who were to appear in that port city's Empire theater, Lime Street, from 30 October. "The Talk of all Europe! The most Curious People ever seen! They are half-way between Anthropoid Apes and Man!"

This newspaper's review was cruel. To the "battering of a wooden box, a member of the troupe commenced the alleged war song, which was, if anything, less musical than the accompaniment." It decided that "The music-hall stage is scarcely the place whence to promulgate the principles of Darwinism." The cheap seats had vociferous rowdies, who seem to have influenced the reviewer who remarked, "After this 'turn,' we gratefully welcomed civilization in the figure of funny May Henderson." She usually appeared in burnt-cork or minstrel style: perhaps genuine Africans were too much for Liverpool, although the city had had a black presence for decades and was Britain's major port for trade with west Africa.

The review in the *Liverpool Post* on 31 October was so different that one suspects that the reviewer might not have actually seen the show. The song was in "a low crooning voice" and the "little people . . . strutted about the stage."

The *Post* said "They were warmly applauded." Perhaps it was an early performance, and the rowdies were still in the pubs.

After Liverpool they opened at the Empire Palace, Nicholson Street, Edinburgh, on Monday, 6 November. The pygmies had considerable experience of British audiences, but the reviewer of the *Edinburgh Evening News* (7 Nov.: 2) regarded the slow start by this "novelty calculated to arouse an interest not usually associated with the music hall" to be caused by the "curious little people" being impressed by "their strange surroundings when the curtain went up." When "the spirit moved them sufficiently" they performed a "native song and a war dance. The latter proved quite interesting."

The African entertainers moved west to Glasgow on Sunday, 11 November 1905. Hoffman's manuscript account, which would have been in the Wellcome archives and thus not available to him when he collaborated on the book published in 1938, states that they reached Glasgow from Preston, which was on the railroad from Liverpool to Scotland. The manuscript also states they returned to Glasgow two months later, to play at Glasgow's Zoo-Hippodrome. That was one of the Empire circuit's theaters, so perhaps the Africans were in Glasgow between the end of their London work and the mid-October start of the national tour.

Both accounts by Hoffman recall problems with accommodation in Glasgow, when they arrived at the hotel from the station "only to be met . . . by an irate landlady who declared that she could not possibly have 'blacks' about the place" (Hoffman 274). His manuscript details that the Africans put beef bones on the open fire to grill, and that the fat caught fire. The landlady objected but Hoffman told her "the little ones are more careful with fires than we are" (Wellcome 5).

The Hippodrome in Glasgow was at the zoo, and the advertising in the *Evening Times* had the anthropoid-ape aspect already seen in Liverpool, but the African entertainers were now the "missing link." They went on stage twice nightly, and at 3:00 on Wednesday and Saturday; and appeared at the zoo for an hour from 3:00 on Tuesday, Thursday, and Friday. Hoffman's manuscript account states, "We saw great fun every afternoon when I took them for a walk" at the zoo. "They would see some of their old friends such as leopards, and elephants, and they were highly interested in the chimpanzee named 'Wee Macgregor'" (Wellcome 6). They were amazed when a white man entered the lions' enclosure.

Hoffman took them to the art museum in Glasgow. Waiting for "our conveyance, a crowd of people gathered" and one remarked that the weapons were merely toys. Hoffman told "Malaka" to hit a blackbird, promising a jar of honey. His arrow killed the bird. Members of the crowd must have talked of that incident, thus encouraging others to see the entertainers at the theater.

The *Glasgow Record and Mail*, which had carried the advertisement on

13 November, had a review two days later. "They are an interesting spectacle and the opportunity of witnessing these entertaining little folk is one not to be missed." The *Evening Times* the day before had called them "midgets" and "little folk," who, "by the way, speak very good English. . . . Last night they executed a war dance in neat style."

As the African entertainers entered their sixth month in Britain, we can still observe the contradictions noted in May and June 1905. There are the press releases and advertising; the war dance; their unknown language; and the professional interest of anthropologists, government officials, museum staff, and journalists. There is their acceptance, albeit as amusing novelties, by Sir Benjamin Stone and his parliamentary colleagues, Lady Stanley, hosts and guests at the royal birthday celebrations, London journalists, and the Earl of Londesborough. Their skills with their ever-present weapons had attracted public comment in London, Yorkshire, and Scotland. Their refusal to be awed by Britons had been noted in rural Sussex and Yorkshire, London, and Glasgow, as well as in the misunderstood delayed start to their stage show. Their status as savages and missing links was at odds with their capacity to learn English and to copy or mimic local tribal habits such as clapping, waving, or kissing hands to indicate farewell.

Hoffman's manuscript, which should be more trustworthy than the ghost-edited account of more than thirty years later, might be hyperbolical in his note that the Africans "have come to the conclusion that England is far better than their swamps" and that they preferred private motor cars to taxi cabs. As the latter, in 1905, were probably horse-drawn, that view seems sensible today. The Africans were taken "to parks and private grounds where there are plenty of trees and bushes. Then they are in their glory." In some urban parks they were stopped by the keeper. Hoffman took them to manufacturing plants to see how things were made, "especially musketry" (Wellcome 7).

They moved south to Birmingham for the week beginning 27 November 1905. They were to appear twice daily, with an afternoon appearance on Thursday, at the Empire Palace theater, which had seating for two thousand (Read 40). Perhaps well over ten thousand Britons were entertained by the Congo pygmies in one week.

The *Birmingham Daily Mail*'s reviewer (28 Nov.) saw human beings. "A very large audience greeted the Central Africa Pygmies with mingled awe and amusement at the Empire last night, but when it was found that the dusky little folks were well-formed specimens of humanity, and, so far from being in the least unpleasant to look upon, could give the common or 'garden' nigger many points as regards manly beauty, the attitude of the house became entirely friendly and ultimately entusihastic [*sic*]. Officially stated to be the missing link between the ape and man, the pygmies, by their appearance, certainly do not suggest the connection; however this may be, the exhibition is an exceedingly interesting one, and during the course of the war-dance which they go through one seems to trace the origins of the cake-walk" (5).

Does the "common nigger" refer to the blackface artists still common in British music halls? That the cakewalk, an African American dance from the 1890s, revived in London in 1903 (Green), was linked to the alleged war dance, strongly suggests that American influences were strong in British musical entertainments. Perhaps that both dances involved dancing in a circle and were performed by blacks was enough?

The Africans moved south, to play the Shepherds Bush Empire in west London, which had a capacity of 1,650, from 4 December (Read 244). Then they returned to Yorkshire, where they appeared from Monday, 11 December. The advertising in the *Bradford Daily Argus* stated that they were "The talk of all Europe" and that they had appeared before the king and queen. The review on Tuesday noted the four entertainers were Bokani and Mongonga, another male, and the younger female. "In a scenic background of forest, with a primitive hut of branches, the Pygmies sit 'squat like a toad,' with bows and arrows in their hands. The lecturer, a member of one of Stanley's expeditions, tells all about their habits and their development since their arrival in this country. The two eldest then execute a war dance and sing a native war song to the tom-tomming of the junior member. The turn is at once interesting and instructive, and should appeal to ethnological students" (4).

The *Bradford Daily Telegraph* had previewed the pygmies on Saturday, 9 December, and made the first reference to technology. "In their primitive state in the lagoons and morasses of Central Africa the Pygmies have managed to discover a method of smelting iron for the purposes of making spears—their only objects and symbols of wealth. These, strange enough, are welded into shape by means of crude stone hammers and anvils" (5). The source must have been a Harrison publicity handout. That seems to have been where this newspaper learned that none of the six were related. Indeed, stating there were six showed that the paper's reporter had not met them (they were still in west London).

Its review noted just four performers, who may well have been ill and surely were fatigued. "The display is not characterised by much vigour; in fact, as their agent states, these diminutive little fellows are not to be hurried. On the whole, the exhibition is of a most interesting nature, and shows what a great work there is for those who have in hand the civilisation of the races of Central Africa."

The announcement of forthcoming turns on the Empire circuit, published weekly in the *Era*, does not mention them after Bradford, just as it had made no mention of them between Glasgow and Birmingham. Hoffman and his wife remained with them into December 1905.

His book says that the Africans "rarely succumbed to the fogs and rains"

AMURIAPE.

Age 33; Height 3 ft. 8 ins.; Mother
of child born in England in
October last

MATUKA.

Male; Age 24; Height 4 ft. 1 in.

Fig. 6.8. Posed in 1906. Four postcards stated their heights. The African
child was apparently stillborn in October 1905. Collection of Jeffrey Green.

but that "one chill December up in Yorkshire three of them went down with
pneumonia" and "really were ill, and we engaged six nurses to look after them."
He also noted that "for a further eighteen months they were allowed to run
wild on his [Harrison's] estate" (Hoffman 277–78).

Although we cannot rely on Hoffman's book, he did recall the wound in
the leg of Amuriape, which had been noted when she was examined by a doctor in Egypt, and appears as a scar in some photographs (Wright). He wrote
that she had given birth but "was determined that no child of hers should be
born in an alien land. . . . the child was born dead." A separate comment,

dating from 1983 or 1984, from a Brandesburton woman then aged eighty-three, holds that "The woman known as the princess had a baby, but it died" (Winter). Awareness that a child had been born, and was buried in Yorkshire, was retained in Brandesburton into the 1990s, no doubt through stories handed down by those who had lived there in the first decade of the twentieth century. A grave in unhallowed ground was indicated, but on investigation by Peter Calvert proved to be irrelevant. These local legends told of more than one death, through influenza, again supporting the substance of Hoffman's account. Certainly Harrison's house servants and the nurses would have been local people, and, as we will see, into the 1980s and 1990s there were a number of people living in Brandesburton with recollections of the Africans.

However, Hoffman was connected with the six Africans into 1906 despite the silence in his book. On 25 September 1906, he wrote to Henry Wellcome, "My old complaint has given me much pain and was obliged to give up the Pygmies, which Lady Stanley spoke so highly of me to obtain the berth, at any rate as they are not doing anything at present it does not matter much, only of course I am earning nothing [*sic*]" (Royal Geographic Society).

We could assume that Hoffman, who spoke German and Swahili, had been with the Africans to the continent earlier that year. The absence of information in the *Beverley Guardian* and the *Era* suggests that they were away for some months, and the *Beverley Guardian* (14 July 1906: 5) stated that they were in Berlin and were due to appear in Yorkshire at the end of that month. The *Grimsby News* (27 July 1906), published in that major fishing port on the Humber estuary across from Yorkshire, announced that the pygmies were coming direct from Berlin and would appear in the town on 7, 8, and 9 August 1906.

The pygmies were to appear first at Withernsea on 27 July, then at another Yorkshire town, Hornsea, on Saturday, 28 July. They were at the larger coastal resort town of Bridlington on 3 and 4 August, for the *Bridlington Chronicle* of 27 July announced the "return visit of the pygmies" on those dates. They were to make four appearances daily at the Grand Pavilion. Then the rest of the public holiday weekend saw them on show at Brandesburton Hall, on 5 and 6 August.

They moved to the north Yorkshire fishing town of Whitby. The summer tourist season had just started, and the *Whitby Times* (10 August 1906: 4) reported that the "interesting little people" would be on show in the afternoon and at 8:00 and 9:00 in the evening at the Spa center, on 13 and 14 August. It added that they were soon to return "to their Forest Homes in Central Africa, whence they were brought last year by Lieut.-Col. J. J. Harrison."

Hoffman severed his association with them by September 1906, but they did not leave for Africa. October saw them in Eastbourne, on the Sussex coast sixty miles south of London. A handbill, announcing their appearance at the Pier Pavilion on 2 through 5 October 1906, states that "Mr. J. Osborne, who was with Sir H. Stanley in these parts, will lecture, and the Little People usually end up with one of their Native Dances." The *Eastbourne Gazette and Fashionable Visitors' List* of 26 September (5) and 3 October (5) repeated the advertisement, while the latter edition stated the times—3:30 on Wednesday, 3 October; 11:30 and 3:30 on Thursday and Friday (8).

The pygmies were still in England in February 1907, two years after they first had met Harrison in Africa. They appeared at the King's Hall in Westcliff on Sea, Southend, on the estuary of the Thames, from 25 February. It was a "farewell performance" and had Osborne lecturing "on their habits and customs." "See them now or never" advised the advertising. The Africans were on display twice daily, for an hour, at 3:30 and 8:15.

Three months later the Africans were entertaining in Bristol. "They return to their home in the Ituri Forest, Central Africa, in July next," was part of the announcement in the *Bristol Evening News* (Saturday, 25 May 1907: 1). It was, again, a "farewell visit." They had been to Bristol before, according to the *Bristol Guardian,* which also went to some lengths to describe the meaning of "pygmy," referring to Homer. Picking up a Harrison claim, this newspaper admitted: "we are inclined to envy the imperturbability with which our visitors from the Ituri forests regard the disdain with which the elements decline to follow the season's theoretical rules!" The advertising also appeared in the *Bristol Echo*. There were no reviews of their show at the Victoria Rooms at the Colston Hall.

The six African entertainers had probably seen more of Britain than the majority of Britons. They had met aristocrats and royalty, numerous people who had paid to see them at receptions and bazaars, and some of the common herd, as noted in Glasgow. They had been filmed on the way to Crawley, made phonograph recordings, been photographed, and ridden in motor cars, taxis, trains, and boats. Bokani had posed for leading sculptor William Goscombe John, and the fourteen-inch-high bronze head had been exhibited at the Royal Academy in 1906 (Pearson 41). They were playing a role as savage entertainers and had done so within days of reaching London, as we have seen through their employment at Buckingham Palace and their presence, fully armed, at Westminster and in Crawley.

One of their postcards had the following message scrawled on it: "I have sent you one of these photo to pick a nice fancy man how do they suite you I thought their face would be fetching what lovely faces they got [sic]." The errors and the script suggest that the writer was working-class.

The inhabitants of Brandesburton whose testimony has survived were also working-class. The Harrison family filled the positions of squire, magis-

Fig. 6.9. The bronze bust of Bokani, by Sir William Goscombe John, was
exhibited in London in 1906. Courtesy National Museum of Wales.

trate, and employer. Those eleven farms included fourteen cottages, and locals
were employed as farm workers, gardeners, and house servants. Other villagers could supplement their incomes by helping when the Harrisons had guests
at the hall or at garden parties. The colonel had given land to the local cricket
club, and, no doubt, employed local people to assist in the care of his horses
and in the upkeep of Brandesburton Hall. Any who disagreed with the status
quo had to keep quiet, migrate, or join the army.

That squire Harrison had six small Africans staying at the hall was not
difficult for the local people to understand; they had seen or heard of his stuffed
heads and other trophies and were aware that the colonel went abroad most
winters. Indeed, the legend that the pygmies were shipped back to Africa be-

cause they had killed too many pheasants with bow and arrow seems to indicate that Brandesburton folk were aware of their own status vis-à-vis the colonel, and that they respected the dark strangers who had not obeyed local game-hunting regulations.

"The most popular theory is that the pygmies, who were expert archers and roamed the squire's acres, shot rabbits and pigeons at first, but then began killing chickens and pheasants and were shipped back to Africa in disgrace" (Winter). Other tales noted by Geoffrey Winter reflected the somewhat feudal nature of Brandesburton in 1905–07, and included a suggestion that Harrison planned to breed them so the children would be servants. Other legends hold that the six were terrified to return to Africa, as they would be slaughtered on their return, and that they all died from influenza.

Tom Haggett, born in the 1890s, said they were his size, and that Harrison "was only a little feller, not a deal bigger nor them [sic]." He recalled that he had somehow upset the chief (Bokani) who "walked away, came back with a handful of green nettles and rubbed 'em all over my face." That story was retold in 1994 by his widow, who had first seen the Africans when she started school in Brandesburton in 1907. She recalled that they looked unhappy and bored.

Winter was told by eighty-six-year-old Haggett and ninety-one-year-old Jim Hudson that the Africans showed no fear of bees when taking their honey. Both Stone and Hoffman had noted their love of honey, but neither had seen what Haggett observed when they found a bees' nest in a hole in a tree: "They'd shin up it, stick their hands in the hole and eat the honey. You couldn't see their lips for bees, but they'd just blow them off." Hudson travelled from Driffield four times to see the Africans, who "were kindly people."

Elsie Dixon cycled from Beverley to Brandesburton at the age of ten or eleven. She thought they looked so pathetic that she patted one woman on the head: angered, the pygmy threw a coin at her head. Edith Beeson recalled their names, perhaps through one of the commercial postcards. She added, "The men pygmies used to go about with some of the teenage village girls, but if there was any romance I was too young to know. A lot of the parents were a bit scared." She said that Harrison spoke their language, which might have been an exaggeration, but he must have known some Swahili. She told Winter, "The pygmies, who were tough little folk, without a doubt, learned to speak quite a bit of English. They went to the village shops and soon got to know how to handle money and get the right change. They were quite brainy, the way they adapted. We village children picked up snatches of their language, and used their words in Swahili, or whatever it was, for going to the toilet."

These recollections, by people who looked back seven decades, are supported by snapshots and posed photographs in the Harrison scrapbooks. The pygmies are seen, playing with a diabolo (a game that was popular in 1907); others have the hall and its gardeners in the background. There are shots of them, on a misty day, mixing with local children.

On 12 February 1991, just before her ninety-first birthday, Grace Watson told of her recollections of the Africans who had shared some of her childhood. They had walked about the village freely, did not attend school or church, always had their bows and arrows with them, were "semi-naked," and "seemed happy enough." "There wasn't a tall one amongst them" she said, and, without a postcard or other souvenir to remind her of that time so long before, she volunteered the name Mongola [sic] (Watson). She confirmed Winter's comments that the pygmies and Brandesburton children had wept when the Africans departed for the long journey home.

Grace Watson and Winter's informants, and younger Brandesburton people who recalled their parents' tales, all spoke of the Africans visiting Blaxendale's forge in the village. The blacksmith shod horses, and the pygmies used the cast-off ends of the horseshoe nails to beat into arrow heads. Some were kept as souvenirs. "They knew what they were doing."

Mrs. Watson also said the pygmies had been accommodated in the coach house at the hall, and that the servants spoke some words in the pygmies' language. A more detailed but unpublished investigation had been conducted in the late 1960s and early 1970s by Stuart Walker, a medical practitioner who had spent some years in Africa and found that elderly patients in Yorkshire had their own vicarious travellers' tales to tell.

Harrison had paid for a large summerhouse to be added to the hall, to create a hot and humid atmosphere for the pygmies. The Africans were so much at home that they were guests at the wedding of one of Dr. Walker's patients' parents. The two women enjoyed dressing up with Harrison staff, and the males played soccer with relish, against children of their own size but less-developed muscle power. The pygmies disliked losing. They liked practical jokes, and they had a passion for red clothing to the extent of exchanging expensive gifts for trivial items that were red; "nearly every one in the late '60s told me how Mafutiminga's chief had found red blankets impossible to turn down" (Walker).

The women made a hut in the grounds of the hall, according to photographic evidence in an article in the *Beverley Guardian* of 20 April 1907, which noted that John Osborne was staying with the Africans. Edith Beeson was to tell Winter, "Squire Harrison employed a Mr. Osborne to be the pygmies' keeper, but exhibiting the pygmies was not the financial success he hoped it would be, and he had to get rid of him."

Osborne was with the Africans in London in the summer of 1907. The six worked at the Balkan States Exhibition at Earls Court, west London. Such shows had all manner of attractions: The *Era* (8 June 1907: 19) noted there was a section called "Old Japan," and that "Just across the way are the Pygmies, an interesting and very happy little family which Colonel Harrison brought from the Congo, and which are going back to their native forest at the close of the Exhibition." It mentioned "Hindoo freaks," fishing cormorants, and a flying machine. There were two bands, too.

The veteran nurse who had recalled the younger woman selling programs in London must have been referring to this exhibition; did the two women, African and Briton, renew their friendship by accident or by design?

The Africans' presence in London was widely known after the humor weekly *Punch* published "Petting the Pygmies" on 28 August 1907 (149). The exhibit consisted of five Africans, who were in front of a double row of chairs. The older woman is seated near a heater, and the younger "is spasmodically accepting invitations to shake hands." The patrons are seen as foolish—throwing a ball to one of them, trying to get their jewelry as a gift, dancing with one of the women, and remarking that the Africans knew the names of the regular patrons. The show closed at eleven; the two women "bestow generous kisses on such fortunate female admirers as have attended sufficient audiences to have earned the distinction. The Pygmy Chief appears to be pondering over the excessive susceptibility of the British Public to the charms of his countrywomen, in whom, though fine women enough in their way, he can see nothing whatever to make all that fuss about. But then these big white folk, though they have their uses in providing him with cigarettes, do seem to him to be rather lacking in intelligence."

The pygmies were mentioned in the London scandal sheet *Illustrated Police News* on Saturday, 26 October 1907 (14). Its usual fare of suicides, murders, trials, tragic events, and natural catastrophes sometimes was expanded to include exotic items. A London court heard jeweler Isaac Mizraki's claim that Osborne had threatened him. Mizraki had sold a watch to the Africans, and afterward "the defendant, who is manager of the Pigmies Troupe, came round and asked what he had meant by selling the pigmies a watch" which was "trashy." It had ceased working. John Osborne and two male pygmies had gone to the shop. One waited at the door while his companion, also carrying bow and arrows, was with Osborne at the counter. Osborne demanded their money back. Mizraki's claim was that in bringing armed Africans, Osborne was threatening him. The defense pointed out that the Africans were "about 2 ft. 6 in. high" (85 cm).

A 1906 postcard of Mongonga, the smallest, states his height was 3 ft., 10 in. However, a "coloured man" named Aaron Martin, who had witnessed the incident, said that the jeweler had been very frightened and was "sick for two hours." The case was adjourned as the magistrate could not find anything threatening in Osborne's behavior; the pygmies received a refund. The matter was reported in the *Beverley Guardian* (9 Nov. 1907: 8).

Two weeks earlier the *Guardian* had reported that the pygmies were back at Brandesburton Hall, in "excellent health," and were to sail to Mombasa, where the colonel was to join them in January. On 16 November the *Guardian* announced the real final public show by the six African entertainers, "in aid of the Hull Royal Infirmary," at the Albert Lecture Hall, Hull, on 16 November. The six were on show from 2:00 to 6:30, and after a break of thirty minutes, until 10:00. Daytime tickets were double the cost of the three-penny evening tickets (5).

The *Hull Times* (16 Nov. 1907: 10) reported that they had obtained consent from Harrison. Osborne was quoted as praising the Africans' "cleanliness and their intelligence," a view very far removed from the nonsense in the press in May and June 1905. Yet again there are contradictions, for the *Yorkshire Post* of Friday, 15 November 1907, stated that the pygmies were on show that night and on the Saturday at the Albion Lecture Hall (9).

On Sunday, 17 November 1907, the six African entertainers and John Osborne were on board the cargo boat *Hindoo* as she sailed out of Hull. The colonel followed later, by a faster ship. His diary notes that he left on 6 December, met up with the others in Mombasa on 24 December, and all were in Nairobi on 26 December. Photographs of the new East African Railway are in a Harrison scrapbook.

They reached Lake Victoria, and on 1 January 1908, Harrison went with the four male pygmies to Government House, Entebbe. Using forty porters, who also carried the ladies, they set off south. Mafutiminga had sunstroke, and both Bokani and Mongonga were "going very lame" by 3 January. They reached Bunyoro four days later and were near the mountains in Toro by 13 January. Harrison noted in his diary that he wrote to "Dr Leslie" and purchased a donkey, and that on 14 January he paid his respects to the local monarch, Daudi Kasigano. The king of Toro planned to visit England, he noted. His palace had "quite an imposing array."

Harrison, Osborne, the porters, and the six pygmies crossed the Semliki river valley on 16 January and soon were in the forests. One week later, Harrison's diary records "3 hours brought us in to Bokani's place in the forest. Track was very bad for our porters—Great excitement. Bokani and his brother, who had been acting chief, thinking he was dead, to complicate matters he had married the old man's wife—when they met they embraced . . . but quite silently—further on we met his wife and they at once sat down, arm in arm—Mafuti also had his arm round another fair damsel."

How Harrison found the "miserable" settlement of eight huts, of which four were complete, is not stated. Seeking nomads in a rain forest, even in the dry season, had taken a week. "Monga does not seem to relish the surround-ings at all—and sits aloof." The two women were "still clad in their red dresses—rather a contrast to the village belles."

The following day Harrison shot an elephant, and two hundred people gathered. "Matuka tried to boss the crowd—they looked very quaint in their smart red dresses—gradually the boys discarded their clothes—and when Bokane fell into a puddle, he at last discarded his trousers—the ladies waited till we had gone & then took of [sic] all their clothes."

At the beginning of February, Harrison received English newspapers from 20 December 1907, and he wrote to Reuters news agency. He left before the rains and walked back to Entebbe, where on 27 March he caught up with his mail. His message reached Mombasa, where it was telegraphed to England. The *Beverley Guardian* of 7 March 1908 reported that the six African enter-tainers had returned to their homes in the rain forests of the eastern Congo (6).

Harrison returned a year later, on another shooting trip, but it was not until 20 January 1910, on another expedition, that the colonel was able to make contact with his black companions. He sent out messengers to "tell my little people I am here" and the next afternoon Matuka came to meet him. "He had his old fustian breeches but not improved in looks. He told me that the others were all scattered about, both his wives had left him. I gave him a lot of presents and he went off back to look for Mafutimingi." Matuka returned the next day, too.

Harrison captured another live prize, in November 1910, when he mar-ried Mrs. Mary Stetson Clarke of Illinois. *Who Was Who 1916–1928* (469) named her as Mrs. Sumner Clarke of Peoria, Illinois. Yorkshire legends have her as the heiress of the Stetson hat company. The wedding was a top social affair in London: three of the four ushers—two baronets and a naval officer—can be found in *Who's Who*, while the best man, Albert Stern, was to be direc-tor of mechanical warfare in 1916 and a director of a nationwide bank until 1939. There was a touch of the exotic in the list of wedding guests, for one was Princess Petriva of Cooch Behar, India.

James Harrison died on 12 March 1923, and was cremated. His widow is believed to have gone to America. She died in 1932. William Hoffman worked in the French Congo for a spell, returned to London in the 1910s, and bothered Dorothy Stanley for money until her death in 1926. He continued to ask for help from her husband's old friend, millionaire Henry Wellcome, in selling docu-ments, photographs, arrows, and five manuscripts. He was the last of the Euro-peans who had crossed Africa with Stanley, and he could damage the explorer's reputation. When Wellcome died in 1936, Hoffman turned to a publisher, and his lifeless *With Stanley in Africa* appeared in 1938. His name was spelled "Hoffmann" and it has been misspelled in every biography and account of

Stanley's travels. Hoffman died in 1941, shortly before his wife, who had comforted the pygmies in 1905.

Twelve years later Macmillan and Co. of London published *Wrack at Tidesend,* a collection of poems by Osbert Sitwell. Born in 1892, he had seen Harrison and the pygmies, possibly at Londesborough Park (his mother was the daughter of the first Lord Londesborough) or in Scarborough, where the Sitwells lived. He immortalized Harrison as "Colonel Grindle," who had "engaged in single—though unequal—combat" an elephant, rhino, zebra, and okapi whose "tusks or rugoose heads now adorned his palladian mansion." Amid the snows of a Yorkshire winter the colonel "spent his days shaking with inappropriate jungle fevers," observed by portraits of his ancestors.

"But his life was still exotic: the sound of strange, unworldly conversations echoed from the direction of the stables, that annexe of the Equator, where lived a whole tribe of pygmies." Describing Scarborough as "Tidesend," Sitwell wrote that the "shivering Colonel" would come there with "a posse of chattering manikins . . . quarelling or grinning on their way to be shown at some Church Fete." The "yellow, bearded, naked, male pygmies" were "German [garden ornament] gnomes dipped in coffee," who were exhibited in aid of charities. "Sometimes they would dance—no decorous measure, but a laughing prophecy of the jazz wind that would soon sweep the world."

What was the impact of the six African entertainers in Britain? One Brandesburton youth who became a farmer migrated to Kenya and there dreamed of following the colonel's footsteps. The children of the Beverley area saw the Africans, who were brought to their schools. The village children mixed with them. The nurse and the younger woman pygmy had a friendship. Hoffman and his wife had a soft spot for them, if her niece's recollections can be relied upon. For the mass of Britons who paid to see them, they were just a novel turn in one program out of a dozen or more at the local variety theater. Any memory of their show, like recollections of most entertainers, faded fast.

Yet the jaded appetites of London theatrical journalists had been sharpened by their presence, and some saw behind the act and observed people. Small strangers from an unknown part of the last inhabited continent to divulge its secrets to Europeans, the pygmies were both part of an imperial display with strong overtones of cultural inferiority, and a group of little people who earned respect. Whatever else the six entertainers did in their years in Britain, that they went, fully armed, to the very heart of the world's largest empire suggests that they were people who earned the trust of the mighty. They earned the trust and respect of the people of Brandesburton, too.

Their humanity reached over the footlights of the theaters and encouraged a sympathetic response from some in the audience. The large white people and the small Africans had a relationship that was, as the phonograph company's catalog said, "punctuated by laughter." We will never know how much was directed at the African entertainers, or how much they laughed at the British. The teenage Osbert Sitwell had seen the colonel and the ladies at garden parties as victims of the pygmies. In the story of the Congo pygmies in Britain 1905–07, even Harrison, the "dwarf impresario," cannot be judged solely as a villainous exploiter; and certainly the six entertainers cannot be seen as victims. There were times when the Africans and the British found themselves sharing joys and laughter.

The barely literate scrawl on one postcard has "what lovely faces they got." What other comments might there be in the ocean of silence that separates performer from audience? "Niggers on a small scale" was the basic impression, certainly, but the six were not representing a defeated people such as the troupes of Dahomey Warriors which toured Britain at this time. The pygmies were ambassadors of Africa, people of legend, dwellers in the darkest forests, whose lack of stature made larger people wonder at their lives.

The British knew almost nothing about the great rain forest, its peoples, and the Congo river system. Morel, in his *Red Rubber,* had to superimpose a map of the river over one, on the same scale, of Europe. In presenting these findings to audiences ninety years later, I have had to use Morel's map, for ignorance of Africa remains strong.

For almost three years, the six African entertainers appeared before nearly one million Britons. We know that some of their audiences were respectful and that others just enjoyed the show.

In the 1920s Paul Schebesta lived among the Mbuti, and later published two books on them. Colin Turnbull's *The Forest People* appeared in 1961 and was republished several times. His acknowledgments stated that Schebesta "was the first to open the way to this wonderful world" of the Mbuti people. Turnbull correctly identified George [*sic*] Schweinfurth's *The Heart of Africa* (1873) as the earliest firsthand account of Congo pygmies. Neither Turnbull nor Schebesta had any knowledge that six pygmies had performed before so many in Britain and Germany in 1905–07. Yet Turnbull noted that the Italian traveller Miani, who had died before he could return from the Ituri in the 1860s, had sent two male pygmies to Italy, where they were brought up in Verona by the president of the Geographical Association, sponsors of his journey. Count Miniscalchi educated them; his relative told Turnbull about them (Turnbull 22). Apart from this, "we remain ignorant of anything but the actual fact of their existence [in the Congo] until a White Father, The Rev. Paul Schebesta, set out from Vienna in the nineteen-twenties to study them" (22).

What is clear is that the warning in the *Household Monthly* has been ignored. The "slightest freaks" have been turned into evidence of the "quaint fancies" of strangers. Schebesta could have met Georg Schweinfurth. Turnbull could have asked in Verona whether the aged botanist who died fifty years after his book had been published had seen the six in Berlin in 1906. They and others sought proof of their "quaint fancies" in the Ituri forest, little dreaming that the two who had gone to Italy were not totally exceptional.

In the long, complex, and often evil relationship between the people of Europe and the people of tropical Africa, the role of African entertainers needs careful consideration. These findings on the six who toured Britain from 1905 to 1907 reveal that our quaint fancies are not imaginative enough.

WORKS CITED

Dictionary of National Biography, Supplement January 1901–December 1911. Vol. 3. Ed. Sir Sidney Lee. London: Oxford UP, 1912.

Edwards, Elizabeth. *Anthropology and Photography 1860–1920.* New Haven: Yale UP, 1992.

FO 123/46, FO 141/390. Public Record Office. Kew, England.

Green, Jeffrey. "In Dahomey in London in 1903." *The Black Perspective in Music* 11.1 (1983): 22–40.

Hall, Richard. *Stanley: An Adventurer Explored.* London: Collins, 1974.

Harrison, James. *Life among the Pygmies of the Ituri Forest, Congo Free State.* London: Hutchinson, 1905.

———. Scrapbooks and diaries. Museum of Natural History, Wood End, Scarborough. Courtesy Ian Massey.

Hoffman. Interview with Hoffman's niece, who requested that her name not be published. London. 3 Feb. 1994.

Hoffman[n], William. *With Stanley in Africa.* London: Cassell, 1938.

Inglis, Brian. *Roger Casement.* London: Hodder and Stoughton, 1973.

Johnston, Harry. *The Story of My Life.* Garden City, NY: Garden City Press, 1923.

Kruszynski, Robert. Letter to the author. 26 March 1991.

Louis, William Roger. "The Triumph of the Congo Reform Movement." *Boston University Papers on Africa 2.* Ed. Jeffrey Butler. Boston: Boston UP, 1966.

National Portrait Gallery, London. Benjamin Stone collection. See also *Sir Benjamin Stone's Pictures.* London: Cassell, 1906.

Neave, David. Letter to the author. 14 Nov. 1992.

Pearson, Fiona. *Goscombe John at the National Museum of Wales.* Cardiff: National Museum of Wales, 1979.

Read, Jack. *Empires, Hippodromes and Palaces.* London: Alderman Press, 1985.

Royal Geographical Society, London. William Hoffman file.

Schebesta, Paul. *Among Congo Pygmies.* London: Hutchinson, 1933.

———. *Revisiting My Pygmy Hosts.* London: Hutchinson, 1936.

Stanley, Henry. *In Darkest Africa.* London: Sampson, Low, 1890.

Stoecker, Helmuth, ed. *German Imperialism in Africa.* Atlantic Highlands, N.J.: Humanities Press International, 1986.

Turnbull, Colin M. *The Forest People.* London: Chatto and Windus, 1961.

Walker, J. E. S. Comments on author's 1991 ts. N.d.

Watson, Grace. Telephone interview with the author. 12 Feb. 1991.

Wellcome Institute, London. Hoffman files 6010, 6011, 6012.

Winter, Geoffrey. "Pygmies of East Riding." Newspaper clipping. N.d. [1983?].

Wright, Chris. Discussion and examination of photographs. Royal Anthropological Institute, London. 19 Jan. 1995.

7

Ota Benga and the Barnum Perplex

Harvey Blume

For all the attention P. T. Barnum has received from biographers and others, his effect on culture, especially the culture of human display, is in many ways uncharted.

True, Barnum's varied contributions to science have been enumerated. We know, for example, that Henry Thoreau thought Barnum's American Museum worth repeated visits and that he particularly valued the sea anemones on view in the fresh water aquarium (Betts 355). (Thoreau's opinions of Barnum's unicorns and mermaids, are, regrettably, not on record.) We know, too, that Barnum fielded a worldwide network of agents in constant search of fresh material; that he cultivated ties with the leading naturalists of his day, Albert S. Bickmore and Louis Agassiz among them (Saxon); and that in his later years, he donated items regularly to the Smithsonian Institution, the American Museum of Natural History, and the Tufts College Museum, which he founded.

But if Barnum's efforts to slake the curatorial hungers of nineteenth-century science have been documented, the contribution science made to Barnumism is less understood. Had there been no P. T. Barnum, science would lack for some of its more enticing displays, such as the bones of Jumbo the giant elephant, on view once more at the American Museum of Natural History. Naturalists would have found themselves less often in the public eye to credit, discredit, or be boggled by one of Barnum's exhibits. And when the time came for scientists to mount their own ethnographic spectacles, as they did at world's fairs, they might have been clumsier were it not for the Barnumesque dress rehearsals. But all in all, science would have developed much as it did without Tom Thumb, Jumbo, or the Feejee Mermaid. Barnum, on the other hand, is a wraith without natural history and ethnography. He is a trapeze artist with no trapeze, a bareback rider minus a mount, a subversive with no government to agitate against.

I want to let Barnum and Barnumism lead into a discussion of the nine-teenth century's twin fixations—authenticity and showmanship, realism and display—elements that when joined together take on paradoxical potency. I will continue by presenting one of many possible visions of Ota Benga, an African Pygmy, when he was, indeed, the Pygmy in the Zoo, and end with some thoughts about how Ota might be received today, and where we might find several strands of contemporary Barnumism.

Let me start by claiming P. T. Barnum for postmodernism, for the melt-down of form, the erosion of convention, the pervasive blurring of genre we now see on every side. Among the hybrids threatening to push out the more traditional forms, Clifford Geertz notes:

> philosophical inquiries looking like literary criticism . . . documentaries that read like true confessions . . . parables posing as ethnographies . . . theoretical treatises set out as travelogues . . . epistemological studies constructed like po-litical tracts . . . methodological polemics got up as personal memoirs. . . .

"One waits only," muses Geertz, "for quantum theory in verse or biography in algebra" (19).

Geertz's essay on genre blurring was written in 1980. That was before Art Spiegelman's *Maus* confronted bookstore workers with an insoluble problem of classification (just where exactly should autobiographical comic books about genocide be shelved?); before historian Simon Schama's *Dead Certainties: Un-warranted Speculations* split the *New York Times Book Review* editorial board neatly down the middle on whether the book was fiction or nonfiction; before Oliver Stone's *JFK* created uproar not least of all because it seamlessly spliced together documentary and fictional footage; and before Pico Iyer learned he could never tell whether, in any given bookstore, his travel books would be billed as history, anthropology, or works of fiction.

It is safe to say the process Geertz described has speeded up. The digital engine has kicked it into overdrive, adding a vast potential for do-it-yourself genre fusion (graphics, text, video, and sound in a single Web site), and confu-sion (extending from the validity of photographic evidence to issues of gender and identity) (see, e.g., Turkle).

We may as well accept the mutability of form as a fundamental law of contemporary culture. This does not, as is often feared, obviate questions of truth and falsity. If anything, they emerge more starkly when no longer camouflaged by, spoken for, or identified with specific delivery systems. Still, no matter how well adjusted you are to the general drift, there can be shock when anomalies crop up in your own neighborhood. Historians, for example, voiced few concerns about the nonfiction novel—so long as it remained a novel and its leading practitioners (Truman Capote, Norman Mailer) were clearly marked as novelists. But when Simon Schama imported the novel's techniques wholesale into works of supposed nonfiction, alarms rang out in history departments.[1]

Genre blurring was always Barnum's neighborhood, the base of operations from which he issued oddities and anomalies to entice the culture into maximum perplexity. In this respect, he is our contemporary. The categories he used for the unclassifiable—the "nondescript" and the "what is it?"—are labels many of today's culture makers might proudly claim for their work. Let me suggest we think of Barnum, then, as an epistemologist in impresario's drag, a philosopher entirely in the American grain, unfastening ideas from things, demonstrating that reality is too slippery, continuous, and manifold to be pinned down by names and notions, and accomplishing all this before a mass audience.

No less a historian of ideas than Arthur Lovejoy vouches for Barnum's philosophical credentials, writing, "that if Aristotle had been permitted to return to the sublunary scene in the eighteen-forties, he would have made haste to visit Barnum's Museum" (236). Lovejoy sees the Barnum of those years as operating well within the structure of the Great Chain of Being, the intellectual scaffolding that held sway for nearly a millennium before being supplanted by Darwinism. It flows from the Great Chain of Being that between any two species there will always be an intermediate species, and so on between the next two, until all conceivable gaps in the continuum of Creation are occupied, else Creation would be less complete than it was required to be by definition.

As Lovejoy notes, Barnum was nothing if not expert in intermediate species. Missing links were his specialty, and he kept his museum stocked with them, whether to flesh out the Great Chain of Being, or after 1859, when Darwin's *Origin of Species* appeared, to buttress the theory of evolution. (Barnum was not choosy about which intellectual framework he simultaneously promoted and subverted.) When his museum burned and Barnum turned his attention to the circus, he continued to work the margins, probing for the unknown (and sometimes unreal) hidden within or just beyond the borders of the seen.

It is inherent in the three-ring circus, a Barnum and Bailey innovation, to tease the viewer with events unfolding at the periphery (Bogdan 288). Animals, clowns, trapeze artists, and strongmen engage in activities that stretch and exceed the range of vision, reminders that no particular point of view is absolute and that no fixed gaze can ever be more than provisional. Barnum carried this teasing emphasis on incompletion and mutability over from museum to circus to text. His autobiography was a hybrid of marketing and conceptual art that he modified regularly by "adding and subtracting chapters so that the tome could be sold again as an entirely new version" (Sante 60).

The genres it was most crucial for Barnum to confound were those of fact and fiction, or, more specifically, science and showmanship. In one sense, Barnum functioned as science's clown: after the strongman poses, flexes, and finally, arduously, lifts the barbell, the clown emerges to clean up the mess the hero has left onstage. Wiggling his behind, he tosses the weight carelessly over one shoulder, his other hand free for a mop and a pail of water. Similarly, after Darwin published his heroically researched *Origin of Species*, Barnum lost no time in resolving the outstanding question of evolution, or at least the one with the greatest purchase on the popular imagination. He invited the viewing public to his American Museum to study no less a personage than Mr. Johnson, the Missing Link between man and ape, just purchased from a band of African explorers, and only now learning how to walk upright. Press and public were thrown into a quandary, suspecting Mr. Johnson was Barnumesque "bosh" but not wanting to rule out the possibility that he was, instead, the "great fact for Darwin" (Saxon 99).

Again, it was not long after the Anthropology Department of the Chicago World's Fair of 1893 was organized by Frederick Ward Putnam and Franz Boas to study and display indigenous peoples that the Barnum and Bailey Circus put forth its own version of an anthropological gala: for the next two years a Great Ethnological Congress, including representatives of seventy-four non-Western people, some drawn directly from the fair, was the featured attraction, on view in the menagerie tent. As Mikhail Bakhtin points out, it is in the nature of carnival, or in this case circus, to take things down a notch or two, confronting form with flux, stability with roiling chaos, and high (anthropological) seriousness with the reverse image of spectacle and fun-house grotesquerie.

But it is not really so easy to determine which comes first here, science or circus, or which is truly the other's shadow. The anthropologists putting people on display were adopting to their own uses a motif of exhibition long in evidence at sideshows, dime museums, and fairs. The showman, in turn, would have failed to realize the full potential of a human exhibit if he did not provide it with a learned label of some kind, if he did not argue for its accuracy and frame it so as to satisfy the ever-increasing craving for authenticity. When it came to human display, science and showmanship, like Eng and Chang, were joined at the hip.

The anthropologists of the St. Louis Fair of 1904 proposed to treat their charges with a seriousness that would once and for all sever anthropology from its lowbrow brother. The 1,200 Filipinos, Ainu, Eskimo, Native Americans, Zulus, and Pygmies were brought to St. Louis to be studied, to be dissolved, if

Fig. 7.1. Pygmy music. St. Louis Exposition, 1904.

possible, into the numerical ordering system provided by anthropometry and psychometry. But the press and the public were only further incited by the overlay of science, the G-string of statistics. The crowds pressed in as if they would not be satisfied with anything less than a piece of Pygmy, stealing from the Kwakiutl, and buying buttons, bows, and arrows from the industrious Geronimo.

The masses resisted inculcation into the higher racism provided by anthropometry, psychometry, and social Darwinism. It was elitist and non-participatory, the real fun restricted to the coterie of anthropologists. It denied the evidence of the senses, all of which were alerted to the presence of spectacle. Barnum, dead for thirteen years by the time of the St. Louis Fair, could never have concocted a more inflammatory piece of showmanship than did the anthropologists with their canny juxtaposition of science and exotica.

Barnumism was no less operative two years later when Ota Benga, one of the Pygmies who survived St. Louis, found himself in the same cage as Dohong the orangutan in the Bronx Zoo. Bronx Zoo director William Temple Hornaday's only initial prop was a sign placed in front of the cage listing Ota's name, height, weight, age, where he came from, who brought him to the United States, and when he would be exhibited, namely, "each afternoon during September." The crowd decoded the bland message precisely as they were meant to: within a few days 40,000 people were jostling each other for a glimpse of the Pygmy in the Zoo.

Hornaday's sign juxtaposed realism, factuality, science—in short, authenticity—over against the archaic, the mythological, the disquieting and grotesque. It used knowledge to frame the wild, the unknown and perhaps unknowable. Everything was in place, everything positioned in proper relationship to everything else—sign, cage, man, ape, science, and spectacle—but in this case probably not all of it was necessary. Ota Benga alone would have been sufficient, as became apparent a few days later, when, released from the monkey cage and roaming Bronx Zoo grounds at will, he attained to the peak of unasked-for popularity.

As a Pygmy, he had not only decades and centuries, but millennia of advance billing. His appearance in the flesh, his authenticity vouched for by a zoo director, could not be anything less than a sensation. Homer had written about the defeat of Pygmies by the cranes descending upon them in their annual escape from "winter time and the rains unceasing." Herodotus had called them a "nation of wizards." Pliny had listed them among the monstrous races and bequeathed them to the Middle Ages for further study. A medieval schoolman argued that the Pygmies' humanity was skin deep, a matter of appearance only; it would fail to pass the test of logic. Pygmies, he postulated, could not reason from a premise to its conclusion. They would fail at syllogisms, and therefore, were merely counterfeit humans, monsters in human disguise.

The ability to chop Aristotelian logic was used as the entrance exam into the human race for centuries. When Samuel Phillips Verner, the man who brought Ota Benga to America, met Batwa Pygmies in Africa in the late 1880s, the question asked by the Middle Ages was foremost in his mind: were the schoolmen right? Could the Pygmies reason? Were they capable of navigating from a premise to its conclusion? (Bradford and Blume 82). As it happened, Verner gave the Pygmies a passing grade in logic.

The taxonomy proposed by antiquity and elaborated by the Middle Ages was built to last. When a schoolman wrote that Pygmies were "deformed and do not build houses but live in mountain caverns and caves," his words were conducted with high fidelity down the ages until they wound up as the learned gloss used by Barnum to frame an exhibition (Friedman 145). According to Barnum, the Earthman (like Bushman, a term used interchangeably with Pygmy in the freak show), is known for

> burrowing holes into the ground, and there finding shelter beyond the reach of man or beast. . . . A colony of them resembles a gigantic warren of rabbits. . . . These holes are so numerous and intricate, that in the course of time whole mountains become honey-combed. . . . (Bogdan 188)

The schoolmen would not have begrudged Barnum his few embellishments; he was faithful to the essence of their teaching. When they declared that the

Pygmy was without real language—"the cause of his speech is as a shadow resulting from the sunset of reason" (Friedman 192)—Barnum once again concurred, advertising that "Earthmen have no recognized language beyond the simple and almost unintelligible patois which designates their simple wants" (Bogdan 189).

The link between learning and human display was old and intimate. When the crane man—identified by his enormous neck and big beak—began to make public appearances in the sixteenth century, he had with him a pamphlet containing an explanatory text by the learned Lycosthenes (Wittkower 194).

Display, on the one hand, the claim of authenticity, on the other, are twin pillars of Barnumism, and with them Barnum exemplifies the fixations of his age. The nineteenth century represented a burgeoning of techniques and venues for exhibition. The scramble for new means of appropriating and representing reality was as typical of the time as the scramble for colonial possessions.

Among the display venues that arose or were given modern form were zoos, museums (with art and natural history museums distinguished for the first time), department stores, and world's fairs, which displayed not only objects but human beings. Among the techniques developed were the diorama, cyclorama, panorama, photograph, and, with the introduction of electricity toward the end of the century, a panoply of modern devices, including the phonograph and motion picture camera.

Louis Jacques Mandé Daguerre's obsession with discovering the perfect instrument for the reproduction of visual reality is instructive, and as riveting in its way as David Livingstone's less successful search for the sources of the Nile. Daguerre, who began his career as a mediocre naturalist painter, gravitated at first toward set design. His successful "striving for extreme naturalism led him more and more beyond the bounds of art into the field of showmanship" (Gernsheim 10). Experimenting further with the interplay of light and paint, he developed the diorama, which presented changing naturalistic vistas, and presaged the popularity of the cinema (Rice 71).

When Daguerre's Parisian diorama burnt down in 1839, he was ready with the next advance in representational fidelity, the daguerreotype. When exposure time was reduced sufficiently to permit human portraiture, the response to the daguerreotype took on religious overtones. Opponents attacked the device and its inventor with the pious rage evident in this German editorial:

> The wish to capture evanescent reflections . . . the mere desire alone, the will to do so, is blasphemy. God created man in His own image, and no man-made machine may fix the image of God. (Gernsheim 2)

The very notion of "mirror pictures made permanent" proved the Frenchman Daguerre to be "the fool of fools." It was one thing to capture space—that was private property—but quite another to trap and preserve time's "evanescent reflections." That was to intrude on a divine prerogative.

The language of Daguerre's supporters was equally fervent, and no less laced with references to the supernatural. In 1843, shortly after the technique was introduced in England, Elizabeth Barrett wrote,

> Think of a man sitting down in the sun and leaving his facsimile in all its full completion of outline and shadow, steadfast on a plate, at the end of a minute and a half! The Mesmeric disembodiment of spirits strikes one as a degree less marvellous . . . the fact of the *very shadow of the person* lying there fixed for ever! It is the very sanctification of portraits I think. (Gernsheim 149)

The image was like a shadow; capturing it on a photographic plate was like detaining a spirit. Whether you were pro or con, this was magic, the magic that emerges from realism pushed so far to an extreme that it doubles back on itself. As Susan Sontag puts it: "What defines the originality of photography is that, at the very moment in the long, increasingly secular history of painting when secularism is entirely triumphant, it revives—in wholly secular terms—something like the primitive status of images" (156).

Photography constitutes one node on a nineteenth-century continuum of display space. The world's fair, which maintained indigenous people in supposed simulations of their natural habitats, in authentic dwellings, and in authentic gear, constitutes another. Anthropological fieldwork, in which the native is arrayed beneath the anthropologist's gaze under conditions, by definition, of maximum authenticity, constitutes yet another.

With the world's fair, the show takes place in the metropolis. In the case of fieldwork, the show is always on the road. The assumption about the anthropological observer remains the same: his gaze is neutral; it belongs not so much to a human being as to a ghostly instrument that leaves no trace on what it touches. The subject does not yet disturb the object; the knower somehow makes no impression on the known.

It is hard to imagine a better illustration of this stringent naiveté than in the case of the Zulus exhibited on a London stage in 1853. According to newspaper reports, the Zulus sang, danced, courted each other, and prepared for war as if oblivious of spectators (Lindfors 146). They were human, yes, but with a defining quality of self-consciousness missing. They were like a hive of bees or a glass-plated ant colony that could be taken from place of origin to the laboratory for study. The analogy to insect life, and even to microbes, is strength-

Fig. 7.2. "The Pygmies on Dress Parade." From Walter B. Stevens, *The World's Fair.*

ened by a remark made by Margaret Mead: "We are just completing a culture of a mountain group here in the lower Torres Chelles" (Clifford 230). A culture, then, could be completed, taken in its entirety, and regenerated without loss of detail in the agar of the anthropologist's mind. Should that culture, for some reason, disappear, it could, in principle, be reconstituted from the field notes.

This naiveté—forced, arrogant, and preposterous from our point of view—was a distinctly non-postmodern element of Barnumism. To the extent that he subscribed to it, Barnum was in accord with his times. All his art was employed to deny the presence of art, to dissolve consciousness into nature. For any of his human anomalies to indicate that they were of normal intelligence, fully aware of the context in which they were viewed and fully capable of judging those who viewed them, would have blown the secret. On the other hand, in Barnum's case, the secret was sometimes meant to be blown: much of Tom Thumb's appeal lay in the contrast between the small body and the sharp mind. Tiny as he was, he could hold his own in repartee with the Queen of England or draw a diminutive sword on her poodle when it threatened to bite.

Barnum was interested in toying with perception, not etherizing it on a table. He throve on the very ambiguities the ethnographers of his day wanted to flatten out. For Barnum, objectivity was a collapsing prop; truth, volatile and elusive. And Barnumism was participatory in a way science could not be: when viewers were faced with the irreducible "nondescript," the inscrutable "what is it?" they had to come to their own conclusions. World's fair ethnographers wanted to spare their charges the indignity of humbug. Barnum may have spared his charges the greater indignity of ethnographers with their calipers, tests, and presumptions of certainty.

Barnumism was supple, adaptable, loose-jointed. Realism was rigid by comparison and kept backing into the very magical-mythological material it hoped to expunge. But this material was transformed in the interim. It was camouflaged and defamiliarized. It regained the element of surprise, absorbed new vitality from the close contact with science. The fetish for authenticity attained to efficacy, became a working fetish, evoking, summoning.

For example, Ota Benga at the zoo corresponds with a terrible if well-disguised exactitude to a prototype harbored by the Middle Ages and passed on to modernity—the wild man.[2] Wild men and women were centers of medieval concern, regulars of tapestries, woodcuts, engravings, and love caskets. They were stalwarts of carnival, heraldry, dance, poetry, and dream. The wild man was a masterpiece of mixed media, the meeting place of man and demon, man and beast, life and death. He was frequently hairy, commonly cannibalistic; the forest was his home and wild animals his only society. The wild man was to civilization what anti-matter is to matter. When the wild man met a knight, the result was instant combat, cudgel against sword, nature against society.

Fig. 7.3. Plaster cast of bust of Ota Benga.

Michael Taussig summarizes the wild man's vocation thus:

> In his wrath he creates tempests and hail—the weather he likes most—condi-
> tions best suited to the return of the dead. Ignorant of God, he wields power
> over the forest's animals. . . . Inferior to humans in the great chain of being, he
> is also superior to them. (213)

With this portrayal of the wild man in mind, let us revisit Ota Benga at
the zoo in 1906. He is a short, dark man, born in Africa's ancient forests, a
forest dweller who has somehow exchanged his habitat of trees for the more
abstractly linear design of steel bars that ring the monkey cage in which he is
displayed. The press and the public seize upon him as a cannibal immediately
and understand implicitly why he is to be found in the same locale as Señor
Lopez the jaguar, Hannibal the lion, Princeton the tiger, Gunda the elephant,
and Mogul the rhino. He is Ota Benga, the wild man, and this, the latter-day
environment of beasts, is designated as his proper home.

If we can for a moment imagine the Bronx Zoo as a wilderness, as the

Zoo founders, with their emphasis on natural habitat, their fetish for realism, often insisted on doing,[3] then the presence of Ota Benga is neither ornament nor accident. It is essential. It authenticates their project and brings it to its climax. When the wilderness is ready for him, then the wild man comes.

That's how Ota Benga was presented near the start of the twentieth century. How might he be presented near its close? Perhaps, like the Batwa who visited American cities in 1990, he would be a musician, leaving his village in Zaire for the very first time to play for *Africa Oyé,* a troupe of African performers on the first stop of their world tour. The Batwa performers were no less embedded in mythological material than was Ota, but this material accorded them dignity and pride of place.[4] As the senior inhabitants of the African forests, they opened the show for the other performers in the expectation that their good standing with the spirits of the ancestors would bring favor on the performances to come.

Or perhaps, in the closing decades of the century, Ota would not be a Pygmy at all. He would return as a performance artist, turning himself into a spectacle, generating for himself those very attributes of marginality and monstrosity that had been thrust on him decades ago. Critic Arthur Danto links the metier of the performance artist to the motif of the wild man by calling performance art disturbatory art, art that assumes a "regressive posture, undertaking to recover a stage of art where art itself was almost like magic—like deep magic, making dark possibilities real . . . summoning spirits from the vasty deep" (127). Of course, the differences between Ota Benga in a monkey cage and any number of contemporary performers who would gladly take up that post are the element of choice and the validation of art, the very things banished from nineteenth-century ethnography—and zoo keeping.

It would be fair, too, to ask where one would look for Barnumism today, except the search would soon collapse under the sheer weight of answers. Barnumism is everywhere—in politics, media, entertainment, and advertising. Ours is as much, or more, a Barnumesque Republic as it is a Jeffersonian Democracy. If, one day, Barnum's signature turned up on an original copy of the Declaration of Independence so that he could be retroactively pronounced a Founding Father, it would be appropriate—and Barnumesque.

Still, there are levels of Barnumism; not all Barnumism is the same. It is easy to detect the lower forms in those television shows where family members seem as if they were beamed directly from their kitchens to the studio where they go on screaming at each other, no less dysfunctional before a national audience than they were at home. The old paradigm really does live on here; the artifice of realism continues to prevail. (Are these families told prior to air time that they are on no account to behave well just because they are being watched? The more dysfunctional, the better?)

But there is also a higher Barnumism. One might find it in an institution like L.A.'s Museum of Jurassic Technology, as documented by Lawrence Weschler. The MJT's founder and director, David Wilson, often sits outside the storefront playing his accordion. Inside, there is a varying display of natural and manufactured objects: for example, a photograph of an African stink ant, a fungus protruding from its head and spearing it in place; documentation pertaining to the minute bat known as the "piercing devil," which has been caught only by putting a wall of solid lead eight inches thick in its flight path; micro-sculptures (Little Red Riding Hood, Donald Duck, Napoleon) set within the eyes of needles; a graphic description of a potion dating from 1579 in which mice, powdered or taken whole, are used as a cure for bedwetting.

The troublesome thing is that many of the exhibits are separated from being completely valid by no more than a detail—it seems the stink ant is South American rather than African, as advertised. Some displays are completely true (horns have been removed from human heads), and others patently false. Five lead walls each twenty feet high and two hundred feet long, somehow deployed in the rain forest to catch a bat? It's hard to know the percentage of truth in any given exhibit, and when to give up trying to find out.[5] In the meantime a kind of derangement sets in, a susceptibility to wonder. Weschler records that one wanderer in the back rooms emerged only to become spellbound by a pencil sharpener: "a regular pencil sharpener," according to the museum's director, "but he couldn't get enough of it" (52).

One museum director characterized the MJT as "a museum, a critique of museums, and a celebration of museums—all rolled into one" (Weschler 40). Weschler himself situates the MJT within the context of the *Wunderkammern*, or wonder cabinets, of the sixteenth and seventeenth centuries. Containing "whatsoever singularity, chance and the shuffle of things hath produced," they were used to top off a gentleman's education and, by dint of sustaining wonder, to make him permanently educable (76).

Looking back from the perspective of the Museum of Jurassic Technology, Barnum emerges as more than the progenitor of screech TV. He was also the impresario of a three-ring *Wunderkammer* and founder of that midtown wonder cabinet known as the American Museum (something for both Aristotle and Thoreau). In the original wonder cabinets, "you had the wonders of God spread out there cheek-by-jowl with the wonder of man, both presented as aspects of the same thing" (Weschler 61). The higher Barnumism resisted the severance of science from spectacle, just when the *zeitgeist* was most determined to pull them apart, housing art, as in New York City, on one side of town, science on the other. The higher Barnumism needed both to work with; they were the building blocks of the Barnum Perplex.

NOTES

1. Novelist Paul West gives this situation a nice reverse spin. After researching a novel about one of the plots to kill Hitler, and finding substantial discrepancies among the historical accounts, he told students the best way to learn to write good novels was to study closely the ways of historians (West).

2. Bernheimer notes that "In the case of the wild man, the testimony from the thirteenth century is often identical with that from the nineteenth" (vii).

3. As Bronx Zoo founders Henry Fairfield Osborn and C. Grant La Farge put it: "This new principle will be to place both native and foreign animals of the tropical, temperate and colder regions as far as possible in the natural surroundings. Thus the larger wild animals of North America—deer, elk, caribou, moose, bison, antelope, sheep—should be shown not in paddocks but in the free range of large enclosures, in which the forests, rocks, and natural features of the landscape will give the people an impression of the life, habits and native surroundings of these different types. We may also present the tropical and equatorial animals to a certain extent in their natural surroundings" (Bridges 16).

4. As was not the case when Ota Benga and Batwa Pygmies, performing at the St. Louis Fair, were mocked by anthropologists and attacked by spectators (Bradford and Blume 119).

5. Weschler reached his limit with the mouse recipe: "Right then and there I made myself a promise; and I've kept it: I have not gone to the library to track down that . . . reference. There has to be an end to all this. No, really" (106).

WORKS CITED

Bakhtin, Mikhail. *Rabelais and His World*. Cambridge: MIT Press, 1968.

Bernheimer, Richard. *Wild Men in the Middle Ages*. Cambridge: Harvard UP, 1952.

Betts, John Rickards. "P. T. Barnum and the Popularization of Natural History." *Journal of the History of Ideas* 20 (1959): 353–68.

Bogdan, Robert. *Freak Show: Presenting Human Oddities for Amusement and Profit*. Chicago: U of Chicago P, 1988.

Bradford, Phillips Verner, and Harvey Blume. *Ota Benga: The Pygmy in the Zoo*. New York: St. Martin's Press, 1992.

Bridges, William. *Gathering of Animals: An Unconventional History of the New York Zoological Society*. New York: Harper and Row, 1974.

Clifford, James. *The Predicament of Culture: Twentieth-Century Ethnography, Literature, and Art*. Cambridge: Harvard UP, 1988.

Danto, Arthur Coleman. *The Philosophical Disenfranchisement of Art*. New York: Columbia UP, 1986.

Friedman, John Block. *The Monstrous Races in Medieval Thought and Art*. Cambridge: Harvard UP, 1981.

Geertz, Clifford. *Local Knowledge*. New York: Basic Books, 1983.

Gernsheim, Helmut, and Alison Gernsheim. *L. J. M. Daguerre (1787–1851): The World's First Photographer*. Cleveland: World Publishing Company, 1956.

Lindfors, Bernth. "Charles Dickens and the Zulus." *Olive Schreiner and After: Essays on Southern African Literature*. Ed. Malvern Van Wyk Smith and Don Maclennan. Cape Town: David Philip, 1983. 142–55.

Lovejoy, Arthur O. *The Great Chain of Being*. Cambridge: Harvard UP, 1936.

Rice, Shelly. "Boundless Horizons: The Panoramic Image." *Art in America* Dec. 1993: 58–71.

Sante, Luc. *Low Life: Lures and Snares of Old New York*. New York: Farrar, Straus and Giroux, 1991.

Saxon, A. H. *P. T. Barnum: The Legend and the Man*. New York: Columbia UP, 1989.

Schama, Simon. *Dead Certainties: Unwarranted Speculations*. New York: Knopf, 1991.

Sontag, Susan. *On Photography*. New York: Dell, 1973.

Spiegleman, Art. *Maus: A Survivor's Tale*. New York: Pantheon, 1986.

Taussig, Michael. *Shamanism, Colonialism, and the Wild Man: A Study in Terror and Healing*. Chicago: U of Chicago P, 1986.

Turkle, Sherry. *Life on the Screen: Identity in the Age of the Internet*. New York: Simon and Schuster, 1995.

Weschler, Lawrence. *Mr. Wilson's Cabinet of Wonder*. New York: Pantheon, 1996.

West, Paul. Lecture. Public Library, Cambridge, Mass. 16 May 1991.

Wittkower, Rudolf. "Marvels of the East: A Study in the History of Monsters." *Journal of the Warburg and Courtauld Institute* 5 (1942): 159–97.

8

"Clicko"

Franz Taaibosch, South African Bushman Entertainer in England, France, Cuba, and the United States, 1908–1940

NEIL PARSONS

Franz Taaibosch appeared in vaudeville in England and France in 1913 as a "wild dancing Bushman." Attempts to liberate him from his manager resulted in his being taken away, possibly to Ireland, and then subsequently to Cuba. From there he was recruited to the United States, where as "Clicko" he became a standard attraction in circus sideshows until his death in 1940. His story is a study not only in the relationship between imperialism and popular entertainment, but also in individual human endurance.

INTRODUCTION

The intimate relationship between popular imperialism, popular entertainment, and popular education was recognized as long ago as 1901 by J. A. Hobson in his book *The Psychology of Jingoism*. Hobson saw "the glorification of brute force and an ignorant contempt for foreigners" being spread among "large sections of the middle and labouring classes" by the entertainment and recreation business—"a more potent educator than the church, the school, the political meeting, or even than the press." The very word Jingoism, meaning "Imperialist sentiment," had after all been inspired by an 1878 music-hall (vaudeville) song.

Hobson blamed the spread of "Imperialist sentiment" on modern forms of communication such as the electric telegraph, on the collective "neurotic temperament" generated by increasing urbanization, and on "rich, able and energetic" capitalists in entertainment and the media who exploited the persistent semi-literacy of the masses. His critique applied not only to Britain but also to the United States, where jingoism over war with Mexico showed that "A pseudo-scientific view of history has been used to support this new predestinarianism in politics."[1]

Such insights have been echoed in recent historical literature on the impact of imperialism in later-nineteenth- and twentieth-century Britain and Europe—notably the ongoing "Studies in Imperialism" series edited by John M. MacKenzie and published by Manchester University Press. Such studies, in parallel with studies of black people and the entertainment business in North America, have focused on the "images" and stereotypes of Africa and Africans as portrayed and developed by British and European entertainment and information media.

This essay is concerned with the stereotypic images in Western society not of people of African descent in general, but of a particular grouping, or so-called race, who were taken to be Stone Age people left over from the remote past. I refer to the "Bushmen" and "Hottentots" of southern Africa, otherwise known by the portmanteau term "Khoisan," derived from the words *khoi* or *khoe* and *san,* used for "person" and "people." Until the 1950s Khoisan people were presented in popular entertainment to the Western public in a manner that conflated them with biological "freaks" like bearded ladies and six-fingered giants; and at least until the 1930s that popular image was not so different from the scholarly image of Khoisan people propagated among Western intellectuals.

The history of Sara (or "Saartjie," a disparaging diminutive) Baartman, the "Hottentot Venus," a woman entertainer presented in London and Paris in the early nineteenth century, has been comprehensively studied.[2] Less well known are the families of Khoisan entertainers, as well as the individual servants, brought to Europe and North America later in the century. These ranged from the family reviewed so disparagingly by Charles Dickens in *Household Words* in 1853, to the people imported to New York's Coney Island and London's Westminster Aquarium by the showman G. A. Farini (aka William Hunt) in the 1880s.[3]

Even less well known is the story of Franz Taaibosch, a dancer who appeared on the London stage in 1913 and who died in New York State in 1940. Taaibosch travelled widely across the United States for two decades, and must have been the best known "Bushman" in North America—until Xiau or N!xau, the star of the 1980s film *The Gods Must be Crazy.*

In this essay, it is possible to put together for the first time an outline of the life story of Franz Taaibosch on both sides of the Atlantic. The story is as yet imperfectly known and by nature episodic, and thus may be best told, in the manner of later-nineteenth-century entertainment, as a series of *tableaux vivants.*

Postcard of the Wild Dancing Bushman, c. 1913.

The Life Story of Franz Taaibosch

Somewhere in the Kalahari, about "7 years" before 1915: *"He was found . . . in the Kalahari Desert. No other human being was seen in the locality at the time. . . . when discovered this Bushman was in pursuit of ostriches, and . . . he was armed with the bow and arrow which he still carries."* Captain Hepston *"was shooting ostriches in the Kalahari Desert and wounded (as he thought) one, but it continued to run away and he mounted his horse and overtook it and then he discovered it was the Bushman disguised very cleverly as an os-*

trich, which he was trying to kill when Captain [Hepston] appeared on the scene. The Bushman was wounded in the leg and was taken down to Kimberley by the Captain who got him well and looked after him." Hepston kept him on his farm *"near Kimberley,"* *"and 'tamed' him by tying him to a post and whipping him every day for six months."*[4]

The tale of a "Bushman" hunter dressed as an ostrich is a type-story which had been acted out in London and New York entertainment as early as 1884, and possibly earlier. As Sir H. H. Johnston was later to remark, the story was also curiously dated, as ostriches had become virtually extinct in the (southern) Kalahari by the end of the nineteenth century and were being raised on ostrich farms instead.

How far can we trust this account of Franz Taaibosch's origins "in the Kalahari Desert"? Even if accepted at face value, it is an example of a style of coercive labor recruitment that was to survive in South Africa at least until the 1950s: a mixture of force and inducement by the supply of tobacco, etc. that removed the person so far from his native environment that he was unable to escape home. The further assertion that Franz was the "only one of his tribe in existence," a common claim in Western exhibitions of "exotic" people, if true, suggests that he was the survivor of genocide.

It is more likely that Franz Taaibosch had been born in "captivity" as a farmworker in the northern Cape Colony, among a Khoisan group who mixed Afrikaans-Dutch culture into their traditional identity and way of life. Both of Franz Taaibosch's names were Dutch or Afrikaans. Franz is typical of the names by which farm servants were called by their masters. Taaibosch, meaning "tough bush," refers to a wild plant. It was also the name of a leading Kora (Khoisan herder) family in the Kimberley-Kuruman area, who were descended from a great bandit leader called Matsetedi or Taaibosch, who rose to power in the area around 1750.[5] Franz's family may have once been servile retainers or even full members of the Taaibosch family.

A farm near Kimberley, South Africa, 1913 or earlier: *Captain "Paddy" Hepston, a "large red-faced, beery moustached" settler-farmer of Irish origin, is preparing to take ship for England in the company of one of his farm servants.*

Hepston had been in South Africa for fifteen years. His military title implies he was a junior army officer who came to fight in the recent South African War, and then decided to settle and farm. (Though at that time aspiring Irish gentlemen traditionally adopted the honorific militia title of "captain," much like the "colonels" of the South in the United States.) Hepston had recognized

London music-hall poster, July 1913.

the commercial potential of Franz Taaibosch and, after years during which drought and livestock disease depressed farming prospects, saw a more profitable career as a show-business promoter back in Europe. Paddy Hepston was assisted by his brother Randolph, an actor-singer who had been touring South Africa spelling his surname as "Epsteyne."

Franz's dancing was "of the nature of 'step-dancing'"—a Khoisan dance style noted by the London *Morning Post* in 1884 as a "well-marked heel-and-toe step" closely resembling "the terpsichorean efforts of 'Young London' in front of a piano-organ."[6]

A venue in Paris, September-October 1913: *"Frantz, the Wild Dancing Bushman," is performing under the management of "M. P. Epstein," the* nom de theatre *adopted by Paddy Hepston. "Frantz" has previously appeared in London and has been examined at the*

207

*Anthropological Laboratory of W. L. H. Duckworth (1870–1956),
author of the popular booklet* Prehistoric Man, *lecturer, and eventually Reader in physical anthropology and Master of Jesus College at
the University of Cambridge. Duckworth is preparing a report declaring the four-foot, three-inch "Bushman" to be physically "genuine." Duckworth's son-in-law, Captain (later Lord) Ironside, prototype of John Buchan's Richard Hannay because of his adventures as
a spy in German South West Africa, declares that the Bushman speaks
neither a Bantu nor a "click" language.*

Duckworth writes a letter to the Times *of London, which
reads more like the "puff" of an advertiser than the opinion of a
scholar. He publicizes the "recent visit (to this country) of an aboriginal Bushman from South Africa." As for the Bushman's dancing, he reports that "to me it appears to be of an extremely high
artistic standard, and indeed of an order approaching perfection.
... I am confident that if the Bushman returns to this country his
performance will attract connoisseurs of dancing no less than expert anthropologists."*[7]

Franz Taaibosch's limited linguistic ability may be explained by the bullying control of Paddy Hepston, who strictly forbade him to speak to anyone
else. Presumably Hepston communicated with Taaibosch in rudimentary Afrikaans. Franz Taaibosch's subsequent stage name, "Clicko," indicates that he
spoke a "click" language; and we know that later in America he showed off his
"clicks" as a party trick.

*The Palace Theatre at Maidstone, Kent, May 1914: "Frantz, the
Wild Dancing Bushman," is appearing at this popular theatre. "Captain Epstein" tells the theatre staff to "keep at a distance" because
the Bushman is "absolutely wild." Taaibosch is also advertised as
being "nearly 100 years of age." After dancing for ten minutes,
"Frantz" is carried off screaming and locked in a cold bare dressing
room. On Saturday night, when "Epstein" goes out drinking with a
friend and does not return until well after midnight, a stage manager
takes pity on "Frantz." He finds the Bushman "quite rational but
unable to speak to me," with no knowledge of English at all, and
arranges for him to be taken back to his lodgings.*

*Outside the theatre, the stage manager and "Frantz" are confronted by "Captain Epstein." According to the stage manager, the
captain becomes "violent and struck me."*[8]

When "Frantz" and "Epstein" moved on to the Grand Theatre, Gravesend, also in Kent, the stage manager wrote to the Anti-Slavery and Aborigines' Protection Society (A.P.S.) in London, recounting the tale: "I consider Epstein not a proper person to have charge of such a being, who is treated like an animal and is powerless to defend himself." A later letter added: "he is absolutely at the mercy of Epstein, who himself told me that he had punished him times out of number."[9]

A.P.S. headquarters, Denison House, at the south end of Vauxhall Bridge, May 1914: *ten days later. Travers Buxton, secretary of the A.P.S., receives a second report about "Frantz, the Wild Dancing Bushman"—this time from R. Douglas Vernon of Emmanuel College, Cambridge. "I wish to draw your attention to what I consider to be a case of great cruelty regarding a native South African Bushman. . . . It does not seem right that a member of a nearly extinct race should be exploited in the music-halls for gain by men who treat him exactly as they would a performing animal."*

"Frantz" is appearing at the Mill Road Empire Theatre, Cambridge. Vernon, who has been allowed backstage in the wings, claims that the Bushman "cannot speak nor in any way understand the language of his keepers (one is an Englishman, the other a Boer) nor can they speak his language; the Bushman is absolutely in their power." The Bushman is "made to dance (in clog-dancing shoes), gesticulate and yell . . . until the man is ready to drop with fatigue . . . he seems to lose all self-control and the shouting is automatic— only to be stopped by forcibly gagging the man."

When the stage is blacked out and the curtain comes down, "one man uses a pocket flash-light to see the Bushman, while the second man forcibly gags him with a rag and wraps a heavy rug around him. The Bushman is then carried off by force while he tries to scream, bite, kick and fight." Vernon is told that this is a nightly scene, and that "there had been some bloodshed at the man's lodging the night before."[10]

Hepston was the "Boer" referred to—no doubt fifteen years in South Africa had changed his accent. The Englishman must have been Randolph Epsteyne. Vernon's account might suggest that Franz Taaibosch was epileptic. Alternatively, Taaibosch might have been resisting interruption of an extremely energetic procedure of psychic preparation for the trance-dancing characteristic of Khoisan hunters and gatherers.

The A.P.S. opened a file on "Bushman, Ill-Treatment of Wild Dancing"—now deposited with the Anti-Slavery Papers at Rhodes House Library, Oxford. Travers Buxton and an energetic organizing secretary of the A.P.S., Rev. John Harris, alerted the Colonial Office, the Variety Artistes' Federation, London's Metropolitan Police Commissioner, the high commission (embassy) of the Union of South Africa, and the anthropologist "Headhunter" Haddon at Cambridge. The aim of Buxton and Harris was to release the dancer from the Svengali-like grip of his manager-master. Haddon had gone off to Australia, but his wife replied, suggesting that the A.P.S. contact "Dr. Duckworth of Jesus Coll.," who had arranged a private showing of the Bushman for fellow academics. The Variety Artistes' Federation, representing vaudeville performers (affiliated with the White Rats' Actors Union of the United States), proved particularly anxious to clear from the music halls a "degrading" performance involving "cruelty to the performer."[11]

The London police tracked "Frantz" and "Epstein" in mid-June to lodgings in the aptly named Kimberley Avenue (next door to Mafeking and Ladysmith Avenues) at East Ham beyond the East End of London. It was established that the pair would soon be going across the sea to Dublin's World's Fair theatre until the end of August. The Colonial Office referred "the matter . . . to the Irish government," while Dublin's Metropolitan Police Commissioner was alerted by a Member of Parliament friendly to the A.P.S. and by the Variety Artistes' Federation.

Duckworth replied indignantly that he could "hardly believe" Vernon's observations of the Bushman's performance, as "What I did see was neither degrading, nor did it involve cruelty of the kind described." He begged to see Travers Buxton in person. Meanwhile "Frantz" and "Epstein" ducked out of sight; the police were unable even to find them in Dublin.[12] Hepston's timing in disappearing was perfect. There was insurrection in Dublin against British rule at the end of July, and the Great War broke out across Europe in August.

Rendezvous amusement park, Margate pier, July 1915: *Franz Taaibosch is appearing daily in a "Fun City" sideshow in this seaside resort on the northeast Kent coast—the area of England in sight and sometimes sound of trench warfare in Flanders. He has a new stage name, "Klikko"—no doubt a ploy to escape detection. Jane Goddard of The Bungalow, Grotto Hill, Margate, presumably a lady in retirement, writes indignantly to E. D. Morel—the humanitarian who has made his name exposing the Red Rubber atrocities in King Leopold's Congo. She is haunted by the "piteous look and evident terror" of "an aged Bushman, said to be a hundred years old, who is being exploited by some white people." "He looks very old and wretched and dances until the perspiration streams off him."* [13]

Morel passed on the letter to the A.P.S., who set investigations going again, fearful that "no sooner do we begin to take action in one place than he appears to be 'spirited away' in another."

Despite Goddard's lack of confidence in her local police force, Margate police were asked to investigate. Detective Constable Frank Ashbee and Police Constable Thorpe accordingly went along, and found "Klikko" dancing in a ten-by-six-foot wooden pit to the sound of a windup phonograph. A man, apparently an employee of Hepston, sat whistling and beating out time with a stick on the edge of the pit. The stick was not a folded whip as previously reported. Though he was advertised as dancing for up to eight hours at a stretch, and the wooden auditorium was open between 10:00 A.M. and 9:00 P.M. every day except Sunday, "Klikko" was dancing for only as long as the public threw coins into the ring. The policemen further reported:

> re. Wild Bushman, showing at the Rendevous [*sic*], Margate. . . . We remained in the show 16 minutes and the Bushman danced three times during that period and the rest of the time was taken up by the man in charge describing how the Bushman came to be captured. . . .
>
> He is supposed to have been examined by Professor Cunningham of Cambridge, who estimates his age as over 100 years, and states the Bushman is the nearest approach to the Ape species he has ever seen. . . .

After noting that Klikko lives on raw potatoes washed down by Bovril beef tea, and four or five pints of dark stout ale per day, the police report continues:

> When the audience applaud the Bushman shouts and always finishes up with a laugh. He has on no occasion ever shown any signs of fear. . . .
>
> During the intervals when he is not dancing he sells postcards of himself (one attached) and laughs to the purchaser and kisses his hand. He then stands on his head and turns somersaults apparently of his own accord. Frequently when the man in charge is describing the Bushman, he throws a kiss to a lady or child in the audience and generally appears to like the attention he creates.

The policemen went on to interview the "landlady" of the lodgings "where Captain Epstein and his wife are staying." "She informs me that the Bushman has a small room to himself and has a warm bath every morning and behaves in the house as an ordinary individual. The Captain takes him up his food. . . ." [14]

"Klikko" certainly appeared to be a more relaxed character than "Frantz" ever was. He was no longer just one short act among many in a theatre, but now had his own show in semi-continuous performance. He was also communicating now with his audience in his own way, especially with the women and children. Perhaps the new "man in charge" at the show and Hepston's new "wife" at the lodgings had improved Taaibosch's circumstances, though Hepston was still keeping him in isolation. Another sinister character with an interest in Taaibosch had also entered the story over the course of the previous year— "Professor" Cunningham, whose racist claptrap is quoted above.

The Union of South Africa's high commissioner, W. P. Schreiner, remarked that the Margate police report, if correct, showed the Bushman "having rather a good time and to be kindly treated." Though formerly South Africa's leading white liberal politician, and brother of the feminist and novelist Olive Schreiner, W. P. Schreiner proved unsympathetic to the case of Franz Taaibosch. While tut-tutting about "such performances by units [sic] of the less civilised races," he refused to have anything to do with the case on the grounds that a Bushman would be most likely to come from the Bechuanaland Protectorate (later Botswana), which was still ruled by Britain. The same argument had been used by the high commissioner three years before to disclaim responsibility for a South African "native" born in Cape Colony, on the grounds that he was Sotho-speaking and must therefore be the responsibility of Basutoland.[15] However, the A.P.S. was still convinced that "The whole thing is part of the wicked exploitation of defenceless natives against which we are always working."

The A.P.S. considered taking out a writ of *habeas corpus* against Hepston for "Klikko." "What is the old man but a slave?" opined Buxton. The A.P.S. legal adviser was more cautious. He referred to the obvious precedent, the case of Sara Baartman, the "Hottentot Venus," in 1810–11. One of the A.P.S.'s predecessor organizations, the African Association, which included Zachary Macaulay, father of the famous historian, had filed for a writ of *habeas corpus* and brought Sara and her manager-master to court. But they had failed to establish that she was in bondage to her master, the court finding that she was under willing contract rather than under durance. There was no reason to anticipate better success with "Klikko." It would be better to get the Director of Public Prosecutions to institute a criminal action against Hepston for "unlawful duress" on the dancer.

The Home Office replied, following the Margate police report, that there was no cause for complaint. The A.P.S. solicitor advised that no case could be made without directly obtaining the complaint by speaking to the "old native African whose language no-one understood."[16]

Harris also turned for advice to Sir Harry Johnston, former colonial administrator now deep into the "awful" task of writing his *Comparative Bantu Grammar*, which "grows and grows" as he struggled to cover hundreds of languages. Johnston reacted with scathing criticism of the "careless indifference of our Colonial Office to the welfare of our coloured fellow-subjects." If the Colonial Office wouldn't act, "THEN WE WILL APPEAL TO THE PRESS." But he feared that his own ill health and overwork precluded his interviewing the Bushman in person. For that task, it would be best to get Sol Plaatje, "probably the only man in Great Britain or Europe able to converse with this Bushman." The Bushman might even speak the Khalagari language, closely related to Tswana and Sotho.

Unwittingly, Johnston had stepped on two of Harris's corns—the press and journalist and linguist Sol Plaatje. Harris believed in lobbying behind the scenes and in not alienating the powers that be by untoward publicity. He was also daggers drawn with Plaatje, who had come to England in 1914 as secretary-general of the South African Native National Congress (later ANC) to petition the imperial government against the 1913 Natives' Land Act in South Africa. Harris and the A.P.S. helped to sabotage the SANNC mission by patronizing it and diluting its representations, pressing instead the policy of "equitable segregation," which Harris was trying to get the British South Africa Company to adopt in Rhodesia. In August 1914, Plaatje had stormed out of Harris's office in a temper and had wrested back control of the SANNC mission from Harris, though too late.[17]

Johnston's advice of "Don't let Epstein slip through our fingers, carrying off the prey" thus went unheeded because of Harris's *amour propre*. Franz Taaibosch lost his one good chance in Britain to break out of solitary linguistic confinement and out of the absolute control of Paddy Hepston, his manager. As later events would show, Plaatje could have communicated with Franz Taaibosch in Afrikaans.

"Frantz" continued to dance in the Margate sideshow during the summer months of 1915, while the A.P.S. fretted about what to do into September. Hepston undoubtedly knew what was going on, as did his collaborator "Professor" George Cunningham.

> A.P.S. offices in London, first or second week of September 1915: *"Professor" Cunningham calls on Rev. Harris. He presents a visiting card describing himself as "Cinema Science Lecturer," tells Harris that he is also a member of the Senate of Cambridge University, and distinguishes himself from another Dr. Cunningham of Cambridge. He turns out to be a dentist.* "He was anxious," Harris writes, "to know the evidence which the society had as he is interested in the Bushman and has, I understand, a contract with Epstein his captor in reference to the production of certain cinema films in which the Bushman figures." "He gives Epstein a bad name and is anxious to get the Bushman out of his hands."[18]

Harris smelled a rat, but Cunningham intensified his bid to gain possession of "Klikko" as a theatrical property. He put pressure on the A.P.S. to undertake the expenses of legal action against "Epstein." Finally on 19–20 September, Cunningham (telegraphic address "Cunningham Dentist Cambridge") wrote two eccentric letters in thick blue pencil on lined pages from a school exercise book. Full of insertions, hesitations and reiterations, the page is dented with different pressures of handwriting. The generally nervous literary style can hardly have impressed the reverend reader:

> I did not know that you were a "Rev." . . . hence I hope you will excuse my exclamation on reading yr letter—DAMN.
>
> Get possession of the Bushman and I undertake to talk with him in 6 weeks (& I believe read his handwriting which looks like shorthand). I may do in less time.
>
> But do hurry up!
>
> V.E.Y.
> [Very Earnestly Yours]
> [signed Geo Cunningham]

A second letter berated Harris for being "cold, formal and official."[19]

John Harris now foresaw that "the old man may before long be stranded in this country," because of the success of the Variety Artistes' Federation in ensuring "difficulty in getting further 'turns' for the Bushman."

The A.P.S. had previously campaigned in 1910–11 against the exploitation of the "Kaffir Boys" choir, a quintet of five children (apparently Khoisan and Mfengu as well as Xhosa) brought from South Africa by a Liverpool minister's son to tour Congregational churches. Buxton and Harris must have also been aware of a number of precedents of theatrical entrepreneurs dumping exotic entertainers on the streets. The most important case was that of the "Zulu" choir, including the future nationalist leader Charlotte Manye (Maxeke), abandoned in Cleveland, Ohio, in 1892–93. A more recent case in England had been that of "Prince Lobengula," left over from the 1900 "Savage South Africa" extravaganza—an attempt by Rhodesian capitalists to match W. F. Cody's "Wild West Exhibition." The prince had been reduced to penury and miner's phthisis (silicosis) as a collier near Manchester. The manager-promoter behind "Savage South Africa," Frank Fillis, had also been responsible in 1906 for abandoning "a troupe of thoroughly traditional rural-traditional dancers" accompanying General Piet Cronje and the "Boer War Show" on Coney Island, New York.[20]

Margate, 3 October 1915: Jane Goddard visits the sideshows next to the pier. Next day she writes the A.P.S. a final letter:

Yesterday I found that the "pleasure fair" where the Bushman has been exhibited as a side show for some months, has been closed. It will not re-open until June of next year. I suppose the Bushman has been taken away.[21]

Hepston and Taaibosch disappear from the record. We now know that, within a year, they must have taken a dangerous transatlantic crossing from Liverpool in England or Queenstown (Cobh) in Ireland across U-boat–infested waters.

> Near Havana, Cuba, late in 1916: *"Klikko" or "Clicko" is dancing in the limelight at a circus outside Havana, patronized by "bored well-nourished and well-wined" local whites and American tourists, who laugh at him. Rich Americans come to the Caribbean around Christmastime, but have come in lesser numbers this year because of the impending entry of the United States into the Great War.[22]*
>
> *One of the American visitors to Cuba is William Mann, a Montana-born entomologist working for the U.S. Department of Agriculture, who is on his way through Havana from a fieldtrip in the Bahamas. Mann, who has been a circus lover since childhood, is fascinated by Franz Taaibosch. Probably by letter, he alerts his friend Frank Cook, the legal agent for America's greatest circus, Ringling Brothers Barnum and Bailey. Cook "at the time managed the importation of all Ringling's international attractions."*
>
> *Cook comes down to Havana and watches Taaibosch in action. He goes round to the star's dressing room and has Franz long enough to himself for Franz "to confirm in a strange kind of English that he was most unhappy and in a plight from which he longed to be delivered." At this point, the Bushman's bullying promoter barges in and ends the interview.*
>
> *Cook is given the impression that Hepston is an "Englishman, who professed to be a captain in the British army." Cook thinks him no patriot, as he is sheltering in the Americas from his military duty in Europe.[23]*

History now seemed to be repeating itself: the scene in a dressing room in Cuba almost exactly replays a previous scene in Maidstone, England, from two years earlier.

Frank Cook decided to import Franz Taaibosch into the United States on a short-term contract, but it was evident that Hepston would have to come too. There was no written contract binding Franz, who was illiterate, to Hepston; the "captain's power over him came entirely from the fact that [Franz] had nobody else to whom he could turn for protection." Once both Franz and

Hepston were in the United States, Cook reasoned that there would be a better chance of liberating the dancer from his manager. Frank Cook made the arrangements, and "Early in 1917 [Franz] Taaibosch and the captain were travelling the circuits of America as members of the circus for which the lawyer worked."

As for Hepston, Cook's plan eventually worked—after some legal and physical wrangles: "within a year or two he had vanished from the scene." Laurens van der Post suggests that the captain, so unprofessional and egotistical, was "out of his depth" in the camaraderie of circus company. Frank Cook became Franz Taaibosch's legal guardian, and "From then on [Franz] spent all the summer months travelling the wide circus beat of America."[24]

> Boston, Massachusetts, or New York City, 1920: *A twenty-three-year-old white South African scholar by the name of Gerard Paul Lestrade, coming to Harvard University to study Hebrew, Chinese, and Arabic, is taken to meet a Bushman. Lestrade amazes his hosts by rapid and complete communication with Taaibosch. Though he is in later years to become the first Professor of Bantu Languages at the University of Cape Town, at this time Lestrade speaks no indigenous African language—only the Afrikaans creole of Dutch. He concludes that the Bushman is really a "Hottentot" or coloured person from the southern Cape.*[25]

Such confusion over the differences between "Bushman" and "Hottentot" identities persisted among ethnologists and historians of South Africa, as much as among observers of the life of "Clicko" in North America. There was no simple equation of "Bushmen" with San-speakers and foragers, nor of "Hottentots" with Khoi-speakers and pastoralists. All these categories overlapped and varied in different periods of time and regions.[26] But Lestrade's discovery of Franz Taaibosch's fuller identity may have been a further liberating moment in Taaibosch's reconnection with the outside world, as he learned to communicate with people directly in a "funny little Bushman-English voice."[27]

If accounts by circus people are to be accepted at face value, Franz Taaibosch, whose theatrical name was now spelled "Cliko" and "Clico" as well as "Clicko," became notable for "his positive adjustment to circus life and his overall happiness. . . . In his own way he was part of the amusement world—a showman of sorts." Franz felt "immediately at home" among "unusually happy, humane and harmonious" folk. "Everyone took him to their hearts," from performers to tent pitchers. According to van der Post, Franz particularly admired the clowns: "as if in their tumbling, constant humiliation and incorrigible capacity for laughing at their misfortunes, he saw his

Ringling Brothers Barnum & Bailey sideshow artistes, c. 1930.
"Clicko" in middle of lower level.

own unrecorded fate portrayed, and thus felt accompanied, needed, wanted and so became content."[28]

During the 1920s and 1930s Franz Taaibosch was one of Ringling's regular attractions in circus sideshows and at "dime museums," travelling all over North America. He entered into the spirit of things as a star attraction who stood next to the fairground barker ("talker"), inducing patrons to enter the sideshow tents. He took to smoking large black cigars, which "became his trade mark," and was known as "the pet of circus executives, who were always bringing him his favorite smokes, or a bottle of beer, his favourite refreshment."[29] On many weekends on the road Franz was taken to a local hotel for a drink.

Taaibosch's turn at places like "Dreamland" on Coney Island, the seaside resort for New York City where he danced one summer season for the "freak show czar" Sam Gumpertz, was essentially similar to his act at Margate's "Fun City" during the Great War. He was now obliged to cover his lithe body in a sacklike leopard skin, presumably for fear of prudery. But he danced shoeless on a platform, rather than in wooden clogs, while letting out his "ungodly yells." At the end of the act he sold a pamphlet about himself, rather than a postcard. The pamphlet described his capture and taming in the Kalahari Desert by a "Captain Du Barry"—a legal ploy to disown Hepston's connection with Taaibosch.

"Clicko" was described as a "Pygmy African Bushman," as the "only genuine" African Head Hunter to be shown in the United States, and even as the "Wild Man of Madagascar." Such confusion over his ethnic identity reflects both his uniqueness in the eyes of circus people, and also the popular conflation in North America of images of non-American aboriginal peoples.

Vermont, 1924: *Franz Taaibosch stands in skis on thick snow, in woolen bobble hat and thick sweater, with ski poles in his hands. As the legal ward of Frank Cook, Franz Taaibosch shares his guardian's life. Cook is divorced and middle-aged, living alone, and he finds Franz a witty, lively, and humorous companion. So Franz comes to stay with him during the winter off-seasons when the circuses are in hibernation and goes everywhere with Cook, even on holiday. In 1922–23 they had spent a winter vacation together golfing in Miami.*

In November 1924 Franz joins Frank in exulting over the re-election of Calvin Coolidge as President. Franz is photographed sunk into a chair in an expensive dressing gown on the morning after the victory, pointing at a headline in a newspaper that he could not otherwise read, with an "expression of utter resolution and unmistakable happiness." Each winter off-season Franz Taaibosch finds it

*easy enough to slip into the lifestyle of the idle rich, but the relation-
ship between Franz and Frank remains patriarchal. Franz, like others in the circus, calls Frank "Papa."*[30]

Photographs show Franz Taaibosch's penchant for cigar smoking. He
exhibited the traditional drawing power of Bushman lungs when sucking at
earth hookahs, and when inhaling cigar smoke so deeply that the smoke only
emerged minutes later, apparently through every orifice of his face.[31] Nor were
his sensual indulgences limited to cigars and beer. Franz's sexual desires were
satisfied inside and occasionally outside the close-knit circle of circus folk. One
show-biz source credits Franz Taaibosch with loving "all the girls" and wanting "a big fat mama" for his wife.

> Omaha, Nebraska, "one Sunday" probably in the later 1920s:
> *"Clicko" sneaks out of his hotel with other circus people late one
> evening to visit the nightspots, and is still not back next morning.
> Papa Cook tracks him to a police station, where he is held for being
> drunk and disorderly. "What's the matter boy, where have you been?"
> Franz tells "Papa" that he had drunk too much "hot water" the
> previous night, and had then gone "to see nice mama"—who had
> taken his gold watch in return for "plenty [more] hot water and a
> big kiss." (Taaibosch leaves all financial affairs to Cook and carries
> no cash.) The police take all this as good fun, and Cook bribes them
> with free tickets for the circus. "Clicko" is released after shaking
> hands all round, to catch a taxi back to the circus.*[32]

This may explain why a photo from about 1930 shows Franz Taaibosch
with two or three police badges pinned to his sleeveless leopard-skin tunic.[33]
That "Clicko" in some ways lived a charmed life, and was made an exception
to rules as an individual, rather than persecuted as a stereotype, is suggested by
another tale about him, in the "deep South." Our source does not indicate the
"race" of the two girls in the story, but remarks cryptically of Taaibosch: "In
the South he was really a problem."

> Tuscaloosa, Alabama, probably in the late 1920s: *"Clicko" dances
> up the steps of the sideshow "bally" platform, as the band strikes up
> "Twelfth Street Rag." He stands next to the barker spieling on the
> platform, ogling the girls and snapping the locks of his springy hair.
> When two girls scream and run off, he gives chase—and is "soon
> lost in the darkness" on the dirt road. About an hour later he is
> picked up begging for liquor at a country store, surrounded by a
> crowd of the curious.*[34]

Ringling Brothers Barnum & Bailey Circus, 1928: *a publicity photo or photographic poster of "Clico, Wild Dancing South African Bushman" is distributed by the circus. In it Franz Taaibosch, looking fiftyish in years, stands at attention in outsize leopard skins, his feet in heavy boots.*

The copy of this picture in the Ringling Museum of Art is marked on the back: "this wild African bushman was actually captured from the headhunters by Capt. Hepston." Another photograph shows Franz in different outsize leopard skins, with a circus wagon and horses in the background. His outward image is that of an obvious circus person, but his shadow, projected onto the circus tent, is that of a Bushman traveller dressed in a large buckskin on a cold desert day.[35]

> San Antonio, Texas, 14 September 1929: *A rival "Clicko," described as "bushman and fire-eater," is appearing in a sideshow of "strange people" at the Sells-Floto Circus. Fellow exhibits include minstrels, a snake-charmer, a sword-swallower, an escapologist, a sword-walker, and "Princess Oskoman, Indian guide and seer." Later the rival Clicko will opt for the new name "Bamboola, fire-eating pygmy," no doubt after a threat of legal action by Papa Cook.*[36]

Photographs taken about 1930 show "Clicko" cheerfully posing with Ringling attractions such as the Doll Family of midget "girls," of whom he was particularly fond.[37]

When Frank Cook married the daughter of a circus family, his new wife Evelyn found that she must care for Franz Taaibosch as their man-child. They spent each winter in a hired penthouse at the top of the Forest Hotel near Madison Square Garden. Evelyn Joyce Cook recalls one occasion with particular humor:

> The Gay Nineties Club, New York City, in the mid-1930s: *Frank and Evelyn Cook, accompanied by "Clicko" and their three-year-old daughter Barbara, are entertained with other circus people by the blonde, cigar-smoking New York socialite Louise Lonsdale. "Now Franz," she tells Taaibosch, "you are to drink only beer, no hard liquor. Understand?" Taaibosch replies in his own brand of Afrikaans-English, "Ach forschstand Maw." Louise Lonsdale, decked in diamonds and sapphires, kisses and presses Taaibosch's face, "nothing loath," into the open cleavage of her extravagant pink and white dinner dress.*[38]
>
> *Later on in the evening, Franz bursts into the downstairs bar of the club, weaving unsteadily and howling so uncannily that the bar bottles rattle.*

Evelyn Joyce Cook observes in her memoirs that Franz "had entertained the guests with his imitations and spoken to them in his clicking, explosive tongue," but had been filled with much liquor and no food, and needed to go home to bed. It was approaching four o'clock in the morning.[39] Another source explains what sort of imitations Franz would present: "lawyers, artists, businessmen, scientists and priests," mimicked precisely but with no hint of malice or mockery.[40]

"Clicko" spent the summers of 1934 and 1936 (the Gumperts-managed years of the Ringling circus) touring with the Ringling Brothers circus side-shows in company with human "freaks," "headhunters," and his friends the "Doll Family" of midget beauties. This contrasted with his winters in the warm family apartment of the Cook family in New York City. A photo of 1936 shows Cook as a father advanced in years with his young daughter Barbara. Barbara grew up with Franz Taaibosch as the third adult in the family. After her father died in 1937, Franz continued to live with the widow and her child, as the only male adult in the household.

Photographs show that Franz Taaibosch aged rapidly at the end of the 1930s. Within the household the death of Frank Cook seems to have transformed him overnight from adult-child to grandfather figure. This is the period when Franz Taaibosch (though called "Hans") also features in the childhood of a Quaker woman who told her story to Laurens van der Post in the 1960s. Van der Post does not give her name, but Franz called her and other little girls "Dolly." This Dolly was one of Barbara Cook's friends from the same apartment block in New York, who grew to regard Franz Taaibosch proprietarily as an immutable part of her childhood. He took enormous delight in dancing for her and other children.

Laurens van der Post has told the tale of Taaibosch and Dolly in fictionalized form as *A Mantis Carol*. No justice can be done here to that extraordinary book by way of summary. The book, like its title, which combines references to the praying mantis "god" of the Khoisan and to the festivities celebrating the birth of Christ, works its way toward the resolution of Khoisan and Christian ideas of religion, sacrifice, and the afterlife. In its pages Dolly recounts how Taaibosch used to perform two dances which van der Post identifies as the "dance of the little hunger" and the "dance of the great hunger"—the two "great terminal dances of Bushman life." Her tale, as told by van der Post, ends with Taaibosch on his deathbed in New York City: "Dolly, dance for me, please. Please dance for me Dolly, [as] I have so often danced for you."

An obituary, published in the show-biz periodical *Billboard*, tells us that Franz Taaibosch in fact died at the home of Mrs. Frank Sullivan, Frank Cook's elder daughter, on 31 August 1940, in the riverside town of Hudson in New York State. After a service at the local Roman Catholic church, St. Mary's, he was buried in Cedar Park Cemetery. That is where his body, since reinterred with Mr. and Mrs. Sullivan under a common headstone, lies today.

The "great hunger" of Taaibosch's dancing, van der Post opined, was the hunger for love—the reconciliation of the great paradox of "history, time and space transcended in terms of its one great and for ever now." In those terms Franz Taaibosch was not and is not yet dead, as he seeks to return home to "find a place in the record of his people."

Laurens van der Post believed that he had been recruited by the spirit of Taaibosch, through the mantis dreams of an American Quaker woman, to find

Taaibosch's way home to his birthplace. But, despite "the most prolonged search-ing," he was unable to place Taaibosch in "the annals of his country and memory of his people."[41]

It is hoped that this paper has brought that resolution one step nearer.

WHAT DOES IT ALL MEAN?

The life of Franz Taaibosch is a story that can be told for its own sake. But each part of the life story needs to be reconstructed, deconstructed, and inter-preted, and the story as a whole has to be teased for meaning on a number of levels.

First, as indicated at the beginning of this essay, for historians it is an exemplar of the relationship between imperialism and entertainment. The capi-talism of imperial expansion and the capitalism of expanding show business grew simultaneously in the later nineteenth century, and maintained connec-tions thereafter. Show business was almost a caricature of capitalist develop-ment. Clikko's early career shows the ruthless appropriation and exploitation of labor characteristic of "primitive" capitalism, while his later career, when he took on the status of a corporate employee, illustrates advanced capitalism.[42]

Second, for anthropologists it is a tale of racial paternalism and ethnic stereotyping. The theme of paternalism is reflected in Franz Taaibosch's mov-ing from utter dependence on a master as a permanent orphan, in the manner of South African settler farms, to his subsequent acceptance of the role of "child-man" in the American lawyer's family.

The ethnic stereotyping of Taaibosch, on both sides of the Atlantic, reflected a tradition in popular entertainment, never far divorced from aca-demic inquiry, which pandered to Western public curiosity about the con-quered and enslaved peoples of empire. The history of this human trophy display goes back in England to the display of Native Americans in Elizabe-than times, and hearkens back to the display of Britons and Angles in Ancient Rome.

In Britain and France, "Franz" or "Klikko" fit into stereotypes of "Hot-tentots" and "Bushmen" constructed in entertainment and academia over the course of the nineteenth century, and closely tied to the development of racist ideas by theorists like Robert Knox and Francis Galton—both erstwhile resi-dents of southern Africa. The image of Franz Taaibosch's small but extremely muscular male body was also appropriated by practitioners of the new "cin-ema science."

In North America, on the other hand, "Clicko" fell within the universal stereotype being constructed of remote hunting peoples of the world in gen-eral—hence the hodgepodge of identities: a headhunter, pygmy, etc. Though

Khoisan studies have undergone a great upheaval in recent years, one can still see the traces of these European/South African and North American traditions of scholarship—one concerned with Khoisan biological traits, and the other with "Man the Hunter."[43]

Third, for students of drama, the story of Franz Taaibosch goes to the shamanistic roots of dance-drama. Taaibosch was an extraordinarily energetic and probably also graceful dancer, but true appreciation of his exotic style was obviously an acquired taste. This did not matter, as Taaibosch was equally if not more happy to accept the derisive laughs and shouts of the masses as expressions of enjoyment. He seems to have been positively inspired by such vocal audience participation.

This can be explained by reference to Khoisan dance culture. Taaibosch may be seen as a "shaman" in the sense that he had apparently reached and could reach again the highest trance state by persistent dancing, achieving contact with the spirits of the recent dead—though we have no evidence that he also acted as a trance-healer. (American children certainly regarded him as some kind of benign dwarf wizard.)

The dancing of Khoisan men around a fire towards this trance state took place over the course of a whole night inside a seated circle of chanting and clapping women. The rhythmic encouragement of the women was absolutely essential to achievement of the trance state. This is comparable to the clapping and vocal encouragement of a theatre audience sitting beyond the lights as the performance rises to catharsis—the purgation of "pity and fear" uniting audience and performer in one spirit.[44]

Finally, the story of Franz Taaibosch is a story of individual human endurance. Evidently, he called on deep inner resources to survive and reconstruct his psyche. Franz Taaibosch underwent a "middle passage" of removal, bondage, and disorientation across the seas, until he found himself once more as a complete human being, first in the circus community and later in the drafty canyons of New York City. The laughter and shouting of the masses, and particularly of children, was for him a new affirmation.

What was this inner resource? The word for it in some Khoisan languages is *n/um*. Comparable to "spirit" or "soul," *n/um* has been more precisely translated as "boiling energy." It lies at the pit of the stomach but can be raised up the spine through dancing, to explode in the brain after a great sweat, like the boiling of fermenting beer. The trance state thus reached, with the world spinning round the dancer, is called *!kia*. Having once achieved *!kia*, the dancer or shaman will seek to return to it on subsequent occasions. Some such ecstasy may be the key to Franz Taaibosch's survival after a long dark night of the soul—even if his "great hunger" for the light was not entirely assuaged at his death.[45]

NOTES

My first attempt to understand Franz Taaibosch took place long before I knew anything about his career after 1915—"The sad story of Klikko," *Kutlwano* (Gaborone) 7.2 (Feb. 1969): 2–3. Taaibosch was included in seminars and talks given by me at Edinburgh (1979), Gaborone (1981) and Berkeley (1985), until I was persuaded by Bob Hitchcock to write up what I knew as "Frantz or Klikko, The Wild Dancing Bushman: A Case Study in Khoisan Stereotyping," *Botswana Notes and Records* (Gaborone) 20 (1988), special issue on Khoisan: 71–76 and "Frantz or Klikko—a Correction," *Botswana Notes and Records* 22 (1991): 154—a paper subsequently discussed in London and Oxford. My thanks go to the late Jack Chirenje, Brian Willan, Robin Palmer, Robin Derricourt, and Andrew Roberts for pushing me along in different ways.

Taaibosch's post-1917 career was drawn to my attention by Prof. Bernth Lindfors of the University of Texas in January 1992, though I should have made some such deduction from a letter written by Harvey Blume of Cambridge, Massachusetts, dated April 1990, kindly shown me then by Prof. Shula Marks. During the course of 1992 I was assisted by the kindness of Sir Laurens van der Post and Prof. Isaac Schapera of London; Dr. R. A. Foley, Director of the Duckworth Laboratory at the University of Cambridge; Deborah W. Walk, Museum Archivist of the John and Mabel Ringling Museum of Art, Sarasota; and Fred Dahlinger, Jr., Director of the Circus World Museum, Baraboo. Fred Dahlinger put me in contact with Frank Cook's widow, Evelyn Joyce Cook, and her daughter, Barbara de Romain. My thanks go to all of them.

1. J. A. Hobson, *The Psychology of Jingoism* (London: Grant Richards, 1901) 3–11, 81.

2. Yvette Ahraham of the Department of History, University of Cape Town, is presently working on Sara Baartman (c. 1787–1815). Publications on Baartman, 1948–54, by P. R. Kirby are listed in his "Hottentot Venus," *Standard Encyclopaedia of South Africa*, ed. D. J. Potgieter (Cape Town: Nasou, 1972) 611–12; Stephen Gray, *South African Literature: An Introduction* (Cape Town: David Philip; London: Rex Collings, 1979) 38–51; Richard David Altick, *The Shows of London* (Cambridge: Belknap–Harvard UP, 1978) 269–72; Bernth Lindfors, "The Hottentot Venus and Other African Attractions in Nineteenth-Century England," *Australasian Drama Studies* 1.2 (April 1983): 82–104.

3. Altick, *Shows*; A. J. Clement, *The Kalahari and Its Lost City* (Cape Town: Longmans, 1967) 175–82; Bernth Lindfors, "Clicks and Clucks: Victorian Reactions to San Speech," *Africana Journal* 14.1 (1983): 10–17; Neil Parsons, "Bushman Troupes and Zulu Choirs: Southern African Entertainers Overseas, 1810–1925," unpublished essay, 1981; Robert Bogdan, *Freak Show: Presenting Human Oddities for Pleasure and Profit* (Chicago: U of Chicago P, 1988) 187–89.

4. W. L. H. Duckworth, letter, *Times* 2 Oct. 1913: 5; Margate Police Detective Department, report to Chief Commissioner's Office, 27 July 1915, enclosed in Chief Constable's Office report to Anti-Slavery and Aborigines' Protection Society (hereafter A.P.S.), 27 July 1915; R. Douglass Vernon, report to A.P.S., 25 May 1914, Mss.Brit.Emp. s.22/G.125, "Bushman, Ill-Treatment of Wild Dancing," Rhodes House Library, Oxford (hereafter RHL).

5. H. H. Johnston to A.P.S., 1 Aug. 1915, RHL; Paul-Lambert Breutz, *The Tribes of Mafeking District* (Pretoria: Native Affairs Department, Ethnological Publications No. 32, 1955–56) 30–31.

6. Clement, *The Kalahari and Its Lost City* 181.

7. Duckworth, letter; E. T. Williams and Helen M. Palmer, eds., *The Dictionary of National Biography 1951–1956* (London: Open UP, 1971) 316–17. (Ironside is now believed to have

been Hitler's choice for Britain's Petain or Quisling in the Second World War.) Duckworth's detailed report on the physical anthropology of Franz Taaibosch has not yet been located. Director of the Duckworth Laboratory, Department of Biological Anthropology, University of Cambridge, letter to the author, 30 Oct. 1992 (interestingly enough on notepaper headed with a Bushman dancer logo).

8. L. Norley, Maidstone, letter to A.P.S., 15 May 1914, RHL.

9. Ibid., 20 May 1914.

10. R. Douglass Vernon, letter to to A.P.S., 25 May 1914, RHL.

11. Miscellaneous correspondence, May 1914, RHL.

12. London Metropolitan Police Commissioner, letter to A.P.S., 18 June 1914; Fanny Haddon, letter to A.P.S., 23 June 1914; W. L. H. Duckworth, letter to A.P.S., 3 July 1914; Chairman, Variety Artistes' Federation, letter to A.P.S., 6 July 1914, RHL.

13. J. Goddard, letter to E. D. Morel, 12 July 1915, RHL.

14. A.P.S., letter to Goddard, 15 July 1915; Chief Constable Margate, letter to A.P.S., 27 July 1915 (with enclosures), RHL.

15. W. P. Schreiner, letter to A.P.S., 29 July 1915; H. H. Johnston, letter to A.P.S., 1 Aug. 1915, RHL.

16. Miscellaneous correspondence, August 1915, RHL.

17. H. H. Johnston, letter to A.P.S., 1 Aug. 1915, RHL; Brian Willan, *Sol Plaatje: South African Nationalist 1876–1932* (London: Heinemann, 1984; James Currey, 1990) 174–80. Plaatje stayed on in Britain into the war years to further his literary career, and was engaged in collaboration with the phoneticist Daniel Jones at University College, London. Jones (the prototype for "Professor Higgins") used Plaatje's unrivaled knowledge of Tswana to make it one of the key languages in the development of his International Phonetic Alphabet (IPA).

18. A.P.S., letter to Vernon, 10 Sept. 1915, RHL.

19. Cunningham, letter to Harris, 17, 19–20, and 20 Sept. 1915, RHL.

20. A.P.S., letter to Schreiner, 13 Sept. 1915, RHL; "Kaffir Boys" file (1911) (RHL: Mss.Brit.Emp. s.22/G.126); David Coplan, "The African Musician and the Development of the Johannesburg Entertainment Industry, 1900–1960," *Journal of Southern African Studies* 5.2 (April 1979): 150; J. R. Coan and Charlotte Crogman Wright, *Beneath the Southern Cross: The Story of an American Bishop's Wife in South Africa* (New York: Exposition Press, 1955) 58–59, 111–25; George Pauling, *The Chronicles of a Contractor: Being the Autobiography of the Late George Pauling,* ed. David Buchan (London: Constable and Co., 1926) 188–93; CO 879/574, 150, Public Record Office, London; Ben Shephard, "Showbiz Imperialism: The Case of Peter Lobengula," *Imperialism and Popular Culture,* ed. John M. Mackenzie (Manchester: Manchester UP, 1986) 94–112.

21. Goddard, letter to A.P.S., 4 Oct. 1915, RHL.

22. Information from Barbara de Romain. See also William M. Mann, *Ant Hill Odyssey* (Boston: Atlantic Monthly Books Club/Little Brown, 1948), though the book frustratingly stops just short of his Cuba trip.

23. Bogdan, *Freak Show* 190–92; Laurens van der Post, *A Mantis Carol* (New York: William Morrow, 1976; U.K. ed., 1975) 190–92. Bogdan reports Taaibosch entering the United States in 1912, which is more likely to refer to his leaving Africa, and cites a 1922 pamphlet, *The Life History of Clicko: The Dancing Bushman of Africa,* in the Hertzberg Circus Collection, San Antonio, Texas (which refers to Hepston as "Captain du Barry"). Van der Post calls Franz "Hans" in *Mantis Carol,* but is now satisfied that "Hans" was Franz. Sir Laurens van der Post, personal communication to the author, 10 Feb. 1992.

24. Van der Post, *Mantis Carol* 71.

25. Albert Tucker, "Strangest People on Earth (Part I)," *Sarasota Sentinel* 7 July 1973: 2–3 (copy generously supplied by Ringling Museum).

26. Cf. Edwin Wilmsen, *A Land Filled with Flies: Political Economy of the Kalahari* (Chicago: U of Chicago P, 1989); Wilmsen, "The Real Bushman Is the Other: Labour and Power in the Creation of Basarwa Ethnicity," *Botswana Notes and Records* 22 (1992): 21–35; Robert J. Gordon, *The Bushman Myth: The Making of a Namibian Underclass* (Boulder: Westview Press, 1992); Andrew B. Smith, *Pastoralism in Africa: Origins and Development* (London: Hurst; Athens, Ohio: Ohio UP; Johannesburg: Witwatersrand UP, 1992).

27. Van der Post, *Mantis Carol* 124.

28. Ibid., 70–71; Bogdan, *Freak Show* 192.

29. Bogdan, ibid. Bogdan thus excludes "Clicko" from the category of "freaks" exploited without their true participation.

30. Van der Post, *Mantis Carol* 77, 80–81.

31. Ibid., 80–82. A photograph in Bogdan, *Freak Show* 191, shows wisps of smoke about Clicko's face.

32. Tucker, "Strangest people."

33. Bogdan, *Freak Show,* photograph on 5.

34. Tucker, "Strangest people."

35. Photocopy, marked "Gift of Geo. Baden," generously supplied by Ringling Museum.

36. "Sells-Floto Circus: The Successful Season of 1929," *The White Tops* Nov.-Dec. 1975: 13–14 (copy generously supplied by Ringling Museum).

37. Bogdan, *Freak Show* 5, 191.

38. Evelyn Cook, "This Little Pig Went Night Clubbing," *Bandwagon* Jan.-Feb. 1992: 42–48 (copy generously supplied by Circus World Museum).

39. Ibid.

40. Van der Post, *Mantis Carol* 74–75.

41. Ibid., 117–18; Bogdan, *Freak Show* 192.

42. Cf. William H. Schneider, *An Empire for the Masses* (Westport, Conn.: Greenwood Press, 1982); John M. MacKenzie, *Propaganda and Empire: The Manipulation of British Public Opinion 1880–1960* (Manchester: Manchester UP, 1984); MacKenzie, ed., *Imperialism and Popular Culture*; Jacqueline S. Bratton et al., *Acts of Supremacy: The British Empire and the Stage, 1790–1930* (Manchester: Manchester UP, 1991); Jan Nederveen Pieterse, *White on Black: Images of Africa and Blacks in Western Popular Culture* (New Haven: Yale UP, 1992; Amsterdam: Cosmic Illusion Productions, 1990).

43. See note 25.

44. J. David Lewis-Williams, *Believing and Seeing: Symbolic Meanings in Southern San Rock Paintings* (New York and London: Academic Press, 1981); E. T. Kirby, "The Shamanistic Origins of Popular Entertainments," *The Drama Review* 18.1 (March 1974): 5–15.

45. Richard Katz, *Boiling Energy: Community Healing among the Kalahari !Kung* (Cambridge: Harvard UP, 1982); Richard B. Lee, *The Dobe !Kung, Case Studies in Cultural Anthropology* (New York: Holt, Rinehart and Winston, 1984).

Bata Kindai Amgoza ibn LoBagola and the Making of *An African Savage's Own Story*

DAVID KILLINGRAY AND WILLIE HENDERSON

In an autobiography sensationally entitled *An African Savage's Own Story*, published first in *Scribner's Magazine* in New York in 1929, and then as a book by Knopf, Kindai Amgoza LoBagola described a life of adventure, fortune, and misfortune.[1] He claimed to be a black Jew from the southern Sahelian region of West Africa who, at the age of six, ran away from home with a group of boys. On reaching the coast all of the other boys died in the shark-infested seas while trying to board a British ship. LoBagola hid on the ship and arrived as a naked stowaway on the dockside at Glasgow in March 1896. A quarter of LoBagola's autobiography is an account of his Scottish childhood, how he was taken into the home of a Glasgow gentleman, his relations with the family, schooling in that city and in Edinburgh, and his eventual flight with the son of the house to England and then to Europe. Thereafter, LoBagola describes his life as an itinerant entertainer and vaudeville artiste, informant to anthropologists, lecturer on African "culture," convict, and soldier in both the United States and Britain; and he recounts his conversion to Roman Catholicism in Palestine. It is an elaborately conceived and questionable life covering four continents. LoBagola's major occupation was as an entertainer. He was a skillful and intriguing storyteller, and truth and falsehood are elaborately woven into his autobiography. His only other known published work was a small book entitled *Folk Tales of a Savage*.

SKEPTICAL CRITICS

LoBagola's autobiography has many obvious hallmarks of fantasy, especially to anyone with a knowledge of West African societies. Melville J. Herskovits, one of the few professional Africanists to review the book, was scathing in the *Nation*: "The internal evidence indicates that this self-termed 'savage' not only did not lead the early life he says he did, but that he never went very far into the interior of West Africa, and could have visited the coastal region only casually." For the most part, reviews of *An African Savage's Own Story* praised LoBagola's abilities as a storyteller but were skeptical as to the veracity of the account. For example, the unsigned writer in the *Times Literary Supplement* said that "the book is ostensibly fact and not fiction but it imposes an inordinate strain upon the reader's credulity."[2] On publication in the United States, the *New York Sun* presented it as "the book of the day" and compared it to René Maran's novel *Bataoula*, which to a storm of criticism won the Prix Goncourt in 1921.[3] Predictably, academic journals on both sides of the Atlantic took little notice of the book; the *Journal of the African Society* gave the autobiography a brief and dismissive mention, while the International African Institute's recently established journal, *Africa*, ignored it.[4] More recent critics have been equally dubious: James Olney has described it as "a sort of *Gulliver's Travels*" (36), and Jahn and Dressler call it "a forgery" (374).

The reviewers were right to be critically suspicious of LoBagola's account of his life; he was not what he pretended to be. At the same time there was considerably more to his life than he revealed in his autobiography. LoBagola was not an African and his book, like much of his life, was a clever misrepresentation, but this does not mean that either man or book should be hastily dismissed. Both raise some interesting questions about the nature of the black experience.[5] Given the extremes of LoBagola's persona, there may be little about black experience that can be generalized from his life. However, the fact that an "ordinary" man wrote about an "extraordinary" life raises interesting questions about autobiography and about who can have a "life" or distinctive voice in the historical record. With the exception of slave narratives, African American autobiography, in common with many other autobiographical traditions, tends to be dominated by the "great and the good." LoBagola constructed an individual life under very difficult circumstances, and this may tell us something about fractured lives in general.

What is to be believed or discounted in LoBagola's autobiography? To what extent can even a questionable account be of use to the historian interested in the black experience in the United States and the United Kingdom during the early decades of this century?[6] If LoBagola was not an African, as he consistently claimed, where did he come from and why did he assume that identity as part of his role as an entertainer? Did being an African become so much a part of him that at times he was no longer acting the part? What does an autobiography by a self-proclaimed African, which is clearly a weave of truth and fantasy, have to tell us about the black lived experience? These are some of the questions addressed in this essay, which tries to get closer to the "real" man who was LoBagola.

THE START OF THE PURSUIT

Many must have read LoBagola's autobiography and given it little thought other than as an interesting but fanciful piece of writing, a curio of the twentieth-century African diaspora. Our scholarly interest in LoBagola was aroused by the chance discovery of a document about his activities, which was found in the Consular papers of the U.S. State Department in the National Archives in Washington, D.C. In a brief letter to the Consul at Dakar, Alfred F. Whitman, Supervisor of Agents for the Massachusetts Society for the Prevention of Cruelty to Children, asked if inquiries could be made about LoBagola's place of origin, given as Dahomey, with a view to deporting him. Whitman described LoBagola as

> a very unusual negro who claims to have been educated at the University of Edinburgh. He professes a strong desire to help the people of his native land and pretends to be making a speciality of our systems of education so that he may introduce a proper one into Dahomey.

In this role, said Whitman, LoBagola had been befriended by a professor of education and had gained access to a number of schools in New York and other cities. He had also been active in the Young Men's Christian Association of Massachusetts and New York. These contacts provided the opportunity for LoBagola to "become widely intimate with young boys [and] he has committed unnatural acts upon them" for which he served eighteen months in the Greenfield, Massachusetts, House of Correction. In Portland, Maine, LoBagola had "secured the confidence of the well-to-do families," but when his reputation became known "he was ordered by the County Attorney to leave town." In other towns he was moved on by the police so that "he simply passes on to the next community." Whitman said that "we have considered the question of his deportation with the Boston and New York offices of the Immigration Department—but he has been here such a long time that this cannot be effected." The consular inquiries proved negative, not surprisingly given the distance of Dakar from Dahomey and the low priority afforded by a busy official to an obscure troublemaker. The Consul, W. J. Yerby, replied: "I presume that he is only another sharper 'Chief Sam.'"[7]

This chance encounter with LoBagola gave a new significance to his autobiography and spurred us to try to piece together his life. The purpose has been to check and reconstruct LoBagola's life, initially using his own account as a touchstone. It has proved a long task and is as yet incomplete, so that this is but a preliminary account of continuing research. There are several good reasons for looking closely at this suspect autobiography. In the first place, it describes the life of an itinerant and restless African American entertainer, someone who in many respects was not an "achiever" in the generally accepted sense of the term, but a failure. So, in some ways it is an extraordinary story about an ordinary man. In the second place, here is a fascinating account of the progress, fortunes, and misfortunes—more of the latter than the former—of a footloose vaudeville artiste and entertainer in Britain and the United States, and briefly in Nigeria. LoBagola followed the path of many travelling "Africans," to be found performing and struggling in every corner of the world, and at times being "studied" and exhibited as creatures of exotic, and often imaginary, cultures. As part of this latter role he served as an informant to anthropologists at the University of Pennsylvania, from which institution, he claims, he was recommended to R. R. Marett at Oxford, who invited him to speak on fetishism to the newly established University Anthropology Society in 1911.[8] Purveyor of ethnographic data and popular entertainment blended into one and, as LoBagola cynically commented,

> I talked to them just as I had talked to the audiences that I had been appearing before. . . . I had no idea that I was supposed to be any more accurate in imparting information to the men who were assigned to question me at the University of Pennsylvania than I had been when talking to a common crowd at a theatre. (332)

A third reason for trying to reconstruct LoBagola's life has very little to do with what most of us count as serious scholarship: it is an intriguing task, to rebuild a picture of the life and times of a man from a variety of often meager references and scattered sources. Provincial newspapers, street directories, single entries in passenger manifests, occasional references in magazines, the rare mention in a public archive, private diaries, and visits to small towns comprise the major sources of our research. Other than his two books, LoBagola appears to have left little in the way of firsthand information about his life. The Schomburg Center for Research in Black Culture of the New York Public Library has a small collection of letters, mainly from his agent, and newspaper cuttings that refer to his activities in the two years immediately following the publication of *An African Savage's Own Story*; his publishers' papers contain a few contractual items. Fortunately the Freedom of Information Act (FOIA) has yielded material from various U.S. Government departments which tells a good deal about LoBagola's life in the United States and also about who he really was.[9]

LoBagola's Autobiography

A substantial part of LoBagola's autobiography is clearly imaginary and set in a West African setting that is false in many aspects—geographically, ethnographically, linguistically, and chronologically. The exotic background appears to be the one that he had carefully developed and assumed over the years in peddling his craft as street entertainer and public lecturer. Interspersed through the book are accounts of African "customs," social life, and folk tales, the latter developed in his second book. On the advice of his friend and literary agent, Frederick Houk Law, LoBagola wrote his autobiography as if he were talking to a live audience.[10] The publication of the book closely followed that of the widely popular life of Trader Horn, *The Ivory Coast in the Earlies,* and no doubt Knopf sought to capitalize on the public interest in tales of exotic lands and savage peoples, particularly focused on Africa,[11] although the publishers had already secured an honorable place in the annals of publishing works by African Americans with books by Walter White, Langston Hughes, Haldane McFall, James Weldon Johnson, and Carl van Vechten. LoBagola's imagined homeland is a savage place of wild and frightening animals; its inhabitants live in a state of uninhibited nakedness, within a primitive social and economic framework and guided by rules and taboos which are different from, but not necessarily inferior to, those of the "civilized" world. Savagery is repeatedly contrasted with "modern civilization" throughout the book. In the words of a promotional circular, LoBagola's book and his public lectures revealed "things no white man could tell, Africa seen with the eyes of a native."[12]

Although LoBagola claimed that he left the "African Bush" many years before, he remains fundamentally a savage, "an alien among his own people and a stranger in the Twentieth Century World." In the industrial world he is an "outsider." "Modern civilization" has had a superficial impact and is but "skin deep"; it "taught me the *surface* of good manners," he wrote, "although at the cost of good *principle*" (100). Throughout his autobiography nakedness is used as metaphor, and the notion of "savage" is ironic and carries with it echoes of "the noble savage." The book is punctuated with stark contrasts: raw and cooked, naked and clothed, clean and dirty, savage and civilized, natural and unnatural, truth and deceit, pure and impure, moral and amoral, and, of course, black and white. LoBagola describes himself as caught in the warp of his savage origins, remaining in part the personality ordained by nature. Deceit, as we shall see, is a central aspect of LoBagola's life. The series of contrasts between "savage" and "civilized" carry the idea of innocence corrupted by civilization.

These ideas, together with the confessional nature of the autobiography, place the work firmly within a tradition established by Rousseau. It is hard to imagine, even given LoBagola's proven skill as a teller of tales, that he hit upon these structures and contrasts by himself. LoBagola's sense of being different has a number of dimensions, including race, religion, and sexual orientation. His life as he tells it is about "deceit" but also about flight, a recurrent theme

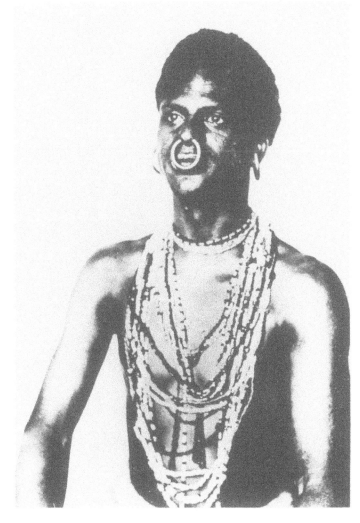

Fig. 9.1. "Amgoza is by far the best exhibit at the Museum." LoBagola at the
University of Pennsylvania Museum, 1911. The University Museum,
Photographic Archives, University of Pennsylvania, Philadelphia, PA
19104–6324.

being a series of "escapes" from mounting personal problems. LoBagola wrote
that he was "neither white nor black" but "a misfit in a white man's country,
and a stranger to my own land" (64).[13] And to visually emphasize this point the
frontispiece photograph has LoBagola seated and naked to the waist while a
later photograph in the book (by the New York photographer Sherrill Schell)
depicts him in a three-piece suit and wearing a wristwatch. These photographs
underscore the point, also made in the text, that civilization has merely clothed
LoBagola in deceit. They also disguise the fact that LoBagola was only 158
centimeters in height.

Fig. 9.2. LoBagola the "savage," the first plate in *An African Savage's Own Story* (New York: Knopf, 1930). Photograph by Sherrill Schell.

The title of LoBagola's autobiography and many of the chapter headings stress his "savage" origins and sense of alienation: "Savage Social Laws and Customs" (chap. III), "Horrible Fetish Laws" (chap. IV), "A Disgusting Savage Learning Deceit" (chap. XX), "A Savage Running Rampant in Civilization" (chap. XXXV), and so on. LoBagola makes much of his confusion over, and ignorance of, the moral and social codes of "modern civilization," which he claims not to have learned. These are rendered more confusing because of the double standard that he claimed pervaded much of Western morality. LoBagola's breach of the Western moral codes is explicable, he says, because he is still a savage at heart; "modern civilization" also had its corrupting effect when as a young and impressionable boy in Scotland he easily acquired "new immoral ways," such as deceit, lying, and, in particular, sexual experiences

(91, 205–206, 211–12). But the opposite is surely the case; if that part of the book were true and he had received his upbringing in a Presbyterian household in Scotland, it would be disingenuous for him to claim such ignorance.

In the anonymous "Introduction" to LoBagola's autobiography, Frederick Houk Law asks, "Is the Story True?" (xix).[14] Law, in introducing the articles in *Scribner's Magazine,* claimed to have corroborative letters, names, and addresses to support the main parts of the story, although these are either omitted or disguised in the book. The "Introduction" also suggested that the book contained plenty of verifiable facts and that

> if the reader will take the trouble to investigate the account he will see that Ibn LoBagola, on the one hand, must write from personal knowledge: or, on the other hand, must have been a profound student of works of reference, which seems unlikely. (xix)

LoBagola also attempted to counter what he knew would be public skepticism:

> It is the same in the United States today. People all over the country try to show that I am deceiving people in this story of my life. They have told me to my face that I never saw Africa; that I was born somewhere in western Pennsylvania or in some place in the South. (257–58)

Although LoBagola had been to Africa, the skeptics were not far wrong about his origins. His persistence in maintaining his African identity was tied closely to his source of income as an entertainer.

LoBagola begins his book with a description of his home in Africa that reads as if derived from a textbook. His native home, he claims, is "the village of Nodaghusah," a short distance south of Timbuktu in the French Sudan. On the next page he contradicts this by stating that "my country is between six degrees and eight degrees north latitude," which would place it within 150 kilometers of the coast. His subsequent descriptions of the "Ondo Bush" and forest region foodstuffs, his references to Yoruba words and institutions, and also to Dahomean social and political structures, describe an area that LoBagola certainly visited, possibly on more than one occasion. The jumble of cultural bits and pieces with which he describes this part of the West African coast could have been drawn from that experience and from random culling of information from a variety of popular travel books.

LoBagola also claimed to be a black Jew, a member of a community which he calls "B'nai Ephraim" (chap. V, "Black Jews of the Ondo Bush"). Throughout his autobiography he makes much of his Jewishness, although a note of caution is entered when he says "there is no absolute certainty about my Jewish origin, but I clung to the Jewish religion . . ." (357).[15] Not that this meant that he was readily accepted by other Jews; LoBagola protested, both in his autobiography and in private letters, about color prejudice by Jews in Palestine, the

United States, and Britain. It is not clear when LoBagola added the Jewish label. It was not as outlandish as it appears, for there were many claims that Jewish communities existed in West Africa and some African Americans also embraced Judaism.[16] A Jewish origin offered storyteller, entertainer, and con man LoBagola a further exotic twist to his tale and possibly a means of gaining access to a variety of Jewish charities. To his Jewish origin he also added a grand, princely title—"Prince Bata Kindai Amgoza Ibn LoBagola." For black entertainers to pretend an African origin and to append a "royal" title was not uncommon in Britain or the United States.[17] Labels are obviously important and at various times LoBagola appends to his African identity a further cultural connection, most particularly a Jewish identity or a Scottish upbringing.

An African Savage's Own Story has many of the ingredients of a popular "thriller": mysterious peoples, wild and ferocious animals, witch doctors, cannibal dwarfs, torture, rogues and heroes, warm friends and betrayers, plus the mildly erotic titillation of "six girls at once." This sexual angle formed a regular feature of LoBagola's public addresses on his life in Africa, toned down for school students. In part the autobiography is a "gripping" tale typical of certain popular magazines of the period. The vocabulary is relatively simple, although the frequent use of the semicolon reveals a fairly sophisticated punctuation. The style of LoBagola's book is clear and concise and more polished than the prose of his few surviving letters, which surely indicates the hand of F. H. Law. The tenor and the language of the book may reflect the audience at which it was directed, one that was dissatisfied with colonial literature and which demanded to read "authoritative" tales of Africa told by authentic Africans who really knew the continent. Certainly it would seem that the book pandered to and helped to reinforce a range of prejudices and stereotypical views held by whites about Africa and Africans.

LoBagola's Identity

Who was LoBagola? He persisted in claiming an African origin, the handle of his trade, even to the extent of taking out U.S. naturalization papers in 1918 and maintaining his false origin while being interrogated by an immigration official as a convict in a New York prison. LoBagola so repeatedly referred one Naturalization Service examiner to his book that the man went and bought a copy. Eventually, faced with the prospect of deportation, LoBagola admitted that he was Joseph Howard Lee, born in Baltimore in 1887, the seventeenth child of African American parents. Even his birth certificate, which was eventually accepted as genuine by the Immigration and Naturalization authorities, did not bear his name, merely stating that he was an "unnamed 17th child."[18]

His father, Joseph Lee, was a cook from St. Mary's County, Maryland, and his mother, Lucy Lee, was a servant from Wilmington, North Carolina.

LoBagola's early years were spent in the family house at 620 Raberg Street (by 1934 renamed Fairmount Avenue). At this stage next to nothing is known of his childhood. He attended the Kasesha Public School and recollected that the principal was a white man, a Mr. Clark, and that he was taught by two white female teachers, a Miss Firth (?) and a Miss Read: "I remember I was about 12 or 13 years old when I completed the 4th grade there." Joseph Lee, senior, was a Roman Catholic, and his young son was sent to St. Francis Xavier Church, "on the corner of Calvert and Pleasant Streets." LoBagola could not remember whether he had been baptized, although he recalled being instructed by a Father Riley or Reilly. According to LoBagola his father died c. 1904 and his mother died in Baltimore sometime between 1906 and 1909, "while I was in Africa."[19]

THE MAKING OF AN ENTERTAINER

This evidence discounts the Scottish childhood claimed in *An African Savage's Own Story*. However, LoBagola said that he had been in Scotland on several occasions, his descriptions of Glasgow indicate that he knew the city fairly well, and various U.S. newspapers report his Scottish accent.[20] At a New York court hearing in late 1927, he said the Presbyterian family with whom he stayed in Glasgow were named Nichols.[21] Considerable effort has been made to find documentary evidence that LoBagola lived in Scotland, but without success. According to the account he gave in his first interrogation, he left Baltimore on a freighter bound for Liverpool sometime in 1906, but he is vague as to dates and times, and in any case falsehood was part of his stock-in-trade. There is firm independent evidence that LoBagola was in the English west Midlands in the fall of 1907, and it may have been there that he began his entertainment career. Places and persons are identifiable, one being Mr. Sumner, landlord of the "Rose and Crown," High Street, Coventry, who promoted LoBagola as one of an "Arab Cycling Club . . . led by Amgosa (West African Chief) in the annual Lady Godiva parade of 1907" (216 ff.).[22] LoBagola also mentions working in the Humber Motor Company factory in Coventry, but this has not been verified. His account of renting a bicycle a few years later in Kidderminster, however, has the mark of truth about it.[23] He told a Naturalization Service official that he returned to Baltimore in 1907 and in that year, presumably November or December, sailed as a seaman to West Africa on a freighter. "I stayed in Africa to 1909 and returned to New York, via Liverpool, on the S.S. Umbria,"[24] though whether as a passenger or a member of the crew is not known. During one of these visits to Britain, LoBagola may have come into contact with African and black entertainers. He claims to have travelled with a cinematograph show run by a Mrs. Collins, whom he met in Liverpool. There is no evidence for this, but there are some disparate clues which may indicate how LoBagola might have gained his early experience of entertaining and also a stage name.

There were many black or African shows in Britain at the time of Lo-Bagola's visit. "In Dahomey" was a popular troupe in London, and also toured the provinces in the first decade of the century, and it is known that LoBagola performed as a Dahomean fire-eater. One troupe of nearly forty Dahomeans had as their director Angazza Bogolo (Coombes, chap. 5; Green).[25] Beah Kindah was the name of a black entertainer at the Liverpool Colonial Products Exhibition in November 1908, while Peter Lobengula had appeared in the stage show "Savage South Africa" in London in 1899, and his name was often in the British press until his death in Salford in November 1913.[26] It is not unreasonable to assume that LoBagola adopted and adapted these names either then or at a later date, thus becoming Bata Kindai Amgoza ibn LoBagola. In Coventry in 1907 he was known as "Amgosa," a name possibly given to him by Sumner, who may have travelled in South Africa, and it is an adaptation of this name that he used professionally. The title "Prince," along with the fez, robe, and sandals which LoBagola added to his wardrobe, were regular stage props for black showmen.

On his return to the United States in 1909, LoBagola stayed in Baltimore for one or two months, which was the last time, he claimed, that he saw his brothers and sisters. He found work in the Eastern states as an entertainer in a dime museum at $25 per week. Shortly thereafter he was seen by a theatrical agent and, starting at $35 a week, began a career as a vaudeville artiste. His earnings mainly went to the agent and to gambling. However, LoBagola claimed, a theatrical performance on board ship provided him with an introduction to a Pennsylvania senator, Mr. K—, whom he met again months later when performing at the predominantly Jewish Mercantile Club on Philadelphia's Broad Street.[27] While in Philadelphia, LoBagola also met "several learned gentlemen" at the University of Pennsylvania, "who asked me to give information about the social organization of the people of Dahomey, where I was supposed to come from." They also "asked me about the Yoruba language, of which my knowledge was very limited. When I found that I could not answer about matters in Dahomey, I simply said anything that came to me" (332–33). These "learned gentlemen" were described by LoBagola as Professor J—, Dr. G—, Dr. S—, and Mr. W—. They did exist and can be identified as Dr. Morris Jastrow, Jr., a professor of Semitic languages; Dr. George Byron Gordon, the director of the University Museum; Dr. Frank Gouldsmith Speck, an assistant professor of anthropology; and Speck's doctoral candidate William D. Wallis, who had been a Rhodes Scholar at Oxford, 1907–10.[28]

Living exhibits were prominent in the University of Pennsylvania Museum program of anthropology, as one local newspaper briefly reported, accompanying the story with two photographs of "Amgoza," who "parades around the halls in native costume much to the amusement of students":

> SHOWS STUDENT REAL NEGRO. Pennsylvania U. Professor Has In Tow South African Specimen. Doctor Frank G. Speck of the University of Pennsylvania Museum has a real South African on exhibition at the Museum. Amgoza is the name of the black man, and every morning, decked in only his native dress, he parades through the halls of the University Museum. The clothing is composed of only a sheep's skin. Doctor Speck is always on the lookout for representatives of the different types of man, and when he heard that Amgoza was to visit Philadelphia he made arrangements for him to visit the Museum. . . . Amgoza is by the far the best exhibit at the museum. While he looks like the wildest black man that came out of African jungles, he is extremely intelligent. The exhibits at the museum have interested Amgoza greatly.[29]

The racist language of the newspaper obscures the motivation of those involved. American anthropologists had only limited access to the field in Africa and generally were becoming skeptical of reports on African law and practice derived from official colonial sources. In addition, popular images of Africa and African culture were derived from living ethnological exhibitions—for example, those in Paris, Berlin, Berne, and Liverpool, where the Ashanti village provided occasional work for local black people, and the various world's fairs and expositions—so that anthropologists were seriously concerned at the distorted nature of public perceptions of the continent (Staehelin). Whatever the motivation, the possibilities for misinterpretation by the public were limitless. Two points are worth making: first, LoBagola was now presented with yet another possibility for earning his living, again as a curiosity, which he took and made use of. At one level he was being exploited, but he was also exploiting the system that employed him and at the same time, if his account is to be believed, successfully misleading the professional anthropologists. Second, in this instance the description of LoBagola as a South African surely has little to do with such an eminent anthropologist as Speck and much to do with newspaper license.

To Britain Again

For some reason LoBagola left Philadelphia on 5 May 1911 as a second-class passenger on board the *Celtic,* bound for Liverpool, travelling as "Am

Goza, Educationalist." Also on the passenger manifest was one Russell Wayman, "a coloured teacher,"[30] an African American on his way to Liberia, who decided to team up with LoBagola on the trip from Liverpool to London. LoBagola claimed that his fare to West Africa was paid by an associate of Mr. K—, and that he travelled in 1910, the date he also misleadingly gave to the Naturalization Service officials (334). He also claimed that he carried with him a letter of introduction from Wallis to R. R. Marett ("Professor M—"), who had recently been appointed Reader in Social Anthropology at Oxford. Invited to speak on fetishism at Exeter College, LoBagola stated that "I [had] specific information on that subject, and, needless to say, I made a hit" (333). Britain was meant to be merely a stop en route to Dahomey, but LoBagola turned, or was reduced, to giving "entertainment in the [London] parks under the title of 'The Fire King of Dahomey'." He also fell afoul of the law. While lodging in East Ham, he stole money from Wayman and was arrested on the night of 11 June 1911, the day before the coronation of King George V. At East Ham police court, LoBagola was sentenced to three months' imprisonment, the first of several periods of incarceration.[31]

ON TO WEST AFRICA

In mid-October 1911, within a few days of his release from prison, LoBagola embarked from Liverpool for West Africa on the SS *Batanga* as a second-class passenger bound for Whydah. This time he was on the passenger manifest as "Mr. Amgoza," "Anthropologist," a "British colonial subject."[32] By his own account his passage was paid for by "Mr. C—, the secretary to Mr. Joseph F—" (both as yet unidentified, although it is known that John Harris paid the fares of impoverished Africans returning to Africa), and he carried with him "a letter of introduction to a Mr. Deeming [*sic*] . . . written by Mr. John Holt himself" (340). A search of the Holt papers has not revealed a copy of the letter, but what LoBagola says may be true. James Deemin had signed a coasters agreement with Holt in 1894 and he was employed by the company at the time of LoBagola's visit to West Africa.[33] This was LoBagola's second visit to West Africa. In 1934 he told the Naturalization Service interrogator: "I went to London and was there several months and went to Dahomey, West Africa. I stayed there and travelled in the bush north of Dahomey until 1912, when I returned to Scotland in May, 1912."[34] There is no supporting evidence of his travels in the interior of West Africa, although he does show some knowledge of coastal Dahomey.

In the autobiography, LoBagola moves people and events around to fabricate his story. For example, he says that the ship in which he stowed away in

1896 to come to Scotland was the SS *Batanga* and that the master was Captain Caley. The ship and master are correct but LoBagola's first contact with Captain W. R. Caley and the *Batanga* was in the fall of 1911, when he was one of two passengers on board en route from Liverpool to Whydah in Dahomey. Similarly, actual people and events in West Africa, mainly in southern Nigeria, are used by LoBagola to elaborate his fictitious and real visits and activities in the region. The autobiography recounts three "return" visits to West Africa before the 1920s: a childhood visit c. 1900, which is obviously false, and trips in 1907–08 and in 1911–12. LoBagola probably made the 1907–08 visit as a seaman from the United States. Whether he travelled in the interior of West Africa as he claimed is not known. It seems unlikely that on that occasion he entertained the Alake Gbadebo, the Egba ruler, by singing Harry Lauder's music hall song "Stop yer tickling, Jock," or that the adventures recounted in his book are in any way true.

However, LoBagola's role as an entertainer in Lagos in 1911–12 can be supported by documentary evidence. Lee or LoBagola, known then simply as Amgoza, seems to have been a very persuasive talker with the knack for eliciting sympathy and help from the prominent and well-placed. He mentioned that he met in Lagos, or had met earlier, David Taylor and also William Shita [*sic*], a prosperous Kruman with a general merchandise store in Balogun Street, who "secured me a place to stay with a very fine family of native Christians, by the name of Savage" in Olowobowo, Lagos (342–43).[35] He also appears to have gained the support and friendship of people such as the Vaughan brothers and particularly Dr. Orisdipe Obasa, the physician and politician who was son-in-law to the merchant R. B. Blaize.[36] With Obasa's encouragement and support, LoBagola, having failed to find a suitable job ("Really, I was a problem"), turned to "the only thing that I seem to be able to do successfully . . . to entertain the public." And an undoubted success he was, especially in his second major performance at the "Night of Merriment" given at the Glover Memorial Hall in May 1912. This included European performers and an audience of Africans and Europeans. The *Lagos Standard* reported enthusiastically: "The 'laurel' of the evening was awarded to Amgoza himself. There is no disguising the fact that he is a born 'light comedian' and his movements on the stage remind one of such Masters of the Art as Eugene Stratton, Harry Lauder, etc. . . . No wonder that the name of Amgoza is fast becoming a household word in Lagos. He knows exactly how to 'tickle an audience'" (343–44; *Lagos Standard* 15 May 1912).

The other claims that LoBagola made were more dramatic and less likely to be true. He wrote that "my experiences in Lagos were not thrilling, outside of being flogged publicly when I took a trip to Northern Nigeria because I refused to prostrate before a white man" (345). This may have happened, but somehow it is doubtful. He seems to be riding the back, so to speak, of the Zaria flogging incident, reported in the *Lagos Standard* in March 1912, when two African government clerks, named Hall and Taylor, were stripped naked and publicly flogged. Or perhaps he came to know about the Bauchi flogging incident of May 1914, which led to the Fitzgerald libel case in London in November 1919 (Duffield). It is likely that LoBagola, as the master entertainer, knew how to embellish his stories. After several months in Lagos, LoBagola's health was threatened by malarial fever and he took ship for Liverpool with a through ticket to New York paid for by his Nigerian friends. The passenger manifest confirms that a "Mr. Amgoza," this time listed as a "U.S. citizen," travelled first class on the *Falaba* to Liverpool, arriving on 30 June 1912.[37]

BACK TO THE UNITED STATES

Two versions of this return to Britain are available. In the autobiography LoBagola wrote that he was footloose in London, and made contact with Mr. C—, who "decided to ship me back to America, where I had made a success of the vaudeville stage" (348). In his official interrogation LoBagola said that he went to Scotland, and "then in September I went to the United States and landed at Philadelphia on SS *Haverford*. I travelled extensively from Philadelphia in theatrical work as LoBagola."[38] In the autobiography LoBagola emigrated to Philadelphia on the *Haverford* in the spring of 1909 (323), another example of the way in which he manipulated bits and pieces of his past. The stage was only part of LoBagola's life. By his own published account, within a few days of his arrival in New York, carrying the tools of his vaudeville trade, "the caftan, fez and sandals," he had been robbed of his money and reduced to begging. His charm, or luck, remained, and he made the acquaintance of a professor of either education or social anthropology at Columbia University (the autobiography says the latter) where he once again became some kind of informant.[39]

This role of African cultural informant, or whatever, was short-lived. LoBagola's real skill, and the source of his income, was on the stage "doing a native dance, in native costume, and a fire-dance; then making a quick change into a Scotch kilt and singing Scotch songs." Another accomplishment, clearly a successful one, was as "The Fireproof Man," which led to theater bookings "all over the eastern part of the United States, and it seemed as if my star were in the ascendant." But, wrote the itinerant entertainer, "good things in my life never had long duration." He described himself as "a savage running rampant in civilization" and reported "naturally that led me into a terrible mess" (351–52). LoBagola did not wish to mention the circumstances that led him into a "terrible mess," other than to say that he was arrested more than once.

Fig. 9.3. The "civilized" LoBagola, 1930. A portrait by the New York
photographer Sherrill Schell, used as a plate in LoBagola's autobiography.

The "mess" that led him into prison was a series of homosexual offenses,
what LoBagola referred to as the abdication of "his throne of manhood" (353).
He was first imprisoned in Greenfield, Massachusetts, in 1913, apparently under the name of Lee, and similar, particularly pedophile, offenses sent him to
prison on several more occasions. For example, in February 1933 his New
York agent, James B. Pond, urged him to be careful:

> We have had a letter of complaint from Bluffton, Ohio, and we have done what
> we can to smooth things there for you. For heaven's sake be careful or you
> won't be able to stay in Bluffton. We can take care of the question with regard
> to your identity, but we can do nothing if you start being indiscreet with the
> boys who hear you lecture and who worship you. You went to Bluffton to
> escape the color line, but you have already aroused suspicions in other lines.[40]

According to the Supervisor of Agents for the Massachusetts Society for the Prevention of Cruelty to Children, LoBagola had befriended a professor of education at Columbia University and thus gained access to a number of schools in New York and other cities. He had also been active in the Young Men's Christian Association of Massachusetts and New York. Such contacts provided the opportunity for LoBagola to "become widely intimate" with young boys and to commit "unnatural acts upon them."[41] Sometime in 1917 he was arrested in Syracuse, New York, and served six months in the county jail for sexual perversion; later that year, or in early 1918, he was again convicted of sexual assault and received a further six-month sentence of imprisonment in the Oswego County jail. Criminal conviction damaged LoBagola's theatrical career: "For a time no one wanted me. The theatres would not engage me" (354). Life was at a very low ebb and LoBagola claimed that the only employment he was able to find was as a bootblack in a barber's shop.

SOLDIER IN PALESTINE AND EGYPT

This was LoBagola's lot when the United States entered the war in April 1917. Stung by a barber's remark about "slack" foreigners, he said that he left the shop and volunteered "for the Allied cause." Whatever the reason, he enlisted in the U.S. Army on 3 August 1918 at Oswego County, New York, as Kindai Amgosa [sic] LoBagola (serial no. 4150887, private 27th Company, 152nd Depot Brigade) and was sent to Camp Upton for initial training.[42] As he had enlisted as an alien, he now applied for and was granted naturalization.[43] Years later when LoBagola was asked why he had taken out citizenship papers, he replied: "In order to always be sure I would have the protection of my country while abroad. I was parading under the name of Lo Bagola [sic] and I wanted something to fall back on in the event of any injustices." LoBagola admitted that no one had ever questioned his nationality up to 1918 and that he had never voted in the United States.[44] As with so many episodes in LoBagola's career, his service with the U.S. Army was to be very brief. Within five weeks he had been "honourably discharged" due to a "physical disability." This hid the real reason, which the Army Department confidentially passed to the Commissioner of Naturalization in 1932. In their report LoBagola was described as suffering from a "constitutional psychopathic state, paranoid personality; history indicates sexual perversion covering an unknown length of time; was arrested on several occasions for practicing unnatural acts; claims that he is hounded from place to place, that he is the victim of an organized plot to keep him from pursuing his vocation, and that the charges of perversion are false."[45]

LoBagola was discharged on 11 September 1918 but within a week or two he had enlisted in the British Army under the name of Kindai Lobagola [*sic*]. He did this through the British recruiting office recently opened in New York City. This office initially sought recruits from British Caribbean immigrants in the United States for the West Indian Regiment, but then, following the Balfour Declaration, it also attempted to enlist Jewish recruits for the 38th, 39th, and 40th Battalion of the Royal Fusiliers.[46] LoBagola was apparently enlisted as Jewish. He claimed to have been sent via Canada to Avonmouth, near Bristol, and from there to Saltash in Cornwall for six weeks of training. The main depot of the Royal Fusiliers was in London but the Jewish battalions (sometimes known as the "Jewsiliers"!) were stationed in Plymouth and Saltash. After training, LoBagola went with the 38th Battalion to Palestine and then to Kantara in Egypt; the main task of the Battalion was guarding Turkish prisoners of war. LoBagola's military discharge papers (photograph facing 358) show that he served for two years and sixty-eight days.[47] Much of what he wrote about his military service in the Middle East seems authentic, and this is partly borne out by the copies of official papers printed in *An African Savage's Own Story*. His account of racial persecution by fellow soldiers also has a ring of truth.[48] LoBagola said that while he was on leave in Jerusalem, he impressed the headmaster of the Collège des Frères, who offered him an appointment as a teacher to be taken up on demobilization. After returning reluctantly with his battalion to Britain, LoBagola applied for and was granted repatriation to Palestine in mid-1920, travelling on a passport issued by the Aliens Branch of the Home Office on 20 July 1920 (photograph facing 364).

Much of what LoBagola had to say about his life in Palestine and Egypt is unconfirmed and needs to be checked by research in the area. His rejection as a black Jew and his social isolation turned him to the Roman Catholic Church. In an undated article entitled "My Religion," LoBagola described the tempestuous background to his conversion in the face of both the hostility of the Jewish community in Jerusalem and the suspicion of the Roman Catholic hierarchy.[49] Through the good offices of a Franciscan priest, Father Barnabé Meistermann, LoBagola decided to become a Roman Catholic. He was eventually baptized at Tanta in Egypt and from then on he was known as Paul Emanuel LoBagola, a name he used for official correspondence in the United States into the 1930s. He further claimed to have taught first at the Collège des Frères in Jerusalem and then later at two schools in Egypt, the Maronite Fathers' School and the Great Benevolent Coptic School in Tanta. In the latter place, so he claimed in his book, he learned to drink heavily, yet another of the problems that dogged his later life. After resigning from the school, LoBagola said, he went to live in Cairo, but after "a long time" he travelled to West Africa. In his published account he returned to New York from Britain as a member of the crew on a cattle boat, although he told the Naturalization Service interrogator that he sailed as a hand on the SS *Louis* from Plymouth in early 1925. His

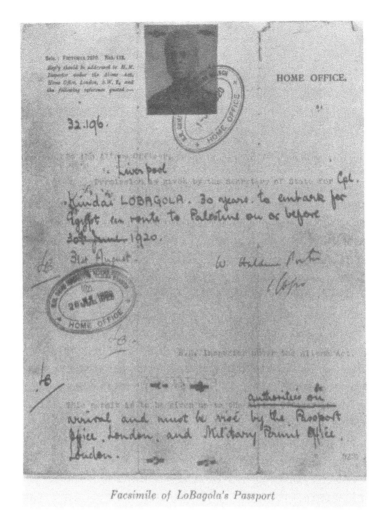

Facsimile of LoBagola's Passport

Fig. 9.4. Facsimile of LoBagola's British passport, issued in London in 1920. This document allowed him to return to Palestine, a territory which had just become a British Mandate.

subsequent Attica prison record states that he served a six-month prison sentence in London in 1925, but this has not been verified. LoBagola also mentions the help and support of the Rev. A. F. Day, SJ, who "was exceedingly good to me." Day had served as a chaplain to the forces in Palestine and Egypt from 1915 to 1919, where he could easily have made the acquaintance of LoBagola.[50]

Lecturer and Author

In the United States LoBagola gave a few lectures but said that he "wished to settle down for life in a cloister." The Maryknoll Fathers accepted him, but

"I remained only a month, and then I fell. Enough said. I had to leave" (369). The Maryknoll records list him but briefly: "Paul Emanuel LoBagola, Home— Jerusalem, Pt. Add. 314 W. 119th St. N.Y.C. Employment—lecturer. Arrived 27 March 1926, left 14 April 1926."[51] The "fall" referred to is perhaps LoBagola's drinking habits or his homosexual practices. Using his Catholic contacts, and through "the kind offices of Monsignor R" (not yet identified), he found a job at Fordham University, where he was employed as a porter and then as an assistant in the Biological Department. After fourteen months LoBagola fell into heavy drinking and was dismissed. On 13 November 1927, while he was living in Harlem, he was arrested and charged with impairing the morals of a minor. According to the court record, he was convicted of seizing a thirteen-year-old boy off the street and "trying to drag him in to a hallway" (*New York Times* 10 Dec. 1927: 18). LoBagola was sentenced to thirty days in the New York County workhouse. On his release he became a vagabond "ignored by all." "In despair," wrote LoBagola, he went on impulse into a New York public school and asked the principal "to pay me for giving a lecture before the school" (370). He was accepted and paid $10. It is not clear when this occurred. It may have been in mid-1928; it certainly proved to be another turning point in LoBagola's life, as he forged a new career on the lecture circuit and became a best-selling author.

The first lectures were given at high schools in New York: Alexander Hamilton High School where on 31 October 1928 he gave the "Address" at the school assembly, Morris High School, Public School 69, and Brooklyn Tech, where he appears to have come to the notice of Maude Winthrop Gibbon, who became his first agent.[52] LoBagola's talks were on African life and customs, which, whatever his origins, he could now give with a degree of authenticity that satisfied his largely unsophisticated audiences. In all probability it is on these various audiences that he honed his imaginary and exotic African background which would then appear as his autobiography. Through his talks to schools, LoBagola came to the attention of first Scribner's and then Dr. Frederick Houk Law, head of English at the Stuyvesant High School in New York and the man who was to turn LoBagola's talks into *An African Savage's Own Story*. Law records in his diary for 11 April 1928: "Dined at the Amherst Club with Mr Lord, Mr Kilbourne [of Scribner's] and Mr LoBagola, a negro."[53]

According to LoBagola, Law encouraged him to write down his story, which was done first in pencil and then laboriously typed on different machines. Law described himself as LoBagola's agent, and he read the proofs of LoBagola's articles for *Scribner's Magazine*, to which he also wrote the brief introduction.[54] He was also the author of the unsigned introduction to LoBagola's autobiography published by Knopf in 1930.[55] LoBagola visited Law at his house in Brooklyn, once arriving with a box of chocolates for Mrs. Law,

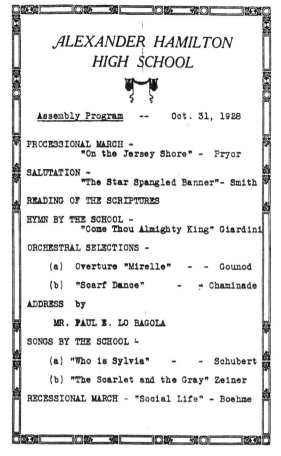

ALEXANDER HAMILTON
HIGH SCHOOL

Assembly Program   --   Oct. 31, 1928

PROCESSIONAL MARCH -
        "On the Jersey Shore" - Pryor

SALUTATION -
        "The Star Spangled Banner"- Smith

READING OF THE SCRIPTURES

HYMN BY THE SCHOOL -
        "Come Thou Almighty King" Giardini

ORCHESTRAL SELECTIONS -

    (a)   Overture "Mirelle"   - - Gounod

    (b)   "Scarf Dance"   - - Chaminade

ADDRESS by

    MR. PAUL E. LO BAGOLA

SONGS BY THE SCHOOL -

    (a) "Who is Sylvia"   -   - Schubert

    (b) "The Scarlet and the Gray" Zeiner

RECESSIONAL MARCH - "Social Life" - Boehme

Fig. 9.5. Program of the Alexander Hamilton High School for 31 October 1928, one of the several schools at which LoBagola spoke in the two years before his books were published.

who was not pleased at his presence.[56] It is difficult to accept that the much-travelled Law did not come to realize at some time that LoBagola was a fraud. However, at Law's urging, LoBagola also acquired a tour manager, James B. Pond of New York, "Manager of American Tours of World Celebrities."[57] With the publication of *An African Savage's Own Story,* Pond argued that "I think the time has come when he [LoBagola] can stand more vigorous exploitation."[58] Pond organized a lecture tour to take in Cleveland and Chicago.[59] That and other engagements included some high schools, but Pond was obviously intent on directing LoBagola's energies toward more prestigious institutions which would pay higher fees, such as the Woman's City Club in Boston, the Adventurers' Club in New York City, and the Woman's Canadian Club in Montreal, plus press interviews and radio talks. The promotional material prepared by

Pond included a number of photographs showing "Chief Ibn LoBagola" in "African dress," the fez and caftan meeting the popular stereotype; he was described as a "fascinating speaker. His English is pure, with the trace of a Scottish accent now and then." Various newspaper reports described LoBagola as "five feet five inches tall, powerfully built with the muscular development of a pugilist," and as a "stocky dark-skinned man with a powerful voice" and "a manner seemingly electrified with enthusiasm."[60]

Appearance was important on the lecture tour, and so was reliability. Despite the economic depression, fees were relatively high in 1930—$100 for the afternoon talks in clubs, $30 for schools, and $200 for evening talks.[61] And when LoBagola turned up and gave his piece, often similar to what he had said in the book, but with questions and answers as well, the press gave approving notices. As a result, by mid-1930 LoBagola was earning a guaranteed minimum income of $300 a month, and had an apartment at 124 East 53rd Street in New York. Had he been able to control his spending, drinking, and sexual activities, the lecture circuit might have held out for him the opportunity for a more stable life. This was dashed by arrest and arraignment when he was charged

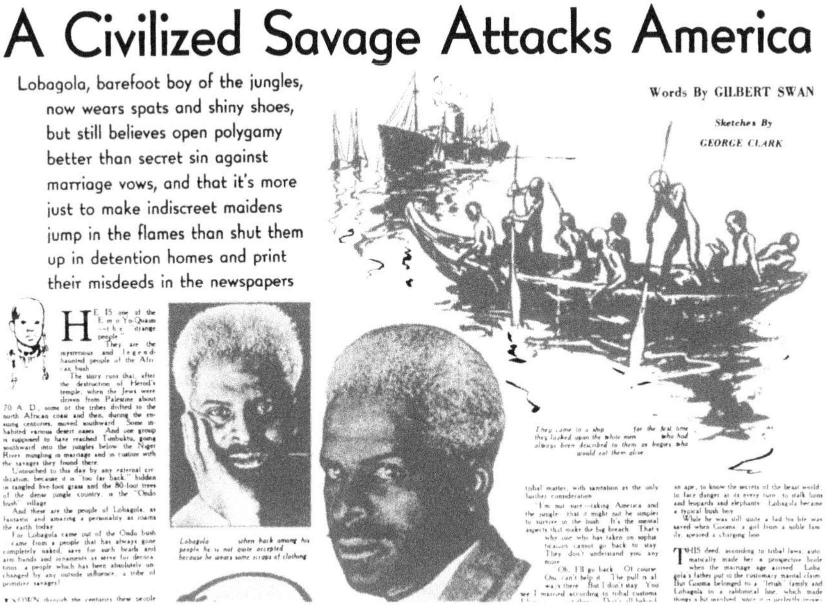

A Civilized Savage Attacks America

Lobagola, barefoot boy of the jungles, now wears spats and shiny shoes, but still believes open polygamy better than secret sin against marriage vows, and that it's more just to make indiscreet maidens jump in the flames than shut them up in detention homes and print their misdeeds in the newspapers

Words By GILBERT SWAN

Sketches By GEORGE CLARK

HE IS one of the E-m-o-Yo-Quaim—the "strange people."

They are the mysterious and legend-haunted people of the African bush.

The story runs that, after the destruction of Herod's temple, when the Jews were driven from Palestine about 70 A. D., some of the tribes drifted to the north African coast and then, during the ensuing centuries, moved southward. Some inhabited various desert oases. And one group is supposed to have reached Timbuktu, going southward into the jungles below the Niger River, mingling in marriage and in custom with the savages they found there.

Untouched to this day by any external civilization, because it is "too far back," hidden in tangled five-foot grass and the 80-foot trees of the dense jungle country, is the "Ondo bush" village.

And these are the people of Lobagola, as fantastic and amazing a personality as roams the earth today.

For Lobagola came out of the Ondo bush—came from a people that has always gone completely naked, save for such beads and arm bands and ornaments as serve for decorations, a people which has been absolutely unchanged by any outside influence, a tribe of primitive savages!

Lobagola ... when back among his people he is not quite accepted because he wears some scraps of clothing

They came to a ship ... for the first time they looked upon the white men ... who had always been described to them as bogies who would eat them alive.

tribal matter, with sanitation as the only further consideration.

"I'm not sure—taking America and the jungle—that it might not be simpler to survive in the bush. It's the mental aspects that make the big breach. That's why one who has taken on sophistication cannot go back to stay. They don't understand you any more.

"Oh, I'll go back. Of course. One can't help it. The pull is always there. But I don't stay. You see I married according to tribal customs ...

an age, to know the secrets of the beast world, to face danger at its every turn, to stalk lions and leopards and elephants—Lobagola became a typical bush boy.

While he was still quite a lad his life was saved when Gooma, a girl from a noble family, speared a charging lion.

THIS deed, according to tribal laws, automatically made her a prospective bride when the marriage age arrived. Lobagola's father put in the customary marital claim. But Gooma belonged to a "letiah" family and Lobagola to a rabbinical line, which made things a bit involved ...

Fig. 9.6. In the several months following the publication in New York of *An African Savage's Own Story,* the book was reviewed by newspapers and magazines all over the United States. This account is from *This EveryWeek Magazine,* April 19–20, 1930.

with sodomy, committed with a fifteen-year-old boy from a New York high school in the Bronx on 19 June 1930; bail was put at $2,500. For Pond it was important to keep news of this unfortunate turn of events as quiet as possible. Under the stress of his impending trial, LoBagola became increasingly unreliable; drink or some other misfortune caused him to miss speaking appointments. Pond, in a brief letter to LoBagola reminding him of engagements to address the Philadelphia Rotary Club and the Brooklyn Masons, desperately urged: "Don't forget these two dates. We both need the money."[62] And they did, Pond to pay for publicity and rail fares, LoBagola to meet an unpaid furniture account of $1,430 with Kors, an East Broadway "Complete Outfitters." Nevertheless, a little over a month before his trial, LoBagola received a congratulatory letter from the parent of a boy at a school in Concord, Massachusetts, thanking him for a "most instructive and enlightening" talk about "a story . . . without parallel," and also enclosing a list of the names of boys who wanted a copy of the book.[63]

PRISON AND OFFICIAL QUESTIONS

LoBagola came to trial in mid-December 1930; he pleaded guilty and in early January 1931 received a one-and-a-half to three-year prison sentence. He was briefly lodged in Sing Sing at Ossining, where F. H. Law visited him,[64] and then transferred to Great Meadow Prison at Comstock. Despite the inconvenience and embarrassment of abruptly losing a star attraction in the middle of a speaking tour—the Hirsch Center in Chicago explained LoBagola's absence as due to his breaking a leg while in Holland!—Pond stood by LoBagola, writing to him, sending him money, making representations on his behalf to various officials, and agreeing with the State Parole Board to reemploy him on his release. There were good commercial reasons for this: apparently Pond had advanced LoBagola several thousand dollars, and now that LoBagola was in prison he was "in no position to repay me the money he already owes me."[65] There were other debts as well and in 1931 LoBagola made over to Kors part of the royalties from the autobiography and the folk tales just published by Knopf.[66] About the same time the copyright of the autobiography was assigned to Frederick Law.[67]

It is not clear whether Pond knew at this time that LoBagola was a fraud. In a letter to the New York State Parole Board in late 1931, he wrote of his imprisoned entertainer that "it is extremely regrettable that he had to deviate from our social conventions."[68] However, by then the Naturalization Service, alerted by a letter which suggested that LoBagola might be an undesirable alien, had already begun inquiries into his status and nationality, and LoBagola had reluctantly admitted to Examiner Siegel that he was really Joseph Howard Lee and a U.S. citizen.[69] Pond was aware of this new interest in LoBagola's origins and it must have soon become clear to him that his "African" attraction was not what he claimed to be. This is obvious from a letter that he wrote to LoBagola in early 1933, in which he said that he would not be able to help if sexual encounters with boys brought about his arrest, but that "we can take care of the question with regard to your identity."[70]

IN THE MIDWEST

When LoBagola emerged from prison in spring 1932 he abandoned the name of Paul and tried to pick up the pieces of his disrupted speaking career.[71] It was not easy. He moved west to Ohio, a state where he was unknown and where he hoped that his prison record would not follow him. Dayton, at the height of the Depression, was not a good place to start. The city was bankrupt and the public schools, an obvious place for LoBagola to give bread-and-butter talks, closed early in the day in order to save money. Without Pond's immediate support, LoBagola had to find his own engagements. "I simply went out and struggled hard to sell my stuff and sold it eventually," he wrote to his distant promoter.[72] Only "puny fees" came from talks to schools, rotary clubs, the YMCA, and Boy Scout camps, while even the three talks given on Dayton radio station WSMK in May 1932 brought notice but little cash. LoBagola had also reflected on how to add to his repertoire and delivery. He wrote to Pond that he had added new materials: "I tell how I came to write the whole story in the beginning and I emphasize the beauty of the 'struggle,' pointing out that 'struggle begets strength' and people just fall over themselves with interest. There is a new note in my tone, a kind of pleading bitterness which catches instantly."[73]

In early August 1932 LoBagola moved to Columbus, lodging first at the YMCA and then with the Salvation Army. His explanation to enquirers as to why a major tour speaker should be among the "rustics" of America, he confided to Pond, was that he had been swindled out of his royalties and was recovering from the shock. The highlight of his time in Columbus was a public debate in late October with Rabbi Jacob Tarshish, on "Is Civilization Worthwhile?" a return to the "noble savage" debate which features so markedly in his autobiography. Tarshish had debated with Clarence Darrow, and LoBagola clearly saw a similar encounter as an opportunity to make a name for himself as well as earn a good sum. Although 1,500 people attended the debate in Columbus's Memorial Hall, LoBagola, "the civilized sage with the Oxford accent," as he was billed, received a mere thirty-two dollars.[74] Throughout mid-1932 LoBagola

Fig. 9.7. LoBagola, the "civilized savage," debates with Rabbi Tarshish at
Memorial Hall, Columbus, Ohio, in October 1932. Source: *Citizen*
(Columbus, Ohio), 22 October 1932.

made frequent complaints about serious racial hostility from whites, especially
Jews; in some of his letters he spoke out against the latter.[75] This may have been
just another sign of the persecution mania that had been diagnosed by the army
doctors twelve years before. LoBagola was unable to get his life sorted out. The
book that he had talked of writing while he was in Great Meadow Prison never
materialized.[76] News of his parole and of his prison record leaked out—he was
rarely discreet in what he said or in how he behaved—rumors were spread, and
promised engagements were cancelled. It was time to move on.

In December 1932 LoBagola arrived in Chicago, where he spoke to the
Executives' Club.[77] Early in the new year he reported to Pond that with the
help of a Midwest agent he was "extremely busy." His program involved a
radio broadcast, sessions for recording the LoBagola story on gramophone
record, and a series of small-time engagements in Ohio, Indiana, and Illinois.
Earning a living by entertainment in these harsh economic years of the Depression was not easy; fees were low and engagements slow in coming. LoBagola
poignantly told Pond that he was having a hard time, "all made worse by news
of my past offenses leaking out and resulting in groups refusing to engage me."[78]
He also wrote that "I am up against it surely" and "at my wits end," and
reported the proverbial "I am broke."[79] At this point, in February 1933, while
LoBagola was in the region of Bluffton, Ohio, his correspondence with Pond

either ceases or has been lost. In a letter to a Mr. Lesser at Knopf, LoBagola wrote from Bluffton that he was "in trouble again," and mentioned debts of one thousand dollars owed to Nathan E. Nelson, an attorney in Decatur, Indiana. He asked Knopf to assign that sum to Nelson from his expected royalties. LoBagola was arrested for a sexual offense in Decatur but did not receive a prison sentence; the debt may have been incurred as legal fees.[80]

At some time between 1932 and early 1934, LoBagola had as his travelling companion and "booking agent" a young white man. According to a member of the young man's family, "the two of them would hit a town and X would line up bookings for him [LoBagola]. The two would go into fancy restaurants, check the menu and order the most expensive meals no matter what it was. When travelling they always booked first class and same with hotels. They also wore expensive clothes."[81] So, Joseph Lee, the poor African American from Baltimore, played the alien African prince and thus was able to thumb his nose at "Jim Crow" laws and travel with a white man.[82] The young white man subsequently married, became a Salvation Army officer, and together with his wife and child visited LoBagola in Attica Prison in the late 1930s. In his will dated early 1946, LoBagola left all that he had (which was next to nothing!) to the man who had befriended him.[83]

When next we hear of the supposed African entertainer, he is being interviewed further by the Naturalization Service, this time by Lawrence Cleaking, in the Wisconsin State Penitentiary, Waupun, on 21 September 1934. LoBagola had been convicted of sodomy in Kenosha, Wisconsin, in April 1934, and sentenced to two indeterminate terms of from one to five years each, his sixth time in prison.[84] Since late 1931 the Naturalization Service had been slowly investigating LoBagola's claim that he was indeed a U.S. citizen. There were doubts about the authenticity of the birth certificate—LoBagola had handed in a copy to the New York office in March 1932—which carried the "strange entry" of "unnamed 17th child." After the Naturalization Service made checks in Baltimore the birth certificate was accepted, and accordingly LoBagola's false certificate of naturalization, taken out in 1918, was cancelled by the U.S. Attorney in New York on 19 March 1934. Apparently further doubts lingered in the minds of officials, so Inspector Cleaking was sent to Waupun to interview LoBagola once again. Cleaking reported that to his satisfaction the subject of his enquiry "is a full blooded negro born at Baltimore, Md. December 15th 1887, correct name Joseph Howard Lee."[85] LoBagola was in prison, penniless, but now no longer caught in the web of his own deceptive claims and facing deportation.

LoBagola spent the final thirteen years of his life in prison. He had been released on parole in New York State in 1932 but that was cancelled by his 1934 conviction in Wisconsin. When LoBagola completed his term of impris-

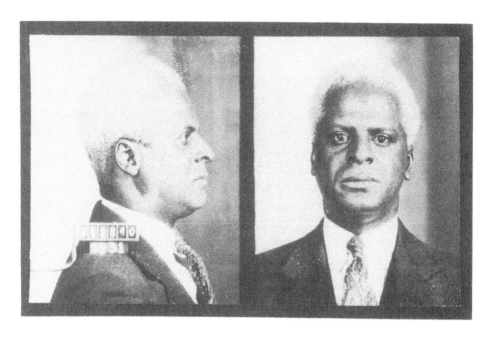

Fig. 9.8. In 1931 LoBagola was again convicted and sent to prison in New York. Official prison photographs from Attica Correctional Facility, Attica, New York.

onment at Waupun in 1938 he was immediately transferred to Attica Prison in Wyoming County, New York. There he received an additional conviction for sodomy committed with another inmate, and a further five- to ten-year sentence. In Attica the prison authorities registered LoBagola as having a mental age of thirteen and an intelligence quotient of eighty-seven, but at that time official IQ tests were invariably heavily loaded against African Americans. He weighed 192 pounds and was diagnosed as suffering from diabetes and defective hearing. His "nearest friend" was recorded as a single lady living on East 117 Street, New York City.[86] From mid-1946 onward LoBagola was in the prison hospital suffering from arteriosclerosis and a cerebral hemorrhage. In early January 1947, with eighteen months of his sentence to go, LoBagola died of a pulmonary edema. He was buried in the Attica Prison Cemetery, in plot 29. His last resting place is marked by a cement headstone bearing his assumed name, prison number, and the dates of his birth and death.[87]

Conclusion

Joseph Howard Lee, an African American born in very disadvantaged circumstances, with little schooling, was clearly in many ways a remarkable, if deeply disturbed, man. His life might have been spent in the poorer districts of his home city of Baltimore or aboard freighters plying the transatlantic routes,

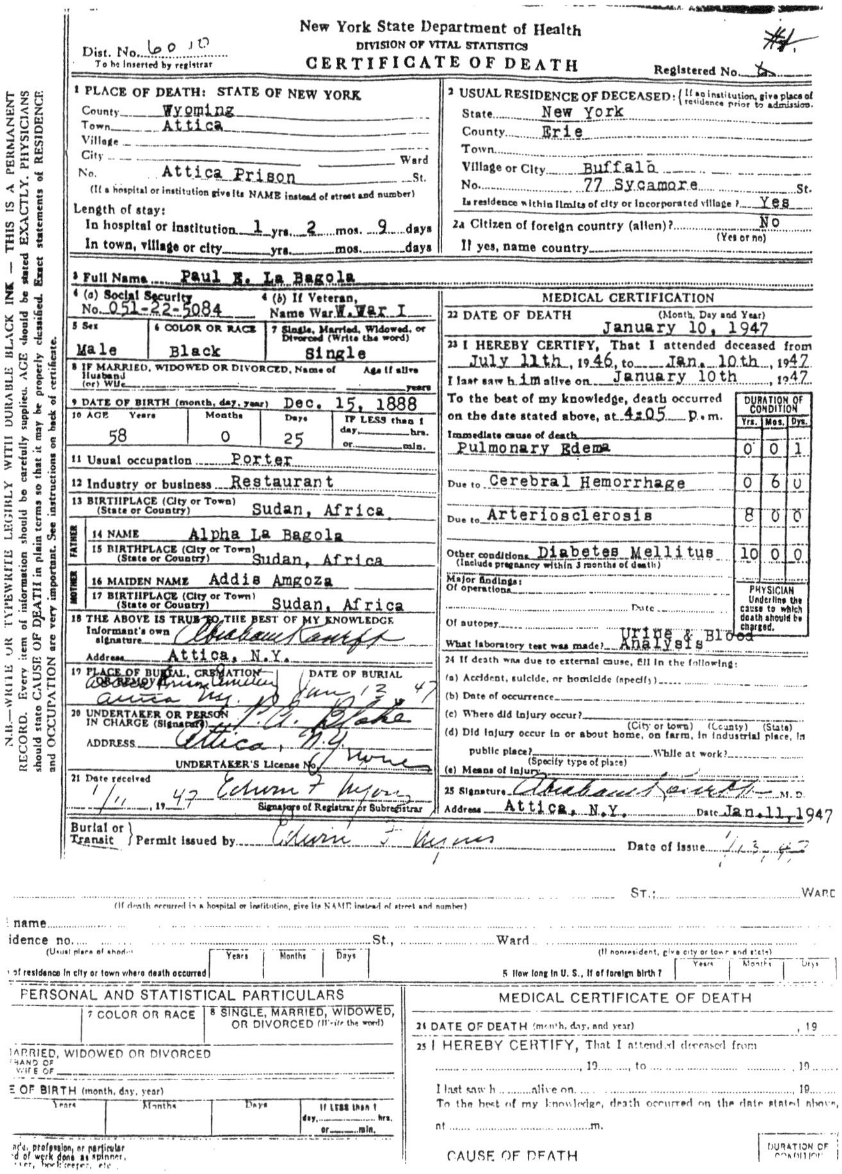

N.B.—WRITE OR TYPEWRITE LEGIBLY WITH DURABLE BLACK INK — THIS IS A PERMANENT RECORD. Every item of information should be carefully supplied. AGE should be stated EXACTLY. PHYSICIANS should state CAUSE OF DEATH in plain terms so that it may be properly classified. Exact statements of RESIDENCE and OCCUPATION are very important. See instructions on back of certificate.

Dist. No. 60 10
To be inserted by registrar

New York State Department of Health
DIVISION OF VITAL STATISTICS
CERTIFICATE OF DEATH

Registered No. 6

1 PLACE OF DEATH: STATE OF NEW YORK
County Wyoming
Town Attica
Village
City Ward
No. Attica Prison St.
(If a hospital or institution give its NAME instead of street and number)
Length of stay:
In hospital or institution 1 yrs. 2 mos. 9 days
In town, village or city yrs. mos. days

2 USUAL RESIDENCE OF DECEASED: (If an institution, give place of residence prior to admission.)
State New York
County Erie
Town
Village or City Buffalo
No. 77 Sycamore St.
Is residence within limits of city or incorporated village? Yes
2a Citizen of foreign country (alien)? No (Yes or no)
If yes, name country

3 Full Name Paul E. La Bagola
4 (a) Social Security No. 051-22-5084
4 (b) If Veteran, Name War W. War I
5 Sex Male
6 COLOR OR RACE Black
7 Single, Married, Widowed, or Divorced (Write the word) Single
8 IF MARRIED, WIDOWED OR DIVORCED, Name of Husband (or) Wife — Age if alive years
9 DATE OF BIRTH (month, day, year) Dec. 15, 1888
10 AGE Years 58 Months 0 Days 25 IF LESS than 1 day hrs. or min.
11 Usual occupation Porter
12 Industry or business Restaurant
13 BIRTHPLACE (City or Town) (State or Country) Sudan, Africa
FATHER 14 NAME Alpha La Bagola
15 BIRTHPLACE (City or Town) (State or Country) Sudan, Africa
MOTHER 16 MAIDEN NAME Addis Amgoza
17 BIRTHPLACE (City or Town) (State or Country) Sudan, Africa
18 THE ABOVE IS TRUE TO THE BEST OF MY KNOWLEDGE
Informant's own signature Abraham Kauff
Address Attica, N.Y.
19 PLACE OF BURIAL, CREMATION OR REMOVAL Prison Cemetery Attica N.Y. DATE OF BURIAL Jan 12 47
20 UNDERTAKER OR PERSON IN CHARGE (Signature) P. A. Blake
ADDRESS Attica, N.Y.
UNDERTAKER'S License No.
21 Date received 1/11, 1947 Edwin F. Myers Signature of Registrar or Subregistrar

MEDICAL CERTIFICATION
22 DATE OF DEATH (Month, Day and Year) January 10, 1947
23 I HEREBY CERTIFY, That I attended deceased from July 11th, 1946, to Jan. 10th, 1947
I last saw him alive on January 10th, 1947
To the best of my knowledge, death occurred on the date stated above, at 4:05 p.m.

Cause	Yrs.	Mos.	Dys.
Immediate cause of death: Pulmonary Edema	0	0	1
Due to Cerebral Hemorrhage	0	6	0
Due to Arteriosclerosis	8	0	0
Other conditions (Include pregnancy within 3 months of death) Diabetes Mellitus	10	0	0

DURATION OF CONDITION
Major findings: Of operations Date
Of autopsy
What laboratory test was made? Urine & Blood Analysis
PHYSICIAN Underline the cause to which death should be charged.
24 If death was due to external cause, fill in the following:
(a) Accident, suicide, or homicide (specify)
(b) Date of occurrence
(c) Where did injury occur? (City or town) (County) (State)
(d) Did injury occur in or about home, on farm, in industrial place, in public place? (Specify type of place) While at work?
(e) Means of injury
25 Signature Abraham Kauff M.D.
Address Attica, N.Y. Date Jan. 11, 1947

Burial or Transit Permit issued by Edwin F. Myers Date of Issue 1/13/47

Fig. 9.9. Death certificate of Amgoza LoBagola, who died in Attica Prison, upper New York State, in January 1947. He was buried in the prison graveyard.

but he escaped from both urban drear and maritime employ. This and his subsequent career reveal a considerable measure of intelligence and a determination or willingness to seize chances as they came his way. Some of those were dead ends that led nowhere; others opened up a range of opportunities. His success, when it came, depended upon his ability to tell and sustain a lively tale and upon his great capacity as an entertainer. By adopting an African identity,

LoBagola was able to exploit his blackness in a way that opened doors that would otherwise have been closed to an African American. In the process he was able to fool a whole range of professional people in the white establishment. Undoubtedly he was exploited, but he also exploited others by his talent for imitation and presentation. As such he entertained at a high standard before large, appreciative, and sometimes critical audiences.

LoBagola's African persona, while both flawed and frequently challenged, was successfully maintained. The series of flights which make up the major part of his autobiography, and of his life as he lived it, were not a consequence of his identity as an African but of his underlying and disturbed personality. His African "mask" represents an imaginative flight, an escape into a fantasy world, lived out as real. His attempt to justify his own deep-seated confusions and inner tensions by claiming to be a "savage" outsider has pathetic appeal. In one powerful image he can gather together the various fragments of his life in a way which both asserts his dignity and shifts the blame: a fractured and disturbed life made coherent, but not healed, by an appeal to an African identity. The various labels applied to LoBagola—by himself, by the courts, and by others—do not represent a full understanding of this troubled man. On stage and in most areas of his life many found him to be an engaging and interesting character, for a time at least. His instability and sexual preferences destroyed him in the end. LoBagola's autobiography well illustrates his ability to entertain and to charm, as well as to manipulate.

Many black entertainers pretended to be Africans and performed "tricked out in all the paraphernalia of imposture."[88] LoBagola played the African prince, a fire-eater, a savage bewildered by modernization, the clown, and much else, but he could also turn his hand to the straight act as singer, Scottish comic, or if necessary, the urbane and disciplined speaker who entranced high school students and well-heeled members of smart bourgeois clubs and confraternities. His ability to keep the attention of all kinds of audiences is well documented in newspaper reports and, later, in letters to Pond from satisfied customers.[89] Undoubtedly LoBagola was an entertainer of considerable verve who could also skillfully deal with questions by turning them back on an audience without actually answering them. He also seems to have had considerable persuasive charm, which led a large number of people to accept his story. For an African American to do this consistently in his own country while pretending to be an African says a great deal about his talent. LoBagola did come up against racial hostility and abuse, but he met this by boldly maintaining his stage life and by claiming that he was an African and not a black American.

It is also clear from LoBagola's letters to Pond, especially those written from Ohio and Chicago in 1932–33, that he thought that various people and institutions were conspiring against him, which perhaps gives some weight to the views of the military psychologists who recommended his dismissal from the army in 1918. Some of his actions, and his lack of discretion, inevitably created suspicions, but the confusion and contradiction which were his life and livelihood appear to have fueled his anxieties, which at times gave vent to bitterly expressed feelings of persecution. The final story in *An African Savage's Own Story* is on "the folly of attempting too much—how a gazelle fooled a leopard." The tale, and the book, concludes with the words: "Now, Mr. Leopard, when you wish to fool somebody, try not to be the fool yourself" (402).[90] It might stand as an appropriate epitaph for LoBagola himself.

NOTES

In our pursuit of LoBagola over the last few years we have been grateful for the help, encouragement, and indulgence of many people, including George D. Brightwell, Michael Cooney, Jean Gaugh, Jeffrey P. Green, Hollee Haswell, Clare Keating, Robert S. Law, Robin Law, Bernth Lindfors, Alessandro Pezzati, Gail M. Pietryzk, John Peel, Patricia Priestley, Janos Riesz, George Shepperson, and Selena Winsnes. Much more research remains to be done, particularly in the United States and in the Middle East.

1. All references in the text are to the 1930 edition, which went into several printings—1 March, 3 June, and 4 June. It sold in the United States for $2, and in the United Kingdom for 10s. 6d. A Blue Ribbon edition appeared in 1932. A Tauchnitz edition in English was published in Germany, as was a German-language edition, translated by Berit Schivatzki (Basel and Leipzig: Kompass Verlag, 1931). In 1931, five thousand copies of a Norwegian edition were published, *En Innfødt Afrikaners Egen Historie* (Oslo: H. Aschehoug, 1931); in the same year a Spanish edition appeared: *Autobiografia de un salvaje africano* (Madrid: Cenit). The next year saw the publication of a French edition, *Lobagola; histoire d'un sauvage africain par lui-meme*, translated by Michel Drucker (Paris: A. Michel, 1932). A Hungarian edition was also published.

2. *Times Literary Supplement* 21 Aug. 1930: 669. See also *New York Times* 16 March 1930: iv, 4; *Brooklyn Eagle* 16 March 1930; *New York Telegram* 22 March 1930; *Evening Post* (New York) 22 March 1930; *Boston Transcript* 29 March 1930; *Books* 30 March 1930; *Every Week Magazine* 19–20 April 1930: 4; *Bookman* April 1930; *Seattle Sunday Times* 1 May 1930; *New Republic* 18 June 1930; *Saturday Review of Literature* 28 June 1930; *Saturday Review* 23 Aug. 1930; and *Spectator* 4 Oct. 1930.

3. *New York Sun* 30 April 1930. The reviewer likened LoBagola's autobiography to Albert Londres's *Terre d'Ebene. La traite des noirs* (trans. as *A Very Naked People*), which appeared in Paris the year before. René Maran, Caribbean-born former French colonial administrator, set his novel in a Central African colony. It is highly critical of the "civilizing mission" of colonialism. Maran turns African "vices" into "virtues" and accuses whites of, among other things, hypocrisy, prudery, and impotence. The novel was translated into English in 1922 and republished in 1973 in the Heinemann African Writers Series, London.

4. *Journal of the African Society* 29 (1929–30): 557. The *Negro Year Book 1931–32* (Tuskegee, 1931), in an extensive review of annual black writing, ignored LoBagola's book. Given his provocative title, that is not surprising.

5. Published autobiographies of Africans in the 1930s were relatively rare. See Perham,

Ntara, Fraser, Westermann, and Nyabongo. The popular idea of an exotic and "savage" origin lingered long with publishers: e.g., Modupe.

6. LoBagola is rarely quoted or referred to by writers on the black experience in Britain and the United States, due more to ignorance of the book than to disbelief in the author's claims. See Jenkinson, W. Thompson, and Kilson and Rotberg.

7. A. F. Whitman, letter to W. J. Yerby, 7 May 1917 RG84, C.387.7, No. 310, Department of State: Consular Papers, National Archives and Records Administration (NARA), Washington, D.C.; and Yerby, letter to Whitman 31 July 1917. The "Chief Sam" referred to by Yerby was Alfred Sam, a Gold Coast merchant, who organized an abortive "back-to-Africa" movement from the United States in 1914–15; see Bittle and Geis.

8. LoBagola identified the "Department of Anthropology, at Exeter College, Oxford." There is no reference to LoBagola's talk in the register of the University Anthropology Society, although that does not mean LoBagola was not telling the truth. R. R. Marett was appointed Reader in Social Anthropology in 1908, a break with the established pattern of physical anthropology. Was Marett taken in by LoBagola? Other scholars were, so why not an Oxford man? Marett wrote a good deal on "savages," and in the text of a talk on "The Making of the Medicine Man," he wrote: "It is important to remember that there is a savage folklore—a mass of fanciful talk conceived in a light vein and with little effect on practice save indirectly, so far as it promotes credulity." I, 18, p. 7, n.d., Marett Papers, Pitt Rivers Museum Archive, Oxford.

9. Freedom of Information Act (FOIA). Material on LoBagola has been released in part by various U.S. government departments. Copies, often of poor quality and difficult to read, are in the possession of the authors. They bear the handwritten reference 2332/C 107949.

10. Dr. Frederick Houk Law wrote the brief introduction to the *Scribner's Magazine* articles, and it would appear that he was also the author of the unsigned introduction to the published autobiography. Forty percent of the royalties from LoBagola's autobiography were assigned to Law. William A. Koshland, letter, with documents, to David Killingray, 9 Aug. 1994.

11. In the United States, Horn's book was adopted by the Literary Guild and went through ten printings in five months, selling 10,000 copies per month in the United States alone. Two further Horn books were published by 1930. The South African novelist Ethelreda Lewis was the literary hand behind the Horn books. For more details, see Couzens, *Tramp Royal.* Several U.S. newspapers drew the parallel between the Horn and LoBagola tales, e.g., "Black Jew's Yarn Recalls A. A. Horn," *World* (New York) 4 March 1929, on the articles in *Scribner's Magazine,* and Greenville Vernon in *Bookman* 71 (April 1930): 226. A further piece of literary fallout from LoBagola's autobiography is in Winifred Holtby's sole African novel, *Mandoa, Mandoa!* (London: 1933; 1982). The capital of the imaginary African state of Mandoa is "Logabola." We owe this reference to Couzens ("Keeping" 44, 52). Holtby was a close friend of Ethelreda Lewis.

12. Maud W. Gibbon, "Lobagola," lecture circular, Knopf Archive, Harry Ransom Humanities Research Center, University of Texas, Austin.

13. This evokes ideas drawn from Rousseau's "noble savage" about the education of the "native" and the corruption of cities. In his "natural" home, i.e., Africa, LoBagola is robustly heterosexual with several wives, but in the corrupt modern world he is actually a homosexual misfit.

14. As Law was the coauthor, the parallels to various books of travel may be by his hand, e.g., LoBagola's account of his childhood adventure on a ship off West Africa, which echoes Olaudah Equiano's experience of being carried on board a slaver (see Equiano, chap. 2).

15. See also LoBagola, "My Religion," ts., MS group 142, SCM 78–13, folder 1, LoBagola Papers, Schomburg Center for Research in Black Culture, New York Public Library (hereafter Schomburg).

16. For example, the West African writers Olaudah Equiano, J. A. Horton, and A. B. C. Sibthorpe all lend credence to the idea of the "Ten Lost Tribes of Israel" being in West Africa. Dupuis mentions reports of a Jewish community in the Sudan (cvi–cviii), while Williams argued that "a Jewish element is to be found in the parent-stock of the Ashanti." There is a growing literature on black Jews in the United States; see Ottley (chaps. 10 and 11) and Brotz.

17. Imitating Africans was a well-established practice among black entertainers. For examples from Britain, see Marke (102, 104), which refers to Edgar B. Knight, the Wombwell "crocuser" ("quack" doctor and herbalist) originally from Demerara, who called himself Abyssinian and dressed in long "African" robes, and Black Dougie, from Jamaica, who worked the British racecourses as an African. The classic black street character was Ras Prince Monolulu (Peter McKay from Guyana) who from the 1920s on entertained people at railway stations, racetracks, and in the streets of London, for which see White. A London pub has recently been named after him. See also the story by Bell, "His Highness Prince Kwakoo," about an African who cons his way around Britain.

18. FOIA. LoBagola's admission to Examiner Siegel, of the Immigration and Naturalization Service, took place in an interview at Great Meadow Prison, Comstock, New York, 9–10 Nov. 1932. On his release from prison, LoBagola delivered a copy of his birth certificate, dated 16 Dec. 1887, to the Naturalization Service office in New York City. The Bureau wanted to investigate the authenticity of the certificate and this was eventually done in Baltimore by Inspector Irwin A. Lex, 4 Oct. 1934.

19. FOIA. LoBagola, interview with Inspector Lawrence Cleaking, Naturalization Service, Wisconsin State Penitentiary, Waupun, 21 Sept. 1934.

20. E.g., *Daily Argus* (Mt. Vernon, New York) 12 Nov. 1930.

21. *New York Times* 10 Dec. 1927: 18.

22. See also *Coventry Times* 7 Aug. 1907. Extract from the order of procession, Lady Godiva Procession Club, 1907: "Arab Cycling Club. Members dressed as Arabs, led by Angosa [*sic*] (West African Chief)." Maule of Nottingham made photographic postcards of all the groups, duly recorded by LoBagola (218), but copies have yet to be found.

23. LoBagola mentions learning to ride a bicycle borrowed from a Mr. Jenks, "a barber by trade" (321). A Thomas Jenks is listed in *Kelly's Directory* 1904 as a hairdresser, and in 1916 as a hairdresser and manager of a motor garage.

24. LoBagola, interview with Cleaking.

25. Various African entertainers adopted the title "Dahomean" for stage purposes; e.g., a group of Sierra Leoneans worked as Dahomey warriors in England in 1908. I owe this information to Jeffrey P. Green.

26. For Beah Kindah, see *Liverpool Courier* 13 Nov. 1908; Peter Lobengula is the subject of Ben Shepherd's articles. On black entertainers, see also Jeffrey P. Green, *Black Edwardians* (London: Frank Cass, 1998) chap. 5.

27. Mr. K— may have been Charles H. Kline (1870–1933), a prominent Pennsylvania Republican who was elected to the State Senate in 1908 and eventually became mayor of Philadelphia (1925–33). The Mercantile Club closed in 1937. We owe this information to George D. Brightbill, Associate Archivist, Samuel Paley Library, Temple University, Philadelphia.

28. We are grateful to Gail M. Pietryzk, Public Services Analyst, and Alessandro Pezzati, Reference Archivist, University of Pennsylvania, for information about the members and activities of the Anthropology Department in the first decade of this century. The entry on Frank Speck in the *Dictionary of American Biography,* Supplement B (1975), written by John Witthoft, includes the following: "His intellectual interests also attracted many visitors, the beginning of a long pattern. A wandering South African Bushman, Amgoza, visited him for several weeks in 1911, and Speck spent his spare time transcribing Khoisan (a southern African language group) texts, which apparently have not survived." A wax disk recording, dated c. 1910, supposedly of LoBagola singing Yoruba songs, was provided by Alessandro Pezzati in 1995. Yoruba speakers have confirmed that this is not their language, and indeed the recording does sound like nonsense. A copy is in the Indiana University Archives of Traditional Music, 60-0190-F.

29. Newspaper clipping, source unknown, 28 Jan. 1911, University of Pennsylvania Archives. Also in *Republic* (St. Louis, Mo.) 9 Feb. 1911. The University of Pennsylvania *Museum Journal* 2.2 (June 1911): 54, also reported that the Museum had acquired the services of Inquatwa, "a young native from the Yoruba country, a part of Dahomey" who was helping to record "native songs" on the phonograph. Thirty years later, in 1942–43, the University Museum was involved in a wartime training program which included courses in "African dialects." The *Pennsylvania Gazette* (Sept. 1942), published by the university, stated that it was employing four "native informants" and was "concentrating on the numerous and devious speeches of Africa. Three dusky natives are informing students about the native tongues of Swahili, Fanti, and Hausa. . . ." One of those informants was Kwame Nkrumah, later the first president of Ghana. See Sherwood, 65–66.

30. BT26/483, passenger manifest of *Celtic,* Public Record Office, Kew (PRO).

31. *Illustrated Police News* 1 July 1911: 14; *East Ham Echo* 24 June 1911: 5; 7 July 1911: 3; *An African Savage's Own Story* (337). Beah Kindah, who has been noted at Liverpool, often worked as a Dahomey fire king.

32. BT26/519, SS *Batanga,* PRO.

33. James Deemin, mss. Afr.s. 1525, with autobiographical notes (1897–1910) written in 1931, box 13, file 1, John Holt and Co. Ltd. (Liverpool) papers, Rhodes House Library, Oxford. Interestingly, Trader Horn also had contact with Deemin in West Africa at an earlier stage (see note 11).

34. LoBagola, interview with Cleaking.

35. David Taylor, born 1865, had "a general merchandise store on the Marina" in Lagos; see Macmillan 108.

36. A William Shitta was proprietor of a haberdashery on Shitta St., Lagos. Dr. Orisdipe Obassa was a leading Lagos physician and cultural nationalist; the Vaughan brothers were involved in a variety of Christian concerns and commercial activities. See Macmillan 108, and E. B. Thompson.

37. BT27/716, SS *Falaba,* PRO.

38. LoBagola, interview with Cleaking.

39. Whitman to Yerby, 7 May 1917, identifies a "professor of education" at Columbia. At this time the social anthropology department at Columbia had an interest in "primitive social organization," but it is difficult to believe that someone as distinguished as Franz Boas could have been taken in by LoBagola. Boas had close relationships with a number of African students, including James Aggrey from the Gold Coast and Kamba Simango from Mozambique. See *Columbia University, Bulletin of Information 1912–1913.* We owe this information to Ms. Hollee Haswell, Curator of Columbiana (letter to the authors, 30 Nov. 1990).

40. Bond, letter to LoBagola, 2 Feb. 1933, folder, 2, Schomburg.

41. Whitman to Yerby, 7 May 1917.

42. FOIA. Maj. Gen. C. Bridges, War Dept., letter, with enclosures, to Commissioner of Naturalization, Dept. of Labor, 1 April 1931.

43. FOIA. Certificate No. 1079749, 26 Aug. 1918, Dept. of Immigration and Naturalization.

44. LoBagola, interview with Cleaking.

45. Bridges to War Dept.

46. "Enlistment of Coloured British Subjects in the U.S.A.," WO 32/4765, PRO; also "Anglo-American Military Service Law 1918," 1/1040, Dept. of National Service (NATS); see Killingray.

47. Even though a page of his military discharge papers was printed in his autobiography, the one-hundred-year rule operated by the PRO prevents a non-relative from looking at the actual documents. The 38th, 39th, and 40th battalions of the Royal Fusiliers were Jewish labor battalions. Many of the details given by LoBagola about his military service in Egypt and Palestine, as to movements, people, and places (359–63), appear to be substantially correct when checked against the following: War Diaries of 38th, 39th, and 40th Battalions, 1918–19, Royal Fusiliers Museum, Tower of London; *Royal Fusiliers Chronicle* 9 (20 Sept. 1920); and Patterson, *With the Judeans*. Patterson was the gentile commander of the 38th Bn., and Lt. Col. E. L. Margolin was the Australian Jewish commander of the 39th Bn., referred to by LoBagola (362). See also Patterson, *The Jews* 21–22.

48. W. Richardson, late Hampshire regiment, letter to "Lobagola," Aldershot, Hants, England, 14 June 1930, Knopf Archive. According to this letter, LoBagola had been company clerk for Sergeant-Major Richardson at Kantara. Richardson wrote that LoBagola, "who the world always treated badly," was laughed at by his fellow soldiers because "you wanted to be repatriated to Palestine." He also referred to LoBagola's abilities to imitate the Scottish singer Harry Lauder and his participation in concerts on the troop ship to Britain.

49. "My Religion," folder 2, Schomburg. LoBagola does not mention the black communities in Jerusalem, and his description of the city is inaccurate. For example, he describes his "daily walk outside the Golden Gate" (365), although the Gate had been blocked up since the sixteenth century, if not earlier, and the area outside had long been a Muslim cemetery.

50. Day (1866–1946) was a Jesuit who served as a chaplain to the British forces in Alexandria and Palestine during the First World War. He was demobilized c. 1920 and was at the Farm Street headquarters of the Jesuits in London until 1939. One of his major interests was Roman Catholic relations with Jews.

51. We owe this information to Rev. Gerald J. Nagle, MM, Director of Development, Maryknoll Fathers and Brothers (letter to David Killingray, 10 Sept. 1990).

52. Alexander High School Program, 31 Oct. 1928, and others, folder 2, Schomburg.

53. Diary of Frederick Houk Law (1871–1957), in possession of his son, Major Robert S. Law, New York. We are grateful to Major Law for providing information from the diaries which his father kept from boyhood (hereafter Law diary). Law, the author of two novels, several school texts, and books on public speaking, lived in Brooklyn and was active in the High School Teachers' Association, the National Education Association, and the National Commission for the Defense of Democracy through Education. See the obituaries in the *New York Times* 9 Sept. 1957: 25; and the *Oxford Review-Times* 12 Sept. 1957. See also the entry on Law in *Who's Who in America 1938–1939* (1491).

54. Law diary, 18 Jan. 1929. Further entries refer to LoBagola's speaking at Columbia

University (9 Feb. 1929) and to Law's receiving a photographic portrait from LoBagola (25 Feb. 1929); one entry mentions: "To office of W.O.R. [a New York City radio station] about LoBagola" (4 April 1930).

55. Law acted both as literary agent and attorney for LoBagola. The copyright certificates for both books, dated 10 July 1929 and 8 Jan. 1930, list the author as Paul E. LoBagola (William A. Koshland, Alfred A. Knopf, New York City, letter, with documents, to David Killingray, 9 Aug. 1994). A letter from Koshland to Harry L. Brown, attorney of Warsaw, New York, 14 Aug. 1957, refers to Law as "co-author" of both *An African Savage's Own Story* and *Folk Tales of a Savage.* In *Who's Who in America in 1938–1939,* Law describes himself as editor of *An African Savage's Own Story.*

56. Major Robert S. Law, letter to David Killingray, 28 Oct. 1995.

57. The firm of James B. Pond had been in the business of promoting "African" entertainment for decades. Pond's father acted as agent for H. M. Stanley on his lecture tour of the United States in the 1890s.

58. J. B. Pond, letter to Frederick H. Law, 21 March 1930, folder 1, Schomburg.

59. James B. Pond, draft note of contract with Paul Emanuel LoBagola and itinerary "Instructions," folder 1, Schomburg. See also *Chicago Daily News* 28 May 1930; and *Chicago Evening Post* 28 May 1930.

60. *Birmingham New-Age Herald* 2 Nov. 1930: 7; *Chautauguan Daily* (New York) 11 July 1930: 1. Warden's Record Card, Attica Prison, New York, 17 Nov. 1938, shows LoBagola as having a height of five feet two inches.

61. Document headed "LOBAGOLA," from a lecture circular by Maud W. Gibbon, with commendation by Claire M. Reis, Executive Director, League of Composers, who wrote that LoBagola spoke to "a gathering of friends at our home" (Knopf Archive). See also "Karl Kitchen presents," *New York Sun,* n.d., c. early May 1930.

62. Pond, letter to LoBagola, 4 Sept. 1930; and letter to LoBagola, 22 Sept. 1930; folder 2, Schomburg.

63. C. W. Locke, letter to LoBagola, Middlesex School, Concord, Massachusetts, 10 Nov. 1930, Knopf Archive.

64. Law, letter to David Killingray.

65. Pond, letter to Sydney E. Kors, 13 Jan. 1931; and letter to LoBagola, 22 Jan. 1931; folder 2, Schomburg.

66. Pond, letter to Kors, 13 Jan. 1931.

67. Koshland, letter to Harry L. Brown, 23 Dec. 1957, Knopf Archive.

68. Pond, letter to Arthur F. Thomas, Parole Office, 31 Dec. 1931, folder 2, Schomburg. And in an 8 Jan. 1931 letter to LoBagola, Pond said: "you are now paying the penalty for a mistake. When the penalty is paid, let us hope that things will run more smoothly for you." LoBagola, writing to Pond on 18 Jan. 1931, says: "I must not do these foolish things again, so now I must run along and get myself out of this mess."

69. FOIA. Examiner Siegel, report on LoBagola, 9–10 Nov. 1932, Great Meadow Prison, New York.

70. Pond, letter to LoBagola, 2 Feb. 1933, folder 2, Schomburg.

71. LoBagola, letter to Pond, 8 June 1932, folder 2, Schomburg.

72. LoBagola, letter to Pond, 29 May 1932, folder 2, Schomburg.

73. LoBagola, letter to Pond, 3 July 1932, folder 2, Schomburg.

74. Columbus *Citizen* 22 Oct. 1932, which contains a cartoon of LoBagola debating "civilization" with Rabbi Tarshish; and Columbus *Sunday Star* 23 Oct. 1932.

75. LoBagola, letter to Pond, 3 July 1932, and 6 Aug. 1932.

76. LoBagola, letter to Pond, 27 April 1931, folder 2, Schomburg.

77. *The Executives' Club News* (9 Dec. 1932: 4–8) contains the address given by LoBagola, which he concluded by saying: "Can you imagine. Thirty-six years ago I was a naked savage and today I tell you to read a book I wrote. Well, it is worth reading for that. The story is true. That is why I recommend that you should read my book."

78. LoBagola, letter to Pond, 16 Jan. 1933, folder 2, Schomburg.

79. Ibid.

80. This correspondence was provided by Koshland. The Decatur conviction is listed on the Warden's Record Card, Attica Prison, New York, 1938.

81. Letter to David Killingray, 24 March 1995. We agreed to maintain the anonymity of LoBagola's white companion, who died in 1992.

82. There are similar examples of blacks, especially West Indian and African students, doing this at the same time; e.g., "Once you had discovered this American folly, you would put on your fez and 'pass' like any other white—even ride on the Pullman. People might think you were an African prince." Makonnen 62.

83. A copy of LoBagola's will was provided from the Attica Prison Records, and for this, and much else, we are grateful to Clare Keating, librarian, Warsaw County Library, Warsaw, New York.

84. Ibn Lobagola [*sic*], 21631, Waupun Prison Record, 9 April 1934, State Historical Society of Wisconsin, Madison.

85. LoBagola, interview with Cleaking.

86. Paul E. LoBagola, T4631, Warden's Record Card, 1938, Attica Prison, Attica, New York.

87. Certificate of Death, 11 Jan. 1947, New York State Department of Health, Wyoming County, New York; Superintendent, Attica Prison, letter to author, 12 March 1995.

88. This splendid phrase comes from Frank Norris's novel *The Octopus* (314).

89. E.g., R. F. Walker, Chairman Program Committee, Rotary Club of Newark, N.J., letter to Pond, 22 July 1930, folder 1, Schomburg: "He [LoBagola] talked for nearly twenty minutes over-time, not a man left the room because of lack of interest." Pond described LoBagola as "one of the most brilliant men I have ever met." See also Pond, letter to Arthur F. Thomas, 31 Dec. 1932, folder 2, Schomburg.

90. This conclusion is not dissimilar to that of Sterne's *Tristram Shandy* (1761–67): ". . . what is all this story about?—A COCK and a BULL, said Yorick—And one of the best of its kind, I ever heard" (674).

WORKS CITED

Bell, Henry Hesketh. "His Highness Prince Kwakoo." *Love in Black*. London: Edward Arnold, 1911.

Bittle, William Elmer, and Gilbert Geis. *The Longest Way Home: Chief Alfred C. Sam's Back-to-Africa Movement*. Detroit: Wayne State UP, 1964.

Brotz, Howard. *Black Jews in Harlem*. New York: Schocken Books, 1964.

Cole, Patrick. *Modern and Traditional Elites in the Politics of Lagos*. Cambridge: Cambridge UP, 1975.

Coombes, Annie E. *Reinventing Africa: Museums, Material Culture and Popular Imagination in Late Victorian and Edwardian England*. New Haven: Yale UP, 1994.

Couzens, Tim. "Keeping the Runway Clear." *English Academy Review* 4 (1987): 39–52.

———. *Tramp Royal: The True Story of Trader Horn*. Johannesburg. U of the Witwatersrand P, 1992.

Duffield, Ian. "John Eldred Taylor and West African Opposition to Indirect Rule in Nigeria." *African Affairs* 70 (1971): 262–68.

Dupuis, Joseph. *Journal of a Residence in Ashantee*. London: H. Colburn, 1824.

Equiano, Olaudah. *The Interesting Narrative of the Life of Olaudah Equiano, or Gustavus Vassa, the African*. London: published by the author, 1789.

Fraser, Donald. *The Autobiography of an African*. London: Seeley, Service and Co., 1925.

Green, Jeffrey P. "*In Dahomey* in London in 1903." *Black Perspectives in Music* 11.1 (1983): 22–40.

Herskovits, Melville J. "The Primitive 'Imagination.'" *Nation* 23 July 1930: 102–103.

Holtby, Winifred. *Mandoa, Mandoa!* London: Collins, 1933.

Horn, Aloysius. *The Ivory Coast in the Earlies*. New York: Simon and Schuster; London: Jonathan Cape, 1927.

Jahn, Janheinz, and Claus Peter Dressler. *Bibliography of Creative African Writing*. Nendeln, Liechtenstein: Kraus-Thomson, 1971.

Jenkinson, Jacqueline. "The Glasgow Race Disturbances of 1919." *Immigrants and Minorities* 4.2 (1985): 43–67.

Kelly's Directory of Merchants, Manufacturers and Shippers. London: Kelly's Directories Ltd., 1904.

Killingray, David. "All the King's Men? Blacks in the British Army in the First World War." *Under the Imperial Carpet: Essays in Black History 1780–1950*. Ed. Rainer Lotz and Ian Pegg. Crawley, Sussex: Rabbit Press, 1986. 164–81.

Kilson, Martin L., and Robert L. Rotberg, eds. *The African Diaspora: Interpretive Essays*. Cambridge: Harvard UP, 1976.

LoBagola, Bata Kindai Amgoza Ibn. "An African Savage's Own Story." *Scribner's Magazine* 85 (1929): 246–56, 405–14, 527–38, 629–39; 86 (1929): 37–50, 426–33.

———. *Folk Tales of a Savage*. New York: Knopf, 1930.

———. *LoBagola: An African Savage's Own Story*. New York: Knopf, 1930. 1933. 1970.

Londres, Albert. *Terre d'ebene: La traite des noirs*. Paris: Michel, 1929.

Macmillan, Allister. *The Red Book of West Africa*. London: Cass, 1920.

Makonnen, Ras. *Pan-Africanism from Within*. Nairobi and New York: Oxford UP, 1973.

Marke, Ernest. *Old Man Trouble*. London: Weidenfeld and Nicolson, 1975.

Modupe, Prince. *I Was a Savage*. New York and London: Museum Press, 1958. Rpt. as *A Royal African*. New York: Praeger, 1969.

Negro Year Book 1931–32. Tuskegee Institute, Alabama: Negro Year Book Publishing Co., 1931.

Norris, Frank. *The Octopus*. New York: Doubleday, Page, 1901. London: Penguin, 1986.

Ntara, Samuel Y. *Man of Africa*. London: Religious Tract Society, 1934.

Nyabongo, Akiki K. *The Story of an African Chief*. New York: Scribner's, 1935. Rpt. as *Africa Answers Back*. London: G. Routledge and Sons, 1936.

Olney, James. *Tell Me Africa: An Approach to African Literature*. Princeton, Princeton UP, 1973.

Ottley, Roi. *Inside Black America*. London: Spottiswoode, 1948.

Patterson, J. H. *The Jews in the Palestine Campaign*. Jerusalem: Menorah Club, 1936.

———. *With the Judeans in the Palestine Campaign*. London: Hutchinson; New York: Macmillan, 1922.

Perham, Margery. *Ten Africans*. London: Faber and Faber, 1936.

Shephard, Ben. "A Royal Gentleman of Colour." *History Today* April 1984: 36–41.

———. "Showbiz Imperialism: The Case of Peter Lobengula." *Imperialism and Popular Culture.* Ed. John M. MacKenzie. Manchester: Manchester UP, 1986. 94–112.

Sherwood, Marika. *Kwame Nkrumah: The Years Abroad 1935–1947.* Legon: Freedom Publications, 1996.

Staehelin, Balthasar. *Völkerschauen im Zoologischen Garten Basel 1879–1935.* Basel: Basler Afrika Bibliographien, 1993.

Sterne, Laurence. *The Life and Opinions of Tristram Shandy.* New York: Modern Library, 1950.

Thompson, E. B. "The Vaughan Family: A Tale of Two Continents." *Ebony* Feb. 1975: 53 ff.

Thompson, W. "Glasgow and Africa: Connexion and Attitudes, 1870–1900." Diss. Strathclyde U, 1978.

Westermann, Diedrich. *Afrikaner erzählen ihr Leben.* Essen: Essener Verlagsanstalt, 1938.

White, Sidney H. *I Gotta Horse: The Autobiography of Ras Prince Monolulu.* London and New York: Hurst and Blackett, 1950.

Williams, Joseph J. *Hebrewisms of West Africa.* London: Allen and Unwin, 1930.

"Bain's Bushmen"
Scenes at the Empire Exhibition, 1936

ROBERT J. GORDON

INTRODUCTION

The 1851 Great Exhibition held in the Crystal Palace heralded a new era: the commodity spectacle for mass consumption. Only recently have scholars started to appreciate the impact of this event. It was the harbinger, Anne McClintock points out, of the shift from scientific to commodity racism. These spectacles were successful because they managed to educate and socialize while the spectators thought they were being entertained. They were successful not only in the metropole but in the "cultural cringe," settler colonies like Australia and South Africa, as well.

In twentieth-century South Africa, undoubtedly the most successful "public display" of indigenes, both in terms of its immediate and long-term impact, was Donald Bain's Bushman display at the Johannesburg Empire Exhibition in 1936. Bain certainly set the standard for the emergent current "tradition" of Bushman displays in South Africa. "Bain's Bushmen" was one of the highlights at the Empire Exhibition, after which he took them down to Cape Town, where they also proved to be immensely popular. His attempt to take them to the United Kingdom did not materialize, and his alternative road show to Port Elizabeth and Durban turned disastrous. In Durban he ran out of money and had to appeal to the government for assistance in repatriating the Bushmen back to their home in the southern Kalahari. Other "Bushman Exhibits" followed, most notably at the van Riebeeck Festival in 1952, celebrating three hundred years of European settlement in South Africa. What is important about these Bushman exhibits is that they were still popular, while in Europe ethnological exhibits had been in disrepute at least since the 1920s.[1] Was this another case of "cultural lag" as the periphery sought to catch up to the continental metropole?

Part of the answer is to be found in the rhetoric accompanying Bain's display. As van Buskirk, a sympathetic journalist, put it:

> At first glance [the display was] the accomplishment of a showman extraordinary. And yet behind it all is the story of a man who for more than 25 years has carried out an unceasing fight for the establishment of a Bushman reserve. . . . The Southern Kalahari Bushmen constitute the greatest potential national monument in South Africa today, and the interest displayed in the Bushmen who have been brought to Johannesburg leads us to believe that such a Reservation would become in time entirely self-supporting. . . . [that] such a reservation will be formed is a practical certainty once the people of South Africa become sufficiently aware of its importance.

So impressed was van Buskirk that he proposed calling the Bushman reserve "Bainesia."

WHAT PEOPLE SAW AT THE EMPIRE EXHIBITION

Located in the corner to the right of the main entrance, the Bushman camp was one of the sensations of the exhibition, according to the daily Empire Exhibition paper. In apprising visitors on "How Best to See the Exhibition," the *Daily-Mail News Bulletin* (17 Sept. 1936) opined that:

> The Bushman Camp is well worth seeing. Although little has been done to give the public an idea of these strange people's natural surroundings—the camp is fenced with corrugated iron—visitors will be given an insight into the Bushman's lives. Old Abraham, the leader, with his body a mass of loosely hanging skin, is possibly the most colourful character.

The Bushman camp proved almost the most popular feature of all; it was constantly crowded, and on many occasions people had to be turned away. During the exhibition the camp drew over half a million viewers, including a record of 7,692 on a single day. And if the exhibit had been open at night the figures would have been much higher. On an average, people spent about 1½ hours "studying these wonderful remnants of one of the oldest races in the world."[2]

What they saw was a camp which lacked ambience. On first being shown it, Bain complained that it looked more like Johannesburg's main street than the Kalahari, and he threatened to withdraw his troupe unless the corrugated fence was appropriately covered. Needless to say, the fence was not covered, but Bain had invested too much to withdraw. Here, in the words of one observer, "their primitive houses contrasted sharply with the modern concrete structures." A few loads of sand had also been deposited to make dancing easier. The Bushmen reportedly threw bones to decide where to build their huts.[3]

We are indebted to an Afrikaans journalist, N. G. Meyer, for a firsthand account of what viewers saw. While waiting for the show to begin, spectators would be entertained and amused by the click sounds of the children. Then Donald Bain would use the public address system:

> Ladies and Gentlemen, the people who you see before you are known as the Southern Bushmen of the Kalahari. Today according to experts there are only some three hundred still living. As you will thus well understand if immediate provision is not made in one or other way to save these children of nature from total extinction, then these original inhabitants are going to vanish from the South African scene for good.
>
> The purpose I had in mind when I brought these people out of the Kalahari was to make propaganda and to educate the public to realize what an unremitting struggle these children of nature are fighting and losing against nature, man and animal. Apart from what they might be, no matter how primitive or rascally (skelm), these individuals are still living beings, and if reserves can be created for wild animals, why can we not stand together and create a reserve for these unfortunates and thus save them from assured extinction. . . . From the historical perspective we can with some regret point the finger to our ancestors because they shortsightedly, irresponsibly and selfishly observed the process of extermination of the Bushman. . . .

The Bushmen would then form a line of about twelve and look at spectators, while Bain continued with the narration, mentioning that the camp consisted of seventy people but that from ten to eighteen Bushmen would be suitable at any time as "Museum" types. The order of procession was led by Old Abraham (!gurice) who, according to Bain, was between 99 and 109 years of age and spoke Afrikaans, which he learned while in jail for breaching the hunting laws.[4] Abraham was followed by his daughter, Anneku (/khanako), "an exceptionally good type." The narration continued:

> I don't want you to think that these Bushmen are organized like our Bantu into tribes or nations. . . . Their social organization is the most primitive known and the social ties are too weak to pressure any of the members. [He then launched into a discussion of their hunting and the use of poisoned arrows.] Today however the Bushmen are exceptionally happy because they have received the good news from the Minister of Native Affairs that Bushmen will not be prosecuted anymore for shooting the occasional big game.

The lecture continued and, in an ad hoc manner, briefly touched the Bushman's use of *dagga* (*Cannabis sativa*), explained how they decorated their faces with ochre, repeated again that Bushmen were not as cruel and cunning as was sometimes maintained, discussed theories about the origins of steatopygia, and claimed that they did not believe in God but were wonderful mimes and could dance all night!

Suitably impressed spectators could then purchase an illustrated brochure for 1s. 6d. featuring an introduction by "Kalahari" Bain and reiterating that the primary object of the camp was educational and that fifty percent of the income from the Bushman exhibit was to go toward establishing a Bushman reserve. He eulogized them as "the last living remnants of a fast dying race. They live as their forefathers lived thousands of years ago, depending on their skillful use of bows and poisoned arrows" and intimated that

> as we view these children of the desert playing their primitive games and dancing their primitive dances before curious spectators in the Bushman Camp at the Empire Exhibition, let us not feel that they are being unduly revealed to the public gaze for the purpose of private gain. Let us rather feel as they feel, that they are working for a home, a land, and for the perpetuation of their race.

The brochure contained numerous photographs, with captions by Wilfred Cassere. The following are typical: "Prehistoric Man, Old Abraham in Philosophic Mood. Abraham, father of the nest, with his youngest son. Scientists estimate Abraham's age at 105 years, his son's at 5 years—only a century difference!" Pseudo-Darwinian approaches were dominant: "A mother of one of the groups. At first sight you thought it was a man!" "Bush-women dancing. Their extraordinary posterior development will be noticed. This is nature's provision for denizens of the desert—like the hump of the camel or the fat tail of the desert sheep"; "The origin of the 'Charleston.'. . . Women dancing to the strains of the first gramophone ever introduced to the desert"; "Nest of Bushwomen and children. These little people take a delight in posing for the camera."

What is striking about the exhibition is how little public criticism there was. A survey of the *Rand Daily Mail* during this period reveals only two letters objecting to the Bushman display.[5] One queried Bain's motives, asserting that it was to make money and not to facilitate ethnological study, since scientists could visit the Bushmen in the Kalahari. The other worried about what would happen to the Bushmen after the exhibition. If they were as "wild" as claimed, how were they persuaded to attend, and if they were not so "wild" then the public was entitled to the real facts about them. Only one newspaper editorial voiced concern. Were the Bushmen doomed because of their inability to readjust after assimilating for four months at the Empire Exhibition? the *Sunday Express* asked. "Will they be able to readjust their diets, or will this effort to perpetuate the history of their race, lead to final extinction?"

It was easy for Bain and his allies to answer these and other coffee-table critics by pointing out, for example, that the Kalahari was actually colder than Johannesburg. Typically they would argue that, far from being "half-starved," the Bushmen had become fat and healthy and that the ends justified the means, as the trip to the exhibition would probably make it possible for a Bushman reserve to be proclaimed in the Kalahari "where these people can live in peace, and thus prevent them from becoming totally extinct. There are reserves for game and natives, so why not a Bushman Reserve? Never before have scientists had such an opportunity of studying these interesting people at close quarters." Thus wrote Bain's son, Robert.

Meanwhile Bain seized every opportunity to propagate the idea of a Bushman reserve and was a much sought-after speaker at service clubs, where he would discuss the future of the Bushmen and how to preserve "these people so intimately bound up in early history":

> Because they have no tribal organization and are inarticulate, they are in imminent danger of being exterminated. . . . They are different from any other native tribe on earth. Their mentality is that of a child and they are absolutely incapable of absorbing modern ideas. From the scientific point of view their physique is interesting. . . . We do not need money to procure this land for them, but what we do want is sufficient public opinion to carry the thing through.

As one columnist put it:

> Mr Bain's simple sincerity about his project for the protection of the Bushmen of the Kalahari made his talk impressive for he speaks with the sure knowledge of those primitive people whom he has studied for years and for whom he is anxious to do so much.[6]

The reserve notion generated some discussion in the press and several writers thought that it would be better to relocate the Bushmen to the Kruger

National Park, where, "when once introduced into the Park, [they] will exterminate the wild dogs in the course of time and will in this respect be an asset to that area."

Public support for a Bushman reserve was overwhelming. All the newspapers I consulted, including both English and Afrikaans, carried editorials, and often repeatedly endorsed Bain's Bushman reserve idea. This publicity (one could hardly call it a debate) served a valuable educational role; at the same time it generated considerable publicity for Bain's Bushman Camp.[7]

FABRICATING THE BUSHMAN EXPERIENCE

Like P. T. Barnum, the famous American showman, Bain consciously or coincidentally appreciated the importance of using the elite and upper classes to build up and exploit an exhibit for the masses. As the great-grandson of the most famous road builder and explorer in South Africa, Andrew Geddes Bain— a fact much advertised by his allies—Bain was able to use his connections to well-placed cabinet ministers like Deneys Reitz and Piet Grobler to gain permission to stage the exhibition over the opposition of senior bureaucrats in the Native Affairs Department. Bain also forged an alliance with his obvious allies, scientists; their expertise countered some of the stereotypes and misrepresentations, especially those of senior Native Affairs Department officials who opposed his plans.

Undoubtedly the skillful use of the press and "Science" ensured the success of the Bushman Camp. But it was on soil already well prepared. Afrikaans writer von Wielligh had published a four-volume study entitled *Boesman Stories* (1919–21); Reenen van Reenen, a Chairman of the Academy for Science and Arts, had written the well-received monograph *Iets oor die Boesmans* (1920); and popular writers like Aschenborn and Sangiro were using Bushman material to great effect. Indeed, the Hobson brothers were to receive the coveted Hertzog Prize for Afrikaans literature in 1930 the same year they published their famous story of Bushman life in the Kalahari, *Skankwan van die Duine.*

Interest in the Bushmen was a lively issue, especially since the 1924 discovery of a potential "missing link," the prehistoric Taungs skull. At the Wembley Exhibition later that year, a banner draped over the entrance to the South African pavilion proclaimed, "South Africa, the Cradle of Humanity." Indeed, in 1928 Hedley Chilvers branded Bushmen one of the *Seven Wonders of Southern Africa,* and the traveller W. J. Makin was only exaggerating slightly when he complained in that same year:

> As is usual with any disappearing race, the Bushmen have now become an absorbing ethnological study to many pundits in the professional world. Every

year white men come to the edge of the Kalahari desert, camp out there with an array of cameras and scientific impediments, and try to entice the nomads of the desert to visit the camp. Tobacco is scattered as lavishly as crumbs to ensnare birds. And the few Bushmen who are in touch with civilization, a type that like a nameless dog will hang about the place where a bone may be flung at them, come into camp and are scientifically examined. (278)

Disgusted, he concluded with remarkable prescience that: "Perhaps someday, the Bushman will degenerate into that final humiliation—an exhibit by a travelling showman" (275).

The Use of Scientists

Scientists had developed a vested interest in maintaining, and indeed elaborating on, the acceptable conventional wisdom concerning those categorized as Bushmen, and eagerly seized upon the opportunity to further enhance their reputations by collaborating with Bain. More importantly, as Raymond Dart, their spokesman and perhaps the most prominent scientist in South Africa, put it, they "were imbued with the desire to bring about the establishment of one or more Bushman Reserves in Southern Africa, where the remnants of this fascinating human group of Bush peoples might be preserved for generations to come . . ." (*Hut Distribution* 167).

At an early stage, in December 1935, Bain wrote to Raymond Dart to invite his participation, and Dart enthusiastically agreed. Not only did he receive financial support from the Principal of Witwatersrand University, but he also induced a large number of colleagues to collaborate as well, attracted no doubt by this "heaven-sent opportunity," since "up to that time, no full study had been made of these tiny, yellow-skinned, wizened creatures" (*Adventures* 66).[8] The scientists were to visit Bain's "holding" camp in the Kalahari to ensure that his Exhibition Camp was an accurate reconstruction. Not only would they have an opportunity for research in the Kalahari, but they would also be able to do follow-up studies during the exhibition. Indeed, the project so excited University Principal Raikes that he considered making a flying visit to Bain's Kalahari camp.

Scientists were crucial in overriding the Native Affairs Department's misgivings, expressed so clearly by the Director of Native Labour:

> It has been the unfortunate experience, according to my advice, that Bushmen separated from their nomadic life and subjected to restrictions observed by European conventions have fallen an easy prey to tuberculosis and pneumonia, and whatever precautions which might be laid down to protect a party visiting or residing in the Rand for 4 or 5 months it would be impossible to guard against the vagaries of the weather and its reaction on members of the party.

> Further, the natural life of the Bushman is usually one long struggle for food in an environment to which he has been acclimatized, and to bring a party to, and keep them for a substantial period at a place where, of course, food will be plentiful, exertion nil, environment totally different and then return to their places would, in my opinion, be a somewhat heartless experiment.

To answer these objections, Bain wrote to Dorothea Bleek. She replied that in her opinion it would not be cruel, especially "If Bushmen are given an open-air camp with some shelter for rain, and blankets for the night. . . . It is confinement in buildings with stone floors that kills them off quickly. The less clothes they wear the healthier them are. . . ." Bain forwarded this letter from "the greatest living authority on the Bushmen" to the Native Affairs Department and offered to place his camp under the aegis of the University of the Witwatersrand, but the secretary, Douglas Smit, remained unimpressed by "the cold-blooded scientists." He wrote to the minister agreeing with the Native Labour Commissioner that it was "a heartless experiment," and questioned Bain's responsibility: "Bain is doing it for private gain and is exaggerating the importance of it from a scientific point of view." Bain's plans to recruit Namibian Bushmen fell through, however, when the Commissioner of Immigration and Asiatic Affairs refused to grant permission for the Bushmen to enter the country even though southern Rhodesian blacks would be attending the exhibition. On 2 July the Bechuanaland Protectorate finally gave Bain permission to recruit Bushmen from the Protectorate. Native Labour Commissioner Medford, as late as 6 August, barely six weeks before the exhibition was to begin, insisted that all the Bushmen be Union nationals. Thus Bain was forced to look within South Africa. Ever diplomatic, scientists downplayed such bureaucratic harassment. Dart reported that what Bain did manage to collect

> represent[ed] the relics of the Southern Bushmen once spread from the Kalahari to the Cape, those generally acknowledged to be the purest of the Bushman type. It was for this reason and at her special suggestion that Mr. Bain followed Miss Bleek's advice of going to this territory at the furthest confines of the Union . . . so that to the limit of human possibility the best examples of the Bushman type should be secured for public exhibition. . . . ("Hut Distribution" 159)

Along with Bain and some exhibition officials, scientists formed a pressure group to have the government create a Bushman reserve. On 30 September they held a meeting at the exhibition with Minister of Native Affairs Piet Grobler and senior aides. Prof. Maingard served as spokesperson and raised several issues. The Bantu were provided for by recent land legislation, but not the Bushmen. Two schemes seemed viable: a short-term scheme which would have the Kalahari Gemsbok Park declared a Bushman reserve, and a long-term one which would involve the administrations of South West Africa and Bechuanaland Protectorate in creating a Bushman buffer reserve running up the length of the Kalahari to Ghanzi.

Grobler's reaction was to reiterate that "when I was Minister of Lands, the Gemsbok Park was established and instructions were issued that Bushmen were to be allowed to live there undisturbed." However, deproclaiming the Kalahari Gemsbok Park was impossible and he had no authority over Bechuanaland. He then dealt the *coup de grâce*: he had no jurisdiction over Bushmen as his department only dealt with natives! To which Maingard quickly asked if that meant that the government disclaimed all responsibility toward the Bushmen. Grobler replied:

> You desire a permanent settlement for the Bushmen but they are not contented to settle in one place; they are always on the move. If the Union has a place anywhere, the matter could be discussed, but there is not a single place in the whole of the Union that is suitable. I would suggest that you form a committee and approach Sir William Clark [British High Commissioner], and put your case to him. He might be able to advise you. After you have seen him I will interview the Prime Minister.[9]

The high commissioner was duly propositioned, but he replied that the Ghanzi corridor scheme was impractical; instead he suggested that an anthropologist be engaged to "properly study the matter." This suggestion eventually led to a committee of both administrators and academics. Apart from a lengthy memorandum by Prof. Schapera, this committee eventually decided it could serve no useful purpose and disbanded on the eve of the Second World War. At the same time, academics got the Historical Monuments Commission to unanimously pass a motion noting the disappearance of the Bushmen with regret and urging the government to create an adequate reserve, to which the minister replied that while he sympathized, there was no land available for a "special reserve for the exclusive use of Bushmen."

But it was as active allies in the public debate about the future of the Bushmen that academics shone, especially Dart, who in an important article in the *Star* (24 Sept. 1936) rebutted critics' claims that the Bushmen were not "genuine" and eloquently made the case for a reserve. He started off by pointing out that there was no such thing as a pure race and that if the fact that a Chinaman spoke English did not make him an Englishman, neither were the Bushmen colored simply because they spoke Afrikaans. The move to the Empire Exhibition had not been harmful. Bushmen were a hardy people who had survived travel to Europe in Napoleonic times. People had forgotten that Bushmen were not naturally desert dwellers but had been driven there. Moreover, in their long periods of imprisonment, they had become used to a European diet.

The basic purpose of bringing the Bushmen was to show to South Africa, and to all who visited, how real they were, how fascinating their customs were, and how worthy they were of being preserved for all time in South Africa. As Union nationals they had freedom of movement [*sic!*]. They were not under contract to Bain but had come of their own free choice. He concluded in a manner which perhaps upset many of the public:

> These children of our human brotherhood . . . have by every criterion accepted by intelligent mankind . . . earned the right to own at least a portion of South Africa for as long as they persist.

Bain might have overdone the use of science to justify his project, indicated by the gently satirical advertisement for *C to C* cigarettes, presented in the form of a newspaper report ostensibly by the South African Smokeological Association, which reported on the "RIDDLE OF SMOKE SIGNALS AT EMPIRE EXHIBITION," and loudly proclaimed "KALAHARI THEORY REFUTED BY LEADING SOUTH AFRICAN AUTHORITIES." The copy went on to report that after "3 months the Bushmen are still children of the desert with many hidden secrets including day by day communication with their Kalahari home. . . . but the smoke rising is not a signal but a crowd of people smoking C to C cigarettes . . . [which] signal[s] more happiness to mankind in five minutes than all the Bushmen in the Kalahari in a thousand years."

THE USE OF GOOD PUBLICITY

Long before the exhibition began, newspapers gave much publicity, frequently of a sensational nature, to Bain's efforts to assemble the Bushmen and also stimulated public appetite to view them. This was done in conjunction with scientists who generated their own publicity. Bain's camp was seen as a locality of national interest, and major South African journalists like Lawrence Green, who accompanied the University of Cape Town expedition, and James van Buskirk FRGS (Fellow Royal Geographic Society) sent special dispatches "by camel police" on the activities of the University of the Witwatersrand expedition led by the redoubtable Raymond Dart.

Their "meeting with the wonders of the white man's civilization for the first time of their lives" provided much copy for the local press, who continuously played the juxtaposition refrain, as when the *Star* reported on the unique scheme

> which aims at temporarily transferring members of one of the world's most primitive races from their "Stone Age" . . . to the "Machine Age" of modern

civilization. . . . They have never seen a locomotive. . . . they still use bows and arrows dipped in deadly poison, tools similar to the relics of the Stone Age. Uncontaminated Bushmen were only found in the center of Kalahari. Those on the fringe had lost their race purity by intermingling. Bain [is] the first man to visit these people in a motor car. . . . It is strange to think that not so many hundreds of miles from Johannesburg as the aeroplane flies live these primitive folk who have made no progress towards civilization for 5,000 years.[10]

It also led to glorification of Bain, whose collection "selected from different parts of the Kalahari" was a result of a "gigantic search almost impossible as they do not live in tribes." And Bain was looked upon as "their very God, their benefactor and their trusted friend." This ensured a publicity buildup unequalled by any other exhibit.

Press attention focused on the venerable patriarch, Old Abraham, who aged some 30 years, from 80 to 110, in the period from the first press report until his death a few months after the exhibition. Even in distant Cape Town the press got involved. The popular column "Talk of the Tavern" reported on "FAME FOR OLD ABRAHAM":

The face in this paragraph will soon be one of the most famous faces in South Africa. Every visitor taking a camera to the Rand Exhibition will want to snap it. Newspapers all around the world will seize on it. For this is the face of Old Abraham the Bushman, who is going to Johannesburg with Mr Donald Bain's collection. Old Abraham is a genuine Bushman, and experts agree that he is at least 100 years old. But he is not a wild man. He is a friendly, cunning old fellow who can smell tobacco a mile away.

Old Abraham was feted along the way to Johannesburg, meeting with local mayors and other dignitaries. On arrival in Johannesburg he was presented with a car for his personal use. While in Johannesburg Bain would take the Bushmen on educational excursions, and the press would follow to adroitly celebrate the technological genius that made the Rand gold mines possible. Shortly after their arrival, for example, Bain took Old Abraham for his first air flight.[11]

A typical headline would suggest that "WHITE MAN'S MAGIC ALARMS BUSHMEN" and the ensuing article would often engage in the well-known phenomenon of collapsing time:

In the past few weeks the old patriarch Abraham has been through a life time of novel experiences, and his natural dignity and philosophy have enabled him to treat even such momentous occasions as his first flight in an aeroplane as if they were everyday occurrences in the Kalahari Desert. . . . His poise almost deserted him [when an] elevator proved altogether too much for his understanding. . . . [H]e shrank back in terror from an apartment window and . . . he was bewildered at the mysteries of the bathroom having a hot and a cold water tap.

Or as the *Rand Daily Mail* headlined it:

BUSHMEN TAKE TO THE AIR OVER JOHANNESBURG

OLD ABRAHAM THINKS "CAMP" IS TOO BIG

"WHERE DO YOU GET ALL THE WATER?"

THOUGHT PLANE WAS GIANT BIRD

Apparently, since he had never seen an airplane crash before, he had no fear.

Most of the coverage focused on the impact of technology; this started in the recruitment phase, when it was reported that:

TRUCKS SCOUR DESERT FOR BUSHMEN

SEVERE TEST FOR DODGES

"OXLESS WAGON" DELIGHTS TRAVELLERS[12]

Naturally the media made their alleged first view of movies newsworthy:

BUSHMEN RUSH SCREEN TO SEE WHERE TALKIE COMES FROM

THEY LIKE MICKEY MOUSE BUT DANCING ZULUS SCARED THEM

ABRAHAM SEES HIMSELF IN KALAHARI FILM

Abraham, the centenarian Bushman chief, will never be surprised again. Where the white man is, anything is possible, he now believes. He has seen and heard the greatest wonder of all—Mickey Mouse. . . .

[Zulu dancing attracted them:] Dancing in any form appeals to the Bushmen and it is impossible for them to keep their feet still in the presence of music. Aniko, Abraham's fifty-year-old daughter leads the dancing.

[When the Kalahari camp scenes were shown:] They made a concerted rush forward. They looked under and behind the screen in an effort to find just where it all came from, but to no avail.

Wherever they went, they were accompanied by the press, who never failed to find something to delight. Thus, on a trip to the Union buildings in Pretoria they were reported to be unimpressed until they saw a fish pond and began scooping fish out of it.

Sometimes their actions were given an overtly political interpretation, as when they visited the British pavilion:

BUSHMEN SEE BRITISH PAVILION

WOMEN DANCE BEFORE BUST OF THE KING

Their reaction to King Edward's bust was interesting to watch. The men all clicked in garrulous astonishment. Two of the women began to dance and beat their hands together in supplication. This was their idea of pleasing the "White King."

They were really terror-stricken when the shooting lights of the great map on the floor of the Pavilion began darting this way and that, to indicate the routes followed by British aeroplanes.

CONTEXT: THE ORGANIZATION OF THE EMPIRE EXHIBITION

To understand and analyze the role and meaning of the Bushman Camp it is necessary to place the camp in the wider setting of the Empire Exhibition. Located on some hundred acres of land in Milner Park and with some two million pounds invested in it, the exhibition was managed by H. M. Ballasis, an Englishman on assignment from the Federation of British Industries. Ballasis had been involved in the organization of a number of expositions including White City (1908), Athens (1918), and more recent shows in Canada, Buenos Aires, and Tel Aviv. Having set the tone of the exhibition, he resigned for medical reasons halfway through the exhibition. The strain of two years' hard work had taken its toll. The exhibition officially opened on 15 September 1936 and closed four months later on 16 January. Its organizers hoped that most of South Africa's whites would visit it, but this was not quite realized. An estimated 2 million people, of whom 1.3 million paid entrance fees, visited the exhibition. And like so many other exhibitions, this one ran at a loss, so much so that Parliament had to subsidize it to the amount of £130,577 in order to balance and close the books, much to the outrage of the Nationalists who wanted to know why they had to pay for imperial propaganda.[13]

The Empire Exhibition was organized to celebrate the fiftieth anniversary of the founding of the city of Johannesburg and was intended to show that South Africa was not some provincial backwater but had finally transcended the "cultural cringe" and become metropolitan in its outlook. The exhibition also addressed domestic political issues, namely the largely English-speaking political effort to maintain, indeed strengthen, links with the Commonwealth in opposition to the then still vaguely articulated republican sentiments of the Afrikaner nationalists. Two years later, in 1938, the Nationalists were to have their moment of symbolic splendor when they reenacted the Great Trek to celebrate its centenary.

The theme of the exhibition was cooperation of the British Dominions or, more accurately, how South Africa was linked to the Commonwealth, and this was reflected in both the layout of pavilions and in the official opening ceremonies. Most newspapers agreed that the United Kingdom had the most impressive display. Its centerpiece was the renowned aviatrix Amy Mollison's airplane, suspended over a globe which lit up the routes of British airplanes. The largest structure, however, was the South African government's four-acre model farm featuring the world's largest rock garden, with some 6,000 plants. Of the Dominions, Canada had a large pavilion, Australia and New Zealand were also well represented, and Southern Rhodesia and an assorted number of British colonies, mostly in Africa, also had displays. To underline the importance of the empire as a communications network, an air race from London and an automobile race from Nairobi, both finishing in Johannesburg, formed part of the official activities. And to emphasize Johannesburg's emerging subregional role, some twenty-seven conferences were held in the Hall of Events during the exhibition, highlighted by a major conference on regional transportation.

The ritual manifestation of dominional/imperial cooperation was clear at the official opening ceremony, which featured the Governor-General, Lord Clarendon, followed by South African Premier Hertzog and his Rhodesian colleague, Godfrey Huggins. Then a message from British Prime Minister Stanley Baldwin was played on a phonograph. Finally, the remaining six empire premiers gave brief telephonic speeches.

The visits of prominent politicians, and especially where they planted their feet, were also heavy with meaning. Premier Hertzog was accorded a sneak preview and had much praise for the rock garden and claimed to be "very pleased that other Dominions are taking part . . . [and] also very pleased to note the manner in which provision is being made for the Afrikaans-speaking section as well as for the English-speaking.[14] Cabinet ministers reported to have visited the exhibition included Smuts, Hertzog, Reitz, Stuttaford, and Pirow. They all visited the United Kingdom pavilion and then invariably toured the East African colonies stands. Interestingly, none, except possibly Grobler, reportedly visited the Bushmen exhibit.

One of the highlights of the exhibition, and certainly its ideological centerpiece, was a nineteen-episode, four-day pageant celebrating the "Story of South Africa." It was scripted by the Afrikaner historical hagiographer Gustav Preller, and started on a day heavy with meaning for Afrikaners, Dingaan's Day, 16 December. It presented an engaging interpretation of history. Thus Episode One was entitled *Zimbabwe* and narrated as follows:

> Africa, the vast and mysterious, has been called the Cradle of the Human Race. The oldest of the continents, cargo of ivory, copper and gold at the docks of Ur, of the Chaldees, while Sargon, the Arcadian, conquered the land of the men of Sumer. The men of Zimbabwe mined for gold and copper and tin—their old workings have been traced as far southward as the Rand.

According to the script notes, "The first episode is a representation of Zimbabwe when it was a hive of industry, showing the treasures sent by caravanserai to the shores of the Mediterranean sea and the courts of Asia."

The second episode was entitled *The Bushmen*:

These people were one time sole owners of Africa—the only living beings who could speak, kindle a fire and fashion implements. Their signature in the shape of rock carvings and paintings is writ large over the face of Africa. All that today remains to them of their mighty heritage is a small portion of the Kalahari desert and the primeval forest to the west of the Albert Nyanza.

The script notes direct: This episode shows them (courtesy of Donald Bain) around their camp fire, dancing and singing their ancient songs, as was their custom on some festive occasion." The third episode has Diaz ("the first Christian") planting a cross at Santa Cruz in "AD 1486" and is entitled *The Beginning of History.*[15]

For day-to-day education and amusement, visitors to the exhibition had a wide choice. They could visit the Hall of Technology to see early pioneering television or enjoy the novelty of watching Oxford play Cambridge at ice hockey. If they favored dancing, they could attend performances by some five "first rate" overseas bands. For a modest shilling they could see one of a number of special exhibits: the Victoria Waterfall replica, which used over 2,000 gallons per minute; a model of the Zimbabwe ruins; "Palestine"; the aquarium; the art museum; or the "Bushman Town." In terms of attendance, by far the most popular exhibitions were the Victoria Falls replica, followed by the Bushman Camp. Other ethnological displays like the Swazi Village or the Tswana craftspeople drew only small crowds.

A QUESTION OF MOTIVE?

Despite all the scientific advice Bain received, much of the Bushman Camp was contrived. Thus we know that he made a special trip up to Ngamiland to obtain "traditional attire" and artifacts, and, according to his son:

insisted that they spoke their own language and anyone overheard using either Afrikaans or Hottentot expressions would forfeit the weekly ration of tobacco or handful of sweets. This had the desired effect, and the use of their language is now habitual.

Nevertheless it is clear that just as he might have fabricated the Bushmen, in a very real sense they constructed him. They represented what Norman Denzin calls a major "turning point" in his biography.

The credibility of Bain's case for a Bushman reserve depended largely on the motives imputed to his act of bringing Bushmen to the exhibition. Those opposed to his idea dismissed him as a showman, while those who supported him attributed more noble motives.

In terms strikingly similar to other contemporary Bushmanophiles like van der Post and Myburgh, Bain explained his particular fixation with Bushmen thus:

> from my earliest childhood . . . my imagination was fired by the mere mention of the name. . . . Perhaps it is that the call of the wild is inherent in me or may be it is my horror of our soul devastating civilization, the ghastly monotony of the individual existence and the thought that perhaps some day I will find myself condemned to confinement in one of those modern monstrosities, a skyscraper, that my sympathies go out to the Bushmen. If I, a product of civilization, can feel about these things as I do what must have been the feelings of the Bushmen when, after thousands or, perhaps hundreds of thousands of years of absolute individual independence, they are confronted with the prospect of joining the shackled slave gangs or the ranks of sweated labour. . . . He made his choice, not because he reasoned it out, but because he was incapable of any other. . . .

Other biographical factors also helped to shape Bain's career. The fact that newspapers constantly mentioned that he was the great-grandson of Andrew Geddes Bain prodded him into playing a certain type of public role in which the spirit of noblesse oblige[16] was prominent. This stress on Bain's lineage was clearly an attempt to vest authority in his competence as an expert on Bushmen. Bain, like explorers and elites elsewhere, derived status and prestige from showing off priceless artifacts and treasures.

If Bain's camp had been designed simply for profit and entertainment, it would not have succeeded. Corbey, in his excellent review of "ethnological shows," points out that by the 1930s ethnological exhibitions were out of fashion as criticism of imperialism and racism increased, and such shows were found objectionable on moral grounds. In terms of a grammar of motives, simple financial gain and amusement would not have been acceptable. Indeed, these were the motives that Department of Native Affairs officials privately attributed to him but could never publicly prove. Such suspicions motivated their resistance to the Bushman exhibition. In short, Bain could not have succeeded had he not framed his motives within an educational and humanitarian paradigm. Certainly "commercial gain" was unacceptable as a motive.

What strikes one about Bain is how very unbusinesslike he was. Thus, while he could easily have settled on the more profitable course of taking only twenty or so "genuine specimens" to the exhibition, in the end he wound up taking everyone who wanted to go, a party of over seventy, including many "dubious" specimens and a number of dogs. More importantly, if the profit motive was the chief driving force, as the Department of Native Affairs suggested, he would have taken his profits and run after the Empire Exhibition.[17] Instead, when he felt that the Bushmen had been wronged he took them on a

march to the Houses of Parliament and tried to take them to the United Kingdom to petition for a Bushman reserve in Bechuanaland. This led directly to his
bankruptcy. In the end, as Berger points out, such a debate about imputed
motives might be irrelevant because one's "role forms, shapes, patterns both
action and the actor. It is very difficult to pretend in this world. Normally one
becomes what we play at" (115).

Bain's show and accompanying rhetoric were devoted to persuasion. He
believed, like so many of his era, that if he simply presented the facts, the public
would react rationally and support his conservation efforts. His interest was in
persuasion, not conviction, and thus he deliberately withheld accusations and
evidence of exploitation of Bushmen by local Kalahari farmers. In fact, the
Bushman reserve rhetoric is striking for its complete glossing over of how Bushmen were historically impoverished and massacred. Bushmen were completely
disaggregated from their context. Bain did not appear to suffer, at least publicly, from a lack of legitimacy. People listened and mostly accepted what was
said. Indeed it was a rare achievement to get both English and Afrikaans newspapers to endorse his Bushman reserve idea.

There was a strong element of performance in what Bain did. It is clear
that he laid great emphasis on *symbolic actions*. This is obvious from the march
on the Houses of Parliament and from the various excursions he took the Bushmen on, like those to the symbolically important Union Buildings and the British Pavilion. Robert Paine argues that legitimation comes particularly through
its form and that persuasion entails a number of forces: (a) the suspension of
disbelief by the audience, (b) an inducement of collaborative expectancy, and
(c) audience complicity with the speaker. As Bain lured the audience into his
project, the performance was shared. Unfortunately the sharing was never con-
summated. Many people offered to make cash contributions for a Bushman
reserve, but Bain initially refused such offers until a legally constituted body
controlling such a fund could be established. By the time such a body was
established, public enthusiasm had diminished somewhat. One can give two
readings to this situation. First, it can be taken as further evidence for Bain's
lack of business acumen; second, it can be read as evidence of his political
naiveté: all that was needed was enough spreading of the message and enthusiasm would do the rest. Paine (19) has noted the similarities between rhetoric—
the interweaving of speech and action—and the performance of magical acts,
especially how in both, word and deed confirm each other. Magic can destroy
magic but not belief, and the same applies to rhetoric. The force of common
assumption between audience and performer is mobilized in both magic and
rhetoric. Both provide the audience with supplements of what they hear or see,
with their own beliefs, experiences, and social knowledge.

Understanding the Success of the Exhibition[18]

If, as Paine claims, "politics is a vehicle for the circulation of symbolic statements about the social order," then the spectators are as important as the exhibition itself, for their values and beliefs determine the meaning of what is said and done. The news media evoked a spectacle, an interpretation reflecting the diverse social situations of the audience and the language and symbols to which they were exposed. The spectacle, Edelman reminds us, is a fetish, a creation of its audience which then dominates the thought and action of its creators. Every instance of spectacle resonates with the memory of other signifiers "so that it create[s] a radiating network of meaning that varies with the situation of spectators and actors" (10).

Teachers and popularizers of anthropology have always realized that the discipline's exotic findings cannot be absorbed unless they speak directly to the innermost preoccupations of would-be students. The audience of would-be students and supporters of the camp, however, was sociologically complex. Bain's intended audience extended beyond the narrow confines of the spectators physically present at the show. The media made sure of this. Indeed, his audience was quite international, although they all shared one common characteristic: they were members of the white middle class, and a conscientious reading of their varied utterances and statements reveals certain preoccupations.

The Empire Exhibition was part of what Ulf Hannerz terms an emergent global ecumene undergirded by a unitary cultural technology for situating metropole and periphery. Every anniversary requires attributing origins, motivating events which are called into mind in various ways as commemorative acts to connect the past with the present. This is what the Bushmen did in 1936. The exhibition was organized in such a way as to reveal an order, and this came out strongly during the official opening. The role of the Bushmen in this order is manifested most strongly in the focal position they occupied in the pageant scripted by Preller. Such spectacles, Corbey notes, "neutralized the cognitive dissonance and the threat to Western middle-class identity constituted by the baffling cultural difference of new peoples. Colonial Others were incorporated narratively" (360) and thus testified to the success of South African colonization. While the Bushmen might have been socially marginal, symbolically they were central to a number of different ideological constellations.

Like other exhibitions, the Empire Exhibition was closely tied to politics, and the theme of metropole/periphery links was dominant. Yet within the "cultural cringe," contending groups placed different interpretations on the Bushman exhibition. In this connection the use of the Bushmen to endorse political ideology was particularly prominent. This period, as was noted, featured conflict between largely English-speaking supporters of the Commonwealth and Afrikaner nationalists who would have liked to secede. Thus it is not surprising that press coverage of the Empire Exhibition tended to be largely by the English press. The Afrikaans press was largely nationalist and thus did not enjoy celebrating the empire and what it stood for. This changed, however, with Bain's visit to Cape Town with his Bushmen troupe. The English and Afrikaans press gave completely different "readings" of the Bushmen visit. The influential Cape nationalist newspaper, *Die Burger*, focused almost exclusively on "Old Fytjie," Abraham's daughter. This striking emphasis on females rather than males, which contrasts with the English newspapers' coverage, is exceptional and bears further exploration. But the Afrikaans press was also using the Bushmen visit to score political points, especially with the royal coronation imminent. Thus, for example, *Die Burger* headlined a front-page article "Old Fytjie and the 'Big Boss' across the sea: Why must I dance for him?" They delighted in quoting her "broken Afrikaans" wisdom.[19]

In contrast, the *Cape Argus* had little time for seventy-year-old Anako, who they described as "stunted, withered and yet highly steatopygous." Instead, their story was headlined: "The Bushmen Come to Town, Weird Desert Troupe Startles City; Appeal to Government for right to live, [Minister] Grobler promises relief; Loyal Outburst on seeing picture of the King." Carel Birkby, the foremost journalist of the time, began his story, "Weirdest of all King George's subjects" and continued: "They also saw for the first time a picture of King George VI and knelt in the street and kissed their hands to the picture while crowds watched this unsophisticated demonstration of loyalty."[20]

Visibility is an important tool of education, and in addition, living exhibits have certain advantages if only because they engage more of the senses. Not only sight, but sound, touch, and smell, as Barbara Kirschenblatt-Gimblett observes, tend to make people into artifacts because the ethnographic gaze objectifies. They could be observed in motion as functioning objects, and the exhibition held out the possibility of envisaging a more scientific breeding of humans to replace and reorder the chaos-of-miscegenation approach. Science was used to appropriate the Bushmen. This was the obvious consequence of the reserve debate, especially where Dart was involved, and was strengthened by Bain's use of a natural history approach, which proved to be enduring because of the dominance of geology and natural history museums in South Africa and, especially, the Transvaal. The narratives used by both Bain and the pageant familiarized, exoticized, and ambiguously defined Bushmen as victims in need of protection, but at the same time debased them. They also played a pivotal role by telling of a heroic ascent toward the natural goal: white middle-class society. The discourse of nonassimilability was important in the development of the mythology of Apartheid.

The exhibition visualized achievement and progress—there was no mention of social problems like poverty, sickness, or racism—and unlike the van Riebeeck Festival of 1952 none of the disfranchised groups tried to use the occasion for symbolic protests. The central role accorded to the Bushmen served to displace other black groups. Thus, for example, the Swazi village and the Tswana craftspeople drew only small crowds. Similarly, on a national level focus and debate on a Bushmen reserve served to anesthetize the crucial debate about the final passage of the Hertzog Native Bills, which legalized the dispossession of vast tracts of black land as well as the disfranchisement of Cape blacks. Not only did the Bushmen displace this potentially explosive and uncomfortable topic for whites, but they also provided an implicit vindication for black land dispossession in the common but unstated belief that because blacks robbed Bushmen, whites were justified in taking the land away from blacks.

Within eighteen months Bain had dropped from public view. His financial embarrassment and lack of success reduced his efficacy as a Bushmen advocate. But even without these problems it is doubtful that the public pressure to create a Bushmen reserve would have continued. Media attention does not depend on the severity of the problem, but rather on dramatic appeals, which are extremely vulnerable, as Murray Edelman remarks, to "satiation of attention" (8).

Bain's naive reliance on public opinion was a major factor leading to the ultimate failure of his mission. Again, as Edelman trenchantly observes, the "public" is mainly a black hole into which the efforts of advocates disappear with hardly a trace: its apathy, indifference, quiescence, and resistance to the consciousness industry are especially impressive. Indifference is the prime weapon of the middle classes. It is demonstrated by the fact that despite numerous newspaper editorial endorsements of his plans to raise £30,000, Bain only managed to raise £60, plus one and a half tons of food.

NOTES

1. For a recent summary of such exhibitions in Europe, see Corbey.

2. *Rand Daily Mail* 5 Oct. 1936; *Cape Argus* 26 Dec. 1936. Where newspapers or sources are cited without proper attribution, they are undated copies from Donald Bain's private files. I am much indebted to Donald Bain's son, John, for allowing me access to these files. Photocopies are available on request.

3. *Rand Daily Mail* 17 Aug. 1936. Initially the exhibition only wanted twenty-five "specimens" to be housed on a one-acre site. Because Bain eventually brought more than seventy Bushmen, he was forced to establish a base camp away from the exhibition and to transfer a selection there every day. The location of this main camp was to be a closely guarded secret. It was the university's botanic farm, Frankenwald, some nine miles away; every day a group of some thirty would be brought to the exhibition so that the rest could relax and play. Data on this point is ambiguous, however.

4. Meyer disputes this claim as unlikely and suggests that Abraham probably learned it in service with Afrikaner farmers. Meyer's typescript "Die Boesmans op die Rykstentoonstelling" is among the Dart Papers at the University of the Witwatersrand Archives.

5. *Rand Daily Mail* 19 and 22 Aug. 1936.

6. *Rand Daily Mail* 15 Sept. 1936.

7. The Bushman reserve did not materialize because powerful forces who were opposed to it, in particular senior civil servants in the Department of Native Affairs and the Gordonia farming lobby, did not participate in the public debate. Instead they repeatedly attacked by anonymous innuendo: The Bushmen were not "pure," but fakes who moreover spoke Afrikaans. To rebut these damaging charges, Bain had to rely upon scientists. This is the topic of a companion essay ("Saving").

8. This is actually erroneous. Many German studies had been done. For a general discussion of the wider context of Bushmen in Southern Africa and the policies toward them, see Gordon, *Bushman Myth*.

9. Later in the interview Grobler repeated this assertion but quickly added "We are mainly responsible for their good treatment here and to see that they are sent back safely" (file NTS 9586 382/400, State Archives, Pretoria).

10. *Christian Science Monitor* 11 Jan. 1936.

11. The executive committee of the exhibition was none too happy with such excursions, especially the air flight, and Bain was accordingly "disciplined," as this was contrary to the undertaking they had given the Department of Native Affairs. See Exco Minutes, Johannesburg Public Library.

12. *Rand Daily Mail* 24 and 29 Aug. 1936.

13. *Rand Daily Mail* 4 Nov. 1936; *Die Burger* 18 Feb. 1937.

14. *Rand Daily Mail* 5 Aug. 1936.

15. In the original script, Preller had entitled Episode Three *Hottentots* and had presented their history as follows:

> Probably of remote Egyptian origin, the Hottentots came south not many centuries be-
> fore the first white man set foot on South African soil. Though akin to the Bushmen they
> proudly called themselves "THE PEOPLE" to distinguish their race from the Bushmen.
> They developed into pastoralists while the Bushman remains to this day a hunter only. A
> thousand years ago they lived about the lake regions of Central Africa, and their Great
> Trek southward has been traced as far as Somaliland. They were the people whom the
> white man found in possession.

The pageant also called for a small party of Hottentots driving cattle before them and three pack oxen, who are "Suddenly attacked by Bushmen. Bushmen terrified flee." This episode was scrapped, probably because they could not find actors to play the Hottentot roles (Minutes, Empire Exhibition, Johannesburg Public Library).

16. Bain was acutely conscious of the fact that the Secretary of Native Affairs had on more than one occasion accused him of the "basest motives," but pointed out in a letter to Maingard that since the exhibition he had continued to feed the Bushmen despite the considerable cost involved:

> but I must go through with it. They know of course by now what I am after and their faith
> in me, as you know, is so implicit, that they are perfectly confident of the result. Were I to
> abandon them now I would not only lose their confidence but they would scatter to the
> four winds and would be very suspicious of any attempt to round them up in the future.

He adds that he was going to the Kalahari to see if he could raise a deputation to take to Cape Town but this "will also depend upon the wishes of the Bushmen themselves . . ." (Dart Papers).

Nowhere is his spirit of noblesse oblige better illustrated than in his letter to the trader Jooste, reprinted in Boydell, instructing him to disband the Bushman Camp:

> In doing so I would be very grateful to you if you would thank them from me for the exemplary manner in which they have behaved themselves in the past and give them my personal assurance that I shall in no way relax my efforts on their behalf. I realize that it is going to be exceedingly difficult for you to explain away Mr Groblers and Gen. Smuts' promises, which as you will recollect, we impressed upon the Bushmen had been made by the "Big Bosses." . . . I sincerely hope that you will deal with the matter in your usual tactful manner. (132–33)

Newspapers reinforced the liberal approach:

> It was an historic event. Not for two centuries has such a band of little people slept on the outskirts of Cape Town. They were driven away like wild animals by the advance of civilisation, far away in Bushmanland.
> Bain is determined to see these last survivors of the Cape Bushmen protected and saved from extinction. . . . all sorts of promises have been made about a Bushman reserve but nothing has been done. Meanwhile the helpless people have been in danger of starvation.
> It was an act of sheer humanity that the old explorer Andrew Geddes Bain would have been proud to see his grandson undertaking.

17. The financial arrangements underlying the Bushman exhibition were quite straightforward: When Bain approached the Executive Committee of the exhibition they enthusiastically welcomed his proposal but pointed out that it was outside their ability to finance the project and that, moreover, the project should be cleared with the Native Affairs Department, "who were not in favor of transplanting Bushmen from their normal place of abode, since they invariably died when any changes were made in their mode of life" (Exco Minutes, 14 Oct. 1935). Bain replied that he was willing to finance the scheme (which would cost him between six and seven hundred pounds) but wanted a guarantee from the exhibition. The Executive Committee agreed to consider the matter favorably provided Bain got the written consent of the Department of Native Affairs. On supplying a letter from the Secretary of South West Africa approving of the display of SWA Bushmen, the committee agreed to the project under which Bain would be responsible for obtaining and transporting the Bushmen as well as for supporting them while at the exhibition. They also agreed that the estimated expenditure of one thousand pounds be charged against the takings of the exhibit and that the balance of takings be split 60 percent to Bain and 40 percent to the exhibition and that they guarantee Bain six hundred pounds (Exco Minutes, 17 Feb. 1936).

To bankroll his project Bain turned to a local Johannesburg businessman, George Naylor. As reported to the Receiver of Taxes, the camp realized a total profit of 5,084 pounds, less 2,537 pounds for expenses, leaving a net profit of 2,547 pounds, of which Bain's 50 percent share amounted to 1273/10/— (Photocopies of correspondence).

18. Parts of this discussion are reproduced in Gordon, "Saving."

19. E.g.: "Ou Fytijie was gistermiddag eers op haar stukke:

Sy loop oor van blydskap; indrukke wat nooit uit boesmans-verstand gewis sal word nie, het sy opgedoen. Gister het sy die museum besoek en haar voorouers in beeldgesien and toe gemsbokke. . . . 'n Boesman geleer homself. Sy gelerentheid kom as hy getroud is en die meeste van ons is of was getroud. My man is geverdring in die groot water, maar wat 'n

Boesman nie sien, hy glo nie en respekteer nie . . . daarom vra ek , , , dit wil gaweet wees, waarom nou vir Boesman bangmaak?" (*Die Burger* 11 May 1937)

Or, the claim that after attending the intervarsity rugby match between Cape Town and Stellenbosch Universities, she wanted to import rugby into the Kalahari (*Die Burger* 22 May 1937).

20. *Cape Argus* 8 May 1937.

Works Cited

Berger, Peter. *Invitation to Sociology.* New York: Anchor, 1963.

Boydell, Thomas. *My Luck's Still In.* Cape Town: Stewart, 1948.

Chilvers, Hedley. *The Seven Wonders of South Africa.* Johannesburg, SAR and H, 1929.

Corbey, Raymond. "Ethnographic Showcases, 1870–1930." *Cultural Anthropology* 8.3 (1993): 338–69.

Dart, Raymond. *Adventures with the Missing Link.* Philadelphia: Institutes Press, 1959.

———. "The Hut Distribution Genealogy and Homogeneity of the /?auni-=khomani Bushmen." *Bantu Studies* 11.3 (1937): 175–246.

Denzin, Norman. *Interpretive Interactionism.* Beverly Hills: Sage, 1992.

Edelman, Murray. *Constructing the Political Spectacle.* Chicago: U of Chicago P, 1988.

Gordon, Robert. *The Bushman Myth and the Making of a Namibian Underclass.* Boulder: Westview, 1992.

———. "Saving the Last South African Bushman: A Spectacular Failure?" *Critical Arts* 9.2 (1995): 28–48.

Hannerz, Ulf. *Cultural Complexity.* New York: Columbia UP, 1992.

Kirschenblatt-Gimblett, Barbara. "Objects of Ethnography." *Exhibiting Cultures: The Poetics and Politics of Museum Display.* Ed. Ivan Karp and Stephen D. Lavine. Washington, DC: Smithsonian Institution Press, 1991. 386–443.

Makin, W. J. *Across the Kalahari Desert.* London: Arrowsmith, 1929.

McClintock, Anne. *Imperial Leather: Race, Gender and Sexuality in the Colonial Context.* New York and London: Routledge, 1995.

Paine, R., ed. *Politically Speaking.* Philadelphia: ISHI, 1981.

Van Buskirk, James. "Bainesia." *Africa* Sept. 1936: 28–32.

CONTRIBUTORS

Harvey Blume is coauthor of *Ota Benga: The Pygmy in the Zoo* (1992) and a contributing editor to the *Boston Book Review*. His essays and criticism have appeared in a variety of books and journals, including *Tolstoy's Dictaphone: Technology and the Muse* (1996).

Veit Erlmann teaches ethnomusicology and anthropology at the University of Texas at Austin. He has done fieldwork in West, Central, and South Africa. Among his most recent publications is *Nightsong: Performance, Power and Practice in South Africa* (1996).

Robert J. Gordon is based in the Department of Anthropology at the University of Vermont. He has also worked in Papua New Guinea, South Africa, Lesotho, and Namibia. His most recent books include *The Bushman Myth* (1992) and *Picturing Bushmen* (1997). He is currently doing a comparative study of colonial societies in New Guinea and Namibia.

Jeffrey P. Green, the author of *Edmund Thornton Jenkins* (1982) and *Black Edwardians* (1998), has written articles on aspects of the black presence in Britain for *Immigrants and Minorities, Black Perspective in Music, International Journal of the History of Sport, Storyville, History Today*, and the *Journal of Caribbean History*. He has presented papers in Europe and America, appeared on radio and television, and written for reference books.

Willie Henderson is Senior Lecturer in the School of Continuing Studies, University of Birmingham, where he teaches economics and African studies. He has published work on economics discourse, on the history of economic thought, and on economic and political development of Southern Africa. He makes regular visits to Zimbabwe. He is currently reviews editor of *African Affairs*, the quarterly journal of the Royal African Society.

David Killingray is Professor of Modern History at Goldsmiths College, University of London. Formerly a schoolteacher in Britain and Tanzania, he has written books and articles on aspects of African, Caribbean, British Imperial, and English local history. He is coeditor of *African Affairs*. His most recent books are *Guardians of Empire* (1998) and *Caribbean Federation* (1998).

Bernth Lindfors is Professor of English and African Literatures at the University of Texas at Austin. Founding editor of the journal *Research in African Literatures*, he has written and edited a number of books on African verbal arts, the most recent being *African Textualities: Texts, Pre-Texts and Contexts of African Literature* (1997) and *Conversations with Chinua Achebe* (1997).

Neil Parsons is Associate Professor of History at the University of Botswana and has taught and researched over many years in Zambia, Swaziland, and Botswana. He is the author of *A New History of Southern Africa* (1982) and of *King Khama, Emperor Joe, and the Great White Queen* (1998).

Shane Peacock is the author of *The Great Farini: The High-Wire Life of William Hunt* (1995). He is a Canadian, descended from pioneers of the same south-central part of Ontario from which Farini came. A graduate of Trent University and the University of Toronto, he has had success as a writer in a number of genres, using journalism, drama, and biography to investigate individual lives, often those of eccentric, daring people.

Robert W. Rydell is Professor of History at Montana State University–Bozeman. He is the author of *All the World's a Fair* (1984) and *World of Fairs* (1993). He has recently been a fellow at the Netherlands Institute for Advanced Study and is currently investigating the globalization of American mass culture.

Z. S. Strother is Assistant Professor in the Department of Art History and Archaeology at Columbia University. She received her Ph.D. in 1992 from Yale University and enjoyed a post-doctoral fellowship in the Michigan Society of Fellows, University of Michigan–Ann Arbor, 1992–95. She has conducted fieldwork in Zaïre (now Democratic Republic of the Congo) (1987–89) and Senegal (1992) and has published *Inventing Masks: Agency and History in the Art of the Central Pende* (1998).

INDEX

Italicized page numbers refer to illustrations.

www.ingramcontent.com/pod-product-compliance
Ingram Content Group UK Ltd.
Pitfield, Milton Keynes, MK11 3LW, UK
UKHW052112140225
455125UK00009B/244